Live & Work
── IN ──
SCANDINAVIA

DENMARK · FINLAND
ICELAND · NORWAY
SWEDEN

Victoria Pybus
Susan Dunne

Published by Vacation Work, 9 Park End Street, Oxford

LIVE AND WORK IN SCANDINAVIA
by Victoria Pybus & Susan Dunne

Copyright © Vacation Work 1995

ISBN 1 85458 121 X (softback)
ISBN 1 85458 122 8 (hardback)

Cover design by
Miller, Craig and Cocking Design Partnership

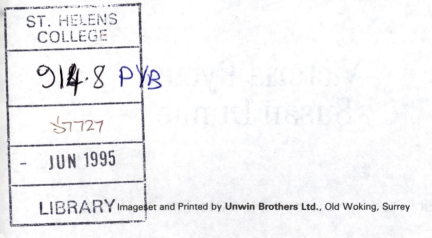
Imageset and Printed by **Unwin Brothers Ltd.**, Old Woking, Surrey

Contents

Denmark

SECTION I — LIVING IN DENMARK

GENERAL INTRODUCTION

RESIDENCE & ENTRY REGULATIONS

SETTING UP HOME

DAILY LIFE

SECTION II — WORKING IN DENMARK

EMPLOYMENT

STARTING A BUSINESS

Finland

SECTION I — LIVING IN FINLAND

GENERAL INTRODUCTION

RESIDENCE & ENTRY REGULATIONS

SETTING UP HOME

DAILY LIFE

RETIREMENT

SECTION II — WORKING IN FINLAND

EMPLOYMENT

STARTING A BUSINESS

Living and Working in Iceland

GENERAL INTRODUCTION

RESIDENCE & ENTRY REGULATIONS

SETTING UP HOME

Norway

SECTION I — LIVING IN NORWAY

RETIREMENT

SECTION II — WORKING IN NORWAY

EMPLOYMENT

STARTING A BUSINESS

Sweden

SECTION I — LIVING IN SWEDEN

SECTION II — WORKING IN SWEDEN

EMPLOYMENT

STARTING A BUSINESS

MAP

APPENDIX

Foreword

Mention Scandinavia to most people and they think of wide empty spaces, unpolluted cities populated by leggy blondes of both sexes, the highest standard of living (and the highest taxes) in Europe, cradle-to-grave welfare that is the envy of many Europeans, true democracy, sexual freedom, liberal attitudes, a class-free society, midnight sun, forests, long, white winters, cross-country skiing, reindeer, the Arctic circle, saunas and wonderful food based around the *smörgås-bord*. Although these images reflect some truth, as is often the case they are only snapshots of the whole.

The Scandinavian nations of Denmark, Sweden, Norway and Iceland are linked by geography and a common Norse heritage giving them history, culture and customs in common, yet there are noticeable variations and more than a little rivalry between these related nations. Finland is the odd one out and furthest from the Scandinavian stereotype. The Finnish language is unrelated to the other Scandinavian languages and its people are not Nordics. Denmark and Norway were united under a single monarchy for several centuries and then Sweden became the dominant power. Norway broke away from Sweden in 1905 and became an independent state. Finland was part of Sweden for more than six hundred years, then, for nearly a hundred years until the Bolshevik revolution, it was a Russian Grand Duchy. Iceland was ruled by Denmark from 1380 with varying degrees of harshness until it too became independent in 1944. Scandinavia in the 1990's comprises two republics (Finland and Iceland) and three, low-key monarchies (Denmark, Norway and Sweden).

The Scandinavian countries have shown no less individualistic tendencies in their approach to the European Union. Denmark was the first, and seemingly the only Scandinavian country willing to join the European Community back in 1972. Norway flirted with the EC and then shied away from full union in 1972 after a negative national referendum of which there was a repeat performance in 1994. Sweden and Finland joined the EU on January 1st 1995 (widely regarded as an impossibility considering the complexity of various issues, including Sweden's neutrality, which had to be resolved in the run up period). Norway and Iceland are however, members of the European Economic Area (EEA) thus giving themselves access to the EU's vast market which boosted their economy almost immediately. During 1994 annual inflation was lower in Sweden, Norway and Finland than the EU average of 3% and all the Nordic countries had higher than the EU average GNP per inhabitant exceeding even Germany.

The relevance of all this to the foreigner considering living and working in Scandinavia is that if he or she is an EU national it is possible to go to any Scandinavian country to look for work without prior permission or the need to obtain a work permit, or in some cases even a residence permit. Considering the previous difficulty in obtaining work except through approved, very restricted schemes or professional relocation, this will make job hunting (though not necessarily job finding) much easier. The previous restrictions on working and duration of stays will however still apply to non-EU nationals, but with the increasing opening up of the Nordic economies, foreign expertise generally will be welcomed and prospects are much better also for non-EU nationals.

This book aims to provide a more complete picture of the different countries that make up Scandinavia and to provide insights into many aspects of daily life that will help the non-Scandinavian who wants to live and work amongst the Nordics and the Finns to settle in with as much ease as possible despite the different languages, customs, laws and attitudes that would otherwise hamper their progress. The fact that the small populations of these countries reveal their ability to speak English with alacrity and often with impressive fluency, means that even non-linguists may consider them places to exercise their entrepreneurial flair.

Each of the five countries in the book is divided into two sections *Living* and *Working* which between them cover all areas of these subjects from opening a bank account, finding accommodation and a job, employment regulations, advice on setting up a small business, not to mention the aesthetics of Scandinavian social mores, language, education and culture.

Much has been written of the reserve of Scandinavians and for the outsider this contrasts strikingly with say the peoples of Mediterranean countries and can be the basis of profound loneliness amongst foreigners intially. It takes perseverance to break the ice, which like the Scandinavian winters can seem unendurable at times. Those who have stayed long enough to do so usually find it impossible to leave Scandinavia permanently. There is no time like the present for discovering the extraordinary beauty of and the opportunities for living and working in Scandinavia.

Victoria Pybus
Susan Dunne
March 1995

Acknowledgements

Vacation Work is indebted to the following for their invaluable help in compiling this book:

Denmark: Sanne Masden for her detailed account of daily life in Denmark, Camilla Marsden for her case history, the staff of the information office of the Danish Embassy in London.

Sweden: Charlotte Rosen for her case history and other insights about living in Sweden, the staff of the Swedish Embassy information department, the Swedish institute and the national employment service of Sweden for their help in providing statistics and information on Swedish life and employment.

Norway: Moira Mitchell and Jim Sinclair for sharing their experiences of Norway and their case histories, Jim Hoskin of Kvaerner Professional Services for employment data and the tireless help of the Norwegian Embassy staff information department.

Iceland: Janet Bridgeport for her case history and Maria and Erlandur Magnusson for their detailed account of Icelandic daily life; also the staff of the Icelandic Embassy for much useful statistical information and the staff of the *Icelandic Review* in Reykjavík for all their assistance.

Finland: Dr Bernadette Ferry for her case history and insights into Finnish daily life and the staff of the information department of the Finnish Embassy.

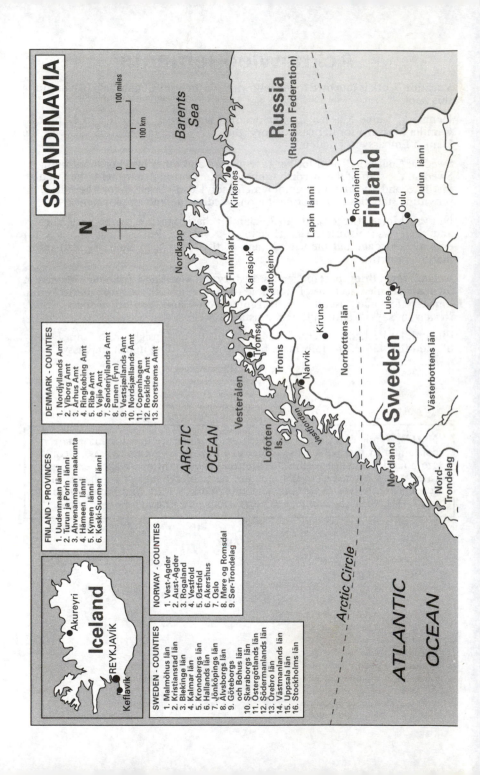

SCANDINAVIA

N

Barents
Sea

Russia
(Russian Federation)

0
0   100 km
100 miles

Nordkapp

Kirkenes

Finnmark

Karasjok

Kautokeino

Finland

Rovaniemi

Oulu

Lapin lääni

Oulun lääni

Tromsø

Kiruna

Luleå

Troms

Norrbottens län

Narvik

Vesterålen

Lofoten
Is.

Vestfjorden

Nordland

Sweden

Västerbottens län

Nord-
Trøndelag

ARCTIC

OCEAN

ATLANTIC

OCEAN

Arctic Circle

Akureyri

Iceland

REYKJAVÍK

Keflavík

FINLAND - PROVINCES
1. Uudenmaan lääni
2. Turun ja Porin lääni
3. Ahvenanmaan maakunta
4. Hämeen lääni
5. Kymen lääni
6. Keski-Suomen lääni

DENMARK - COUNTIES
1. Nordjyllands Amt
2. Viborg Amt
3. Århus Amt
4. Ringkøbing Amt
5. Ribe Amt
6. Vejle Amt
7. Sønderjyllands Amt
8. Funen (Fyn)
9. Vestsjællands Amt
10. Nordsjællands Amt
11. Copenhagen
12. Roskilde Amt
13. Storstrøms Amt

NORWAY - COUNTIES
1. Vest-Agder
2. Aust-Agder
3. Rogaland
4. Vestfold
5. Østfold
6. Akershus
7. Oslo
8. Møre og Romsdal
9. Sør-Trøndelag

SWEDEN - COUNTIES
1. Malmöhus län
2. Kristianstad län
3. Blekinge län
4. Kalmar län
5. Kronobergs län
6. Hallands län
7. Jönköpings län
8. Älvsborgs län
9. Göteborgs
   och Bohus län
10. Skaraborgs län
11. Östergötlands län
12. Södermanlands län
13. Örebro län
14. Västmanlands län
15. Uppsala län
16. Stockholms län

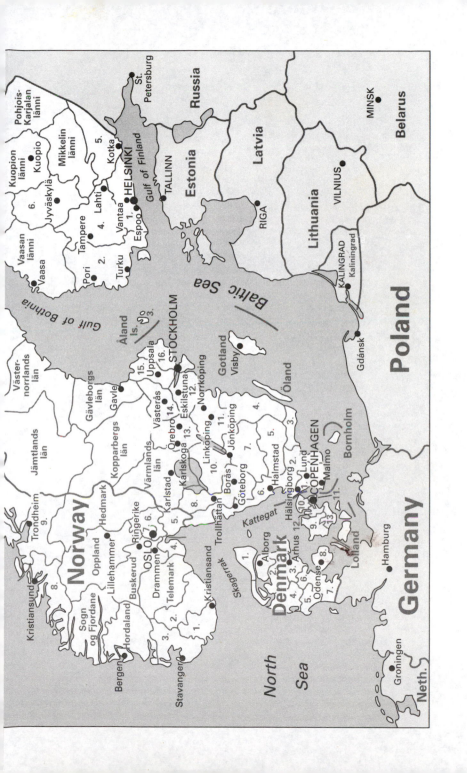

Denmark

SECTION I

Living in Denmark

General Introduction
Residence and Entry Regulations
Setting Up Home
Daily Life
Retirement

General Introduction

Destination Denmark

At one and the same time occupying the the the northern extremity of continental Europe and the most southern part of Scandinavia, it is perhaps not surprising that Denmark (Danmark to the Danes), being the physical and cultural bridge between the two, was the first Nordic country to join what was then called the European Community (now known as the European Union) following a national referendum which came out in favour in 1972.

The golden age of Denmark can well be said to have been during the reign of the Danish King Knud (Canute) who, from 1016-1042, ruled a northern empire that stretched from England through Scandinavia and as far as the Baltics. During the Middle Ages the power of Denmark was in decline as conflicts between church and state disunited the country. This in turn allowed the power balance in the area to be dominated by Sweden and the nearby German states. Until the last quarter of the eighteenth century, German was the official language of the Danish court. Despite various military defeats, Denmark continued to enhance its reputation as a great trading and seafaring nation (as befits the descendants of the Vikings).

The Napoleonic Wars, in which Denmark unwisely allied herself to the French, ultimately led to defeat and bankruptcy for the Danes. In the ensuing Treaty of Kiel, Denmark was forced to surrender Holstein to the Confederation of German states. By 1848 Denmark was well along the route of prosperous industrial revolution when a series of constitutional reforms made it one of the most democratic nations of Europe. Novelties for the time included a code of civil liberties, free speech and a new parliament the *Rigsdag* with an upper (*landsting*) and a lower (*folketing*) chamber; the latter elected by popular vote. Further military disasters led to the ceding of Schleswig to the German Confederation. At this point, Denmark became the smallest it had been for centuries.

Danish politics, as elsewhere in northern Europe, were a hotbed of radical ideas by the 1870s. These accompanied the industrial and agricultural revolutions which were progressively transforming the political and cultural outlook and increasing the expectations of the population. Proposals for reform included the outline of a welfare state including sick pay, maximum working hours and old age pensions. Denmark's champion of these tenets was the *United Left*, a party whose manifesto also included demands for universal suffrage and equal taxation. Their demands led to a backlash from the rightist parties and eventually a compromise was reached. Full parliamentary democracy was not instituted until 1901. At the onset of the First World War, Denmark, which had good relations with both Britain and Germany, declared itself neutral. In the ensuing peace settlement (Treaty of Versailles) Denmark regained northern Schleswig but not southern Schleswig which voted in a referendum to remain part of Germany. The new Danish-German border was fixed just north of Flensborg. In the years between the two World Wars, Denmark became progressively more enlightened and liberal, notably in the removal of discrimination against illegitimacy and the legalisation of abortion. National engineering achievements included the building of the bridge linking Jutland and Funen Island.

As the price of remaining neutral during the Second World War Denmark conceded to inevitable Nazi occupation. The Germans wanted to use Denmark as a base for an invasion of Norway and after threats that refusal would result in a German bombardment of Denmark the Danes allowed the Germans in. Resistance came later when it was obvious the Germans were losing. For the duration of the occupation normal parliamentary government was replaced by a national coalition and German currency replaced the Danish krone. Despite the fact that Denmark had escaped the devastation wrought in much of Europe after the Second World War, the economy had collapsed and needed a generous infusion from the Marshall Plan funds. Denmark became a member of the United Nations in 1945. Aware of a fast developing polarisation of Europe into east and west, and notwithstanding a consistent policy of neutrality, the Danes joined the North Atlantic Treaty Organisation (NATO) in 1948 albeit with an anti-nuclear proviso which it still maintains today.

The postwar years were marked by political upheavals as the various parties including the main ones, the Social Democrats and Conservatives, jostled for the upperhand and fell in and out of coalitions with smaller parties. Meanwhile the liberal ethos of Denmark continued to evolve. This has been a mixed blessing, admirable in its equal treatment of all citizens; for instance homosexuals can enter into a kind of legalised marriage and the equality of women has gone further in Denmark than in many other European nations; but perhaps less successful in others where an element of exploitation may have crept in. Having abandoned all forms of censorship in the 60s, Denmark generally, and Copenhagen in particular is considered the porn centre of Europe. Copenhagen even has its own museum of erotica, the top floors of which are devoted to the most extreme varieties.

Denmark's other well publicised but less lurid products include Hans Christian Anderson (who emanated from Odense), Lego, and its eponymous offshoot Legoland (an entire model village made from Lego at Billund), Bang and Olufsen high tech consumer durables, Carlsberg-Tuborg lager, Danish bacon and Danish blue (cheese not films), the 'bog people' — 2,000-year-old human remains found perfectly preserved in the peat bogs of Denmark, contemporary furniture, and (arguably) Hamlet.

To summarise: Denmark is well organised and efficiently run and typical of the Scandinavian countries whose small, well disciplined populations facilitate administration. In addition, Danes tend to be politically aware and contemporary in outlook, with a practical approach to everyday things and an attention to detail. Underlying this pragmatism is a strong sense of history reaching back beyond the Vikings to antiquity, and an ability to incorporate the past in their lives without living in it. Take for instance the Danish attitude to the monarchy, which is reduced and democratised but still an important part of their national identity. It stands as an example of how to incorporate a monarchy into the edifice of a modern state, another, which other small, former empire-owning nations might care to emulate.

It would be wrong however to portray Denmark or any other Nordic country as Utopian. The other side of the coin that extols individual freedom as paramount and the right of all citizens to be cared for by the state, is a seedy underside of social problems and delinquency, not just in the capital and large cities but in the remoter communities. Denmark also has one of the highest suicide rates in the world. About one tenth of the population are Inuit (Eskimo) immigrants from Denmark's other territory of Greenland. Greenlanders are widely regarded as second-rate citizens by even the liberal Danes and alcoholism and social problems are rife among them. As unemployment continues to rise the welfare burden is increasing to the point that it is clear that Denmark cannot maintain such exemplary standards indefinitely.

Another perceived ill is that there is a growing rationale among young people that employment is no longer a priority or even a necessity. In other words, those who have become used to relying on the state no longer see earning a living and paying taxes as their part of a social contract.

Pros: Rates of pay are higher than in the UK.
Denmark is a well-organised country with a reasonably unobtrusive bureaucracy.
The state provides womb-to-tomb care for all citizens.
Standards of medicine and public health are amongst the highest in Europe.
The Danes are very good linguists, so no problems communicating.
They also have a tradition of tolerance and championing the freedom of the individual.
Women are accepted as equal to men by the state.
The standard of living in Denmark is generally higher than in the UK at only a slightly higher cost and with all the benefits above.
Denmark's climate is the mildest in Scandinavia.
The business sector is diversified and well-developed offering plenty of opportunities for entrepreneurs.

Cons: There is a high rate of unemployment, currently the third highest in the EU, so jobs are not easy to find.
Prime holiday time mid-June to mid-August is virtually a write off for anyone wanting to do business in Denmark.
An appreciation of Danish culture and Nordic history is essential as much of the social life revolves around them.
Although everyday relations are easy, Danes take time to open up and may seem withdrawn and cold.

Political and Economic Structure

Government and Politics

Denmark is divided into eighteen major regions each of which elects representives for the national parliament (*Folketinget*). Each major region is broken down into smaller units.

The Danish parliament (*Folketinget*) is uni-cameral and has 179 seats. In addition frequent referenda provide the population with a direct say on major issues. Elections are held every four years. Each of the eighteen regions elects its representatives to the Folketinget and supplementary seats are allocated on the basis of the percentage of votes gained overall by the political parties. A minimum of 2% of all votes is needed in order to get into Parliament. This system of proportional representation ensures a more accurate representation of the wishes of the electorate but inevitably leads to no one party governing the country. Over the past couple of decades Denmark has been ruled by coalitions made up of varying parties. The highest number of parties in parliament has so far has been eleven.

The last major parliamentary crisis was brought on by the Danish rejection of the Maastricht Treaty in a 1992 referendum. A suitably revised version with negotiated opt outs relating to common defence, common currency, union citizenship and pan-EU legal directives was again put to the electorate in a second referendum in May 1993 when it was accepted.

Political Parties
The eight parties represented in parliament are: *Socialdemokraterne* (Social Democrats), *det Konservative Folkeparti* (Conservative People's Party), *Socialistisk Folkeparti* (the Socialist People's Party), *Venstre* (the Liberal Party), *Fremskridstpartiet* (The Progress Party), *det Radikale Venstre* (the Radical Liberal Party), *Centrum Demokraterne* (Centre Democrats) and *Kristeligt Folkeparti* (Christian People's Party).

Historically the Social Democrats have been the largest party and held the balance of power the longest. However from 1983-93 the government was led by a liberal minority with a Conservative Prime Minister, Poul Schlüter. In the January 1993 elections the Social Democrats again formed a coalition government headed by Nyrup Rasmussen who is the current (1994) prime minister

Apart from getting the Maastricht Treaty endorsed, Mr. Rasmussen's government has also distinguished itself by introducing major income tax reductions including lower taxes for the most wealthy, effective from 1994 (see *Daily Life — Taxation*) which it is hoped will provide a consumer-led boost to the economy.

Approximately 30% of those elected to the parliament and local councils are female. It is estimated that about 10% of the population are members of political parties. The high national turnout of voters at parliamentary elections has so far ranged from 82% to 89%.

The Economy
The Danish economy is based largely on industry including electronics, technochemicals, pharmaceuticals, furniture making, paper and printing, textiles and cement. Food processing and drinks, especially beer are also important. This is supported by a high level of agricultural output which needs little introduction: bacon, butter and cheese being some of the most exported products.

The lack of indigenous raw materials means that these have to be imported which leaves the Danish economy vulnerable to price fluctuations and supply. However the discovery of offshore oil in recent years has helped to offset a previous large drain on the economy and even contributed to a small net trade surplus in the 1980s. Natural gas is another resource that has had an economic benefit. Denmark produces enough for its own use and also manages to export the surplus.

At the start of the 1990s Denmark's economy was given a thorough boost through membership of the otherwise ill-fated ERM (European Exchange Rate Mechanism) which resulted in Denmark having the lowest inflation in the Common Market. Less beneficial however, was the large increase in unemployment, one result of which has been cutbacks in welfare provision.

According to the Gross National Product per head of the population, Denmark ranks at the world's twelfth richest country and GNP is also 8% above the EU average.

Geographical Information

Area and Main Physical Features
Of the countries in the European Union only Belgium, the Netherlands (just) and Luxembourg are smaller than Denmark. It is the smallest of the Scandinavian countries at 43,093 sq kms (16,638 sq miles). Denmark consists of the province

of Jutland, which projects from Germany into the North Sea and the Danish archipelago, of over four hundred islands many of them tiny and uninhabited while one of the two largest, Zealand, contains the capital Copenhagen (*København*) and most of the commercial and industrial activity. Copenhagen is on the coast and is separated by the Öresund from Sweden, a mere half hour away by ferry. A bridge ten-miles long is being constructed across the Sound, linking Denmark and Sweden, but the project has been the object of intense opposition from environmentalists in Sweden. All being well, its completion will bring immense prosperity to Copenhagen and the enthusiastic Danes have already started construction. A bridge and tunnel linking Zealand and Funen on the other hand, is nearly finished; from 1996 it will be open to traffic.

Other important islands are Funen, the nearest large island to Jutland to which it is physically linked by road and rail, Lolland and Falster two artificially linked islands off the south of Zealand and the isolated island of Bornholm which lies far east of the rest of Denmark in the middle of the Baltic Sea between Poland and Sweden.

Denmark is a low-lying country with the somewhat ambitiously named Himmelbjerget (Sky Mountain), the highest point, reaching only 550 feet (173 metres). The landscapes are open, and offer a great expanse to the eye especially the coastline of which there is 7000kms. The stretch of coast from the Skaw and Blaavands Huk is the longest sand beach in Europe. Nowhere in Denmark is more than a 52kms (32 miles) from the sea.

Greenland and the Faroe Islands

The predominantly Arctic island of Greenland, which is bigger than all of Scandinavia and has a population of 55,117 has belonged to Denmark since Viking times, and still comes under Danish sovereignty, as do the seventeen, distant Faroe Islands (population 47,287) which are marooned in the Atlantic between Scotland and Norway. Both are self-governing but have two seats each in the Danish parliament. Neither area belongs to the EU but Greenland was a member of the EC until 1985 when it voted in a referendum to secede.

Most of Greenland lies permanently under an icecap and the immense island has some of the earth's most stunning scenery, especially if you like icebergs. In the short Arctic summer the coastal areas undergo a transformation as they explode into a mass of wildflowers and teeming wildlife. Iceland has invested much money in Greenland bringing its tourist facilities up to date and the islanders' housing wouldn't look out of place in a modern city suburb. The tourist potential, fishing grounds and probable mineral resources are Greenland's biggest assets.

The Faroe islands on the other hand are a twitcher's paradise offering an unrivalled range of seabirds in quantities which make you wonder why Hitchcock didn't film *The Birds* there. Unfortunately the islanders' annual, bloodthirsty tradition of hacking to death a school of migratory whales has upset many tour operators, not to mention their clients and at the time of going to press has caused an almost total touristic boycott.

Internal Organisation

For administrative purposes Denmark is divided into fourteen districts plus the two cities of Copenhagen and Frederiksberg. These *amter* are the equivalent of counties. The smaller units into which the amter are divided are the municipalities (*kommuner*) of which there are 275. Both these entities have a small amount of autonomy in their localities but federalism is much less well-developed than in Germany or Spain.

Population

The population of Denmark received additions during the Middle Ages from German, French, Dutch and Polish stock. Until the 60s, the only 'foreign' population was the 20,000 strong German contingent in North Slesvig. In common with many other countries, so-called guest workers, mainly less prosperous nationals from Turkey, Asian countries and Yugoslavia were invited to Denmark as a source of cheap labour for the growing economy. Many have now settled there. In addition, several thousand asylum seekers, mainly from Iran, Sri Lanka and Vietnam were taken in by Denmark during the past couple of decades. Most recently, a few thousand refugees from ex-Yugoslavia have been granted asylum in Denmark. Overall however, Denmark still has one of the smallest immigrant populations of any European country at 3.1% of the population of a mere 5.5 million Danes. At least a quarter of Denmark's entire population is based in the capital, Copenhagen.

Climatic Zones

Being more southerly, Denmark has a continental climate rather than the typical Scandinavian one of extreme and long winters. In fact Danish winters can be very wet. Long lasting frosts tend to be a bigger feature of the cold months than snow. However the difference between summer and winter temperatures rarely exceeds 20°C. The average January temperature for Copenhagen (which is on the same latitude as Edinburgh) is 0.4°C and July 17°C. The coldest month is generally February.

Spring and autumn can be very mild but the windswept agricultural plains of the Jutland peninsular can be a trial to farmers at sowing time; the seeds are literally tossed to the wind and may never reach the furrow.

Regions Report

Jutland (Jylland)

The largest part of Denmark is the peninsular of Jutland which projects 250 miles (400kms) from the 42-mile (68kms) land border with Germany into the North Sea. Although appearing to be named for its jutting appearance, it actually takes its name from the Jutes, a tribe originally quite separate from the bloodthirsty Danes who overran and absorbed them sometime in the ninth century. Modern day Jutland is highly cultivated, indeed the south is known as the breadbasket of Denmark, but with more variations of landscape than may be found anywhere else in Denmark. Schleswig in the south is home to 20,000 ethnic German, but Danish citizens. The town of Ribe, once a medieval port has long been silted up, but the ancient town has been lovingly preserved and is an obvious tourist attraction. The main southern city is Esbjerg mainly known as the docking place for Scandinavian Seaways ferries and fish-oil processing. The after effects of the latter hang heavily on the air.

The eastern side of Jutland is hilly and in many parts wooded, unlike the windswept western side. It also provides the driving-off point for Funen Island to which Jutland has a road and rail connection. Frederica which is also one of the country's main railway termini. Just north of Frederica is the more attractive harbour town of Vejle whose prime industry is sausage-making. Anyone who harbours fond memories of interlocking little plastic bricks in semblance of motors, houses, boats and the like, may indulge in the ecstasy of viewing over 43 million of them clamped together to form both fantastic and familiar structures (and Legorado Wild West) at the Legoland Park at Billund. The name Lego is derived from the Danish *Leg Godt* (good play).

Moving further north, but still in the east, is the area known as the Danish Lake District which extends roughly as far north as Viborg. The area is characterised by gentle, wooded hills, some rather diminutive lakes and is a popular camping area in summer. It contains the towns of Skanderborg, Silkeborg and the undisputed cultural gem of Århus. Århus is a lively university city and port of 200,000 residents that has its origins in Viking history, it is also the sailing off point for the ferries to Denmark's largest island, Zealand. The city itself is a mixture of old and new. The medieval heart of the city is the cathedral from which radiate narrow twisting streets. In contrast impressive architecture from recent decades is much in evidence in the outer part of the city. For instance the Musikhuset, the concert hall/opera house complex is a 1980's building, and comprises the first phase of the The new Scandinavian Congress Centre which opened in 1995. Its completion is expected to make Aarhus the leading conference centre of Northern Europe. In addition to this architectural panoply is the collection of about seventy-five original buildings from the 16th to the 19th centuries brought from around the country and re-erected on a special site *Den Gamle By* (the Old Town), to recreate the atmosphere of market town life through the centuries. The entire city provides an atmospheric backdrop for The Århus Festival, a week long arts extravaganza which takes place annually at the beginning of September.

Yet further north is the town of Randers and, almost in the centre of Jutland, the city of Viborg. As befits such an importantly sited city, Viborg was the coronation place of successive Danish kings, but only until 1655. Viborg had continued to decline in importance: two hundred years ago it was the provincial administrative centre. These days however its chief importance is as a market centre for the surrounding agricultural district.

The nothern part of Jutland is actually an island, separated from the rest of the peninsular by the Limfjord. The northwest (known as the Limfjordslandet) is a popular holiday area attracting hordes during the summer months with its expanse of excellent beaches and a kind of Arthur Ransome paradise, sea sailing on what is virtually a vast inland lake. However it is only for those who like their sea air fortissimo, as the area is generally blasted by the wind coming off the North Sea.

The northwest of Jutland is dominated by Denmark's fourth largest city, Aalborg which is situated on the southern bank of the Limfjord. Beyond Aalborg, on the northern side of the Limfjord reached by the Limfjord bridge, the landscape is windswept, bleak and fairly uninviting. Aalborg has a rich mercantile past from which its wealth and importance sprang. It is also the home of the Danish Worldwide Archives whose records, (a vast collection of them), detail the migration of every Dane who moved overseas. The archives can be used by the public to trace the emigration of individuals. The grim northern port of Frederikshavn is principally known for being overrun by other Nordics who come to drink alcohol in life-threatening quantities, thanks to the less stringent drinking laws of Denmark and the ferry companies which dock there. The dramatically sited Skagen however, on the narrow projection of land that is the most northerly point of Jutland, is a magical place with inspiring light effects much favoured by indigenous painters in the nineteenth century. Some of their resulting canvases can be seen in the local museum.

Funen (Fyn)

With good reason is the second largest of the islands, Funen, which lies between Jutland and the largest island of Zealand, known as the 'the garden of Denmark'.

Typical of Danish cultivation is the symmetry and orderliness of the fields on Funen from which a vast quantity of fruit and vegetables is produced. The main city, and third largest in Denmark is Odense which was also the birthplace of Hans Christian Anderson, though there is nothing very fairytale-like in the city's appearance today. Its famous son has however spawned a large tourist industry, high hotel prices and a week long festival celebrating his life and works every July. Odense has a pleasant old centre away from which modern industrial development has sprawled along the canal bank. In the nineteenth century, the canal brought increased prosperity to the city by connecting Odense to the sea and facilitating export of the island's produce.

Denmark's largest engineering project to date is the 18km-long road and rail link (a bridge and a tunnel) between Funen and Zealand. The rail link, which will run through the tunnel for most of the crossing, is due for completion in 1996, while the road link which involves a two-stage bridge is scheduled to open a year later. The strip of water between the two islands traversed by the new links, is known as Storebaelt (Great Belt).

Funen is a busy holiday area and the many harbours and marinas in the south attract a large number of the yachting fraternity, principally Danes and Germans. The hub town of the south is Svendborg from where you can also get ferries to the smaller islands such as AErø or take the road bridge across to the island of Langeland. There is a host of small islands in this region and numerous ferries to reach them. Another southern town Fåborg is also popular with tourists, but tends to be less frenetic than Svendborg. The museum of the Funen painters is a major attraction of the town.

Zealand (Sjoelland)

Zealand is the largest of the Danish islands (roughly the same area and shape as Northern Ireland), and also the site of the capital, Copenhagen (København) which acquired this honour in 1443. Inevitably Zealand is where most of the population, production and commercial activity of Denmark is located.

Copenhagen: The founding of Copenhagen can be dated from the building of a castle in the twelfth century, of which only ruins remain on the site of Christiansborg, the parliament complex of modern Denmark. Major construction of the capital's landmark buildings began in the sixteenth century under the auspices of Christian 1V and the royal palace of Amalienborg is a seventeenth century edifice.

Modern Copenhagen is considered one of the friendliest capitals of Europe and certainly the most welcoming in Scandinavia. It is also one of the most pleasing, due thought having been given to the requirements of pedestrians and human beings over those of motor vehicles and corporate interests. The old city fortifications have been re-sculpted into parks and small lakes and the wharves and quaysides of the old 'merchants' harbour' have become public walkways. The general atmosphere has the reputation of being one of the most laid back and Bacchanalian (especially the nightlife) in Europe. The Christiania area of the city has been largely taken over by those who prefer an alternative lifestyle. The first hippies arrived there in the 1960s and there is a commune of about 1000 people now living there. They pay no taxes, build without permission and deal openly in soft drugs. The Danish government is not entirely happy about this situation, especially the drug dealing which it is trying to limit by interrupting supplies as much as possible.

Surprisingly, Copenhagen is not one of the most expensive capitals in which to live although in Denmark generally the cost of living is extremely high. Despite its reputation for the uninhibited pursuit of pleasure, the city is not without its moments of reflection: the red and white Danish flag (*Dannebrog*) flies at half mast on the morning of the 9th April, the anniversary of the German occupation.

Copenhagen is separated from Sweden by the Øresund, a narrow strip of water 16.8kms wideacross which a road/rail tunnel and bridge link is due to be built during this decade. Once in place, it will be possible to drive from Germany to Sweden without taking a ferry as the bridge/tunnel links between the main Danish islands will be complete. The original settlement on the site of Copenhagen grew rich from the levying of tolls on ships which passed through the Øresund. With the proposed bridge/tunnnel link, the so-called Øresund region will be truly common to both Denmark and Sweden, and is destined to be one of the fastest growing commercial areas of Europe. The combined conurbation of Copenhagen and Malmö (the latter in Sweden) when fully developed by the end of the millenium will have a population of over 2½ million and will be a Nordic version of Antwerp-Rotterdam.

Getting to Denmark

High street travel agents can, of course offer advice on travel to Denmark by air, train or ferry. But there are also a number of travel agents in the UK that specialise in offering discount fares, particularly, but by no means exclusively for young people. London Campus Travel (headquarters at 52 Grosvenor Gardens, London SW1W OAG) is one of Britain's largest specialists in discount travel for students, young people and independent travellers.

The EURO 26 Youth Travel Scheme, for under 26s, was revamped in 1993 with the introduction of a British Council sponsored card available from specialist youth a and student travel agencies. The card users' entitlements include discounted fares and access to a 24-hour helpline offering advice before you go and assistance if you get into difficulties abroad. Further information from Under 26, 52 Grosvenor Gardens, London SW1W OAG; tel 0171-823 5363; fax 0171-730 5739.

AIR

Both British Airways and Scandinavian Air Systems (SAS) operate regular daily flights between London and Copenhagen starting at about £150 return. SAS also run flights from Manchester, Aberdeen, Glasgow and Dublin to Copenhagen and London to Aarhus. Maersk Air flies from London Gatwick to Copenhagen and Billund. Aer Lingus operates flights from Dublin to Copenhagen and Manchester to Copenhagen. Business Air flies from Aberdeen, Dundee, Edinburgh, East Midlands and Manchester to Esbjerg in southwest Jutland, but these flights are pricier than others at £224-£249. Birmingham Executive Airways operate flights from Birmingham to Copenhagen and New Air flies from Birmingham and Manchester to Billund for a return fare starting at £219. Maersk Air has a seven-day apex return from London for £145 which is probably the cheapest regular fare available. Flights take under two hours which is a cinch compared with the 27-hour train journey from London.

Useful Addresses

Birmingham Executive Airways, Jetstream House, Birmingham International Airport, Coventry Road, Birmingham (0121-782 0711).
British Airways, 156 Regent Street, London W1 (0181-897 4000).
Business Air, tel 01382 66345.
Maersk Air, Terminal House, 52 Grosvenor Gardens, London SW1 (0171-333 0066).
New Air, tel 0161-489 2800.
SAS, 52-53 Conduit Street, London W1 (0171-734 4020).

FERRIES

Scandinavian ferries tend to set the comfort standards for ferries anywhere in the world. You can take a Scandinavian Seaways (tel 0171-409-6060) ferry from Harwich or Newcastle in the UK to Esbjerg. The overnight journey takes about 19/20 hours depending on the route. The Newcastle-Esbjerg route operates only from March 27th to October 31st with two departures a week. For a single foot passenger the 1994 return fare was from £69.

RAIL

An important organisation for anyone who prefers to avoid aeroplanes is Wasteels Travel in London which is Europe's largest international rail specialist. In the UK they offer ROUTE 26 tickets for the under 26s. These tickets carry large discounts on standard rail fares to Europe. All tickets are valid for two months and allow stop offs en route. The 27-hour train journey from London to Copenhagen via Harwich Esbjerg is an odyssey compared with flying (see *Air* above). Maersk Air (tel 0171-333 0066) has a seven-day apex return from London for £145 which is slightly cheaper than the competition. You can take a quicker (24-hour) route via Ostende/Hamburg or Amsterdam/Hamburg. The Eurotrain under 26s fare from London to Copenhagen costs £124 return; £80 single.

Not surprisingly considering the length of the land journey, flying can work out cheaper for anyone paying the normal fare.

British Rail European Travel Centre, Victoria Station, London SW1 (0171-834 2345)

Wasteels Travel, 121 Wilton Road, London SW1 (0171-834 7066).

BUS

Coaches take just as long as trains to reach Denmark but are cheaper: National Express Eurolines charges £103 for a round-trip to Copenhagen (£89 for anyone under 26). BB Travel offer return fares from London to Copenhagen or Aarhus from £75 return.

BB Travel UK, 12 St. George's Drive, London SW1V 4BJ; tel 0171-834 7999; fax 0171-821 0040.

National Express Eurolines (52 Grosvenor Gardens, London SW1 (0171-730 0202).

PACKAGE TRIPS

Because of the expensiveness of all Scandinavian countries, package trips are worth considering if you are thinking of going to Denmark to do a reconnaissance of job prospects: Scandinavian Seaways (01255-241234) do a six-night package staying in Danish Inns from £175 per person including ferry crossing with cabin, and bed and breakfast. Even better value are their out-of-season city breaks with 2/3 night stays.

Residence and Entry Regulations

The Current Position

Denmark is a member of the European Union which guarantees free movement of goods, services and labour anywhere within the Union. This chapter may therefore seem superfluous for EU nationals. Unfortunately this is far from the case as despite the EU, Denmark still has its own regulations which govern other EU nationals taking up residence there. The simplest regulations are for other Scandinavians who are entitled to identical rights as Danish citizens. For citizens of countries belonging to the EU (see below), there are registration procedures to be followed on arrival, for stays of longer than three months. Nationals of countries outside the EU are the most restricted and normally need to apply before departure from the home country.

EU and EEA Nationality

Nationals of other EU countries namely Belgium, Britain, The Netherlands, Germany, France, Ireland Luxembourg, Italy, Spain, Portugal, Austria and Greece have the right to work, and if they wish, settle permanently in Denmark. Nationals of The European Economic Area which includes Lichtenstein are also entitled to the same rights as EU nationals.

Entry for EU and EEA Nationals

Nationals of the above countries are free to go to Denmark to look for work for up to three months with no prior permission. In other words, there is no difference at this stage whether someone is entering Denmark as a tourist or as a potential resident. It is necessary to register with the labour exchange (A.F.), within seven days of arrival. Although this may not necessarily be the best way to find a job (see *Employment* chapter) it is a formality which should none-the-less be fulfilled as it shows the authorities that your intentions to find work are genuine. In order to look for work in Denmark you should be able to prove that you have sufficient funds to support yourself which may include entitlement to unemployment benefit at the time of your departure (see *Employment* chapter). Once you have obtained a job it must fulfil minimum conditions as regards working hours and remuneration.

The Danish Ministry of Labour also stipulates that foreigners (only other Scandinavians are not counted as foreigners) must contribute to the social security fund of Denmark. Exempted from this regulation are foreigners who have paid into a Danish unemployment fund (*arbejdsloshedskasser*) for two consecutive years previously, those who are working in Denmark as au pairs, foreigners born in Denmark or married to a citizen of that country, or foreigners who are self-employed or carrying out services in Denmark.

Residence Permit

If employment is found within the three-month period a residence permit (*opholdstilladelse*) should be applied for at the Directorate for Aliens (*Direktoratet for udlaendinge*) ideally two weeks before the three-month period is up. Applicants will need to take their national identity card or passport, two passport photographs and confirmation that they have a job and have joined an unemployment fund. The job must pay a living wage (as a rough guide a minimum yearly salary of kr50,000 net).

Personal Code Number

Anyone who is staying in Denmark to live and work, rather than as a tourist, must have a *personnummer* (personal code number) made up of their date of birth plus a selection of other digits. This is an indispensable part of the life of any Danish citizen or foreign resident. You need it for opening a bank account, joining a library, moving house, paying taxes, going to the doctor etc. Danes are given a personal code number (a.k.a. a CPR number) at birth, and foreigners have to apply for one as part of the residency procedure. You are often asked for your personal code number before you are asked to give your name which can seem somewhat impersonal.

In order to be given a CPR number certificate you must have obtained the residence permit and have a permanent address (poste restante addresses are not acceptable, nor is a youth hostel or hotel). If you change your address, you are obliged to register details of your new abode within five days.

The personal code number certificate (*personnummerbevis*) is issued by the *Folkeregisteret* (National Register). Once you are registered there you also get a social security certificate (*sygesikringsbevis*) which entitles the holder to use the free national health service of Denmark.

Identity Cards

Danish citizens may voluntarily carry national identity cards with all the information mentioned above on them. Recently a new type of card was issued with a magnetic strip containing the information previously printed on the card. There is potential for a card with a microchip containing useful data such as a person's entire medical history. However despite their willing acceptance of the identity card as a necessary and useful item, even the Danes see limits to the amount and type of personal information they wish to be stored on them. They objected strongly to a proposal to record all prescribed medicines on them linked to a central computer by a number on the card. It was proposed the information be used for research purposes.

Entry for Non-EU or EEA Nationals

Nationals of countries other than Scandinavian ones and the countries already mentioned above are not allowed to work doing paid or unpaid work during a stay in Denmark unless they have arranged a work and residence permit in advance with the Danish Embassy or Consulate in their home country, or the country in which they have had legal residence for the previous six months. Permits are in no way automatically forthcoming and will only be granted in specific circumstances only if there is no one available on the Danish labour market to do the job. For details of employment possibilities, see *Employment* chapter.

Danish Citizenship

The minimum period of residency required to apply for Danish Citizenship is four years for anyone who has been through legal marriage to a Dane, or seven years for a single person. Other essential requirements are an ability to speak Danish and an exemplary record of good conduct. For non-EU nationals, the citizenship requirements are theoretically the same, but it is more difficult to enter Denmark to live and work in the first place.

EU Citizenship

Following the Edinburgh Summit in 1993, Denmark finally accepted the Maastricht Treaty of European Union, with certain opt outs, one of which was union citizenship which was accepted by all other member states. However under the Maastricht Treaty, all EU countries including Denmark agreed measures allowing the five million EU citizens living in countries other than their own to vote in the European Elections (from 1994) and local elections (from 1995) held in their adopted country.

Useful Addresses

Royal Danish Embassy in London, 55 Sloane Street, London SW1X 9SR; tel 0171-333 0200; fax 0171-333 0270.

Royal Danish Embassy in the USA, 3200 Whitehaven Street, NW, Washington DC 20008-3683; tel 202-234 4300; fax 202-328 1470.

Royal Danish Embassy in Canada, Suit 702, 85 Range Road, Ottawa, Ontario K1N 8J6; tel 613-234 0704; fax 613 234 7368,

Direktoratet for udlaendinge (The Directorate for Aliens), Absalonsgade 9, 1658 København V; tel 31 22 08 77. EU and Austrian citzens apply to this Directorate for Aliens for a residence permit.

Direktoratet for udlaendinge, Ryesgade 53, 2100 København Ø; tel 31 39 31 00. Non EU nationals have their paperwork dealt with at this directorate.

Folkerregisteret (The National Register), Dahlerupsgade 6, 1640 København V. Open Monday to Friday, 10am-2pm and Thursdays 10am-2pm & 4pm-6pm. Tel 33 66 33 66.

Use It, Youth Information Copenhagen, Rådhusstraede 13, 1466 København K; tel 33 15 65 18. Young people's advice centre.

Setting Up Home

Rent or Buy?

The majority of foreigners setting up home in Denmark at least initially, will have to rent rather than buy because of the Danish Law of Aquisition which says that only residents of Denmark can purchase real estate there. Finding somewhere to stay that is not too expensive or inconvenient requires quite a lot of hard work as there is a considerable demand. It is a question of trying everything: newspaper adverts, notice boards in pubs and supermarkets etc. Information centres can also be helpful as can the district housing office which may have non-profit housing at their disposal. Another useful address, particularly for short-term accommodation (private rooms and communes) is Copenhagen Youth Information,(13 Rådhusstraede 13, 1204 Copenhagen K; tel 45/33 15 47 99).

The Legal Aspects of Renting

Tenancy Agreements

According lawyers in the Danish Ministry of Housing in Copenhagen, the laws governing Danish property are probably the most complex in Europe. Suffice it to say that when you rent a property, strictly speaking, a written tenancy agreement is not required as all such arrangements automatically come under the law of tenancy. However it is not a bad idea to have a written agreement just to avoid misunderstandings. Under the law, if either party insists on a written contract then it is obligatory to draw one up. A standard type of contract can be bought from stationers and bookshops. It is important to realise however that while such special contracts exist and may be duly signed by both parties, the tenant still has statutory rights which cannot be superseded.

Deposit and Receipts. The landlord also has statutory rights: he or she can charge a prepaid deposit of up to six months rent before you move in, but three months rent is more usual. The tenant should always obtain a receipt for any money paid as a deposit and for the monthly rent payments. Rent automatically falls due on the first working day of each month and if the tenant fails to pay in time, the landlord is entitled to cancel the tenancy as the failure to pay is interpreted under the law as giving a notice to quit.

It is difficult to be precise about monthly rents but you should expect to pay at least kr1600 per month. If you have to pay three months' deposit before you move in you will need at least kr5000 at the outset of your stay.

Notice to Quit. A landlord and tenant are both obliged to give notice to quit a minimum of one month in advance. A longer period may be agreed by both parties if a special contract is drawn up. Notice to quit should always be given on the last day of the month otherwise you cannot quit until the end of the subsequent month. i.e. If you give notice to quit on December 1st, the moving out date would be February 1st.

Moving Out. When you leave your accommodation it should be in the same state as when you moved in. It is a sensible idea to take a series of photographs (preferably with a camera that dates the photos), when you move in, especially of items of decor that are in a dilapidated state. Then if there is a dispute you will have evidence to support your argument.

Lodgers' Associations. Denmark has a national network of tenants' associations which come under the umbrella organisation Lejernes Landsorganisation (LLO). For further details of your local one you can contact the LLO's Secretariat (Rewentlowsgade 14, 4. 1651 København 5; tel 31 22 68 69.). As a member of this organisation you are entitled to professional advice with any problems relating to your tenancy.

Unfair Rents. Under Danish tenancy law you can only be charged what the room is worth. If you wish to appeal against what seems to be an overhigh rent you should contact the rent arbitrators (*Huslejenaevnet*) in your locality. Not all municipalities have these, so if there is not one available contact the nearest advice centre instead.

Home Exchange

As a way of giving yourself time to find somewhere to rent you might like to consider arranging a home exchange. Normally these occur between families, rather than individuals. The following organisations specialise in home exchanges for short periods:

Danske Bolig Bytte, Hesselvang 20, 2900 Hellerup; tel 31 61 04 05.
Intervac, Denmark, c/o JCH Lauritzen, Postboks 34 3000 Helsinger; tel 42 19 00 71.
Haney's Bolig Bytte, v/Ingrid and Erik Haney, Byvaernsvej 3, 2730 Herlev; tel 3043 17 79; fax 42 84 77 79.

Buying Property

At the time of going to press, there is a controversy about the restrictions Danish property purchase laws impose on prospective buyers from outside Denmark. The Danish Law of Aquisition is one of the most restrictive in the EU. As things stand, there is a residency qualification, in that only residents of Denmark who have lived there for five years are eligible to purchase property under Danish law. There is however an exception made in the case of citizens from EU countries who may buy property provided that it is for personal use, year-round i.e. a principal residence or business premises, and provided that they are an employee or self-employed in Denmark. In the case of a secondary residence, EU nationals have to obtain the permission of the Ministry of Justice unless they have already lived in Denmark for five years. Non-EU nationals have to hold a Danish residence permit to buy a primary residence and permission to buy a secondary residence is only granted 'in a few exceptional cases and only if the party concerned has very special, close ties with Denmark'.

The residency clause has been challenged by Germans in particular as many German citizens would like to buy holiday or retirement property in Jutland, which has a border with Germany, and in island regions where many Germans like to take sailing holidays. Not only are property prices cheaper in Denmark than in Germany but financial terms are much easier. It is a peculiarity of the Danish property purchasing system that the mortgage is left with the property, so that whoever buys the property also gets the mortgage, usually on very favourable terms.

For details of any changes in the law and for general information contact: The Ministry of Justice (Justitsministeriet), Slotholmsgade 10, 1216 Copenhagen K; tel 33 92 33 40.

Loans from Mortgage Credit Institutions

It is less usual for foreigners to buy property in Denmark than in other European countries because of the restrictions (see *Buying Property* above), but for those who do there are sound and favourable financial facilities. As in other countries there exist specialised mortgage credit institutions whose principal activity is to grant long-term loans for the purchase of real estate. The way in which these funds are traditionally raised is however unique to Denmark in that they are raised purely from the issue of bonds on the Copenhagen Stock Exchange. These have long been the staple of both the stock exchange and the non-speculative investor as they provide rock solid investments regarded as gilt-edged stock along with government issued bonds. The practice of issuing such credit bonds arose out of a need to rebuild Copenhagen following two disastrous fires which consumed much of city in the eighteenth century. A balance between the volume of loans granted and the volume of bonds issued is carefully maintained so the interest risk to mortgage credit institutions is minimal. Borrowers can obtain loans for all the usual range of buildings and renovations. Lending limits are prescribed by law at 80% maximum of the value of residential property and repayments take place over ten to 35 years. There are several types of mortgage loan with varying methods of repayment:

1. *Serial.* Repayments by equal capital instalments, and reducing interest instalments.
2. *Annuity.* Repayments are constant throughout the loan period.
3. *Bullet.* Interest repayments only, with all the capital being repaid at the end of the loan.
4. *Index.* (for new construction only). Variable instalments depending on the changes in the price index.

Useful Addresses

UK Addresses of Danish Mortgage Institutions:

The Mortgage Credit Association Denmark KD, 43 New Bond Street, London W1Y 9HB; tel 0171-491 0404; fax 0171-629 0362
Nykredit Mortgage Bank plc, Nykredit House, 26 Lockyer Street, Plymouth, Devon PL1 2QW; tel 01752-669286; fax 01752-666922.

Addresses of Mortgage Credit Institutions in Denmark:

Byggeriets Realkreditfond (The Building Mortgage Fund), Klampenborgvej 205, 2800 Lyngby.
Kreditforeningen Danmark (The Denmark Mortgage Credit Association), Jarmers Plads 2, 1551 Copenhagen V.
Nykredit (New Credit), Otto Mønsteds Plads 2, 1563 Copenhagen V.
Dansk Landbrugs Realkreditfond, Nyropsgade 21, 1602 Copenhagen V, Denmark (Danish Agricultural Mortgage Fund).
Industriens Realkreditfond, Nyropsgade 17-19, 1602 Copenhagen V (specialists in industrial mortgages).

The Danish Mortgage Credit System

The Danish Mortgage Credit System differs from systems in many other countries which tend to be based on an assessment of the individual borrower's financial circumstances. In Denmark the granting of loans is solely against mortgage in real estate, a system which has several advantages. There are limits on the proportion which can be lent and in addition, if a change of ownership occurs it is not normally necessary to re-assess earlier loans.

Mortgage rights in individual properties are protected by a national registration system. Everytime that a mortgage is taken out it has to be registered. This protects mortgage rights in any given property.

The Danish Mortgage Credit System in the Future

Unfortunately the Danish Mortgage System is under threat from the Single Market of the European Community which enables foreign mortgage institutions to set up in Denmark on perhaps not quite as secure a basis as the traditional ones. Danish mortgage legislation has been changed to take this into account. The legal form of new mortgage credit financing institutions will be a limited company with capital of at least 150 million Danish kroner.

Loans from Banks

Those who obtain a mortgage from a bank are subject to fewer restrictions than someone who borrows from a mortgage credit institution as the terms of the loan are based on the bank's assessment of the borrower's ability to repay, rather than on legalities. It may thus be possible to get a 100% mortgage if the bank deems the risk acceptable. Alternatively it might be possible to obtain the maximum 80% from a mortgage credit institution and the balance from a bank.

Repayment periods and rates of interest vary depending on the bank and the amount of the loan. Long-term (i.e. up to 30 years) loans are generally possible.

Utilities

Electricity & Gas

The electric current is 220 Volt AC. (50 Hz) and plugs are of the two-pin variety, so bring continental adaptors if you don't want to change them.

For a small country, Denmark has a lot of electricity companies; 68 to be precise. Furthermore each community is free to choose its own sources. Many automatically opt for ecologically sound ones which in Denmark often means wind. Thanks to a long North Sea coastline and an average windspeed of 7 to 8 m/sec throughout the year, this is a very practical option. It has also made wind companies a profitable investment in Denmark. Wind power is now a highly developed Danish industry and one maker of wind turbines, Vestas, exports them all over the world. Trying to find ways of minimising the visual effect of wind farms on the landscape will no doubt improve the popularity of wind farms in other countries where the landscapes are not as suitable as in Denmark. Siting them on offshore platforms is one possibility.

It is not unusual for an electricity supplier to utilise more than one source. For instance one small community in Jutland uses natural gas, biodiesel and over 200 wind turbines. Suppliers sell any surplus energy to the national grid.

Thanks to a homegrown supply of natural gas, Denmark has adequate for its needs and the surplus is exported.

Removals

Anyone who chooses not to transport their belongings to Denmark will certainly save money on removal expenses. However, nearly everyone possesses something to which they feel inextricably attached and it is always comforting to have something to remind one of home. Additionally one should take into consideration that some goods are much cheaper in the UK than in designer conscious Denmark and it may therefore be worth transporting them by sea or land.

Always start with a list of 'essential items'. Then try to cut it down to a minimum. Electrical items and gadgets are always much more expensive in Denmark and it may be worth taking them if they are compatible. However, repairs may cause difficulties if they are makes not normally sold in Denmark.

Anything of substantial weight will be very expensive to move and some furnishings may not be suitable to keep in a centrally heated flat, for instance delicate antiques made from wood which are vulnerable to temperature and humidity.

If one intends to take only a small quantity of items, it is possible to transport them oneself, using a hired van. It will however be necessary to obtain clearance from the hire company.

If you are paying a removal company then choose a company experienced in overseas removals and which can readily provide a quotation for any destination.The British Association of Removers (BAR, 3 Churchill Court, 58 Station Road, North Harrow, Middx. tel 0181-861 3331) will provide a list of firms and general information on moving possessions overseas. Individuals normally have to pay the removal company up front for the removal so if you are worried about the removal company going bust or what will happen if your most precious items are damaged or lost, BAR has set up International Movers Mutual Insurance so that clients of any of the companies belonging to BAR will be compensated for loss or damage, or in the case of bankruptcy the removal will be taken over by another member company.

Daily Life

Anyone who goes to live in a foreign country, will initially find that the multitude of daily rituals, previously taken for granted, now pose seemingly insurmountable problems. Admittedly in the small, well organised country of Denmark this is likely to be less of a problem than in some other countries and Denmark has the added advantage, that a high proportion of its citizens speak English very proficiently. There are estimated to be over 28,000 nationals of other EU countries living and working in Denmark, which considering its small size and population is a significant number. The intention of this chapter is to provide as much as possible of the practical information required to cope with the daily aspects of Danish life. If you have already experienced living or working in another Scandinavian country, much of the information will probably seem familiar.

The Danish Language

Danish has some similarities with German, which many Danes also speak, and is related to Swedish and Norwegian. Many Low German words entered the language in the Middle Ages from Denmark's connection with the Hanseatic Traders. Swedes and Danes are mutually intelligible to each other as their languages are both rooted in East Norse, a language of the Viking period. Norwegians and Danes can also understand each other (more or less) though Norwegian evolved from the slightly different West Norse. However, Danish was the official written language in Norway until the nineteenth century. A 'purification' of Danish took place in the eighteenth century when many French words in common usage were replaced with newly created Danish ones. As recently as 1948 the spelling of Danish was reformed to more closely resemble that of related languages (Norwegian and Swedish). Helpful as this may have been to other Scandinavians it has little effect on the ability of foreigners to understand Danish. As with some other languages the pronunciation sometimes seems wildly at odds with the written appearance of the word, as Danes tend to use the glottal stop (swallow whole syllables in the middle), or at the end of a word, and many letters are unvoiced. Danish has three extra letters: å (written aa before 1948), ø and ae which come at the end of the alphabet.

Is it essential to learn Danish?

On the whole you might wonder why you should bother. Most Danes speak English, and Danish is a difficult language to master and is certainly more difficult to speak than to read. Many foreigners give up and lapse into English. However, if you are planning to live and work or stay in Denmark for any length of time it would be advisable to make some attempt to get to grips with it, although you will almost certainly find your efforts to practise thwarted by Danes who will inevitably reply in English. One good reason for acquiring a basic knowledge of Danish, is that if you are job hunting, you will need to be able to understand the situations vacant adverts, which are invariably in Danish.

Learning Danish
Most people will be starting from scratch as unlike French, German, Spanish, Italian and Russian, Scandinavian languages are not taught in European state schools. There are various ways to go about learning the language which are dealt with below.

Self-Study Courses
You are fairly unlikely to find an evening course in Danish which will mean that you will probably have to resort to a self-study programme, backed up by, if you are lucky, a private tutor. Unfortunately, the most popular exponent of self-teaching language packages, the BBC, does not extend its range to any of the Scandinavian languages. The main possibilities are the American company Audio-Forum, which has a UK distributor, and Linguaphone whose Danish starter courses cost about £105 and £169 respectively.

There are other teach yourself courses available, and new ones are always coming on the market so it is worth browsing in the foreign languages department of a good bookshop.

Useful Addresses
Audio-Forum, UK Distributor: Sussex Publications, Microworld House, 2-6 Foscote Mews, London W9 2HH; tel 0171-266 2202; fax 0171-266 2314.
Linguaphone (head office: St. Giles Road, 50 Poland Street, London W1V 4AX; tel 0171-287 4050.

Language Courses in the UK
You may be lucky enough to live near a university that has a Scandinavian department where you can attend a course in Danish language and culture on a part-time basis. If this is not the case, a possible alternative would be attending a course at a commercial language school:

The Berlitz School of Languages, 9-13 Grosvenor Street, London W1A 3BZ; tel 0171-915 0909. This is an international organisation that offers language tuition specifically tailored to the individual's requirements. In the UK Berlitz can arrange one-to-one Danish courses with native speakers. The cost varies but this is generally the most expensive way to learn a language. One advantage of the Berlitz schools is that courses begun in the UK can be completed or continued abroad. Berlitz Branches in the UK are also located in Birmingham, Manchester, Leeds and Edinburgh. Danish courses may not be available in all these localities because of the comparative rarity of Danish teachers.

In Britain, the Danish Cultural Institute (3 Doune Terrace, Edinburgh EH3 6DY; tel 0131 225 71 89) can advise on Danish courses in Scotland.

Private Tutors
If you live outside London or away from big cities, you could try to find a private tutor. You can post a 'Danish Tutor Wanted' advertisement on suitable notice boards in schools, sports centres, supermarkets, colleges and universities or in a local paper. It is advisable to try to teach yourself some Danish before you begin looking so that you are not starting completely from scratch.

Language Courses in Denmark

The good news is that if you do have time to learn Danish before you depart, then there are courses in Denmark itself. Danish courses for foreigners are available in all main cities. As in most countries, the cheapest courses are those which are connected to the state education system and in Denmark they are heavily subsidised so the cost to the student is minimal. However, to be eligible for enrolment you have to have a *personnummerbevis* or personal code number (see *Residence and Entry Regulations* chapter). Another possibility is to attend a course in Danish at the local Folk High School, a kind of community and adult education centre of which there are about 100 throughout Denmark. Courses are residential and last one week to ten months. Private schools offering courses can be found under *sprogundervisning* in the telephone directory (yellow pages), but these are generally very expensive.

Useful Addresses

Højskolernes Sekretatriat, Farvergade 27G, 1463 Copenhagen K; tel 33 13 98 22. Can supply a list of all the Danish Folk Schools and the courses available.
The Danish Club, 62 Knightsbridge, London SW1X 7JX; tel 0171-235 5123. Potential members have to be approved, but the Club is for all ages and there is a special youth subsription rate. The Club may be able to help with finding contacts or private tutors through newsletters, notice board etc.

Schools and Education

Education in Denmark

There are nine years compulsory schooling between the ages of six and sixteen with additional years: one year pre-school class and also a tenth school year. Children begin formal schooling at the age of six or seven. Nearly three-quarters of children aged three to six years go to pre-school kindergartens and other child-minding concerns.

Parents can choose to send their children to a municipal school which is free, or to a private elementary school where they have to pay 15% of the tuition fees; about 10% of pupils go to the latter. The emphasis in Danish education is making sure that all students get the most appropriate education for their needs and abilities. Thus slow learners are offered special education in smaller classes so that they do not lose out by not acquiring basic numeracy and literacy skills. Over the years the educational system has adapted to take account of the diversity of the pupils themselves. Children can, in the eighth or tenth years choose an extended syllabus in a range of subjects. In the tenth form there are a range of highly practical options as an alternative to the more academic subjects.

The school year normally lasts about 200 days. The overall framework of basic schooling is defined by legislation and administrative regulations but within this framework schools can work out their own curriculum. Teachers enjoy a lot of freedom with regard to the planning and organisation of their classes within this framework.

Upper Secondary Schooling. After completing basic schooling, students may go on to the three-year academic and general cycle at the *Gymnasium* which culminates in the *Studentereksamen* (the upper secondary school leaving examination) that qualifies the holders for admission to universities and other higher education. About 33% of pupils qualify for the gymnasium which is open to those who have passed the leaving examination of the Folkeskole which includes

Danish, arithmetic/mathematics, and languages (English and German) or physics/chemistry

The gymnasium syllabus can either have a mathematics or a languages bias. In addition to these core subjects of the syllabus, students select three or four elective subjects.

In 1988 a major education reform stated that education should tend more towards increasing historical awareness in students, promoting languages and an international viewpoint while strengthening science and incorporating new subjects such as computer science, business economics and technology.

Most of the Gymnasia are publicly funded and run by the counties but roughly 6% of gymnasium students are at private institutions governed by private boards which receive state grants for most of their operational costs.

It is also possible to attend a two-year course leading to the Higher Preparatory Examination (HF), which also qualifies for entrance to higher education.

Vocational Education and Training. More than half of young people enrol on a vocational education and training course which may be technical, commercial or a health education course. The last is normally oversubscribed. The basic vocational education and training comprises a combination of on-the-job training and theoretical and practical training in college. In addition to the vocational subjects, general subjects are also taught. This kind of education allows for a great deal of flexibility of content, duration and structure. Courses last two to four and a half years, the college attendance element is six months to two years.

Courses are regularly updated to take into account the current job market and, in the area of advanced technology particularly, there are plans to double the capacity over the next few years.

Agricultural Training, also contains an element of theoretical instruction and practical training. There are approximately 30 agricultural colleges whose course content is regulated by the farming organisations with very limited input from the Ministry of Education.

Further Technical and Commercial Education. Such courses usually come after vocational and educational training have been completed and are primarily theoretical advanced courses lasting one to three years. In combination with the Vocational Education and Training, they are a preparation for jobs in production, marketing, service and other activities such as the health sector.

Higher Education

Danish higher education is yet another area of Danish life governed democratically. Most institutes of higher education are autonomous under Danish law. Students, through various student organisations, have joint voting rights with staff in the governing bodies of such institutions on integral matters concerning curricula, syllabi and the distribution of financial resources.

About 15% of young people enrol in higher education in one of Denmark's five universities or other higher education institutions like the Royal Dental College of Copenhagen and the School of Architecture in Aarhus, all of which institutions are financed by the state. Only business schools are private foundations while some teacher-training colleges, engineering and social work colleges may be private or state foundations. The annual quota on an individual course is fixed by the ministry of education, the so-called *numerus clausus*. There are not always sufficient places to meet demand in some areas, notably health education.

There has been a tendency in recent years for universities to adapt courses to the needs of the private business sector and to restrict those oriented towards the public sector. Before 1988 most university courses lasted for five or six years. From that year bachelor programmes lasting three or four years were finally introduced.

General Adult Education

It is estimated that about one million Danes a year participate in leisure-time education. A special feature of Denmark are the *Folkehøjskoler* (Danish Folk High Schools) which were created in the nineteenth century as an integral part of the socio-cultural political movements of the time. There are about 100 Folk Schools which are free, residential and which offer a range of subjects from general to practical. Certain schools run courses for specific groups, for instance retired people, while others are suitable for sports and physical education courses. Courses can last up to an academic year, but there are many short courses lasting one to four weeks. Those on the longer courses tend to be the young unemployed. Anyone can attend a Folk High School provided they are over 17½ years old and there are no entrance or exit examinations.

In addition, all lectures at Danish universities and institutes of higher education are open to members of the public and students alike, the only limitation on access being on space available. All universities and other higher education institutions also also allow anyone to follow single-subject courses. However it is not possible to piece together a degree from such studies.

The 1990 Act on Open Education

A few years ago Denmark took steps to promote continuing further education and training for adults already in the workplace in order to keep up with new technology and an expanding marketplace, with particular emphasis on the type of skills required by export and import companies. Such courses not only benefit the nation as a whole by improving companies' performances, they also benefit employees by giving them the opportunity to be promoted through acquiring additional qualifications. Some firms run their own staff training courses but at least half of the courses are publicly run and 80% funded by the state; the participant pays the remaining 20% of the operational costs. Training courses are normally attended on a part-time basis and must be available out of working hours.

The admission rules for part-time students are normally the same as for full-time students but these can be waived if the candidate has real-life qualifications, i.e. those learned at work.

In addition to part-time training courses a new scheme allows those in employment to take a sabbatical year off to study, on 80% of their normal full employment pay. This is part of the new government's scheme to bring down unemployment. Another is to offer the long-term unemployed the opportunity to attend a course of up to one and a half years' duration, and to receive education benefit for this in place of unemployment benefit.

State Educational Support

The Danish state scheme for educational grants is the *Statens Uddannelsesstøtte* which provides grants to students over eighteen years old as support towards living costs. The grants are means tested and may be available for study periods abroad.

Foreigners in Higher Education in Denmark

Students from other EU countries wishing to study at a Danish University or other higher education institution should bear in mind that a knowledge of Danish is essential. Some institutions require prospective students to take a Danish test before acceptance. Foreign students participating in a Guest Student scheme for students from other countries who wish to study at a Danish University for one or two terms if their studies are already well-advanced in their own countries, also need at least a working knowledge of Danish.

There are however special university courses conducted in English through Denmark's International Study Programme (DIS) for which American, Canadian or Australian students can apply through affiliated universities in their own countries.

Useful Publications

Danish Cultural Institute, Carlsberg House, 3 Doune Terrace, Edinburgh EH3 6DY. Publishes a useful booklet, *Studying Abroad — Why Deny Denmark* about the higher education system and student life in Denmark, available on request.

The Royal Danish Ministry for Foreign Affairs, produces a leaflet called *Studying in Denmark* obtainable from the Danish Embassy.

The European Commission Information Office, Jean Monnet House, 8 Storey's Gate, London SW1P 3AT; tel 0171-973 1992 publishes a free booklet *Higher Education in the European Community* which describes courses and qualifications and gives advice on scholarships, insurance and living costs.

Useful Addresses

Central Bureau for Educational Visits and Exchanges, Seymour Mews House, Seymour Mews, London W1H 9PE; tel 0171-486 5101. A useful organisation that arranges many types of European exchanges for a range of ages and qualifications.

Commission for Educational Exchange between Denmark and the United States of America, (The Fullbright Commission), Rådhusstraede 3, 1466 Copenhagen K.

The Further Education Euro Network, FE Euro Network Coordinator, AVC International, Middlesex University, Tottenham, White Hart Lane, London N178HR. The FE network was started to provide information on further educaton throughout Europe. There are FE Euro Network contacts all over the country; contact the above address to find the nearest.

National Union of Danish Students, Danske Studerendes Faellesråd, DSF, Knabrostraede 25, 1210 København K; tel 33 11 82 60; fax 33 14 30 76.

Denmark's International Study Programme, (DIS) at the University of Copenhagen, Vestergade 7, 1456 Copenhagen K.

Erasmus UK, University of Kent, Canterbury, Kent CT2 7PD; tel 01227-762712. Distributes the grants for students from the UK who want to conduct part of their studies at another university in an EU country under the ERASMUS scheme. Applications for a place should be made to the ERASMUS Bureau, rue Montoyer 70, 1040 Brussels; tel +32 (2) 233 0111; fax +32 (2) 233 0150. Note: from the end of 1994 ERASMUS and the EU's LINGUA programmes will probably be taken over and extended by a new programme SOCRATES which will also embrace inter-EU exchanges at school level.

The Media, Post and Telecommunications

The Media

Television and Radio

Denmark has a state-owned radio and television corporation which competes with several independent channels which have restricted access to broadcast advertising. The two national television channels and three national radio services are supplemented by over 80 local television stations and 270 local radio stations. Of Denmark's estimated 2.3 million households approximately 539,000 homes have satellite television dishes. In the near future, two-way communications including home monitoring, home banking and television shopping, will be potentially available to 565,000 households via cable transmission.

Books and Newspapers
Traditionally, the Scandinavians watch less television and read more than other Europeans. Denmark claims annual book publications of about 10,000 titles and publishes 48 daily newspapers of which Danes are avid readers.

Post
Post offices are open 9 or 10am-5 or 5.30pm, Monday-Friday, and 9pm-1am Saturdays. The central post office in Copenhagen is behind the Central Station at Tietgensgade 37, 1500 Copenhagen. There is also a branch office in the central station that opens 7am-9pm daily.

There is a free poste restante service at all main post offices.

The correct way to address mail is; name, then street (name, then number), then town, preceded by a four-figure code (which is in turn preceded by the country code DK-if writing from abroad). Copenhagen is followed by a letter indicating the postal zone in the city.

Telephone
The important thing to remember is that in Denmark telephone number area prefixes must be used even if you are dialling inside the prefix area. Copenhagen numbers are prefixed with a number between 31 and 39 or 42 and 49. Other codes are listed in all directories. The international access code is 009. For the UK dial 009 44 followed by UK area code (minus initial 0) and the local number. The international country code for Denmark is 45.

Public phones take kr1, kr2, kr5, kr10 and kr20 coins. A local call costs kr1. You put the money in before dialling, but no coins are returned even if you fail to make your connection, so insert only the minimum. On the other hand, you're allowed more than one call for your money, if the time hasn't run out. With newer coin boxes you don't have to insert money until there is an answer. All public telephones permit international calls. For collect (reverse charge) and BT Chargecard calls dial 0015 for operator; from some payphones you may need to insert kr1 first. A cardphone system is also in use. Phone 0030 for help, 0034 for information. The emergency number to call for the fire brigade, police or an ambulance is 112.

All public telephones should have a directory, which comes in the usual two parts — personal and commercial. The letters AE, Ø and Å come at the end of the alphabet. The Copenhagen personal directory is in two parts: A-K and L-Å. There is some information in English and German.

Telegrams. Are sent from telegram offices and post offices. In Copenhagen, the office at Kobmagergade 37 (tel 33 12 09 03) is open 24 hours. Telegrams can also be sent by phone — dial 122.

Broadcasting. The news is broadcast in English on Danish Radio 1 on 90.8 MHz at 8.10am, Monday to Friday; short reports on what's on in Copenhagen are also sometimes included.

At the time of going to press the privatisation of the The Danish telecommunications giant, Tele Denmark is underway.

Cars and Motoring

Driving Licence
Visitors to Denmark can drive on a licence issued by any EU or EEA country, without any further formalities. An international permit is neither required, nor recommended. However, provisional driving licences are not acceptable. The minimum age for driving is 18 years and for car hire 20 years.

Importing a Car
You can import a car into Denmark, as part of removal goods, exempt from VAT, provided that the vehicle has been owned and registered by you for at least six months. If you are already in Denmark you must produce proof of residence there for the previous six months. Motor vehicles for commercial use such as taxicabs or vans are not exempted from VAT. If you sell the vehicle, lend or hire it within 12 months of importation the VAT exemption will be nullified.

Registration Tax
Once the vehicle is imported the owner has to be registered. Registration tax is high andis paid to the Danish Customs and Excise authorities. The tax varies according to the age of the vehicle. Expatriates staying in Denmark for less than a year can bring in private cars provided that they do not have a Danish home. Non-Danish expatriates whose stay in Denmark will not exceed three years are only required to pay 1% of the normal registration tax, per month.

A list of the addresses and telephone numbers of local customs and excise offices can be obtained from the Danish Embassy in your home country.

Roads
The road system in Denmark is modern and extensive. Needless to say anyone travelling widely in Denmark will need to make use of the excellent car ferries, or where available, the bridges linking the major islands. Danish drivers have a reasonable safety record and it would appear that they are becoming progressively safer: the mumber of traffic accidents decreased in the ten years from 1981 to 1991 from 14,311 to 10,871. Fatalities also declined from 662 to 606 in the same period.

Parking. Parking is controlled by discs, available from police stations, post offices, banks and petrol stations. In Copenhagen, the time limit is shown on signs. Meters (limit: 3 hours) are also in operation in Copenhagen and in some other towns, and take Dkr. 1,5, and 10 coins. The sign *Stopforbud* means no waiting; *parkering forbud* no parking.

Petrol. Denmark's petrol is the cheapest in Scandinavia at about 54p a litre for unleaded; diesel costs about 48.27p per litre. Fill up before joining a motorway as they are devoid of petrol stations. A maximum of ten litres of petrol may be carried in safe containers as a reserve. Many petrol stations are automatic and accept Dkr 20 notes.

Touring Club. The Danish motoring organisation is Forenede Danske Motoreje (FDM), Firskovvej 32, Postboks 500, 5800 Lyngby (tel 45 93 08 00).

Accidents & Breakdowns. There are emergency telephones on motorways and emergency road patrols on all the main highways. A national rescue towing service run by the *Falck Organisation* can be called out 24-hours a day. For the nearest, consult the yellow pages. In Copenhagen dial 15 18 08.

In cases of accident involving injury or material damage, the police must be called (tel 112). VAT at 25% is added to garage bills.

Rules of the Road

As in all Scandinavian countries, it is compulsory to drive, or motorcycle, with dipped headlights during the day, regardless of the brilliance or otherwise of the prevailing weather conditions. However it is necessary to do this only outside built-up areas.

The speed limits are 31mph/50kmh in built-up areas, 50mph/80kmh outside built-up areas and 68mph/110kmh on motorways. Town limits are indicated by a town silhouette on a white background.

Children aged from three to seven years are legally required to have a properly fitted safety seat when travelling in the front of a vehicle.

The penalties for drinking and driving are severe. The blood/alcohol limit is the same as for the UK and there is random breath-testing of drivers.

Transport

Air

SAS runs Denmark's domestic network. In such a small country it takes under an hour to fly to all destinations within the Danish peninsular and archipelago. As the overland public transport is efficient and fast, there is not much need to use domestic air services. However, for certain age groups such as under 26's and over 60's as well as for families, it is possible to get substantial reductions on standby tickets. The details can be obtained from any SAS or Tourist office.

Fares come in three categories: The two cheaper ones are Red Departures (*røde afange*) which are return tickets for use on weekdays and Green Departures (*grønne afange*) for weekend returns. The most expensive are blue departures which are valid anytime.

Airport bus. Airport buses run from the SAS terminal in Copenhagen Central Station to Kastrup Airport every 20 minutes (kr28) and take 25 minutes. There are also direct land/sea connections between Kastrup airport and Malmö in Sweden.

Rail/Bus

Denmark has an excellent railway system. Trains are run by Danske Statsbaner (DSB) the Danish State Railways, who have information points at all major rail stations (in Copenhagen, dial 33 14 88 00). Some trains should be amphibious as they spend as much time being transported across water as they do on railway lines. There are ferries specially adapted to take trains between the islands. Rail passengers can leave the carriages and stroll about on board.

A few areas are not covered by the rail network, for instance the remote north east island of Jutland and the island of Funen. In these areas there are bus services often linked to the train timetables. Supplements are payable for *Lyntog* (lightning) express trains, on which reservations, which cost kr30, are compulsory. Other types of train are the ICB and IC3 intercity trains for which seat reservations are also obligatory. The IC3s are the newest addition to the network and connect all four major cities.

Regionaltoget are the slower trains that link the small towns, while S-tog are integrated bus and train transport in cities.

Fares are based on a zone system and are priced according to the number of zones the journey covers. Some examples of adult, single fares: Copenhagen-Vejle (213km/30zones) kr166; Odense-Esbjerg (137km/18 zones) kr106; Copenhagen-Frederickshavn (443km/62 zones) kr231.

Cheap Deals. In addition to cheap deals like the Scanrail pass which is a holiday pass valid for all the Scandinavian railways and the Euro Domino pass which is a holiday pass sold by British Rail International (tel 0171-834 2345), there are reductions of up to 50% for students and anyone over 65 years old on Danish railways. Children under 4 years travel free and those aged 4-12 years pay half. Young people aged 12-25 can get a youth card which entitles the holder to discounted tickets all year round. There is a nationwide discount card valid for 3,6 or 12 months which entitles the holder to discounted tickets on any day. Cheaper day tickets are available on Tuesdays, Wednesdays, Thursdays and part of Saturdays except in high season and group discounts are also available. Commuter passes for a regular route are available on a monthly or annual basis.

Long Distance Buses
In some instances it may be easier to take a bus than struggle with complicated train connections. The main long distance services are from Copenhagen to Aarhus and Esbjert to Aalborg/Frederickshavn.

Sea
The peninsula and islands of Denmark are linked predominantly by ferries (and the occasional bridge/tunnel). The larger ferries linking Zealand, Funen and Jutland are train-bearing (giving a new meaning to roll on, roll off ferry) with numerous on board facilities for passengers, while others are just functional car ferries and there are even more basic ferries for the smallest island communities.

Copenhagen is linked to Malmö in Sweden by hydrofoil, (hourly from 6am to midnight: dial 33 12 80 88 for information) and ship (three daily: tel 32 53 15 85 for details). Prices start at around Dkr45 one-way by ship, double by hydrofoil. The main link from Denmark to Sweden is the ferry from Helsingør (Elsinor) to Helsingborg, which runs every 15 minutes from 5am-2am for about Dkr30 each way. To Germany, the Rødbyhavn — Puttgarten ferry costs the same and runs hourly. There are numerous other ferries linking Jutland and the islands of Denmark to Iceland the Faroe Islands, Scotland, Norway and Poland.

City Transport
Bus/S-tog. Transport around main cities is normally by bus. Buses are one-person operated; board at the front and buy tickets from the driver. Copenhagen has both buses and electric trains. The city is divided into zones, the first three being designated the inner city area. Bus tickets cost Dkr9 each for travel in 3 zones with one hour on all buses and the S-Bahn; add on kr4.50 per zone extra.

Other tickets vary in price and scope: you can buy a discount card (*rabatkort*) worth ten 3 zone fares for kr80. The tourist office will have details of the discount day card which is valid for unlimited travel on urban transport for 24 hours.

Tickets are stamped with the date and time of issue. Smoking is not allowed on any buses. S-Bahn tickets are only valid if stamped in the machines on station platforms. The S-bahn is covered by Eurailpass and Inter-Rail tickets.

The set fine (called a 'surcharge') for travelling without a valid and time stamped ticket is Dkr 150 on buses and kr250 on trains. Buses and trains run from 5am (6am on Sundays) to around midnight, with a reduced bus service continuing until 2.30am.

Regular commuters can get weekly or monthly bus passes or a multiride ticket allowing 10/20/40 rides.

Bicycle

The flat terrain of Denmark (highest point 531 feet) is ideal for cycling holidays or excursions and also for getting about in towns. This is evidenced by the fact that there are over two and a half million bicycles in Denmark. Cycles can be hired from main railway stations for about Dkr 40 a day but if you are living and working in Denmark it would certainly be worth bringing your bicycle or buying one either to get to work or for recreation. If you wish to buy one in Denmark, it is worth considering the police auctions of unclaimed lost property. Details are published in local papers and you can inspect the goods before making a bid. Danes are very keen on cycling holidays and organised tours are run by various tourist offices, affiliated to the *Dansk Cyklist Forbund* (Kjeld Langesgade 14, Copenhagen; tel 33 32 31 21), a helpful organisation that can answer any particular queries about cycling in Denmark. Funen Island is a popular area for cycling holidays. The Danish Tourist Office produces a useful leaflet entitled 'On a Bike in Denmark'.

If you get tired of cycling, it is a simple matter to take your bike on most kinds of public transport. Trains and long distance buses make a small charge, Dkr 75 is charged for flights, while ferries usually take bikes for free.

Hitch-Hiking

It is the general wisdom that hitch-hiking in Denmark is extremely difficult. It certainly will be if you try to hitch on motorways as this is illegal. If you are dropped off in a lay-by or car park you can approach parked motorists. Otherwise try to hitch from somewhere the traffic has to slow down, like a slip road.

Banking and Finance

During the three years up to 1993 Danish banks ran up billion kroner losses. Fortunately the top three banks (Den Danske Bank, Unibank and the savings bank Sparekassen Bikuben) reversed this trend when they managed to move back into the black in 1993. The banks generally are expecting improved performance and a turn around from 1994 however this optimism is somewhat tempered by the fact that many smaller and medium-sized provincial banks are still in financial trouble. The larger banks have been able to recover more quickly partly because of their ability to drastically cut staff and improve profit margins. Den Danske Bank, the largest, was formed by a merger of Den Danske Bank, Copenhagen Handelsbank and Provinsbank. The new entity cut staff numbers by 22% to 12,540 and reduced the number of branches from 613 to 501.

The largest provincially based bank is Jyske Bank whose headquarters is in Silkeborg.

Until recently it was possible for banks to lend money to their own customers to buy bonds in the bank, but after a recent fiasco involving the small Himmerlandbank whose shareholders lost all their money, this practice has now been made illegal.

The privatisation of the Girobank in autumn 1993 brought a big new player into the Danish banking arena. The Girobank was formerly part of the Post Office and was widely used for transactions by government utilities, companies and individuals. It was not however allowed to lend money. Now that it is a limited company there are no such restrictions and its loyal customers provide a sound basis for its operations. At present it is the fifth largest Danish Bank.

The Copenhagen Stock Exchange. The CSE was founded in 1619 which makes it one of the world's oldest stock exchanges. A major modernisation programme was instituted in 1986 which cost one billion Danish kroner. The exchange now has a staff of about 50 who oversee all trading which takes place from stock-brokers' offices via one electronic system aptly called ELECTRA. Settlement times are usually three days. However, despite such streamlined operation the CSE is at present a minor European exhange whose future after the 1996 introduction of almost barrierless international trading, is uncertain. Many shares are strategically held as an attempt to ward off bids from unwelcome outsiders (i.e. foreigners) and thus a strong element of protectionism pervades dealings. The CSE also suffers from a scarcity of big share issues but is hoping to build up a reputation by handling major Danish privatisations, having dealt with the Danish Girobank in 1993 and currently (1994) Tele Danmark, the state telecommunications giant. The other problem is that Danes tend to buy bonds which are extremely reliable, rather than shares of which they are generally wary. The CSE future prominence would depend on it being a main international financial centre. It has already been linked with other Scandinavian exchanges via NORDIX and international ones by Telerate (a Dow Jones subsidiary).

Personal Banking. Opening a bank account in Denmark is straightforward. If you are a cautious type you will probably choose one of the big five banks mentioned above, depending on your location. As tends to be the case with banks other than those in the UK, there will be charges for servicing your account even when it is in credit. Banking hours are normally 9.30am to 4pm on weekdays, except Thursdays when they are extended to 5.30pm.

Generally, the Danish banks are flexible when it comes to tailoring products to the individial customer. As they are largely computerised, their computers generate the required financial package. Danish banks also provide wider services, for instance insurance packages, while some Danish insurance companies also provide banking services.

Money Transfers. There are several possibilites for transferring money to and from Denmark through banks but British banks charge a fee of between £5 and £80 depending on the bank and the amount. The lowest fee is charged by the Co-op bank (£5 to customers and non-customers). The cheapest and slowest way is a money transfer by post. It is advisable to check that the UK bank and the Danish bank involved are 'correspondents'. If they are not the transaction may take longer. The procedure can take five to ten working days depending on the banks involved. The fastest way to transfer money is by SWIFT. Most big UK banks are members of SWIFT which takes no more than two days and costs about £15 from the UK or Dkr 1000 plus a commission of ½% of the amount transferred. Another useful system is the EuroGiro which claims to have 40 million private and business customers and operates an international electronic payment system for a fixed scale of charges and will handle any transaction large or small for a fixed charge of £7.50 plus £2.50 paid by the recipient. It takes four working days to reach any Girobank in Denmark. It is possible for new customers to open an account solely for international transactions, separate from any other arrangements with Girobank. For further details contact: Girobank plc. (Midlands Region, Lydon House, 62 Hagley Road, Birmingham, West Midlands, B16 8PE; tel 0121-454 9876).

Internal Payments System. Danish banks have a very efficient credit card system as they all share the same one *Dankort* which can be used in over 46,000 shops as an instant debit card and in all cash points. About 42% of adult Danes use a Dankort. There is also a Dankort/Visa for use in Denmark and Abroad but the most popular foreign credit card is Eurocard which has twice as many holders as the Dankort/Visa.

Tax and the Expatriate

In the future it is conceivable that tax systems throughout Europe may become completely integrated, but at present this is far from the case despite the Maastrict Treaty of European Union and all its implications.

As a result of the different tax regimes which exist in different countries there are major complications involved in a move overseas. This does not just apply to tax affairs in the host country; a move will conjure up many tax implications in one's home country also. The situation is rather more simple, however, if one is leaving the UK, and thus the UK tax system for good. Tax regulations are more complex if one is buying a second home but this is much less likely to occur if one is moving to Denmark, rather than say France or Italy where the likelihood of property purchase, (rather than rental) by foreigners is considerably higher because of the comparative cheapness and availability of land and buildings.

It is advisable to take individual and independent financial advice before committing oneself to a move to Denmark. This will ensure that no unecessary tax is paid, and should also minimise eventual tax bills. Tax advisers can be located through specialised magazines including *The Expatriate*.

The Question of Residence

Anyone who spends more than six months (183 days) per year in Denmark has to pay Danish tax on his or her worldwide income unless they are eligible for the Expatriate Tax Regime (see below). Taxable income includes income from work, letting and leasing, trade enterprises, returns on investment, annuities and speculative capital gains. Before moving to Denmark it is therefore important to consider where one's main residence will be for tax purposes. The important point to note is that one does not necessarily escape one country's income tax and become subject to another's just by moving there. It all depends on where the tax authorities consider one is resident for tax purposes, and also where one is domiciled — not necessarily the same thing.

Procedure for Residents. The situation is reasonably straightforward if one is moving permanently abroad. You should inform the UK Inspector of Taxes at the office usually dealt with of this fact and you will be sent a P85 form to complete. The UK tax office will usually require certain proof that you are leaving the UK, and hence their jurisdiction, for good. Evidence of having sold a house in the UK and having rented or bought one in Denmark is usually sufficient. If you are leaving a UK company to take up employment with a Danish one then the P45 form given by your UK employer and evidence of employment in Denmark should be sufficient. You may be eligible for a tax refund in respect of the period up to your departure in which case it will be necessary to complete an income tax return for income and gains from the previous 5 April to your departure date. It may be advisable to seek professional advice when completing the P85 which needs to be completed carefully. Once the Inland Revenue has been satisfied that an individual is no longer resident or domiciled in the UK, they will close the appropriate file and not expect any more UK income tax to be paid.

Procedure for Non-Residents. If one is buying a second home in Denmark whether for long holidays or retirement, then the situation as regards taxation is more complicated in that one remains liable to UK tax but may also acquire liability for Danish tax. This may also be the case if one is maintaining any sort of financial connection with the UK, e.g. if one still owns and rents out a home in the UK, thus generating an income. If this is the case then an accountant in the UK must be consulted for individual advice, otherwise you may find that both the UK and Danish tax authorities will consider you liable for income tax, no matter where it is earned. Some people who move to Denmark but spend long holidays or business trips back in the UK may find that the UK Inland Revenue still consider them domiciled in the UK for tax purposes.

At the time of going to press the question of whether non-residents of Denmark can buy property there had still not been resolved so the problem of buying a second home there may not arise.

Personal Income Tax

It is widely-known that taxes in Scandinavia are some of the world's highest, mainly in order to support the welfare largesse and superb infrastructure. Denmark is no exception. However, in a major reform of the tax system, implemented in 1994, there have been some dramatic (for Scandinavia) reductions in income taxes from 68% to 62% for those earning over kr240,000 (the higher end of the scale) and from 51% to 43% for middle and low incomes. In addition, the tax on the very wealthy has been cut from 78% to 68%. Despite the reductions, income tax in Denmark is still much higher than in other countries. For instance, France has a top rate of income tax of 56.8% and the UK's rate of tax on low incomes is 25%. In Denmark taxation of the individual comprises income tax and a flat rate local tax which ranges from 23% to 33% depending on the municipality. These are combined to produce the total tax on individual incomes.

The thinking behind the latest tax reductions is that a sudden lowering of income taxes will help to kick start the economy with a consumer led boom. The treasury will not however be losing out entirely or for long as there will be a gradual introduction of new taxes on fringe benefits and increases in other taxes.

Since virtually all public expenditure in Denmark is covered by the direct and indirect taxes there are almost no other taxes for individuals to pay (see *Church Tax and Property Tax* below). The other burden of taxation falls on companies and organisations see below.

Tax Administration. In Denmark tax assessment for employees is almost completely automatic. The employers pass on employees' details direct to the tax authorities as do banks and insurance companies which gives details of salaries paid, interest received and payments to pension schemes and individuals pay provisional monthly tax calculated on an estimate of taxable income. Thus the taxpayer in effect receives a tax bill, fully itemised which he or she can check and make a note of any items not taken into account such as tax-deductible expenses. In effect about half of all tax bills are dealt with in this simplified manner and thus do not require completion of a tax form. The self-employed generally have to complete a tax form.

Tax is assessed on the previous year's income and tax returns must be filed with the municipal tax authority not later than 1 May each year. Failure to file in time carries a penalty of kr2,000. Any difference between the assessment and actual tax liability will be refunded in the year following the year of income.

Conversely, underpayments of tax have to be paid in three instalments in September, October and November.

Appeals. You can appeal to the municipal assessment board if you do not agree with your tax assessment. Tax appeals can go all the way up to the Supreme Court of Judicature. The Danish government provides a subsidy of 50% towards the expenses of appeal matters of an individual.

Those in search of temporary work who get a job, however temporary may have to rush off and get their own tax card (*skattekart*) from the Skatterforwaltning (Gyldenlovesgade 15, 1639 Copenhagen; tel 33 66 33 66) and give it to the employer themselves the same day. The reason for not delaying is that otherwise tax will be deducted at the emergency rate of 60% and you will not be able to claim it back until six months after the calendar year in which you worked. The office opens from 10am to 2pm daily with an extra hour (4pm to 5pm) on Thursdays.

Other Taxes

At the time of going to press major reforms were being implemented in the tax system. From 1994 the reduced income taxes (see above) will be partly supported by widening the tax base generally. Higher taxes will be imposed on fringe benefits and capital gains and there will be tax increases on energy, water and waste (the so-called 'green' taxes). All these are however taxes paid by companies, rather than individuals. These reforms will be implemented over a five-year period but by immediate reduction of income taxes the government hopes to stimulate the economy.

Church Tax and Property Tax

As in some other European countries the municipalities impose a church tax on members of the Danish Christian Church which amounts to between 0.5% and 1.7% of individual incomes depending on the area. It is somewhat surprising that although most Danes hardly set foot inside a church during their lives, 88% of them elect to pay the church tax. You have to formally opt out of the church in order not to pay it.

Owners of real estate are subject to a local property tax calculated on the value of the land. Rates vary from about 1.6% to 3.4%.

Tax on Pensions

Denmark is the only EU member that imposes a tax on the returns of pension savings. Through the single market Danes with pension savings are now able to shop around outside Denmark for a better deal. This is causing some concern to Danish insurance companies who are lobbying for the tax to be abolished as it constitutes a major infringement of a principle of the free market.

A Note for Non-Residents

It may be a good idea for those intending to live in Denmark on a temporary basis not to register with the Danish authorities, nor to advise the UK authorities of their new situation until professional advice has been taken: to do so may result in paying tax unecessarily. The best way of proceeding will depend largely on how much time each year is spent in the UK. An accountant will advise whether it is better to be resident in either the UK or Denmark for tax purposes and what to tell the authorities in each country.

In 1991 Denmark introduced a special Expatriate Tax Regime available to those who are assigned to work in Denmark for a period not exceeding three years. Under this, expatriates need only pay a 30% rate of tax on salaries.

Previously expatriates were liable to the same rate as residents. Expatriates can opt for the special regime provided that they are on the payroll of a Danish resident employer and their salary does not exceed Dkr500,000 per annum. Only salaries are taxed at the beneficial rate; benefits in kind are taxed at normal rates.

Indirect Taxes

In contrast with some other EU states, notably France, Denmark relies more on revenues from direct rather than indirect taxes. However, as in most European countries the largest indirect tax is VAT which in Denmark is levied at a standard rate of 25% on most goods and services. The EU is aiming towards standardisation of VAT rates throughout the EU but this is some way from fruition. In the meantime, Denmark has no graded rate of VAT but some services, notably banking, real estate and medical are exempted. Exports are zero-rated. The other major indirect tax is car tax.

Information on Tax

Once you have the Personal Code Number (see *Residence and Entry Regulations*) your tax will be automatically deducted from your pay by the employer. Any questions on your tax can be addressed to the employer or failing that the Ministry of Taxation, Slotsholmsdade 10, 1216 Copenhagen K(tel 00 45 33 15 73 00; fax: 00-45 33 32 14 45).

Health Care in Denmark

The Health Care System

The health care system of Denmark is part of the overall state health and welfare policy whose high standards are characteristic of the Scandinavian countries. The policy assures the entitlement of all citizens to good housing, wholesome food, good working conditions, pollution control and an adequate social network of back-up organisations. The health sector is administered by the local authorities who operate virtually all health care facilities. Everyone in Denmark, regardless of income, social and employment status is entitled to almost all health care services free of charge. The health care services are virtually financed through general taxation.

The main elements of the welfare system were instituted in the first half of the twentieth century when the organisational framework was created at a national level to supervise the health conditions of the nation and to supervise the local health personnel. Another major reform came in the 1970's when local government entities were expanded and given more responsiblities which led to a decentralisation of health care to a local level.

As in many other developed countries, soaring health care costs and changing health patterns arising from an increasingly stressful environment and social upheavals, has led to policy changes. This is particularly notable in the emphasis on disease prevention rather than curative medicine. The Danish health system therefore comprises primary health care services (including preventative health programmes) and hospital and social sevices care.

The Ministry of Health is responsible for legislation on health insurance, medical and non-medical personnel, hospitals, pharmacies and the marketing of pharmaceutical products, maternal and child care and other fields.

To coordinate the activities of various bodies concerned with health matters the government runs two central agencies: The National Food Institute (responsible for administering legislation on food, food analyses, foodstuffs, additives etc.) and the National Board of Health

The counties, of which there are 16 including the cities of Copenhagen and Frederiksberg, are responsible for running and planning the main health care services, i.e. hospitals and primary health. The districts (*amter*) which are the local authorities (275 in all) are responsible for running and planning most of the social welfare system and also for certain auxiliary medical services: home nurses, infant health visitors, school health and dental services.

General Practitioners and Specialists

As in the UK, often the first point of contact with the health service is one of Denmark's approximately 3,000 GPs. Anyone from the age of 16 is allowed to choose his or her GP. It is usual for families to keep the same doctor for a number of years which helps the doctor build up a rounded knowledge of the medical histories of individuals. GPs can refer patients to specialists in primary health care or hospitals; also to social services, health visitors and home nurses. All such facilities are free of charge.

The GPs' income derives in part from services performed for the National Health Insurance Board. Specialists, of whom there are some 1,850 in Denmark are also connected to the NHIB. The largest groups of specialists in primary health care are ear, nose and throat and eye specialists. As in the UK most specialists have jobs within the hospital system and carry on their own private practices on a part-time basis.

Physiotherapists

Physiotherapists are allowed to set up in private practice. Patients can be referred to them by GPs. They work under an agreement with the NHIB whereby the fees paid by their patients are partly reimbursed. It is usual for local communities to employ physiotherapists, for instance in nursing homes.

Dispensing Chemsists

All dispensing chemists in Denmark are authorised by the state which decides their number and location. The National Health Insurance Scheme refunds some of the patients' prescription costs. The elderly, the chronically sick, and the infirm pay no charges for medicines.

Dentists

Most Danish dentists operate from their own premises, but they have an agreement with the NHIB whereby, in some cases patients can be reimbursed for some of the costs of medical treatment. All children up to the age of 18 are entitled to entirely free dental care.

Some Preventative Health Measures

Each county has a child guidance clinic whose psychologists and child psychiatrists deal with children with emotional or other psychological disturbances.

All schools have sex education in their curriculum at various levels. Everyone is entitled to free examininations and advice on contraception with their own doctor or family planning clinic.

Every adult above 25 years old is entitled to sterilisation on request. All sterilisations must be reported to the National Board of Health.

Abortion is available on demand up to the twelfth week of pregnancy. Under the law a woman must be counselled as to the nature of the operation and be informed of the social benefits available should she decide to have the baby. A termination later than twelve weeks, has to be considered by a special board on an individual basis.

Everyone who wishes is entitled to an anonymous test for AIDS anti-bodies, with a GP, a clinic for venereal diseases, or at special health clinics. However, anyone who has AIDS has to be reported to the health authorities, but not if they only test HIV positive.

Hospitals

There are over a 115 hospitals in Denmark. Of these 10 are large specialised hospitals with national or regional functions which centralise specific treatments. There are a further 18 large specialised hospitals, roughly one per county, to provide specialists for each county. There are nearly 70 local general hospitals and 15 specialised psychiatric hospitals.

The E111

Anyone who is staying in Denmark for up to three months, perhaps on a speculative trip to look for work, or on a course of study, should obtain an E111 to obtain free, or mainly free, treatment under a reciprocal agreement which exists between most European countries including Denmark. The E111 (known as the E-one-eleven), is available from the DSS Overseas Branch (Newcastle-upon-Tyne NE98 1YX; tel 0191-213 5000) or Department of Health and Social Services, Overseas Branch, Lindsay House, 8-14 Callender Street, Belfast BT1 5DP (for those living in Northern Ireland). Once in Denmark anyone who requires minor treatment should go to any doctor, dentist, hospital or any other part of the health care system where they will be treated free of charge as long as the procedure detailed in the E111 is followed. However, you should note that as a percentage of the treatment costs are still not covered by the E111 is is still necessary to have travellers health insurance cover for the balance.

An E111 normally expires after a three-month period and is not valid once one has left the UK permanently or is employed in Denmark. It can sometimes be renewed and it is also possible to get an 'open ended' E111 if one is making frequent trips abroad for a longer period than three months. However, once a residence permit has been applied for (i.e. after three months in Denmark) permanent arrangements should have been made. Explanatory leaflet SA29 gives details of social security, health care and pension rights within the EU and is obtainable from main post offices, doctors' surgeries, hospitals and also from the DSS Overseas Branches in Newcastle and Belfast. It may be of use to those intending to move to and work in France. Leaflet T4 gives general health advice to travellers, contains the application form for an E111 and gives a country by country breakdown of what treatment the E111 entitles you to.

Private Medical Insurance

Those who are going to Denmark seeking work, or who spend a few weeks or months a year there, may require private medical insurance to cover the balance of the cost not covered by the E111 (see above). If you already hold private health insurance for the UK, you will find that most companies will switch this for European cover once you are in Denmark. With the increase of British and foreign insurance companies offering this kind of cover, it is worth shopping around as cover and costs vary. One of the best known UK companies is the British United Provident Association (BUPA) International (Imperial House, 40-42 Queen's Road, Brighton BN1 3WU; tel 01273-323563). BUPA offers a range of schemes from insurance aimed at holders of the E111, to full-scale private patients' plans (International Lifeline, and Senior Lifeline for retired people living abroad). In 1994 BUPA introduced two new insurance schemes designed to provide comprehensive cover for expatriates living or working abroad. This includes specialist's fees and optional repatriation.

The the standard of healthcare in Denmark is uniformly high, those who take out private patient's plans that allow for treatment in Denmark should have no qualms and it may cut the waiting time which may otherwise be necessary for some treatments.

Care of the Elderly

As is the case in most other EU countries Denmark has a large proportion of elderly citizens: 15.5% are over 65 and there is a very high number of over-eighties thanks to improved health care and conditions. Many countries are having to find alternatives to putting the elderly in special institutions which are liable to become old-age ghettos, or subsidising female relatives to care for them. In Denmark the latter is not a viable option as three-quarters of women of working age are in the national workforce. Denmark has developed a policy of maintaining the elderly in their own homes and thus helping them to keep their independence, for as long as it is practicable. This is acheived by supplying, at the state's expense, a back up network of visiting nurses, 24-hour emergency call out systems, home helpers, meals on wheels and cleaners. This auxiliary sector of health care employs 28,000 personnel and eats up a quarter of the entire budget spent on the elderly. With rising healthcare costs the Danish government is looking at ways of contracting out such services. ISS, one of the world's largest industrial cleaning and building maintenance groups which is based in Copenhagen, has put together a package which it hopes the Danish government will accept. The government's main worry seems to be that although the care will be of a high standard it will not be as personalised as at present and will contribute to the loneliness and isolation to which many of the old are vulnerable.

Crime and Police

The Police

As elsewhere in Scandinavia crime is not rampant on the well-lit streets. However it would be a mistake to assume that they are devoid of danger. Denmark has its share of anti-social and criminal elements often linked, with drugs and other addictions.

Should you need their assistance, the police are typically polite and helpful. It was therefore with some surprise that a foreigner in Copenhagen at the time of the Maastricht referendum witnessed them firing ammunition at an unarmed crowd of rioting protesters in Copenhagen, wounding several in the process. The Danes may be one of the most liberal nations on earth in some ways, but the limits of tolerance would not appear to embrace permitting civil disturbance.

The courts come under the Constitution and they operate at three levels: The Lower Courts of which there are eighty-four, deal with the majority of cases; the High Courts of Justice, of which there are two, handle cases not handled by the Lower Courts; The Supreme Court of Judicature deals with appeals from the Lower Courts.

In addition there are three specialised courts: The Maritime and Commercial which handles trade and shipping disputes and the Rent Tribunal and the Labour Tribunal which handle their relevant disputes.

Local Government

In addition to the national parliamentary elections, local elections are held every four years. Local mayors and chairs for local committees are elected by the locally elected councillors from among themselves.

The municipalities are very important at local level. They collect both national and local taxes and are responsible for providing most of the social welfare budget of their area. In addition they run the local schools, libraries, rest homes and other public institutions. They are also responsible for administering various authorisations such as building permits.

Elections for Denmark's sixteen county councils are held simultaneously with local government elections. A county council is mainly the local executive of the country's political administration and as such has limited powers. Each county usually comprises more than one municipality.

In April 1994 the European Commission endorsed proposals to give EU citizens living in another Member State the right to vote and stand in local elections.

Social Life

Anyone considering living and working in Denmark might wonder whether Danish social life would make a vivid impression on the foreigner. Less is known of how Danes tend to enjoy themselves than of some other nationalities. Most people have an idea of southern European social life from holiday or cultural visits, or have an idea about what the Germans or Belgians do to amuse themselves. The Danes too are not without their hedonistic side. In common with Britons they tend to be much more outgoing when the sun is shining and in summertime they inhabit the outdoors as much as possible; campsites, beaches, cycling tours and yachting are all good ways to meet the Danes at their most enjoyable pastimes. In winter they become more hearth-oriented and practise the Danish art of *hygge*. This modern version of wassailing involves inviting some well-chosen friends to one's well-heated and insulated home to share a cosy and intimate evening with plenty of skoaling (toasting). The creation of a convivial atmosphere is probably the Danes' way of creating a bulwark against the isolation and suicidal tendencies to which Scandinavians, enduring a long winter seem particularly prone. Fortunately for anyone living and working in their country, the Danes tend not to be as reserved as Norwegians and they probably have a more British type of humour than the Swedes and Finns. On the whole Danes are informal, easy-going and welcoming to outsiders. As a foreigner you may have to wait a bit longer to be invited to *hygge*. When you are, remember to take flowers for your hostess and not to drink from your glass or make a toast before your host does and not to make jokes about their Royal Family.

The Danes

Although the Danes are easy-going, tolerant and friendly, their reactions will be quite different to those of southern Europeans. Whereas some nationalities will plunge into a heated discussion on some controversial subject with a total stranger, the Danes are less likely to be drawn into such a fray; preferring instead to do the opposite — withdraw almost completely which gives the impression of emotional shallowness or lack of interest. In fact passionate outbursts are not a Danish characteristic. As acquaintance develops you may eventually receive the benefit of their carefully considered and matter-of-fact opinions. If you are used to southern Europeans then the Danes may strike you as a little cold and reserved at first. They will not, as one visitor put it 'invite strangers into their houses'. However, once the ice has been broken, Danes are very amicable and apt to make staunch friends. As in Scandinavian countries generally, individuals do not like to stand out from the crowd. Danes are also very nationalistic and it is therefore inadvisable to make jokes at their expense or about neighbouring Sweden, even if the Danes do it themselves.

Social Attitudes and Practices

One aspect of the Danes which people may find refreshing is their relaxed, no-nonsense way of dealing with most things including social and sexual issues and the openness about sexual matters generally. Danes are not at all easy to shock. Danish women are emancipated, straightforward and broad-minded. They have achieved an equality within their culture that few other European nations can boast. As sex is no longer a taboo subject there is no mileage in jokes about sex which are rather incomprehensible in such an open society. Such open-mindedness and indpendence, underpinned by a welfare state that ensures that all situations are supportable has led to an increase of partnerships that are not formalised by marriage. Denmark has the highest percentage (46.4%) of babies born outside wedlock of any EU nation, and one of the highest divorce rates — two out of every three marriages fail. However, owing to a policy of providing sex education in all schools, unwanted teenage pregnancies account for many fewer births than in other developed countries, like Britain and France.

Not being punctual is considered extremely impolite on social occasions and bad practice in business. Danes are also compulsive in expressing gratitude and appreciation so going round saying *tak* (thankyou) several times to anyone who does you a favour or a kindness is essential.

Entertainment and Culture

The nearest the Danes get to the festival of the midnight sun (which occurs further north in Scandinavia), is June 23rd (St. Hans Eve) when huge bonfires are lit across the country and particular songs are sung.

The Danes are reputed to be great readers (perhaps something to do with the long winters). Public libraries are well stocked and carry a large foreign language section (mainly English and some French). To join a library you will need a *sygesikringskort* (social security card). The Danes are also fervent patrons of their many annual arts festivals including the Roskilde Rock Festival end of June/beginning of July and the Copenhagen Jazz Festival and many more. Details can be obtained from the Danish Tourist Office in your own country. In Denmark itself look for flyers and free sheets advertising events or get the complimentary music monthly *Kappa*. In the arts generally, Denmark is well regarded: the Royal Danish Ballet, based in Copenhagen is considered of a very high international standard.

Sport

Football is regarded as the national sport of Denmark which takes great pride in having been the European football champions in 1992 although they have been slipping down the league ever since. The Danish fans are known as *roligans* (a pun on the word for quiet) which makes them somewhat different in reputation from their British counterparts.

In a country as flat as Denmark it is hardly surprising that cycling is very popular. Additionally, it is the main form of transport for many Danes, and cities and main roads are equipped with numerous cycle paths. Such is the consideration given to cyclists, they also have right of way over other traffic.

Sailing is another favourite Danish pastime and with many coastal villages and havens with marinas it is no wonder that almost every locality has its own little regatta as well as other events. Windsurfing has also gained in popularity during the last decade. Finding the wind is no problem, but you need to be well insulated.

Disabled Sports. As in other Scandinavian countries the disabled come in for exemplary consideration and disabled sport facilities are very well organised. The Danish Sports Organisation for the Disabled (DSOD) has 20,000 members.

Shopping

Normal shopping hours are from 8am or 9am to 5.30pm. Large supermarkets are often open later on most evenings but there is general late shopping on Fridays until 7pm or 8pm. Most shops are closed on Saturdays from 1pm until Monday morning with the exception of bakers which (sometimes) open on Sunday mornings. On the first Saturday of the month, shops are allowed to open from 9am to 5pm. There are also kiosks (*døgnkiosker*) which keep longer daily hours and are open daily. Supermarket chains include Brugsen, Irma and Netto. The last, Netto is a minimalist retailing concept which involves displaying goods in cardboard boxes on the floor, in a warehouse environment. This concept of shopping which emerged from the recent recession, has just begun to catch on in the UK and Germany. More convivial perhaps are the fresh produce markets which most towns hold on Wednesdays and Saturdays.

You can buy groceries until midnight each day at the City Market, Central Station in Copenhagen, and at railway stations in Odense, Åarhus and Aalborg.

Part of the high cost of shopping in Denmark is the sales tax of 25% which is levied on most goods and is included in the price.

Women's Issues

Denmark had its share of feminist hype in the seventies and eighties when its radical feminists were known as the *Rødstrømper* (red stockings). Although they are now older and calmer, they have left a legacy of their heyday in the network of feminist groups and women's advice and support centres.

Useful Addresses
Women's Organisations:

Dannerhuset:, Gyldenlovesgade, Copenhagen; tel 33 14 16 76.
Kvindehuset:, Gothersgade 37, Copenhagen; tel 33 14 28 04.

Pets

According to the British Ministry of Agriculture, Fisheries and Food (MAFF) dogs and cats can be imported into Denmark from the UK without any restriction provided that they have travelled to Denmark direct. Those that have not travelled direct require a rabies vaccination not less than 30 days and not more than 12 months before export and the animals must be accompanied by an EXA26 certificate.

Unaccompanied animals must enter Denmark at one of the frontier points where there is a veterinary surgeon authorised to inspect animals. These are: Billund, Copenhagen, Elsinore, Ebsjerg, Frederickshaven, Padborg, Rodby and Ronne.

Anyone exporting their pets back to the UK from Denmark should bear in mind that current regulations stipulate that all such animals will have to undergo a six-month period of quarantine on arrival in Britain during which time they will be vaccinated against rabies. Additionally, an import licence should have been previously granted on behalf of MAAF.

As regulations are subject to constant review it is in any case advisable to contact the Ministry of Agriculture, Fisheries and Food to check before making any arrangements to import pets into Denmark: MAFF, Government Buildings, Hook Rise South, Tolworth, Surbiton, Surrey KT6 7NF; tel 0181-330 4411; fax 0181 337 3640.

Public Holidays

Denmark does not have an excessive number of public holidays, but they are taken seriously with all shops etc. firmly closed on the appropriate day. The main public holidays are:

1 January — New Year's Day	Palm Sunday
Maundy Thursday	Good Friday
Easter Sunday	Easter Monday
4th Friday after Easter (*Store Bededag*)	May Ascension Day
5th June Constitution Day	June Whit Sunday
June Whit Monday	Christmas Eve
Christmas Day	Boxing Day

Metrication

Denmark uses the metric system in all respects and in the long run it is much easier to learn and think in metric if you don't already do so; otherwise you are always trying to convert from metric to imperial.

Retirement

Background Information

By all accounts the Germans are more likely to want to retire within Denmark (which has a common border with Germany), than Britons are. Many Germans enjoy regular holidays in Denmark and have built up the kind of relationship with areas of the country that the British have with certain parts of France. An additional attraction for Germans is the German-speaking population of southern Jutland. The Germans would not even find the Danish winters particularly severe. Britons on the other hand traditionally seek to retire to climes sunnier than their own where the property and the living expenses generally are cheaper than at home. Denmark does not fulfill any of these criteria and so would probably only be considered as a place to retire to by those who had a connection with Denmark built up over many years.

Theoretically however, those of Danish retirement age (67 years) and older can be well off in Denmark with its generous welfare provisions. Health and hospital care is almost totally free and there is extensive provision for care in their own homes for the very elderly and infirm. Where special housing has to be built for the elderly it takes into account that each resident should have an independent apartment and facilities, in other words the institutional approach to care of the elderly has all but vanished except in the case of the very old, the very frail and the demented.

An old-age pension is about kr5000 monthly for a single person and just under double that each for a married couple. Pensions can be supplemented by government grants for such things as rent, spectacles and television licence fees. In addition, to top up their government pension, many retirees have paid into pension funds or private pension plans.

Those who plan to have an active retirement in Denmark will have no difficulty finding things to do. Danes are born clubbers and form associations at the drop of a hat. There are many pensioners' societies and clubs for socialising and also courses, excursions and entertainment. There are cheap travel deals (usually at 50% reduction) for retired people on all public transport and internal air services. There are also reductions for pensioners doing evening classes.

At day care centres and other centres for the old, there is an increasing emphasis on getting the old to take a greater part in the organisation of their daily lives by means of user councils which can influence the way local authorities plan the future in the field of management of the elderly so that they get the most out of their lives.

It would be wrong however, to paint an entirely rosy picture of retirement in Denmark as it is as possible to become just as isolated there as anywhere else and as a foreigner it could be doubly difficult unless you were already fully integrated. One small consolation is that you would not yearn for a typically British cold wet winter's day as Brits who retire to Florida or Malaga are said to.

Once retired people finally become octogenerian (and many in Denmark do), Denmark's reputation for pioneering care for the over 80s enables them to stay in their own homes or alternatively in sheltered housing combined with activity centres. Those in their own homes are visited regularly by medical and home help staff as required and on an entirely free basis.

Nursing Homes. Where nursing home accommodation becomes unavoidable, residents have to pay rent amounting to a percentage of their pension and other income depending on the system of payment in force in their locality. Local councils have a choice of ways of making the residents pay for stays in nursing homes. Under a new scheme introduced in 1980 they can pay 15% of their income plus electricity and heating. Charges are also made for other benefits (meals, occupational therapy and so on) received in the nursing home but the benefits are normally optional.

Special Considerations

Until 1990 it was not possible for any foreigners other than those who had held residence permits for at least five years previously to buy property in Denmark. This regulation was changed to bring Denmark into line with other EU countries where free movement of all citizens, workers, pensioners and students from a another member state means they can buy property in Denmark without having to fulfill this qualification (which does however, still apply to non-EU nationals). This means in effect that freedom of movement for persons other than employees in Denmark is now assured and that pensioners now have right of residence in Denmark, though they might not be as keen to rush there as they have been to go to France, Spain and Portugal.

Retired people should note that they will need a residence permit in order to get a personal code number which is a prerequisite for using the national health service (see *Residence and Entry Regulations*).

UK State Pensions

Should anyone be in a position to move to Denmark to retire and wish to collect their British pension, there is no reason why they cannot have it paid to them in that country in local currency as this is provided for under EU regulations. It will probably not work to their advantage though as the cost of living is much higher in Denmark than in Britain and Danish pensions take this into account and are more generous (see above). Additionally there are currency fluctuations to take into account as sterling is less predictable than when in was in the European Monetary System (to which the Danish kronor still belongs).

If a pension is sourced in the UK but paid in Denmark, it is index-linked and will be uprated in line with levels in the UK.

Both those who have yet to claim and those who are already claiming a state pension should contact the DSS Overseas Branch (Venton Park, Newcastle-upon-Tyne NE98 1YX; tel 0191-213 5000) for details of payment arrangements for UK state pensions. For those who do not plan to spend periods longer than three months at any one time in Denmark, the easiest course of action is to leave the state pension to mount up in the UK and to cash it in on returning. In the case of a longer or permanent stay in Denmark the pension can still be paid to a UK bank account or to an agent or friend in the UK; alternatively you can have the pension paid to you in Denmark, usually on a monthly or quarterly basis by filling in form E121 issued by the DSS in Newcastle-upon-Tyne (tel 0191-225 3827).

As stated a UK state pension will be paid at UK rates and also in UK currency as long as any contributions still due are paid up: consider this point carefully in the case of early retirement.

If someone has worked in one or more EU countries then they will receive pensions from each country but only in proportion to the number of years worked.

UK Personal Pension Plans
Rising costs of welfare provision everywhere are causing governments to reduce
the levels of benefit on offer. This increasing cost of provision is coupled with
the explosion of pensioners which is going to reach its peak in two or three
decades, so it is no wonder that the personal pension plan business has taken
off in the UK. However those with personal pension plans should contact the
company or financial consultant concerned for details of how the money can be
paid in Denmark. Usually the money will be forwarded in sterling, but some of
the larger personal pension plan insurers can send foreign currency cheques,
though an annual fee will be charged. You will need to ascertain the most
financially advantageous way for receiving payment of the pension. If it cannot
be paid in Denmark, you may need to maintain a UK bank account and stand
the cost of currency exchange yourself.

   You should note that contributions to a UK personal pension fund are not
accepted if the person is not earning a UK income. Expatriates are however able
to invest in offshore pension plans run from offshore centres such as the Isle of
Man and the Channel Islands. There would be no UK tax demands on the
interest on such pensions which would be paid in full, but they would almost
certainly attract tax in the country where they were being paid.

Foreign and UK Wills

It is usually advisable to have a will made in the country where you have
acquired assets rather than to rely on a will made in the UK. Although a will
made in the UK should be executable elsewhere, there may be delays while it it
translated and verified which could be avoided if there is a will dealing with
local assets in the language of the country where the assets are located. The
foreign will should deal only with the property and assets held in that country
and its existence and contents should be made known to the person who has
charge of the UK will and vice versa. It is important that the two wills do not
conflict or duplicate each other and that they take into account any changes in
assets in either country.

SECTION II

Working in Denmark

Employment
Permanent Work
Temporary Work
Starting a Business
Directory of Major Employers

Employment

The Employment Scene in Denmark

Denmark became industrialised comparatively late by European standards, and industrial manufacturing reached its peak after the Second World War. Before that, the economy was largely based on agriculture. The number of independent farmers in Denmark is about 79,000 one of the highest percentages of the population of any EU state, but two-thirds fewer than at the end of the Second World War. However, Denmark's agricultural legacy can be seen in the high level of agricultural exports, though these days it is is technological methods which predominate. Processing is largely managed by farmer-owned cooperative societies. Disappointingly, from an employment point of view, only one-seventh of them employ permanent help.

About 65% of products are livestock based; Denmark is one of the world's leading suppliers of bacon and processed meats. In fact, the pig population of Denmark is a staggering 12 million (more than twice the human one). The farmers' cooperatives have made invested considerably in projects for additional meat processing, ready meals and so on in anticipation of expanded export markets.

Horticulture is also important with flowers and potted plants for export being the mainstays.

The food and drinks industry is dominated by five giant companies: Carlsberg (whose British venture, Carlsberg Tetley has a large brewery in Northampton), Danisco, MD Foods, Danish Crown and Vestjyske Slagterier. Two of Denmark's largest companies, MD Foods (a dairy giant) and Danish Crown (the largest abattoir and meat processing group) are co-operatives.

Danish food companies have clocked up some notable successes in recent years, thus ensuring a high international profile. One such is the company Chr. Hansen Laboratorium which established its reputation as a producer of rennet (essential to cheese-making), but with its eye firmly on future trends it rapidly expanded into natural food additives, and allergy treatment and testing, with the result that its shares have rocketed up the KFX Index (the key index of the Danish Stock Market). A Danisco subsidiary, Danish Sugar has taken over plants in Germany and Sweden and has become Europe's fourth largest producer of beet sugar.

Denmark made its industrial mark through the production of components, rather than glamorous completed products and nowadays produces a range of small, very sophisticated items dependant on a high level of technology. Such products as thermostats, refrigerator compressors, hi-tech pumps, cement-making machines and high tension cables together comprise 70 per cent of Denmark's exports. FLS Industries is the world's leading supplier of cement mills and the machinery and equipment that equips them. While business at home has been slack owing to the recession, the Danish-American subsidiary, F.L. Smidth Fuller Engineering has been doing well in South-East Asia. FLS also comprises road haulage (DanTransport) and an aircraft maintenance group. In telecommunications GN Great Northern and Telecom Danmark have between them completed the ground breaking project of linking Russia to Western Europe by an underwater fibre-optic cable, while the Danish mobile telephone company Cetelco (part of the German Preussag group) has pioneered a mobile telephone which reduces the risk from antennae radiation thought to be a cause of brain cancers amongst frequent users of mobile phones.

Danish pharmaceuticals have also made their international mark. The Danish company Novo Nordisk is one of the world's two leading producers of insulin for diabetes treatment and a world leader in industrial enzymes.

Denmark's biggest single export market is Germany, followed by Sweden and the UK. Denmark has also achieved the rare distinction of being the only country in the EU which has a trade surplus with Japan. Fresh pork, is the most lucrative export to Japan.

Another Danish speciality is furniture design (particularly tables and chairs) and manufacture. Denmark has been making itself highly competitive in this area and is currently in the process of a major export drive which has produced opitimistic forecasts in financial circles, about the growing importance of this industry to the Danish economy.

Traditional luxury Danish exports include Royal Copenhagen china and silverware which have a considerable worldwide reputation.

Like many of its European partners, Denmark has moved steadily in one generation from largely industry-generated manual employment to a white-collar and services employment base. About 36% of all those employed in Denmark are in the public sector which is an increase of over threefold since 1960. The service sector is another area that developed immensely during the 1980's as shipping, aviation, transport, trade in goods and money and tourism all became much more important. The trend away from manufacturing to services, coupled with the fact that there are no extremely low incomes in Denmark means that the need for militant trades unions to resolve disputes between employees and owners over wage increases has largely disappeared. An indication of this is that the post-industrial Danish employee now rates job interest and security as higher priorities than the size of the wage packet.

Since about 1987 most industrial expansion has taken place in new development areas rather than in the old industrial centres. One area that has experienced notable commercial growth is the Jutland peninsular which now provides just over half of all jobs in the manufacturing industry. Denmark has about 11,700 factories of which fewer than 100 have have more than 500 employees. About 43% of the work force is employed by companies with a workforce of under 100, 36.5% in companies with 100-499 employees and 21% in companies of more than 500 employees. There are over 7,000 enterprises with a total work force of about 393,000. Employment breaks down regionally as follows:

Copenhagen	25.7%
Copenhagen metropolitan area	25.7%
Jutland	55.5%
Zealand, Funen and Islands	18.8%

Residence and Work Regulations

The way in which residence regulations for foreigners are generally linked to one's employment position in Denmark means that it is not easy to remain in the country indefinitely while looking for work. Nationals of all EU countries have the right to go to Denmark for up to three months to look for work. If they find employment during this period they must go to the nearest *Direktoratet for Udlaendinge* (Foreigners Bureau), where they will be granted a residence permit. Normally you should apply to the Foreigners Bureau before your three months is up. There are certain conditions for getting a residence permit, even when you have been offered a job. Certain minimum conditions as regards working hours and salary are required and also and that you have joined an unemployment fund. It is required that the salary should be enough to live on. A minimum after tax of kr50,000 per annum is usually acceptable.

When applying to the Foreigners Bureau, you should take your passport or other travel documents, a confirmation from your employer that you have a job including details of duration, salary and so on and confirmation that you have joined an unemployment fund.

If you are not a national of another EU, EEA or Scandinavian country then you are not allowed to work during your stay in Denmark (this prohibition applies even to unpaid work), unless you have obtained a work permit from the Danish Embassy or Consulate before leaving your own country, or the country in which you have had legal residence for the previous six months. As employment prospects in Denmark are somewhat limited by very high domestic unemployment, labour and residence permits may only be obtained in very specific instances where there is need of a foreigner, rather than a Dane to fill the vacancy or in the case of highly specialised skills which may be in demand.

Uemployment Fund Exemptions for Foreigners

There are some specific cases in which a foreigner does not have to belong to a *arbejdsløshedskammer* (unemployment fund) in order to get a residence permit. These include those who have been a member of a Danish unemployment fund for more than two consecutive years previously. Foreigners who are born Danish or who are married to a Danish citizen and foreigners who are self-employed or are carrying out services in Denmark. Nationals of all other Scandinavian countries are also exempted.

Unemployment

It is perhaps no wonder that many Danes put job security at the top of their priorities. The government's tough economic policy of the 1980s and 90's aimed at bringing down inflation and the budget deficit, resulted in rigorous rationalising across the board from some of the country's biggest institutions to the smaller companies. As domestic demand fell and then export demand as Europe generally went into recession, unemployment shot up and is currently running at 12.4%, which is the third highest in Europe after Spain (23.1%) and Finland (18.9%). However the real unemployment rate in Denmark is closer to 17% as revealed by the social security statistics. At least 23% of people of working age (16-66), an approximate total of 510,000 are living on social security incomes related to unemployment benefit. Of these about 100,000 are covered by an early retirement scheme, one of the government's recent measures designed to help younger people find work. Another scheme is to pay those in full-time work 80% of their salary for a sabbatical year to be used for study and updating their skills.

Thus the government's main strategy to combat unemployment and at the same time boost exports and production is to regularly upgrade the skills of the labour force by providing job training and educational programmes so making the labour force rotating and flexible to the demands of the market. It remains to be seen how effective these measures will be in the long-term.

Demand for Foreign Staff

Even before the European recession of the early nineties Denmark was not the easiest of EU countries in which to find work as there is a high level of skills amongst the workforce and great effort is made to update skills to fulfil the latest demands of the workplace. Unemployment, especially amongst young people, is high which diminishes the chances for foreigners even further. Unless you have some highly marketable skill and experience and you are prepared to learn Danish the options will be minimal. One way you can get to know the country is by going there as a guest student on one of the EU schemes such as SOCRATES (formerly ERASMUS), PETRA (c/o Central Bureau London tel 0171-486 5101) and TEMPUS (c/o The British Council in Manchester). That way you will have time to make contacts at Danish university and attend Danish language classes while receiving a bursary that is almost enough to live on.

A better prospect might be available to the international business executive. Although the majority of Denmark's companies employ fewer than 50 staff, there are some multi-national groups such as Asea Brown Boveri (a Zurich-based engineering giant) which have subsidiaries in Denmark and which could provide employment at the higher levels. ABB, is one of the largest and employs 4,600 staff in Denmark alone. Smaller companies are not internationally proficient and might welcome the chance to employ a manager with suitable skills and experience of the European and worldwide markets. See the *Directory of Major Employers* for a list of the largest Danish companies.

Working Conditions

Any British person who has visited Copenhagen or elsewhere in Denmark is usually attracted by the laid back lifestyle and the air of affluence. However, there is a world of difference between visiting a country and living and working there with all the frustrations of daily life which Danes experience just as much as anyone else. However Denmark attracts an increasing number of foreign workers who find it congenial not only from a work point of view but who also find the high Scandinavian ideals about the treatment of the individual are not practised better anywhere in Europe. Denmark is also at the forefront of expertise in certain high technology products including precision components machinery and larger products such as the electronically advanced sailing vessels of the the shipping group J Lauritzen.

Although, like Britain, Denmark has no official minimum wage, salaries are nonetheless much higher in Denmark (as are taxes), than in Britain. The lowest wage paid in Denmark is about £8 per hour. The high taxes finance a meticulous welfare state and superb infrastructure and most Danes are able to enjoy an enviable lifestyle. Industrial relations are good and companies adopt a humanitarian attitude towards their employees as does the Danish state generally. However, typical of their no-nonsense approach to most things in life, firms do not hesitate to divest themselves of excess labour when rationalisation is required. Perhaps the knowlege that the welfare state and state retraining programmes are there to take care of the needs and prospects of the unemployed makes it easier for them. Working surroundings are generally ergonomic and the Danes are punctual, polite and enjoy a relaxed working atmosphere which makes them easy to work with.

Denmark now seems to have inflation under control although it will rise slightly as the new environmental taxes come into effect. Generally prospects for the economy look positive for the future.

Transfer of UK-acquired Skills to Denmark

Working overseas temporarily or permanently, can either be a way of furthering one's career or a means to fulfill an ambition to live abroad: this chapter aims to cover both situations.

Since Denmark became part of the Common Market in 1973, there has been nothing to prevent any UK national in possession of skills and talents which are in demand from working or seeking work in Denmark. However it is only comparatively recently that a system has been worked out for recognising professional qualifications obtained in one country but used in another. Moving between EU countries is now easier from an administrative point of view than it was hitherto. Initially, directives for the mutual recognition of qualifications were dealt with individually, for instance architects in 1985 and general medical practitioners (GPs) in 1986. It is estimated that of the 600,000 GPs in the EU, only a small number, about 2,000 have taken advantage of the directive and so work abroad.

In 1990, another directive ruled that all remaining professional qualifications not yet covered by European Commission directives should be left to the discretion of individual national governments as to whether to allow foreigners from another member country to use them with or without a period of probation or to take a further examination before practising. In general, qualifications obtained in one member country are now recognised in another as from June 1994 when the directive came into operation.

If your qualifications are vocational or in hotel and catering, the motor trade, travel and tourism or office work and you want to know how your qualifications stand up against the Danish equivalent, you can consult the Comparability Co-ordinator through your local job centre or direct: The Comparability Co-ordinator, Employment Dept. Qualifications and Standards Branch (QS1), Room E454, Moorfoot, Sheffield SP1 4PQ; tel 0114-2594144 (answer-machine).

Any EU national, regardless of skills and qualifications, can go to look for a job in Denmark. They must find work within three months in order to be granted a residence permit and ultimately, if they so wish they can settle there. Non-EU nationals however will find the process less straightforward, but if they have a desirable skill or have been offered employment by a Danish company, or a Danish subsidiary of the company employing them, it will be much simpler.

Sources of Jobs

Newspapers

UK Newspapers and Directories

The combined effect of the single European market and the implementation of the European Commission's Professional Qualifications Directives (see above) has not triggered a spate of trans-continental job recruitment but there is a steady crop of advertisements from other EU countries appearing in the appointments pages of UK newspapers such as *The Times, The Financial Times, The Guardian, The Sunday Times* and so on, and this trend is likely to continue now that job mobility has become practicable. In May 1994, *The Sunday Times* carried an advertisement placed by Maersk Olie og Gas AS (Maersk Oil), for a petroleum engineer to be based in Copenhagen. A specialist fortnightly newspaper, *Overseas Jobs Express* available only on subscription (P.O. Box 22, Brighton BN1 6HX) carried an advertisement for school teachers for Denmark in February 1994. OJE also carries articles on working abroad by a range of working travellers and a substantial jobs section.

Alternatively a range of casual jobs in Denmark is included in the annual directory *Summer Jobs Abroad* (£7.95) available from Vacation Work, 9 Park End Street Oxford OX1 1HJ; tel 01865-241978, or from W H Smith and bookshops nationwide. Another useful publication is the magazine *Jobs in Europe* published monthly and available on subscription (52 Queen's Gardens, London W2 3AA; tel 0171-724 5346).

International and European Newspapers
International Newspapers are still a fairly new development in newspaper publishing; these publications circulate editions across several national boundaries and usually carry a modest amount of job advertising. The number of adverts carried and the number of such publications is likely to increase in the near future. Presently, the newspapers to consult include *Wall Street Journal, Financial Times, The International Herald Tribune* and *The European*. As well as employers advertising in these papers, individuals can place their own adverts for any kind of job, although bilingual secretaries and assistants, marketing managers and other professionally qualified people seeking to relocate abroad, are in the greatest demand. Obviously advertising rates vary, but will be several £'s per line, per insertion. For details contact the classified advertising departments at the addresses below.

Useful Addresses

The European, Classified Advertising Department, European Liaison, The European, 5 New Fetter Lane, London EC4A 1AP; tel 0171-822 2458; fax 0171-822 3730. The European, published weekly in the UK on Thursdays and distributed in every EU country on Fridays.

The Financial Times, 1 Southwark Bridge, London SE1 9HL; tel 0171-873 3000. The FT is printed in English in the UK, Germany, France, the USA and Japan and distributed worldwide. International appointments appear on Thursdays in all editions.

International Herald Tribune, 63 Long Acre Street, London WC2E 9JH; 0171-836 4802; international recruitment appears on Thursdays.

Wall Street Journal, The International Press Centre, 76 Shoe Lane, London EC4; tel 0171-334 0008 — European edition published in Brussels: Wall Street Journal Europe, Bld Brand Whitlock 87, 1200 Bruxelles; tel 00-32 27 41 12 11. The recruitment section which covers appointments and business opportunities worldwide appears on Tuesdays.

Danish Newspapers

The potential for finding a job increases if one is able to obtain and read Danish newspapers. The Sunday issue of *Berlingske Tidende* has the biggest number of appointments and jobs while *Politiken* is also worth consulting (though of course they will be in Danish). If you wish to place an advert for a job wanted in either paper you can do so from the UK: Frank L Crane Ltd. 5-15 Cromer Street, Grays Inn Road, London WC1H 8LS are agents for *Berlingske Tidende* and Powers Overseas Ltd. 46 Keyes House, Dolphin Square, London SW1V 3NA deal with *Politiken*.

Other Danish Publications. It is possible to place a free advert in the bi-weekly Copenhagen paper *Den Bla Avis* (the Blue Paper).

Professional and Trade Publications

Professional journals and magazines are another possible source of job vacancies abroad, from British companies wishing to set up offices elsewhere in Europe and foreign firms advertising for staff e.g. *The Architects' Journal, The Architectural Review, Accountancy, Administrator, Brewing & Distilling International* and *The Bookseller* to name but a few. Anyone in the air transport industry should consult *Flight International* while those employed in the catering trade could try *Caterer and Hotel Keeper* and agricultural workers *Farmers Weekly*. Although published in the UK, some of these magazines are considered world authorities in their field and have a correspondingly wide international readership.

An exhaustive list of trade magazines can be found in media directories, for example *Benn's Media* and *Writers' and Artists' Yearbook*, both of which are available in major UK reference libraries.

Danish Publications. Jobs on farms might be obtained by advertising in the farming magazine *Landsbladet* (Vester Farimagsgade 6, 1606 Copenhagen K). A leading publishing house *Teknisk Forlag A/S* (Skelbaekgade 4, 1780 Copenhagen V), produces many journals for technical industries including engineering electronics, chemistry and plastics.

Professional Associations

UK professional associations are a useful contact point for their members with regard to practising elsewhere in the European Union. During the negotiations involved in finalising the directives concerning the mutual recognition of qualifications throughout the EU, many professional associations negotiated with their counterparts in other member states and can therefore be helpful in providing contacts.

Details of all professional associations may be found in the directory *Trade Associations and Professional Bodies of the UK* available at most UK reference libraries. It is also worth trying to contact the Danish equivalent of UK professional associations: the UK body should be able to provide the address. Alternatively you can consult your trade union for information, as they may have links, however tenuous, with their counterpart organisation in Denmark or contact the Danish Federation of Trade Unions (12 Rosenørns Allé, 1634 Copenhagen V; tel 31 35 35 41; fax 35 37 37 41).

A list of addresses of the more mainstream professional organisations is given below.

Useful Addresses

Institute of Actuaries: Napier House, 4 Worcester Street, Gloucester Green, Oxford OX1 2AW; 01865-794144

Faculty of Advocates: Parliament House, 11 Parliament Square, Edinburgh EH1 1RF.

Royal Aeronautical Society: 4 Hamilton Place, London W1V OBQ; fax only 0171-243 2546.

Architects Registration Council for the United Kingdom: 73 Hallam Street, London W1N 6EE; tel 0171-580 5861.

Chartered Institute of Bankers: 10 Lombard Street, London EC3Y 9AS.

General Council of the Bar: 11 South Square Gray's Inn, London WC1R 5EL.

Biochemical Society: 7 Warwick Court, Holborn, London WC1R 5DP.

Institute of Biology: 20 Queensberry Place, London SW7 2DZ.

Institute of British Foundrymen: 3rd Floor Bridge House, 121 Smallbrook Queensway, Birmingham B5 4JP.

Chartered Institute of Building Services Engineers: Delta House, 222 Balham High Road, London.

Chartered Institute of Building: Englemere Kings Ride, Ascot, Berks SL5 8BJ.

Institute of Chartered Accountants: Chartered Accounts' Hall, Moorgate Place, London EC2P 2BJ.

Institute of Civil Engineers: 1-7 Great Ceorge Street, London SW1P 3AA.

British Computer Society: 13 Mansfield Street, London W1M OBQ.

General Dental Council: 37 Wimpole Street, London W1M 8DQ; tel 0171-486 2171.

British Dietetic Association: 103 Daimler House Paradise Circus Queensway, Birmingham B1 2BJ.

Department of Edcuation and Science: Elizabeth House, York Road, London SE1 7PH.

Institution of Electrical Engineers: Michael Faraday House, Six Hills Way, Stevenage, Herts SG1 2AY.

Institute of Chartered Foresters: 22 Walker Street, Edinburgh EH3 7HR.

Institution of Gas Engineers: 17 Grosvenor Crescent, London SW1X 7ES.

Institute of Housing: Octavia House, Westwood Business Park, Westward Way, Coventry CV4 8JP.

Library Association: 7 Ridgmount Street, London WC1E 7AE.

Institute of Marine Engineers: The Memorial Building, 76 Mark Lane, London EC3R 7JN.

Chartered Institute of Marketing: Moor Hall, Cookham, Maidenhead, Berks SL6 9QH.

British Medical Association: BMA House, Tavistock Square, London WC1H 9JP.

Institute of Mining and Metallurgy: 44 Portland Place, London W1N.

British Society of Music Therapists: Guildhall School of Music and Drama, Barbican, London EC2Y 8DT.

The Registrar and Chief Executive, United Kingdom Central Council for Nursing, Midwifery and Health Visiting: 23 Portland Place, London W1N 3AF; tel 0171-637 7181.

General Optical Council: 41 Harley Street, London W1N 2DJ.

Royal Pharmaceutical Society of Great Britain: 1 Lambeth High Street, London SE1 7JN; 0171-735 9141.

Pharmaceutical Society of Northern Ireland: 73 University Street, Belfast BT7 1HL.

College of Radiographers: 14 Upper Wimpole Street, London W1M 8BN; tel 0171-935 5726.

Institute of Chartered Secretaries and Administrators: 16 Park Crescent, London W1N 4AH.

Institute of Chartered Shipbrokers: 24 St Mary Axe, London EC3A 8DE.

College of Speech Therapists: Harold Poster House, 6 Lechmee Road, London NW2 5BU; tel 0181-459 8521.

Royal Town Planning Institute: 26 Portland Place, London W1N 4BE; 0171-636 9107

Royal College of Veterinary Surgeons: 32 Belgrave Square, London SW1X 8QP; tel 0171-235 4971.

Employment Organisations

UK Job Centres

It may not be the first place that springs to mind but job centres in the UK are linked to a network that includes details of vacancies abroad as well as nationally. The Overseas Placing Unit (OPU) specialises in trying to match up applicants' qualifications and experience with European vacancies registered on computer at their headquarters (OPS 5), c/o Moorfoot in Sheffield. Applicants who wish to use this system do not contact the OPU direct but visit their local job centre to fill in two copies (one in English and one in the language of the country where they wish to work), of form ES13. The OPU receives an updated list of European vacancies each month which is then checked against the details individuals have registered. After six months, if no suitable vacancy has been found, the application automatically lapses.

In theory, this system sounds fine; in practice only a relatively small number of vacancies, (tens, rather than hundreds) are registered. There are plans to increase the number of vacancies and streamline the service. The types of vacancies likely to be found through the OPU (also sometimes known as SEDOC) are skilled construction craftsmen and women, and also occasional vacancies for hotel and catering staff, teachers of English (though probably not for Denmark) and office and secretarial workers.

UK-based Private Employment Organisations

There are some employment agencies in the UK which specialize in finding overseas jobs for clients. In many cases these agencies deal with a specific sector e.g. electronics, secretarial, medical, etc.; they tend to recruit only qualified and experienced staff, and deal mainly with regions of the world, e.g. the Middle East where there is still a shortage of home-grown specialists, rather than Europe. Most agencies are retained and paid by employers to fill specific vacancies and do not search on behalf of employees using them. An exception would be agencies, including Drake International which recruits bilingual staff, mainly secretaries and p.a.'s but also receptionists, customer services employees, administrators, interpreters and translators.

Details of employment agency members of the national organisation, the Federation of Recruitment and Employment Services Ltd. (FRES) can be obtained direct from their London address (see below). Those interested should ask for the Overseas Agency List and enclose an A4, self-adressed envelope and a fee of £2. The agencies listed deal mainly with specific sectors, e.g. electronics, secretarial, accountancy etc. and will only handle qualified and experienced staff.

Useful Addresses

CEPEC: 62 Jermyn Street, London SW1Y 6NY; tel 0171-930 0322. A large UK management outplacement and consultancy which publishes the CEPEC Recruitment Guide, a directory of some 550 recruitment agencies and search consultants in the United Kingdom. *The CEPEC Recruitment Guide* is available in reference libraries or from the above address for £21.95 including postage and packing.

CLC Language Services: Buckingham House, Buckingham Street, London WC2 6BU. Offers opportunities for Europeans and North Americans (where valid work permits apply) to work in EU countries at all levels from junior secretary to senior sales executive. Sectors include: sales, marketing and market research, banking, import-export, translating, interpreting, management consultancy, pharmaceutical, media sales and general commerce for secretaries.

Drake International: 57, Brompton Road, London SW3 1DP; tel 0171-823 9233; fax 0171 823 9182).

Eagle Recruitment: 57 Brompton Road, Knightsbridge, London SW3 1DP — specialises in multi-lingual recruitment for all types of permanent and temporary work, secretarial and administrative, across a wide range of professional, commercial and media employment, mostly in Europe.

Federation of Recruitment and Employment Services Ltd: 36-38 Mortimer Street, London W1N 7RB.

Sheila Burgess International: 4 Cromwell Place, London SW7 2JE; tel 0171-584 6446; fax 0171-584 1824. Also has a Paris Office: 62, rue St. Lazare: tel 1-44 63 02 57; fax 1-44 63 02 59. In business over ten years. Specialises in multi-lingual secretaries and personal assistants.

The Danish State Employment Service & Private Agencies

The Danish state employment service (*Arbejdsmarkedsstyrelsen*) has its headquarters at Blegdamsvej 56, 2100 Copenhagen (tel 45-3528 8100) and runs a chain of local labour exchanges (*Arbejdsformidlingen*). The addresses of AFs can be found in the telephone directory. There is a special branch in Copenhagen called *Arbejdsmarkeds-Markedsservice* at Kultorvet 17, Box 2235 1019 Copenhagen K (tel 33 93 43 53) which deals just with students who visit in person. The central *Jobcentret* in Copenhagen is at Jultorvet 17, 1019 Copenhagen; tel 33 93 43 53).

It is advisable not to rely entirely on the effectiveness of the AFs as with high unemployment in Denmark they will not have a vast selection of jobs on their books. It is therefore advisable to arm yourself with the jobs offered section of one of the main newspapers mentioned above and visit employers yourself in person.

Private Agencies: There are a number of chains of general employment agencies that may have jobs in offices, factories, hotels and so on to offer to personal callers. In Copenhagen, two of the largest are *Adia* (N. Volgade 82) and *Western Services* (Kobmagergade 54). The grandiose-sounding *Royal Service Agency* (28B Norregade), was reported a couple of years ago as being a good source of casual jobs, supplying much of Copenhagen's hotel industry. Other agencies can be found under *Vikarbureaux* in the telephone directory.

Embassies and Consulates

Embassies and consulates will not assist members of the public to find jobs. Not only are they unable to deal with the amount of administration involved, but they are not keen to encourage foreign workers to take jobs away from nationals. However they can be a source of contact addresses. It may be worth contacting them by post, or in person to see if they can assist. Most of them produce a few typed pages of information for foreigners about living and working in Denmark. The Danish Embassy sends a free sheet on employment in Denmark and the British representations in Denmark generally have some information sheets for British residents in Denmark.

Chambers of Commerce

Chambers of Commerce exist to serve the interests of businesses trading in both Denmark and the UK, they do not operate as employment agencies. However they may be able to offer background information which can be helpful in the job-hunting process. Denmark has 30 chambers of commerce in Denmark which are part of the national association. In addition there are about 200 local units. Local chambers of commerce can be a useful source of information on a word-of-mouth basis, though it should be stressed that they would only be able to help on a goodwill, casual basis as helping job-seekers is not part of their remit.

Perhaps the best way in which the national chambers of commerce can assist is by providing the names and addresses of member companies. The member companies are medium-sized or large organisations which may well have current or prospective vacancies. Thus, it is worth enquiring on the off chance that there is a job available at the time at which you apply. The chamber of commerce in Copenhagen can supply a the addresses of others throughout Denmark.

Useful Addresses

The addresses of the main chambers of commerce are:

Jutland — *Den Jydske Handelsstands Centralforening*, Ny Banegårdsgade 45, 8000 Århus C; tel 86 13 53 55.

Fyn — *Den fyenske Handelsstands Centralforening*, Albani torv 4, postboks 308, 5100 Odense C; tel 66 14 47 14.

Zealand — *Sjaelland og Lolland-Falsters Handelsstands Centralforening*, Børsen, 1217 Copenhagen K; tel 33 91 23 23; fax 33 32 52 16.

Company/Organisation Transfers

One alternative to finding work in Denmark by applying direct or in person, is to find a position within a company or organisation in the UK which offers the possibility of being transferred to Denmark. Currently few companies will guarantee staff that they will be posted to a specific country after a certain period. However, both the request and the practice are becoming more common as companies take advantage of the single European market for goods and services by expanding their operations in the EU. Ideally, it could be envisaged that companies will post staff as readily from Cardiff to Copenhagen and they do now from, say London to Bristol.

Danish Companies Operating in the UK. A number of Danish companies have entered the UK market in fields as diverse as brewing and banking. However check first that the company you target is a Danish one as many importers of Danish products are British companies.

British Companies Operating in Denmark. Although UK companies have been slower to enter the Danish market than other more obvious ones, notably France, there are many more large British companies now actively involved in Denmark. Since the relaxation of financial controls and the opening up of the free market, many more are likely to follow suit, not least in the financial sector. The British Embassy in Copenhagen (36-40 Kastelsvej, 2100 Copenhagen Ø; tel 35 26 63 75; fax 35 43 14 00) can supply a list of the major companies operating there.

International Companies. There are an increasing number of multinational companies whose branches and subsidiaries are found all round the world and these can offer possible employment prospects. Many addresses of such companies can be obtained through the respective chambers of commerce as discussed earlier. The company name may be different in each country for instance the Danish-based MD Foods International has invested in dairies in the UK, so often a certain amount of detective work is necessary to discover the extent of a particular company's operation in the UK and Denmark and the consequent potential for later being posted elsewhere.

Useful publications

The Financial Times European Top 500 is a reference guide ranking the top 500 European companies by turnover and sector and employee numbers. A comprehensive address list is also given. It can be consulted in libraries or costs £22 to buy.

Who Owns Whom, available in main reference libraries and provides the names of British companies with Danish subsidiaries.

Methods of Application

On Spec Written Applications

You may wish to compile an address book of companies likely to have a use for your particular skills and/or qualifications. Any reference library is a good starting point for compiling such a book. Possible sources of addresses include the Chamber of Commerce Yearbooks, the Danish yellow pages and various professional and industrial directories.

The main drawback of this method is that it can be a very arbitrary, not to mention lengthy, procedure and can cost a small fortune in postage. It will be necessary to compile a great many letters in order to gain even a few leads; the acknowledgement rate may be higher from Denmark which tends to be more meticulous in these matters than some other countries, but postive replies are likely to be very few and far between. Probably the best system is to maintain a rolling list: write a set number of letters each week and regularly replace the addresses used with new ones.

Unless you have a personal contact, the letter should be addressed to The Head of Personnel, or in the case of a multinational, Head of International Human Resources, and if you can discover their name, by means of a quick telephone call, so much the better. Include a c.v. with your letter. If necessary both letter and c.v. should be professionally translated into Danish. A professional agency such as the Institute of Translation and Interpreting (377 City Road, London EC1V 1NA; tel 0171-713 7600), will charge from £80 for 1,000 words, so it is worth checking other possibilities, e.g. local colleges of further education, for this purpose. The best and most convenient method of preparing such letters is by word processor; photocopied circulars tend to receive a much lower response.

Note that such letters need not be restricted to companies, you can also send copies to recruitment agencies and search consultants whose advertisements appear regularly in the main Danish newspapers, weekly news magazines and trade publications. You can also send them to international recruitment agencies in the UK.

A directory of Denmark's top twenty-five companies is provided at the end of this chapter and can be referred to as a starting point from which to begin targeting potential employers. You can also attend trade fairs in your own country or Denmark in order to collect the particulars of potential employers.

Personal Visits

Anyone who is in Denmark looking for a job may want to make enquiries in person as to the availability of employment. This involves not only responding to jobs advertised, but also canvassing potential employers on the spot. Usually an exhausting business entailing much wear and tear to shoe leather and the human spirit, it may still be possible to obtain a job this way. After all, all you need is one positive response so this technique is worth a try.

Before making an approach to a potential employer decide how you can best sell your skills, talents or experience. For example those looking for casual work in the tourist industry will find the fact that they speak English will not over impress the Danes as most of them do so as well. You will have to emphasise instead your relevant experience and interpersonal skills.

When making impromptu personal visits to potential employers, ensure that you have a stock of c.v.'s with you to leave at the personnel department or with the manager, and that you have a contact telephone number where you can be reached. If you hear nothing for a few days it is advisable to follow up your visit with a telephone call. Of course, you may be lucky enough to be telephoned by the employer, or in exceptional cases, offered a job on the spot.

Form, Content & Style of Written Applications

In the vast majority of cases, no matter how one finds out about a job, it will be necessary to write a letter of application. This applies at all levels, except perhaps, for unskilled work or casual employment. Unless an advertisement clearly states that a personal or telephone application is required, a letter is the best choice. The letter will normally have to be written in Danish and it is quite in order to have a professional translation made. On the other hand it is not advisable to suggest that one's command of the language is substantially better than it is.

In many ways the process of doing business in Denmark is relaxed and informal. This does not however apply to job applications, and impressions gained from correspondence are very important. In particular, the letter should be hand written, and tailored to the company/type of job for which you are applying, and appear individually prepared. The temptation to pour out reams of personal history should be resisted as the full dynamism and drive of your personality should be revealed at interview, and not at the application stage. The letter should be formal and respectful in style, clearly stating your reasons for application and the relevance of your qualifications and experience to the employment available. Abbreviations should be avoided, as should jokes which may not be understood. For further guidance on writing business letters, consult *How to Address Overseas Business Letters* by Derek Allen (Foulsham).

Curriculum Vitae

At the core of any application is the curriculum vitae (c.v.). The c.v. should contain concise information and should if possible be no more than one page (two pages maximum), and the information should create the best possible impression. For this reason, many people entrust the preparation and presentation of their c.v. to a company that specialises in this kind of service. They can usually be found by looking in the Yellow Pages under Employment Agencies. The cost is usually about £25 for a one-page graduate c.v. Alternatively, refer to the publication *The Right Way to Write Your Own CV* by John Clarke (Paper Fronts) and *CVs and Written Applications* by Judy Skeats.

Note that for a potential Danish employer the c.v. should be modified to remove any abbreviations and explain any qualifications and so on which could confuse a foreign reader. A c.v. should be on A4 paper and it is acceptable to send out photocopies or print outs of this (unlike the letter of application which should appear personalised). Generally it is better to provide a succinct c.v. that you may consider too short than one which the employer will think overlong. You could then add in your letter of application that if any further information is required you will be happy to supply it. Do not send any certificates or documents with an enquiry or application as these stand little chance of being returned. If they are requested, or you feel they would help, then send photocopies only.

Aspects of Employment

Salaries

Danish salaries compare favourably in both world and European terms and anyone moving from the UK to an equivalent job in Denmark, unless it is at top executive level can expect a higher salary there. However, although top executives are paid more in Denmark than in the rest of Scandinavia, they are paid less than in the UK, France, Italy, Germany and Austria. There is also the burden of high personal taxes and the living costs, both of which are generally above other European countries (excepting other Scandinavian ones). Foreigners living and working in Denmark will benefit most if they are receiving a Danish level salary but only paying 30% tax as under the Expatriate Tax agreement, as long as their stay in Denmark does not exceed three years (see *Daily Life — Taxation*).

There is no statutory minimum wage in Denmark, instead the trades unions and employers' organisations agree on a minimum wage as part of the *Common Consent* (see below). This agreement sets the standard for the basic wage on the general labour market. For instance the hourly rate, as agreed with the unions for employees in the industrial sector is currently kr 70, or over £7 an hour. However, taking into consideration vacation, sickness and overtime allowances, it is estimated that the average minimum value in real terms is about kr122 an hour.

Employer and Employee Organisations

There are two main employers' organisations of which the Danish Employers' Confederation (DA) is the larger and three main employee unions of which The Danish Confederation of Trade Unions (LO) is the largest.

Employer Organisations: The entire labour force of Denmark constitutes about 2.9 million. Approximately 45 employers' organisations, representing 29,300 employers, who between them employ about half a million people, belong to the DA.

Employee Organisations: There are about 90 Danish trade unions with 2.1 million members (roughly 70% of the workforce). This trade union membership level is one of the highest in Europe and gives the Danish trades unions a more significant role than in neighbouring countries.

Most trade unions belong to the LO which represents about 1.4 million workers. In some companies, you have to join the trade union before getting a job.

As in the UK, there is no minimum wage legislation. Instead there is a binding agreement known as The Common Consent between the employers' organisations and the unions. This sets the working hours and wages and is usually drawn up every two years. Normally a new agreement is concluded before the old one expires. If it is impossible to reach an agreement a conciliation officer will be appointed to mediate.

Working Hours, Overtime and Holidays

Scandinavians traditionally have the shortest working week and the worst absenteeism in Europe. In Denmark, the normal working hours are 37 per week. Employees are usually paid overtime but may also be given time off in lieu. The conditions vary depending on the company and are covered by the Common Consent agreement. Working conditions may also be negotiated between an individual and employer, as in the case of small companies. Executive positions, are not covered by the overtime agreements.

Employees are entitled to five weeks paid holiday a year. Unlike wages, holiday pay is fixed by law. The employer pays a supplement of 12.5% of each employee's salary into a central vacation trust (*FerieGiro*). In April, the employee receives a money order from the FerieGiro, which can be cashed by the employee at any post office when it is accompanied by an endorsement from the employer saying when the holiday is to be taken. Even if you have only worked for a few weeks you are still entitled to holiday pay in proportion to the period worked.

For longer-term employees the holiday period can be divided up over the course of the year but every employee has the right of 18 consecutive days of holiday during the main holiday period of 2 May to 30 September.

Any problems with holiday pay can be addressed to to FerieGiro (ATP-Huset, Kongens Vaenge 8, 3400 Hillerød; tel 48 24 11 00).

Women in Work

There are currently 76 women to every 100 men in the national workforce. Although this is one of the highest ratios of women to men in work in Europe, it is not unusual in the Scandinavian countries. Women have equal status with men in the work place and claim equal pay on principle. One of the factors in Scandinavia generally which has contributed to having such a large number of women in the workplace, is the availability of child care services outside the home. By 1991, 73% of of pre-school (3-6 years) children were using day care facilities.

Over recent years, the number of women at work has been falling as an increasing number of young women are choosing to take courses in higher education.

Maternity Benefits and Parental Leave

All women are entitled to four weeks leave before a birth and up to 24 weeks post natal leave. From the fifteenth week after the birth the mother can opt to transfer all, or a part of the remaining leave to the father. Otherwise all fathers are entitled to two weeks paternity leave starting from when the baby is brought home.

While she is on maternity leave, a mother has a right to 50% of her salary during the first four months. Any additional leave is paid by social welfare of about kr2,556 per week.

Social Security and Unemployment Benefit

Claiming UK Unemployment Benefit in Denmark

One of the facilities of labour mobility within the European Union is that it is possible for those who are currently unemployed and claiming benefit, or eligible to claim benefit, to have this paid in another EU country if planning to go there to look for work. You have to have been claiming UK benefit for at least four weeks prior to departure and you can arrange to have the benefit paid in Denmark at UK rates, for up to three months while you are looking for a job. In order to do this you should inform the UK office of your intention to seek work elsewhere in the EU. The leaflet UBL22 *Unemployment benefit* for young people going abroad or coming from abroad contains an application form for transferring benefit.

Your local UB office will inform the Overseas Branch of the Department of Social Security (DSS) who will provide you with form E303 which is the standard EU form authorizing another member state to pay your benefit. when you go to Denmark you should present the form to the authorities in the area where you intend to work. The DSS Overseas Office in the UK will give you advice on where to register abroad. As there may be delays in payments received abroad, even when the procedure is meticulously followed, it is advisable to have some emergency financial resources of your own to fall back on.

Please note that anyone tempted to chuck in their present job to go on the dole for the requisite number of weeks before departing for Denmark will be disappointed: by making themselves voluntarily unemployed they render themselves ineligible for Unemployment Benefit for six months. Even if you are eligible you should note that not only does the benefit run out after three months, but one would also require a permit to stay in Denmark after this period and this is unlikely to be granted if one does not have a job.

Social Security in the UK

Anyone who has been living and working in the UK will have been paying UK national insurance contributions which will entitle the contributor to various social security benefits, including unemployment benefit and a state retirement pension. However, if you are about to embark on a job hunt in Denmark your position does need careful consideration. If you do not intend ever to return to the UK, there is unlikely to be a problem. However, if you are planning to return at a later date and you are not working, then it is as well to ensure that contributions are kept up, otherwise you may not be entitled to all the usual benefits.

If a UK national works in another EU country and then returns to the UK, the fact that contributions have been paid there should keep their UK contributions record up to date. However, if the individual has not worked in Denmark, that record may lapse, although one is usually given the option to pay off the shortfall within a certain time limit. The best policy is to clarify one's position before leaving the UK with the DSS Overseas Branch (Venton Park Road, Newcastle-upon-Tyne NE98 1YX; tel 0191-213 5000),

Social Security in Denmark

Denmark has a highly developed system of social security which has come under criticism from opponents of its policy of paying young people more money than they would receive if they were a trainee with an employer. About 23% of people of working age (i.e. 16-66 years old) are living on social security. About 340,000 received unemployment benefit in 1993 and a further 170,000 were receiving other social security benefits. Social security is enormously expensive for Denmark and is funded by high personal taxation (see Chapter Four, *Daily Life, Taxation*). Until the 1960s unemployment benefits totalled a mere 40% of earnings up to a maximum of 90% of the earnings of a skilled worker (about kr143,000 per annum) which is available more-or-less indefinitely.

Unemployment insurance (*A-kasserne*) in Denmark is administered by the Trade Unions. You have to have paid into a trade union fund for at least one year and have worked at least six months during that year, before you can claim social security. In order to be able to pay into a fund, you have to prove you have worked at least five weeks full-time (or are about to). If you only work part-time then you pay less into the fund and claim correspondingly less unemployment benefit should you need to.

Danish Pensions

The Danish pension system is more generous than that of the UK. The approximate pension is Dkr 4,700 per month for a single person. The pension is tax free if there is no other income. In addition to the pension, allowances are given for general living costs which include rent, spectacles and television licences. Many employees supplement their old age pension by participating in pension funds or private pension schemes.

The normal age for a retirement pension is 67 but entitlements to early pensions are made in specified circumstances. The minimum period of residence before a pension can be claimed at all is three years. In order to receive a full old-age pension 40 years of residence is required between the ages of 15 and 67. If the period of residence is shorter, the pension is calculated in fortieths of a full pension, proportional to the number of years of actual residency. Applicants for an early pension must have lived in Denmark for at least four-fifths of the period between the age of 15 and the age at which the pension is awarded. Where the period of residence is shorter, the amount of the pension is calculated in proportion to the actual number of years of residence.

Recently introduced is a new pension scheme whereby people from the age of 60 can reduce their working hours and receive compensation from the state. Or they can take early retirement at that age. In the latter case they are entitled to kr2,500 per week for the first two years and then kr2000 a week until the age of 67. This is part of a government strategy to create vacancies for the unemployed.

Foreigners can claim a Danish pension provided they have lived in Denmark for at least ten years between the ages of 15 and 67 with five of these years immediately prior to the application for a pension. A special allowance is made for refugees accepted by Denmark who may now claim the years of residence in their own country as residency in Denmark for the purpose of calculating their pension.

Unemployment Benefits & Sickness Pay

Just under three-quarters of the national labour force (over 2 million employees) pay into an unemployment fund. Should they become unemployed, the fund will pay out a proportion of unemployment benefits. The main cost of unemployment benefit is however borne by the government. Membership fees of an unemployment fund vary among the different trades and the average is about Dkr5,000 per annum.

Unemployed people, who are members of an unemployment fund receive benefits which amount to about kr2,500 weekly up to a maximum of 90% of their former salary. If the individual is not a member of an unemployment fund then social welfare provides all benefits due.

Sickness Pay: An employee is entitled to sick pay if they have been working for a minimum of thirteen weeks, and if they have worked for at least 120 hours in the 13 weeks before becoming ill. Often under employer/employee agreements employees are entitled to receive full pay during the first 120 days of illness. If you are paid by the hour however, you can claim only a maximum of 90% of your salary up to a ceiling of about Dkr2,500 per week.

If you are ill for longer than three days and up to five, your employer can ask you to sign a declaration stating that you are ill. For illness that lasts longer than five days your employer has the right to a medical certificate (for which the employer pays), from a doctor stating the nature and expected duration of your malady.

Permanent Work

Computers/Information Technology

Those who work in computing and can speak another European language are almost always able to find jobs in the European Union. British computer science graduates are also highly thought of and many get jobs by approaching recruitment agencies that specialise in computer personnel.

Useful Addresses & Publications

Computer Contractor/Computing: two magazines published by VNU Business Publications, 32-34 Broadwick Street, London W1A 2HG; tel 0171-927 9003. Both carry masses of advertising by computer contractors wanting to hire personnel for Britain and abroad.

Dux International: Riverbank House, Putney Bridge Approach, London SW6 3JD; tel 0171-371 9191; fax 0171-371 7409. Specialises in computer vacancies in Europe.

OCC Computer Personnel: 108 Welsh Row, Nantwich, Cheshire CW5 5EY; tel 01270-627206; fax 01270-629168. In 1994 was advertising for Sybase analyst programmers to work in Copenhagen.

Medical Staff
Qualified medical staff who are interested in working in Danish hospitals can try consulting the weekly journal of the *Danish Medical Association* which can be obtained directly from the DMA (Trondhjemsgade 9, 2100 Copenhagen O) in which hospital staff vacancies are advertised. A complete list of hospitals and other medical institutions can be obtained from the same source for kr300, as well as a useful booklet *Information for Doctors Migrating to Denmark.*

In order to obtain authorisation to practise as a doctor in Denmark, the *National Board of Health*, 13 Amaliegade 1012 Copenhagen K) has to be contacted after an offer of a job is received, but before it is taken up. Generally, the DMA emphasise the difficulty of finding a post in Denmark as there is likely to be a surplus of doctors for some years to come. The DMA may be able to advise which specialties might be in demand.

The regulations governing applications from foreign Doctors to work in Denmark are given in the leaflet *Guidelines for the Registration of Doctors of Medicine with a Degree from Abroad*, available from the Danish Naional Board of Health (Sundhedsstyrelsen) at the above address.

Teaching English
As already mentioned, there is less demand for English teachers in Scandinavia generally than elsewhere in Europe because of native proficiency. Contracts are therefore more often than not part-time and tend to be focussed on English for business. Danish language schools are also very much geared to preparing candidates for the Cambridge English Examinations. An advantage of working in Denmark is that wages are controlled by law. For teaching these are a minimum of kr174.40 per lesson. However taxes are also very high (see *Daily Life — Taxation*).

Useful Addresses
List of Schools:

Cambridge Institute Foundation: Vimmelskaftet 48, 1161 Copenhagen K; tel 33 13 33 02. Contracts generally last from October to May and are renewable.
FOF (Folkeligt Oplysnings Forbund), Sønder Allé 9, 8000 Aarhus C; tel 86 12 29 55; fax 86 19 54 35.
FOF, Lyngby-Taarbaek, Hovedgade 15D, 2800 Lynby; tel 42 88 25 00; fax 42 87 28 46.
Frit Oplysningsforbund, Vestergade 5, 1, 5000 Odense C; tel 66 13 98 13; fax 66 13 90 04.

The European Environmental Agency
In February 1994 the European Commission announced a number of new European Institutions would be located in various major European cities with briefs as diverse as harmonising trade marks, design and models in the internal European market, and a monitoring centre for drugs and drug addiction. The institution allocated to Copenhagen is the European Environmental Agency (not to be confused with the European Economic Area whose acronym it confusingly shares). The EEA moved to Copenhagen (6 Kongens Nytorv, 1050 Copenhagen), from Belgium in autumn 1994, and has a permanent staff of about 50, recruited through, amongst other publications, the *Official Journal of the European Communities* which can be consulted in the UK, at any of the regional offices of the European Commission. Competition for the main posts is however extremely tough: in the EEA Newsletter of February 1995, it was reported that over 10,000 applications were received for 28 posts advertised in the *Official Journal* of

October 1994. Clerical staff are likely to be recruited locally in Denmark while there may be some scientific positions advertised internationally as they fall vacant. The Agency will be entirely independent of the European Commission and will be an environmental liaison office for all the EU countries.

Useful Addresses and Miscellaneous Publications

European Commission: Jean Monnet House, 8 Storey's Gate, London SW1P 3AT; tel 0171-973 1992. Regional UK offices also in Edinburgh, Cardiff and, Belfast. Also in Dublin.

International Jobs (A Guide for UK and Overseas Students): Published by the University of London Careers Advisory Service, 50 Gordon Square, London WC1H OPQ; (tel 0171-387 8221). Contains details of multinationals who often recruit in Britain.

Solicitors in the Single Market: (£22.90) & *Free Movement of Lawyers* (£80), both available from the Law Society Shop, 227 The Strand, London WC2.

Working in the European Community: (Hobsons). Includes employment possibilities, placement agents and general advice on the mobility of graduates.

The following UK recruitment/search agencies specialise in technical, professional and other senior executive appointments in Denmark:

Beechwood Recruitment Ltd. 221 High Street, London W3 9BY; tel 0181-992 8647; fax 0181-992 5658. Very specialised field. Keeps a technical appointments register for qualified engineers with experience.

Berndtson International, 6 Westminster Palace Gardens, Artillery Row, London SW1P 1RL; tel 0171-222 5555; fax 0171-222 5180. Associate office in Copenhagen: tel +45 1 143 636.

Dennis & Gemmill Ltd. 2 The Courtyard, Smith Street, London SW3 4EE; tel 0171-730 7138; fax 0171-730 6983. Associate Office in Copenhagen: W Wachmeister, tel +45 1 150 107.

Egon Zehnder International Ltd., Devonshire House, Mayfair Place, London W1X 5FH; tel 0171-493 3882; fax 0171-629 9552. Associate Office in Copenhagen: Egon Zehnder International SA, Fredericiagade 25, 1310 Copenhagen K; tel +45 33 11 13 53; fax +45 33 32 23 10.

Egor International Ltd., Metro House, 58 St. James Street, London SW1A ILD; 0171-629 8070; fax 0171-493 4320; Associate office in Copenhagen: Egor Skandinavia, Nybrogade 8, 1203 Copenhagen; tel +45 33 15 45 15; fax +45 33 15 30 40.

Marlar International, 12 Well Court, London EC4M 9DN; tel 0171-248 9614; fax 0171-489 8316. Associate office in Vedbaek: Marlar International Denmark ApS, Enrum, Vedbaekstrndvej 341, 2950 Vaedbaek; tel +45 45 66 06 99; fax +45 66 03 99.

Norman Broadbent International Ltd. 65 Curzon Street, London W1Y 7PE; tel 0171-629 9626; fax: 0171-629 9900. Also has associate in Copenhagen.

P-E International plc: Park House, Wick Road, Egham, Surrey TW20 OHW; tel 01784-434411; fax 01784-437828. Associate office in Copenhagen: Finn La Cour, Finco Ltd. 28a Emdrupej, 2100 Copenhagen; tel +45 1 27 0300; fax +45 1 27 0303.

Scientific Resources: King's Court, Kirkwood Road, Cambridge CB4 2PF; tel 01223-420129; fax 01223-424281; Associate office in Copenhagen: Scientific Generics, 33 Toldbodgade, 1253 Copenhagen K; tel +45 33 93 76 03; fax +45 33 15 77 10.

Wessex Executive Search: 1c Wildown Road, Southbourne, Bournemouth, Dorset BH6 4DP; tel 01202-417254. Subsidiary office: PFM Consultants, 50 East Road, Lincoln; tel 01522-514335.

Temporary Work

This section deals with seasonal jobs for instance in agriculture, childcare and tourism as well as a variety of possibilities through agencies. Temping is something which many people might have to do before they find a long-term post. Teaching English as a foreign language is dealt with also under *Permanent Work*, but the possibilities for this are generally far fewer anywhere in Scandinavia than in many other European countries.

Agriculture

Agriculture is an important part of the Danish economy. Denmark produces about three times the agricultural produce, and consumables from food technology subsidiaries, that it needs for home consumption. At least 70% of Danish agriculture produce is exported and about 60% of food products. Its world share of the bacon market is 33%, 22% for fresh pork and 14% for combined dairy products. The food industry provides 30% of Denmark's industrial turnover. More interestingly it has a 32% share of the grass and clover seed market. Although the industry is dominated by farmer-owned cooperatives, often with a short-term profit motivation, there are still a reasonable number of fruit picking jobs, especially on the island of Funen. The most prevalent crops are tomatoes, (grown all summer), strawberries (picked in June and July), cherries (picked in July and August) and apples (picked in September and October). It may be necessary to travel quite widely in Denmark to find work as there is no concentration of fruit farms in one area although some of the larger farms are to be found around Aarhus and east and west of Odense.

The work is paid quite reasonable piece rates at about Dkr 5 per kilo but starting dates and working hours are unpredictable.

Surprisingly, it may also be possible to find a job on a farm by advertising in the farming magazine *Landsbladet* (Vester Farimagsgade 6, 1606 Copenhagen K). The best results have come from those who have mentioned previous farming experience (which might include working on a kibbutz/moshav) in their advert. It is also important to provide a contact telephone number. A typical monthly wage after tax and including bed and board might be £400.

Organic farms are another possibility and you could start by contacting the Danish version of WWOOF, the worldwide organic farm organisation which is VHH (c/o Inga Nielson, Asenvej 35, 9881 Bindslev, Denmark). You will need to send £5/US$10/kr50 for a list of about 25-30 organic farms in Denmark which you then contact individually. The problem with organic farms in Denmark is that they are usually run by alternative communities of which there are many in Denmark with the result that they may not be very compatible with the market economy. Thus though you may be fed and housed, learn valuable agricultural techniques and be otherwise well looked after, remuneration will be minimal.

The Agricultural Council (3 Axeltorv, 1609 Copenhagen V; tel 33 14 56 72; fax 33 14 95 74), is the umbrella organisation for all major farmers' organisations in Denmark.

Useful Addresses

The International Agricultural Exchange Association. NFYFC Centre, National Agricultural Centre, Kenilworth, Warwickshire CV8 2LG. Arranges placements on Danish farms for British subjects with at least two years practical experience of farming/horticulture.

Exchanges from the USA and Canada to Denmark can be arranged by:

The International Agricultural Exchange Association (Servicing Office) 1000 1st
   Avenue South, Great Falls, Montana 59401 United States of America; IAEA
   (Servicing Office), No. 206, 1505-17 Ave. S.W. Calgary, Alberta T2T OE2
   Canada.

The following farms have all taken casual foreign pickers in the past:

Alstrup Frugtplantage, Alstrup 8305 Samso; tel 86 59 31 38; fax 86 59 31 38.
   Strawberry picking can be between May and July but usually from beginning
   of June. Free campsite but no accommodation provided.
Anders Ploug-Sorensen, Broholm, Tastebjerggyden 13, Horne, 5600 Faborg; tel
   09 60 10 28.
Birkholm Frugt & Baer, V/Bjarne Knutsen, Hornelandevej 2 D, 5600 Faaborg;
   tel 62 60 22 62. Strawberry picking. Campsite and washing and cooking
   facilities provided.
Graevlerupgard Plantage, Egsgyden 38, Horne, 5600 Faborg; tel 62 60 22 31.

Au Pair and Nannying
Going as an au pair to Scandinavia, might seem like taking the proverbial coals
to Newcastle, since au pairs from Scandinavia have become something of a
cliché. Despite its potential drawbacks (awful parents, abominable children and
sexploitation) being an au pair/nanny/mother's help in Denmark, which has
signed the Council of Europe's Agreement on Au Pair placements, is well
regulated. It is also probably the best way to learn the language inexpensively,
though not necessarily by chatting with the family who will probably speak
English, but by attending subsidised or free classes locally (see *Daily Life —
Learning the Language*).

   Two of the main au pair organisations in Denmark are *Exis-Europair* and
Scandinavian Au Pair Service. Although both are involved in sending young
Danes abroad as au pairs, they also have a foreigners section which deals with
incoming au pairs. Pocket money starts at about kr1,200 per month.

Useful Addresses
The following UK-based agencies deal with Denmark:

Anglia Au Pair & Domestic Agency, 70 Southsea Avenue, Leigh-on-Sea, Essex
   SS9 2BJ. Tel/fax 01702-471648.
Bingham Placements, 9 Bingham Place, London W1M 3FH; tel 0171-224 4016.
Euro-Pair Agency, 28 Derwent Avenue, Pinner, Middlesex HA5 4QJ; tel 0181-
   421 2100; fax 0181-428 6416.
Highgate Nannies, 21 Pond Square, Highgate Village, London N6 6BA; tel 0181-
   340 0966.
Solihull Au Pair & Nanny Agency, 87 Warwick Road, Olton, Solihull, West
   Midlands B92 7HP; 0121-707 9841.

In Denmark:

Exis-Europair, Skeldevigvej 12, 6310 Broager; tel 74 44 22 33; fax 74 44 21 26.
Scandinavian Au-Pair Service, Dag Hammarskjolds Alle 40, 2100 Copenhagen;
   tel 35 43 60 07.

Teaching
Most teaching English as a foreign language is done in Denmark's *Cambridge
Institute Foundation* which has about 40 branches throughout Denmark and
specialises in English for business. There is a strong emphasis in Denmark on
preparing candidates for the Cambridge Exams. It may be possible to get a

temporary contract, though work is nearly always part-time. There is a British Council office in Copenhagen which can provide a list of private language schools of which there are about fifteen, and also the addresses of folk high schools (see *Daily Life — Education*) where it may be possible to teach English on a temporary basis.

For other teaching possibilities, see *Permanent Work* above.

Tourism

Although Denmark's summers tend to be brief, much like Scottish ones, they can be very fine. In any case, the country has much to offer besides a healthy climate as the rapid expansion of the tourist industry shows. In the last couple of years however there has been a decline in custom caused by the latest recession which resulted in regular clients from Sweden and Germany being more thrifty or staying away altogether.

Four per cent of the total number of jobs (roughly 107,000) in Denmark are in the tourist industry and the government intends to increase this number by about 17,000 by the end of the millenium. Many of the new jobs are likely to be in new tourism organisations. The Danish government also plans to target marketing at southern and central Europe, so anyone with a proficiency in languages from these areas might be able to get a job in the Danish tourist industry.

Menial temporary jobs in hotels in main tourist cities are reasonably easy to find, though you will probably have to do a lot of leg work going round in person to ask for work in hotels and restaurants. It may pay off to start with the biggest establishments as vacancies obviously occur on a large scale. This has happened in the past at the Copenhagen Sheraton where you are likely to get the unskilled jobs like chamber staff and kitchen porter.

Another common source of jobs is the foreign, fast food restaurants such as Burger King and McDonalds whose turnover of staff is almost as fast as their food. Their wages are comparatively low but still a useful standby.

For those who prefer not to be cooped up indoors, the British company Eurocamp runs a campsite in Denmark for which it needs campsite couriers, children' couriers and administrative couriers. Further details from Eurocamp (Summer Jobs, P.O. Box 170, Liverpool L70 1ES).

Voluntary Work

There is a variety of possibilities for volunteer work in Denmark. If you are applying from the UK, you can apply through various umbrella workcamp organisations such as the Christian Movement for Peace, Quaker Work Camps, or the United Nations Association.

If you are already in Denmark you can contact Mellemfolkeligt Samvirke, Borgergade 14, 1300 Copenhagen K. This is one of the few ways you can get a job in the Danish territories of Greenland and the Faroe Islands as well as in the main country of Denmark. MS organises from 20 to 30 workcamps which usually last two or three weeks. The camps mainly involve construction work, either renovatory or from scratch of communal buildings or facilities, located in small communities for whom such buildings are an important part of daily social interaction. Volunteers pay their own travel costs but everything else is provided.

Another Danish-based organisation is the Swallows of Denmark (the Danish Branch of Emmaus International which raises funds for projects in India. They organise fortnight long work camps in Denmark which involve collecting saleable goods.

Useful Addresses
Christian Movement for Peace (CMP), 186 St. Paul's Road, Balsall Heath, Birmingham B12 8LZ.

Quaker International Social Projects (QISP), Friends House, 173/177 Euston Road, London NW1 2BJ; 0171-387 3601, ext. 255.

Swallows of Denmark, c/o Ulandsforeningen Svalerne, Osterbrogade 49, 2100 Copenhagen O; tel 35 26 17 47.

United Nations Association (UNA) Wales, International Youth Service, Welsh Centre for International Affairs, Temple of Peace, Cathays Park, Cardiff CF1 3AP; tel 01222-223088.

Training and Work Experience Schemes
One of the problems for those leaving school or university is competing in the job hunt with those who already have a proven track record, who understandably appeal more to employers than those with no experience of the work place. The European Commission has come up with various schemes for young people aimed at giving them an advantage with regard to European opportunities. The most ambitious of these schemes is PETRA.

COMETT: (COMMETT Liaison Office, Department of Education, FHE2, Sanctuary Buildings, Great Smith Street, London SW1P 3BT; tel 0171-925 5000; or EC Commission, University Information, rue de la Loi 200, 1049 Brussels, Belgium). The Community Programme in Education and Training for Technology (COMMETT), is an EU-sponsored scheme launched in 1986 and aimed at those studying new technologies (e.g. satellites, IT, telecommunications etc.) at university. It aims to encourage cooperation between university and industry by enabling undergraduates and graduates to train in companies and learn new technological skills in another EU country. COMMETT also covers exchanges for university staff.

ICYE: (International Christian Youth Exchange): Dansk ICYE, Sønderport 7, Postbox 642, 8100 Aarhus C; tel 86 11 60 33. ICYE organises stays for those aged 16-30 in over 25 countries worldwide. The normal stay is for one year and comprises college work combined with social work.

LINGUA: c/o Lingua Unit, Seymour Mews House, Seymour Mews, London W1H 9PE; tel 0171-224 1477; fax 0171-224 1906, or Lingua Office, 10 rue du Commerce, 1040 Bruxelles, Belgium; tel +32 2-551 4218; fax +32 2 511 4376. An EU scheme set up in 1990 at aimed at, among others, foreign language teachers. Under the scheme teachers can spend time in the country whose language they propose to teach. Lingua funds scholarships and exchange visits for teachers and also groups of young people.

PETRA: (c/o The Central Bureau for Educational Visits & Exchanges, Seymour Mews House, Seymour Mews, London W1H 9PE. tel 0171-486 5101; fax 0171-935 1017). Petra is an inter-EU scheme which enables young people to undergo short term training or work experience in another EU country. The scheme is open to those aged 16-27 and most programmes are for a period of three weeks (for those in training) or three months (for young workers). There are also possibilities for longer placements of up to a year. To qualify, applicants should be: enrolled on an advanced course of vocational training that is not degree level and, either in employment or unemployed but available for work. Under the scheme, bursaries of £500 to £2000 intended to help with the costs are available depending on the location and duration of the placement. Apart from the office in each EU country appointed to administer the scheme, there is a technical assistance unit based in Brussels: IFAPLAN (tel 00 32 2 511 12 10; fax 00 32 2 511 1960).

Directory of Major Employers in Denmark

The following are Denmark's top 25 companies in terms of turnover and number of employees.

Company	Employees	Type of Company
FDB	14,005	Supermarkets
A.P. Moller Group	30,000	Shipping, oil & gas, shipbuilding, air services, industry & commerce
EAC	17,025	Trade
Tele Danmark	17,701	Telecommunications giant (privatised 1994)
Carlsberg	13,777	Brewing
J Lauritzen Holding	14,000	Shipping, shipyards
Danisco	10,851	Food and Drink
MD Foods	5,684	Dairy Products
FLS Industries	12,268	Cement Machinery
ISS	115,000	Office Maintenance Industrial Cleaning Services
Novo Nordisk	10,733	Pharmaceuticals
Danish Crown	5,910	Meat Products
Skandinavisk Holding	6,059	Tobacco & furniture
Norsk Hydro Danmark	3,249	Oil Refinery
P & T	33,342	Postal Service
Vestjyske Slagterie	4,773	Meat Products
Ess Food	1,387	Meat Wholesalers
Danfoss	13,423	Thermostats
Sophus Berendsen	19,300	Pest Killers
Dansk Shell	2,899	Oil
Superfos	4,581	Conglomerate
Det Danske Traelastkompagni	3,478	Timber
Monberg & Thorsen Holding	4,647	Construction
IBM Danmark	2,643	Documentation
DSB	20,998	Railways

British & Multinational Companies with Branches, Affiliates or Subsidiaries in Denmark

The Associated Press (London EC4), Kristen Bernikowsgade 4ii, 1105 Copenhagen K. (Printing, publishing and graphics).

The Barclays Group of Banks (Representative Office), London EC3; Bredegade 23, iii, 1260 Copenhagen. (Banking, finance and investment).

Baxenden Scandinavia A/S (Accrington BB5 2SL), Fulbyvej 4, Pederborg 4180 Soro.(Chemicals and pharmaceuticals).

Beecham Scandinavia A/S (Brentford). Transformervej 16, 2730 Herlev. (Chemicals and pharmaceuticals).

Black & Decker A/S (Maidenhead). Bistrupvej 172, 3460 Birkerod. (Machine Tools).
Boeg-Thomsen A/S (London W3). 4390 Vipperod. (Foodstuffs and beverages).
British Airways (Hounslow). Vesterbrogade 2B; 1620 Copenhagen V. (Airlines and aerospace products).
British Railways Board, (London SW1), Montergade 3, 1116 Copenhagen K. (Tourist agencies and travel services).
British Steel Corporation (London SW1), Norre Voldgade 68, 1358 Copenhagen K. (Metal products)
British Tobacco Co ApS (Woking). Strandvaeget 43, 2100 Copenhagen 0. (Tobacco and tobacco machinery).
Castrol A/S (Swindon). Esplanaden 7, 1263 Copenhagen K. (Petrochemicals).
Courtaulds Danmark A/S (London W1). Falkoner Alle 53, 2000 Copenhagen. (Clothing).
A/S Dansk Shell (London SE1), Kampmannsgade 2, 1604 Copenhagen. (Petrochemicals).
DEB Swarfega Denmark (Derby), Teglvaerksvej 6, 5620 Glamsbjerg. (Chemicals and pharmaceuticals).
DER A/S (London WC2H 6ED), Gungevej 17, 2650 Hvidovre. (Computers, electrical and electronic equipment).
DOW Chemical A/S (Hounslow). Vedbaek Strandvej 350, 2900 Hellerup. (Chemicals and pharmaceuticals).
Dunlop A/S (London SW1). Tagensvej 85b, 2200 Copenhagen N. (Rubber goods)
EMI (Dansk-Engelsk) A/S (London W1). Hoffdingsvej, 2500 Valby. (Computers, electrical and electronic equipment).
European Plastic Machinery Manufacturing A/S (Brentford). Euromatic, Krimsvej 29, 2300 Copenhagen S. (Plastics).
Ferrymasters A/S, (London E11), Fabriksparken 8, 2600 Glostrup. (Freight storage and transport).
Fisons A/S, (Loughborough). Rosenkaeret 22A, 2860 Soborg. (Chemicals and pharmaceuticals).
Flymo A/S, (Darlington). Lundtoftevej 160, 2800 Lyngby. (Electrical and electronic equipment).
Hoover El-Udstyr ApS (Perivale). Gasvaerksvej 16, 1656 Copenhagen V. (Electrical and electronic equipment).
ICI Denmark A/S (London SW1). Islands Brygge 41, 2300 Copenhagen S. (Chemicals and pharmaceuticals).
Ilford Foto A/S (Ilford). Gadelander 18, 2700 Broshoj. (photographic equipment).
Int'l Computers Ltd. A/S (London SW15). Klampenborgvej 232, 2800 Lyngby.
International Factors A/S. (London W1). Bredegade 29, 1260 Copenhagen K. (Freight transport and storage).
Johnson Matthey A/S (Royston). Norre Farumagsgade 33m 1364 Copenhagen. (Metal products).
Leyland-DAB A/S (London NW1). Kajlstrupvej 71, 8600 Silkeborg. (Vehicles).
Lloyd's Register of Shipping A/S (London EC3M 4BC). Kronprinsessgade 26, 1264 Copenhagen. (Insurance).
Max Factor & Co ApS (Bournemouth). Naerum Hovegade 2, 2850 Naerum. (Cosmetics & toiletries).
Nordland Trading (London W1P OAA). St. Strandstraede 9, 1255 Copenhagen K. (Security).
John Player ApS (Bristol). Ndr. Fasanvej 108, 2200 Copenhagen F. (Tobacco and Tobacco machinery).
Price Waterhouse (London EC2). Norre Farimagsgade 64, 1364 Copenhagen K. (Accounting and auditing).

Radical Radar Aktieselskab (London SE1 7SW). Mitchellsgade 9, 1568 Copenhagen V. (Telecommunications).

Rank Xerox A/S (London NW1 3BH). Borupvang 5, 2750 Ballerup. (Office equipment).

Reckitt & Colman A/S (London W4). Industrivej 14, 2600 Glostrup. (Foodstuffs and beverages).

Renold A/S (Manchester). Skelmarksvej 6, 2600 Glostrup. (Machinery and industrial equipment).

Thorn Electric A/S (London WC2). Brogrenen 6-8, 2635 Ishoj. (Electrical and electronic equipment).

United Biscuit A/S (Middlesex). Sdr. Ringvej 41-45 2600 Glostrup. (Foodstuffs and beverages).

Whitbread & Co (Scandinavia) (London EC1). Strandboulevarden 130, 2100 Copenhagen O. (Brewing).

Starting a Business

The majority of foreigners residing in Denmark are there for work or career reasons. However, there is another option available in the single European market and that is to set up or buy a business in another EU country.

Starting a business abroad need not necessarily be reserved for established business people or multinational companies. In addition to the regular large-scale opportunities, recent administrative simplifications within the EU have made a point of providing encouragement to small and medium-sized businesses and individual entrepreneurs to set up businesses in other EU nations. Such businesses can take almost any form: running small shops, art courses, letting agencies, providing bed and breakfasts, operating a radio station and providing building and plumbing services are just some of the commercial enterprises started by foreigners in other EU countries. Other professional services from farming to landscape gardening and from English-or Irish-style pubs to franchise operations also offer potential livings.

Inevitably the cultural differences between Denmark and the UK may further complicate an already nerve-racking undertaking. However, it is likely that those who set up business in Denmark will already have some connections there. In Denmark, unlike France, Spain and Portugal, you cannot expect some types of business to thrive on the custom of fellow expatriates, or holiday-makers of your own nationality visiting the country. In addition, the extra difficulties caused by a lack of familiarity with foreign procedures could prove a serious drawback. This is less of a problem in Denmark, where you are likely to have reasonably straightforward procedures explained to you in English, than in many other countries where the bureaucracy might be incomprehensible in any language. Initially though, it may be wise to seek out a Danish business partner or company with compatible interests with which you can have a joint venture until you have found your feet.

Denmark has recently become alert to the potential of the newly opened-up markets of Eastern Europe and the Baltic Republics, which it is strategically positioned to exploit. Foreign investors may also like to consider ways of cashing in on these markets. Furthermore, Denmark has already begun talks with Germany and Sweden on the possibility of building a fixed link between Lolland (the island artificially linked to southern Zealand) and Germany across the Fermarn straits. This would reduce distribution time not just to Germany but to the new markets of eastern Europe.

The Business Climate
There are estimated to be about 2,000 foreign-owned businesses operating in Denmark. While some of these are high profile companies with international interests (e.g. Lego, Carlsberg, East Asiatic Company, Sophus Berendsen), large multinationals, do not predominate over Danish commerce. The majority of enterprises (about 75%) have fewer than 50 employees, and the government has a policy of encouraging business start-ups by individuals. However although small companies have some advantages, notably in lead in times (i.e. the speed

with which they can produce new products), they are at a disavantage in a pan-European field when competing with big companies in research and export drives. The government has therefore encouraged Danish companies to merge or to network with other small and medium-sized companies with which their interests are compatible in order to produce a greater momentum in these areas. The government has also invested heavily in efficient distribution systems reducing the time from the order to the receipt of goods by the customer, to one of the shortest in Europe.

The small population of Denmark means that it has strict limitations as a market. Most Danish companies are therefore expanding through exports. For anyone, competent and experienced in international marketing there are opportunities as this is one of the few areas where the Danes lack expertise although they are more likely to turn to their neighbours and commercial collaborators, the Swedes, before they headhunt non-Scandinavians.

Hitherto, an important trading union for the Scandinavians has been the forty-year-old Nordic Union. Since 1954 citizens of Nordic states have had a common labour and trade market. There is also a Nordic investment bank and shared commercial and environmental protection laws. In addition the Nordic countries have harmonised their technology in practical ways so that it is for instance, possible to use the same mobile telephone in Copenhagen or Helsinki. Although the NU has worked beneficially for past decades in the areas of agriculture, industrial policy and natural resources, the economic necessity for, and the enticement of the wider market of the European Union means that Denmark is now no longer the sole Nordic country to enjoy the benefits of EU membership as Finland, and Sweden joined on 1 January 1995.

The largest sector of the Danish economy is that of commercial services (40%), followed by manufacturing (28%). Agriculture, which dominated the economy in the earlier part of the century now is the fifth largest source of GNP.

The EU working definitions of company sizes are generally based on staff levels rather than turnover: micro company (0-9 employees); small company is 10-99 employees and medium 100-499 employees.

Financial Considerations

Loans. Businesses can use the banking services of both commercial and savings banks while mortgage credit institutions can give loans for commercial agricultural properties, companies and ships as well as residential dwellings. The choice of the type of loan will depend on tax considerations and the assessment of individual business income. One mortgage credit institution, Industriens Realkreditfond specialises in mortgages for businesses. About half of all mortgage credit in Denmark is loaned to commercial enterprises. Further information on mortgage credit institutions can be found in the chapter *Setting up Home*.

The institution Finance for Danish Industries (Fiansieringsinstituttet for Industri of Håndvaerk A/S, LaCoursVej 7, 2000 Frederiksberg; tel 38 33 18 88) will provide medium and long-term financing for various business requirements including machinery and building acquisitions, marketing and for mergers and takeovers. Generally serial loans are granted and the first repayment is deferred until the third year and entire repayment lasts over a period of four to 20 years.

Listing on the Stock Exchange. The decisions as to which companies can be listed on the Copenhagen Stock Exchange are taken by the Exchange's own Board which must be satisfied that certain criteria are fulfilled. Companies seeking a listing must disclose information as required by the Board and publish details relevant to future operations. Companies in Groups I and II must have a share capital of Dkr. 15 million or share capital and reserves of Dkr.30 million at the time of listing. Additionally Group I companies must have a minimum of 500 shareholders.

In line with its policy of promoting the interests of small companies there is a Group III for small companies. These must have a share capital of Dkr 2 million, of which one million must be on offer to the public.

The rules of the Copenhagen Stock Exchange are generally considered less rigorous than those of other international exchanges, but have been tightened up in recent years.

Useful Addresses and Publications

The Copenhagen Stock Exchange (Københavns Fondsbørs), Nikolaj Plads 6, 1067 Copenhagen K; tel 33 93 33 66.
Industrial Mortgage Fund (Industriens Realkreditfond). Nyropsgade 17, 1602 Copenhagen V; tel 33 14 80 00.
Information Office for Foreign Investments in Denmark (Informationskontoret for udenlandske investeringer i Danmark), Søndergade 2, 8600 Silkeborg; tel 86 82 56 55.

Ideas & Procedures for Setting up Business in Denmark

Help and Information

In order to help foreigners who want to invest in Denmark, the Ministry of Foreign Affairs has set up an Investment Secretariat. This bureau offers a range of services which include establishing contact with the various authorities, other organisations and commercial companies. It also, helps to arrange fact-finding visits; provides information on investment conditions and help with feasibility studies and market research. The Secretariat will also undertake to find a Danish business partner for foreigners wishing to form a commercial liaison. Even once the desired contacts have been made, assistance is sustained during the setting up of business and afterwards.

Danish embassies and consulates general can also assist in providing information for proposed business set-up and investment in Denmark as can chambers of commerce and special agencies in Denmark.

Useful Addresses

Agency for Investment and Development of Trade and Industry in Greater Copenhagen, via Copenhagen Science Park Symbion; tel 39 17 99 99; fax 31 20 55 21. Started in January 1994 the agency is a partnership representing the following areas: Copenhagen city, Frederiksberg municipality and the districts of Copenhagen, Frederiksborg and Roskilde. The agency aims to offer specific business service programmes to foreign companies considering the Copenhagen area as a possible location.
Danish Chamber of Commerce (Det Danske Handelskammer), Børsen, 1217 Copenhagen K; tel 33 91 23 23; fax 33 32 52 16.
The Danish Federation of Small Industries: Gammelvagt, 8800 Viborg; tel 86 61 49 21.
Ministry of Foreign Affairs (Udenrigsministeriet), Asiatisk Plads 2, 1448 Copenhagen K; tel 33 92 00 00.
National Bureau of Statistics, 11 Sejrøgade, 2100 Copenhagen Ø; tel 39 17 39 10; fax 31 18 48 01.

Royal Danish Embassy, 55 Sloane Street, London SW1X 9SR; tel 071-333 0200.
Royal Danish Embassy, 3200 Whitehaven Street, NW Washington DC 20008-
3683; tel 202-234 4300.
Royal Danish Consulate General, 825 Third Avenue, New York, NY 10022-
7519; tel 212 949 2333; fax 212 983 5260.

Registration of Foreign Enterprises

Citizens from the EU are free to set up a business in Denmark on the same
terms as Danish citizens. For other details of residence regulations in Denmark
for EU citizens, see *Residence and Entry* chapter.

All new foreign commercial enterprises have to be registered with the Danish
Trade and Companies Agency, *Erhvervs & Selskabsstyrelsen*, (Kampmannsgade
1, 1604 Copenhagen K; tel 33 12 42 80), and must be managed by one or more
persons whose residence is in the European Union.

Normally, if a non-EU citizen wishes to establish a business in Denmark it
can only be done if Danes have a reciprocal right with the country concerned.
Non EU-nationals have to obtain authorisation from the Ministry of Justice/
Justitsministeriet, (Slotsholmsgade 10, 1216 Copenhagen K; tel 33 92 33 40) if
they wish to purchase commercial (or residential) property. It is usually easier
for non EU-nationals to obtain permission to buy industrial property than
residential property.

Government Investment Incentives for Foreigners

Denmark operates several business subsidy programmes none of which is particularly substantial except for shipping and agriculture which are earmarked for
preferential treatment. Incentives generally take the form of financial support
such as loans or guarantees which may or may not have to be paid back either
in part, or in full. Other incentives include free export assistance and other
information and advice. Many similar investment schemes are run in other EU
countries. Anyone interested in investing in Denmark should contact the Ministry
of Industry and Coordination, Investment Secretariat (10-12 Slotsholmgade,
1216 Copenhagen K; tel 33 92 33 50; fax 33 12 37 78), for further information.

The areas for which incentives can be provided are:

1. Product development and enhanced production methods — state grants and
subsidised loans.
2. Expansion of small companies including refurbishing/constructing premises
and upgrading equipment — interest subsidised loans.
3. For small companies' export, environmental and energy projects — interest
subsidised loans.
4. Shipping: for building of new ships of minimum gross 100 tons and rebuilding
same in a Danish shipyard — interest subsidised loans.
5. Energy: — for installation of renewable energy sources (solar, wind, compost
heating) and cost efficient energy projects — subsidies.
6. Environmental technology: subsidies for investment in reducing pollution.
7. Hiring & Training Staff: subsidies for the hiring of long-term unemployed if
this causes an increase in overall staffing, retraining subsidies and subsidies for
staff participating in research and development outside Denmark.
8. Export: assistance to enable enterprises to carry out research to find new
export nmarkets and to prepare sales material. A definite export project qualifies
for a guarantee against losses on foreign debts and security for export loans.
9. Consultation: export assistance and counselling on production methods is
available free or at a low cost. Also counselling on product development, market
information and management.
10. Regional Development: the Danish state subsidises development in high

unemployment areas. Subsidies or subsidised loans are granted to companies prepared to establish or relocate in such areas where they provide jobs and raise income levels.

11. Agriculture: The European Commission guarantees mininum prices and guarantees export subsidies for farmers. In addition, there is a range of support schemes aimed at the agricultural sector including subsidies for consultants who provide an advice service to farmers and temporary assistance in case of illness.

12. Information Technology: subsidies for research and development are available where they are deemed valuable to Danish business conditions.

Useful Addresses

Ministry of Foreign Affairs, Investment Secretariat, 2 Asiatisk Plads, 1448 Copen-hagen K; 45 33 920000; fax 45 31 540533.

Regional Investment:

Horsens Trade Council, Tobaksgaarden, 10 Allégade, 8700 Horsens; tel 75 61 18 88; fax 75 61 31 99

Randers Trade Office (& Business Centre), Erhvervenes Hus, 12 Tørvebryggen, 8900 Randers; tel 86 40 10 66; fax 86 40 60 04. Has an excellent data base on companies in the region.

Trade Office for Silkeborg, 4 Godthaabsvej, PB 8500, 8600 Silkeborg; tel 86 81 54 67. Very active trade office for Silkeborg and the region keen to help companies wishing to set up a new enterprise.

Viborg Industrial Development Council, Gammel Vagt, Postbox 4, 2 Ll Sct. Hans Gade, 8800 Viborg; tel 86 62 67 77; fax 86 61 35 50. Viborg.

Business Structures

There are various legal entities which a business can form:

Limited Liability Companies

Denmark has two types of limited company: private and public, and the legislation to which they are subject differs for each of the two types.

Public Limited Company (Aktieselskab A/S). The minimum capital required for the formation of a public company is kr500,000. The main difference between a private and a public company is in the minimum capital required for formation. Also if the capital is reduced to less than 50% of the registered capital by losses, the board of directors (*Bestyrelse*) is required to call a general meeting of shareholders to consider remedial measures.

A public limited company must be incorporated by at least three founders. It is not essential that the founders subscribe capital and the company may be owned by an individual shareholder.

At least two of the founders must be residents of any EU nation (exceptions can be made by special agreement with the Minister of Industry). The founders have to sign a formation agreement. The company must have articles of association which must include the name and objectives of the company, the resident address of the company, the amount of share capital, the number of board members and the accounting year, which need not follow the calendar year.

All companies have to apply for registration with the Danish Commerce and Companies Agency within six months of the formation agreement being signed. Companies may however, begin carrying out business as soon as the formation agreement is signed. However rights against third parties are not possible until registration has taken place. Until the company is registered, The General Management, the Board of Directors and the founders are personally liable.

All public limited companies must have a minimum of three directors on the board. The board is elected by the annual general shareholders' meeting. The board of directors elects at least one general manager (*direktør*). The general manager can be elected to the board but not as its chairperson.

Private Limited Company/Anpartsselskab(ApS). For an ApS, a minimum capital of kr200,000 is required. If the company sustains losses of more than 50% of the registered capital, a reorganisation is compulsory, to comply with the minimum capital requirements.

Generally the formalities for the formation and increases in capital are less restrictive for private than for public companies. Also, the minimum formation capital is less for a private company. A private company is required to have a board of directors, unless it is a small private company, in which case the articles of association may allow that a board is not created. However this exemption will not apply if staffing reaches a level where there is a statutory obligation to have employee representation on the board. This type of entity is designed to facilitate the establishment of small companies with limited liability, for example strictly family held businesses.

The presentation and audit of annual accounts is the same for both private and public companies. There is an additional requirement for a private company to make its annual accounts public through the Trade and Companies Agency (*Erhvervs & Selskabsstyrelsen*, Kampmannsgade 1, 1604 Copenhagen K; tel 33 12 42 80).

If a private company is reorganised into a public one, a special valuation report must be prepared and endorsed by external valuers, regardless of the capital status of the company.

Partnerships

A partnership is not governed by a rigorous framework of regulations and composition and methods of operation are flexible. There are two main types and partners can be individuals or limited liability companies:

A general partnership (Interessentskab, I/S), can be formed by two or more persons that operate a business as co-owners for profit. For instance many professions form partnerships. Although partnerships are free to operate in a manner of their choosing, the method of operation must be set down in a formal set of agreements.

Tax is levied on the share of the profits taken by each member of a partnership. If they wish, partners can elect to be taxed in accordance with the Business Tax Act which enables them to be taxed in part, similarly to an enterprise operating as a single company.

Limited Partnership/kommanditselskab (K/S). A limited partnership is useful where some partners wish to invest in a company but do not want liability. A limited partnership is taxed similarly to a full partnership. In a limited partnership which may comprise two or more individuals or companies of which at least one (the general partner) must be fully liable for all the liabilities of the partnership. Other members are liable only to the extent of the financial stake they have in the company.

Limited partnerships are often used by high tax individuals to raise funds for the aquisition of of depreciable assets such as machinery and buildings. The General Partner in such instances would be a financial company. The assets would then be leased commercially. Leasing is generally cheaper than interest expenses owing to capital allowances. By claiming these allowances, taxes payable are postponed until the assets are disposed of.

Joint Ventures

A joint venture is defined as 'any combination of two or more enterprises associated for the purpose of pursuing a business objective'. Legally two unrelated, incorporated or unincorporated businesses conducting business as a non-corporate joint venture are treated as a partnership, albeit one with limited scope and duration. For tax purposes they are also treated as a partnership.

Sole Proprietorships

Sole proprietors have a special place in Danish economic history as many Danish firms began as single person enterprises including some international Danish companies. The Sole Proprietorship (*Enkeltmandsfirma*) is suitable for those engaged in trading, farming and in the provision of professional services. There is no specific legislation for this type of enterprise. Registration at the registry of trade is optional.

For tax purposes sole proprietors are taxed on business and any other additional income. The Business Tax Act (1987) allows the proprietor to choose to be taxed in the same way as a limited company.

Trusts and Foundations

Trusts are not recognised in Denmark. However both commercial and non-commercial foundations can be established. In order to qualify as a foundation there are certain criteria which must be met:

1. The capital must be separated from the founder's capital so that it cannot be re-acquired by the founder, founder's spouse or their offspring under 18 years.
2. A board of directors must be appointed and include at least one independent member.
3. The foundation must have one or more clearly defined objectives.
4. The foundation must be a separate legal entity responsible for its actions and able to assume rights.

Foundations exist in various types in Denmark. The two main distinctions are between commercial and non-commercial foundations. The former must be registered with the Trade and Companies Agency while non-commercial ones do not have to register. Both types are liable for tax.

Branches of Foreign Companies

A foreign company wishing to establish a branch in Denmark has to register with the Danish Trade and Companies Agency who require specific information regarding the identity and particulars of the parent company. The parent company's annual accounts and annual reports must be filed with the DTCA. A branch has also to file a tax return, which must include details of taxable income and capital and debts.

For tax purposes branches of foreign companies are handled like incorporated companies. The branch and the parent company form an entity. The branch cannot deduct interest on loans granted by the parent company or deduct royalties that are paid to the parent company for the use of rights. Such transactions are deemed capital transfers and do not confer any fiscal benefits.

Running a Business

Employing & Dismissing Staff

Denmark's social security system is almost entirely funded through the tax system. There are two schemes which require compulsory employee contributions: *Arbejdsmarkedets Tillaegspension* (ATP) Pension Scheme (*Arbejdernes Tillaegspensions*) which is run by employers conjointly with the labour organisations, and the *Lønmodtagernes Dyrtidsfond* (LD). In 1993 a new fund was started for about a quarter of a million workers who were not at the time contributing to any pension scheme. Contributions for this sheme which is aimed mainly at non-professional workers are extracted from both employers and employees and amount to about 3% of the salary. There is also an education and training scheme for young workers and the unemployed, *Arbejdsmarkedsuddanelsesfonden* (AUD) which is run by the Ministry of Labour and to which employers contribute.

Useful Addresses

Arbejdsmarkedets Tillaegspension (ATP), ATP Huset, Kongens Vaenge 8, 3400 Hillerød; tel 48 24 11 00; fax 48 24 00 88. (supplementary labour market pension fund).

Lønmodtagernes Dyrtidsfond (LD), Vendersgade 28, 1363 Copenhagen K; tel 33 13 04 42; fax 33 32 44 42.

Dismissing Staff

The notice period of termination of employment is fixed by the Employees Act which stipulates the following notice periods:

Length of Employment	Period of Notice Required
up to five months	one month
up to 2 years & 5 months	three months
up to 5 years & 8 months	four months
up to 8 years & 7 months	five months
thereafter	six months

For employees who have been employed for 12, 15 or 18 or more consecutive years there is a supplementary compensation of one, two or three months salary respectively.

The employment terms for hourly paid employees are governed by collective agreements. There is no legal minimum notice period. An example of an agreement with skilled industrial workers could be:

Period of Employment	Period of Notice Required
less than nine months	nil
more than nine months	21 days
more than three years	49 days
more than six years	70 days.

For employees over 50 years of age whose employment period exceeds nine/twenty years, the notice period would be 90days/120days.

Taxation

The Danish tax system depends more on direct taxes (income tax and corporate tax) than on indirect taxes. In many EU countries the reverse is the case. Whereas individual income tax in Denmark is levied by both central and local governments, corporation tax is levied only by the central government. Although personal taxation in Denmark is notoriously high, the corporation tax, which is the principal tax on businesses is only 34% which is one of the lowest in the EU: in France it is 37% in Germany 50%, Belgium 39% and the UK 42%.

Tax is paid on a current year basis in two tranches on 20 March and 20 November.

The main indirect taxes are VAT at a uniform rate of 25% on most goods and services, and various excise duties of which car tax is one of the most excessive. Most banking, real estate and medical services are exempt from VAT and exports are zero rated. The threshold for compulsory VAT registration is a turnover of Dkr10,000 per annum.

Excise duties are levied on tobacco and spirits, wine, beer, motor vehicles, most energy sources and petroleum.

Useful Addresses

British Embassy Commercial Department, Kastelsvej 36, 2100 Copenhagen Ø; tel 26 46 00. Produces a detailed report *Financial Services in Denmark* covering banking, mortgage credit, insurance and pension funds. Also provides much other useful information for British businesses setting up in Denmark, from business practices and etiquette to a list of Danish lawyers with expertise in drawing up agency/distributor agreements.

Danish Chamber of Commerce, Main office: Børsen 1217 Copenhagen K. tel 33 95 05 00; fax 33 32 52 16. Branches and sub-branches all over Denmark. The Danish chamber of commerce is the principal organisation for international trade and industry and the service sector. For many foreigners it is the first point of contact for those starting a business in Denmark.

Den Danske Bank: International Trade Promotion, 2-12 Holmens Kanal, 1092 Copenhagen K: Visitors Centre: Adelgaarden, 5-7 Adelgade, Copenhagen; tel 43 43 86 00. Produces a leaflet *Taxation of Business Operations in Denmark* and offers a range of banking services to companies in Scandinavia and worldwide including helping establish business contacts and in the acquisition of Danish companies by foreign ones.

Det Danske Handelskammer: Danish Chamber of Commerce, Børsen, 1217 Copenhagen K.

Ernst & Young, National Office, Tagensvej 86. 2200 Copenhagen N, Denmark; tel 35 82 48 48; fax 35 82 48 00. International accountancy firm with over a dozen offices in Denmark. Publishes free booklet *Doing Business in Denmark*.

Industri-og Handelsstyrelsen/National Agency of Industry and Trade, Regional Development, 137 Tagemsvej, 2200 Copenhagen N.

KPMG C Jesperson, Borups Allé 177, P.O. Box 250 Frederiksberg; tel 38 18 30 00; fax 38 18 30 45. KPMG is one of the world's largest accountancy firms and has branches throughout Denmark. Publishes a free guide to *Investment in Denmark.*

Mortensen & Beierholm, Vester Sogade 10, 1601 Copenhagen V; tel 33 12 68 11; fax 33 32 37 73. Part of the worldwide organisation of accounting firms known as HLB International. Has eight other branches in Denmark especially experienced in co-ordinating activities between different countries.

Useful Publications

Business Denmark, Business Denmark Publications ApS., Vimmelskaftet 42A, 1161 Copenhagen K; tel 33 32 75 29; fax 33 93 80 32. A glossy annual free publication financed by advertising but containing useful background on the business scene.

The Scandinavian Economies, Vimmelskaftet 42A, 1161 Copenhagen K; tel 33 14 21 27; fax 33 93 80 32. A monthly business-economic newsletter covering the main Scandinavian countries (i.e. not Iceland).

Finland

SECTION I

Living in Finland

General Introduction
Residence and Entry Regulations
Setting Up Home
Daily Life
Retirement

General Introduction

Destination Finland

Like Sweden, Finland joined the European Union in January 1995 following a yes vote in the autumn referendum of 1994. Fifty-seven percent of voters (the turnout was about 75%) voted for membership. The remaining 25% of non-voters included the notoriously dissenting Finnish farming community who stand to have their income reduced by 15-20% when prices are brought into line with those in the rest of Europe. However, the instability of the former Soviet Union (with which Finland shares a long border), is the main reason why many Finns regard their country's membership of the EU as vital; it will they hope, give them a large measure of security.

Additionally Finland has to repair the damage wrought on the economy by the worst recession for sixty years, which began in 1990 and was exacerbated by the loss of about 60% of their regular export market as a result of the disintegration of the Russian empire, with which trade was mostly on a barter basis.

Preoccupation with the economy and concern about events in Russia are two things uppermost in the minds of most Finns. Fortunately, there has been a discernible improvement in the economy. In January 1994 Prime Minister Esko Aho declared that more than two thirds of foreign trade was with the EU and EFTA nations and that Germany, Sweden and Britain are amongst the top trading partners. In addition the capital Helsinki, freed from Russian influence has blossomed and is fast becoming a cosmopolitan and trendy place for foreigners and expatriates among them top executives and academics. The other pleasant surprises Helsinki offers the newcomer are a fully integrated transport system which runs like clockwork, a virtual absence of atmospheric pollutants and very low crime levels compared with other grand European cities.

Despite the burgeoning delights of the post cold war capital, where new restaurants and nightclubs pop up like mushrooms, some foreigners have remarked on what they perceive as the xenophobia of the Finns and their supposed small nation mentality. Evidently, not all Finns are narrow-minded about foreign parts as it is estimated by the the publishers of *Emigrantti* (a quarterly magazine written by Finnish journalists who are themselves emigrants) that 10,000 Finns emigrate a year. However, membership of the European Union is likely to have a positive effect leading many Finns to change their isolationist attitudes as they begin to benefit from and make their impact on the European Union. The EU however, will be no substitute for the ancient and singular culture of the Finns of which they are justly proud and anyone living and working there should take pains to learn something about it and if possible to learn some Finnish. Mastery of such a difficult language will however probably be beyond the ability of all but the most talented linguists.

Although Finland has the smallest number of foreigners who are resident, than any other European country (about 1% of the population, or 57,000 people), it may well attract more in the future. About 1,500 of the foreign residents are British of whom 408 are female. Finland is an increasingly attractive proposition as a place to live and work. It also has great potential to become an important hub between west and east.

Pros and Cons of Moving to Finland

Those seeking employment in Finland will find an affluent country, but one which is seeking to emerge from a devastating recession that reduced national output by 13% in three years and has seen unemployment climb to one in five of the workforce, by July 1993, and an all time high of 21.8% in December of that year. Optimists forecast this will be reduced to 15% by the end of 1995 when the economy will begin to show signs of recovery.

Pros: Stronger reasons than Norway or Sweden to be in the EU.
Has strong political and trade ties with the new republicised Baltic states, especially affluent Estonia.
Helsinki is one of the least polluted capitals in the world.
Has extremely efficient transport systems.
Skiing and fishing are universal pursuits depending on the season.
Has some of the world's most advanced and streamlined communications systems.
Very low national crime rate, even in Helsinki.
Most Finns speak some English; many fluently.

Cons: The economy is very weak and only a gradual recovery is anticipated.
Unemployment is the second highest in Europe after Spain.
Small range of specialised industries so job and entrepreneurial possibilities not extensive.
Helsinki has a noticeable problem with drunkenness, especially at night.
Seasonal depression is acute in the long winters.
Winters are so cold that the sea around Helsinki freezes (but you can skate on it).
Alcohol is expensive; more than double UK prices
Finnish is an extremely difficult language to learn

Political and Economic Structure

The key to the contemporary politics and economy of Finland lies partly in knowing something of its national history. For more than a century, from 1809 when the Russians invaded, Finland was in Russian hands. Before that it was Swedish-held and until the 1870's Swedish was the official language even though only one-seventh of the population spoke it. The nationalist movements which developed from the 1860's ensured the status of the Finnish language was enhanced to the point that it became the main language until the turn of the century, when it was the turn of the Russians to become heavy-handed. From the early part of the nineteenth century Finland had a Russian Governor General who liaised with the Tsar through a Minister in St. Petersburg. Finland's status as an autonomous Grand Duchy with its own consitutional laws lasted until 1899 when Russia decided to 'Russify' Finland by making Russian the official language of the top administrative cadres and by banning indigenous newspapers. Thus began a period of Russian opression which entered a more domineering phase from 1908 when Russia also assumed the mantle of government in Finland. The downfall of the Tsarist regime in Russia, signalled by the October Revolution, relieved the Finns of Russian domination, and separatists seized the chance to declare Finland independent on October 6, 1917. However the Bolshevikinspired radicals in Finland had another agenda and a bitter Finnish civil war broke out between the nationalists and the radical revolutionary party. The government forces prevailed and early in 1919 Finland finally became a republic.

Government

The Finnish constitution has altered little since its enactment in 1919. Two hundred members of the uni-cameral parliament are elected every four years (next elections 1999). The country is divided into fourteen electoral districts from which representatives are elected by proportional representation. In addition there is a representative from the self-governing province of Åland Islands.

The head of state is the President of the Republic (currently Martti Ahtisaari, expected to serve until 2000), elected by direct popular vote every six years. Before 1988 the President was selected by an electoral college of 301 who were themselves chosen by proportional representation. There are two ballot papers for presidential elections one for the presidential candidates and the other for the electoral college. If there is no outright winner for President then he or she will be selected by the electoral college.

As the highest executive of power in the land, the President has the authority to dissolve Parliament prematurely and order fresh elections. He or she also appoints the Prime Minister (currently Esko Aho) and the other ministers of state.

Political Parties

Historically, post war Finnish political parties represented two main areas of interest: urban and rural. This distinction has become less obvious since the Agrarian Union party changed its name in 1965 to the Centre Party (KP) which is basically liberal and currently the party with the most representatives in Parliament. There are two other main parties: the Finnish Social Democrat Party (SDP) which represents the moderate left, and the National Coalition Party (Kokoomus/KOK) which is the conservative party.

Other Parties in declining order of importance in Parliament are:

Left-Wing Alliance communist and socialist. Polled 10% of the votes in 1991,
Swedish People's Party (RKP), Represents the Swedish-speaking minority.
Greens: They were elected to Parliament for the first time in 1983 and currently have ten representatives.
Finnish Christian League (SKL): Gained first parliamentary seat in 1970, then resigned in June 1994 over Finland's application for EU membership which it has opposed since 1992.
Finnish Rural Party (SMP): Splintered from the Agrarian party in 1959.

The Economy

Finland's industrial base was still embryonic in the early part of the 1950's. Agriculture and forestry were the main occupations of a large part of the working population and forestry products were the main export. In fact Finland's reliance on forestry exports is still the most prodigious element of the economy making up some 40% of export volumes and about half of all revenues. In the fifties individual incomes were very modest. A rapid period of growth at 5% per annum from the fifties to the seventies lead to a great expansion of the cities, (over half of the housing in Finland was built in twenty years from the mid-sixties). This meant that in two decades Finland reached a very high standard of living, became specialised in new industries and experienced considerable urbanisation. From the 1950's exports had been led by metal and engineering industries which did much to promote the growth of the economy. Later, imports of crude oil from the Soviet Union under a bilateral trade agreement also helped the expanding economy. From the 1980's Finland's economy joined the worldwide boom and became over-heated due to excessive borrowing to fund corporate investment mainly in real estate, trading companies, tourism and construction. It is estimated that Finnish banks had to write off a total of FIM22 billion in unrecoverable debts by 1993. With very high foreign debts to pay off Finland has to achieve a balance of trade surplus for several years at the rate of FIM30-40 billion. Such levels have only been notched previously by Germany and Japan. To reach this target would mean a consistent rise in exports by 6% per annum has to be maintained until the end of the millenium. The government has already made historic changes to national legislation to facilitate investment from abroad. For the first time, in 1993, foreign companies were allowed to own Finnish ones; an innovation that sparked a share-buying boom from abroad. It is hoped that foreign companies will increase their operations in Finland, though so far, Scandinavian companies have shown the most interest. Apart from the well-established traditional industries already mentioned, there is no obvious speciality for foreign companies to exploit, except for telecommunications. BT linked up with Telecom Finland (and also the telecoms of Norway and Denmark) in September 1994. It is expected that this kind of international cooperation will extend as Finland develops new industries capable of satisfying the demands of the European market.

The economy base is a mixture of private and state ownership. Finland has been much slower than most European nations to carry out plans for the privatisation of the big state industries like Valtionrautatiet (railways), Finnair the national carrier, Neste (oil refining) and Imatran Voima (the national grid). The government has reduced its holding from 90% to 50% in the metals group Tampella and has earmarked Neste, Kemira (chemicals), Outokumpu (mining and metals) and Velmet (paper machinery and engineering) for part or whole privatisation. For instance a total of 30% of Kemira stock was sold off in October 1994 from the international and domestic retail sectors. Although many reports have been produced and debated on the subject of privatising Finnish industries, progress is generally very slow and comparatively little has so far been effected in this area.

Geographical Information

Area and Main Physical Features

Suomi Finland, the Republic of Finland, is one of the Nordic countries located in the far north-east of Europe; only Iceland lies further north. One third of its area of 338,000 square kms/130,000 square miles lies within the Artic Circle. In total area, Finland is the fifth largest European country in Europe after Germany, France, Spain and Sweden. At its widest point it is 543 kms (337 miles). In the north of the country is Lapland, a part of a huge wilderness area that cuts a swathe also across Norway and Sweden, and which has its own regional culture and traditions.

Finland is a long, thin country (maximum length 1160kms/720 miles), and therefore, not surprisingly, there is considerable difference in the landscape from north to south. The south is characterised by gently rolling landscapes which become hillier and more forested as you go north. About 60% of Finland is tree-covered, which makes it the most densely forested country of Europe. Physically, much of the country is lowland which falls gradually to the south and south-east. The only mountainous region is the north-west tip of Enontekiö towards

Norway, where there are peaks of 1,000m/3,280 feet. The highest point is Halti, 1,328m/4,356 feet.

Like Canada, Finland is a country of lakes. There are about 188,000 in total representing 10% of the surface area of Finland. Statistically, this works out at 37 metres/121 feet of lakeside for every inhabitant. The largest, Lake Saimaa (4400 square kms/2734 square miles) is also Europe's fourth largest expanse of water. However, the lakes tend to shallowness with an average depth of 7m/22 feet and the deepest at 95m/305 feet.

Neighbouring Countries and Coasts

Finland has a frontier of 2570kms/1,596 miles, of which 1269kms/788 miles is with Russia, 716kms/444 miles with Norway and 586kms/364 miles with Sweden.

To the south and west Finland is bounded by the Baltic Sea and the Gulfs of Finland and Bothnia. The shallow Baltic is the largest area of brackish water in the world. The coastline is approximately 1,100kms/683 miles. Finnish islands are as profuse as its lakes: about 30,000 of them lie scattered mainly off the south and south-west coasts. The autonomous region of the Åland Islands is among those to the south-west.

Regional Divisions and Main Towns

For regional administration the country is divided into 12 provinces (*lääni*) which are Uusimaa, Hame, Turku-Pori, Kymi, Mikkeli, Keski Suomi, Vaasa, Pohjois-Karjala, Oulu, Lappi and Åland. The general administration in each province is carried out by a provincial board headed by a governor appointed by the President. Under the provincial board come the local authorities *nimismies* (sheriffs) of which there are 224. In the ancient historical boroughs, a magistrate may be appointed instead of a sheriff. Both functionaries represent the highest legal authority in their province.

Helsinki (Helsingfors in Swedish), the nation's capital since 1812, is the largest city with a population of almost half a million. The populations and the Finnish/Swedish names of the other largest towns are:

Espoo/Esbo	175,692	Oulu/Uleåborg	102,280
Tampere/Tammerfors	173,803	Lahti/Lahtis	93,413
Turku/Åbo	159,399	Kuopio	81,595
Vantaa/Vanda	157,303	Pori/Björne	76,435

Population

The original inhabitants were a combination of settlers (Lapps) who arrived after the last Ice Age and tribes who arrived most probably from the East Baltic region at the beginning of the Christian era. In the 1750's, the population for the whole Finnish land was under half a million (the population of Helsinki today). By 1870 it had reached 1,769,000 and in the next 45 years it doubled. It was not until after the Second World War that it reached four million after which the birth rate declined. The current population of five million was reached in 1992 which makes Finland one of the most sparsely populated nations in Europe. Only Iceland and Norway have fewer inhabitants. There are minority groups: the Lapps/Sami of whom there are about 4,400 the majority of whom live in the Lapp/Sami districts of Enontekiö, Inari, Utsjoki and Sodankylä and the gipsies of whom there are about 5,500. who live mostly in the south. The population of the Åland Islands is Swedish speaking as they were part of that country in former times.

In the Helsinki metropolitan area which includes the towns of Espoo, Vantaa and Kauniainen, there are over 770,000 inhabitants making it easily the most densely populated area of Finland. Over half of the country's total population live in the three southwest provinces comprising 15% of Finland's area.

It has been forecast that the population of Finland will actually decline. This is in part due to the low birth rate (ironically Finnish males have the highest sperm count in the world), and partly due to emigration. A total of about 250,000 Finns are estimated to have left the country for Sweden, while 280,000 have gone to the US about 20,000 to Canada and 10,000 to Australia during this century.

Climate

The Finnish climate is classified as temperate, but winters are extremely cold. However other seasonal temperatures are influenced by the internal waters of Finland and the surrounding oceans: for instance the west winds blow from the Atlantic after warming up over the Gulf Stream.

There are two main climatic zones in Finland: the arctic north and the temperate south. In summer temperatures in the north are about 3°C lower than in the south. The average for July is about 20°C. Winter lasts from November to mid-March and is very cold with average temperatures in Helsinki of-20°C with the coldest months being January and February. The north is much colder and there, snow cover lasts from mid-October to mid-May and in the extreme north, the sun does not rise for nearly six months. In contrast there can be as many as 70 nightless days in the brief Arctic summer. In both north and south Finland summer temperatures of 30°C have been recorded in the past. The warm summers invariably cause a plague of mosquitos and gnats, worst in the north and lakelands where liberal use of insect repellant is essential.

The parts of the country which are consistently the warmest are the southwest and the Åland Islands.

Regions' Report

Information Facilities

Although Finland does not suffer the annual tourist invasion of other, more sun-baked European destinations it nevertheless provides an important source of revenue, and tourists are well-catered for with offices and organisations provided nationally. The most important is the Finnish Tourist Association which publishes the official guides. All large tourist centres have a tourist office and most districts have a tourist manager responsible for developing and co-ordinating tourism in their area. Addresses of some of the main tourist offices are given below under the appropriate region. The regional divisions which follow are geographical rather than political.

The Southwest Including Helsinki

Helsinki, known as the 'daughter of the Baltic', was founded over 400 years ago in 1550. Set on a peninsular, it is a growing city with an increasingly cosmopolitan atmosphere, improving image and an enlarging contingent of foreign residents. As you might expect Helsinki and the southwest are the cultural and industrial hub. The huge post-war expansion of industry took place mostly in this area. Among the southwest's cultural attractions are the former capital Turku as well as Porvoo and Pori. The latter is where an international jazz festival is held annually. Old Rauma, on the other hand is a beautifully preserved town of immaculate wooden houses.

The Coast, Archipelago & the Åland Islands: The mass of islands off the southwest are known as the Turku archipelago and the area has been a maritime national park for over ten years. This region is a popular one for visitors and Finns alike and many Finns have holiday cottages there. It is a much favoured recreation area especially for sailing; tides are minimal and the water of the Baltic is less salty than many seas as little salt water percolates through the straits of Denmark. In fact the Baltic is mainly topped up by the rainfall and rivers of Finland. As you might expect, the warmest part of the country has no shortage of popular resorts including Ekenäs, Hanko, Hyvinkää, Hämeelinna, Kotka, Kouvola, Kuusankoski, Naantali and Lohja.

The Åland Islands (6,500 of them), are set in the Gulf of Bothnia between Sweden and Finland. For historical reasons they are Swedish-speaking, although an autonomous region connected to Finland. They have cultural ties with both Sweden and Finland. The main, indeed only town of any size is Mariehamn. The main industry of these islands used to be shipping and fishing but these days tourism vies with both as the main earner. 'Rod-and-line safaris' are big business in these parts.

Main Tourist Offices
Pohjoisesplanadi 19, 00200 Helsinki; tel 1693757.
Raatihuone, Hallituskatu 9A, 28100 Pori; tel 39 335 780.
Käsityöläiskatu 3, 20100 Turku; tel 21 336 366.
Åland Tourist Office, Aleksandtreinkatu 1, 7900 Lovüsa; tel 15 533 212; fax 532 322.

The Finnish Lakeland

The part of Finland known as the Lakeland or Saimaa Lakeland, after its largest lake, is where the majority of Finland's 180,000 lakes are situated. This veritable maze and mass of waterways lends itself to exploration with its links formed by rivers, straits and canals which in former times provided the principal communication routes. There are many lake steamers offering varied itineraries and because the lakes are shallow they are not too cold for swimming (unless you are used to the Bahamas). The mosquito is the biggest threat to enjoyment of this beautiful region.

The biggest tourist centre and Finland's second city is Tampere on the western edge of the Lakelands which extend as far north as Iisalmi, and east as far as the frontier with Russia. The western edge of Lakelands also includes Hämeenlinna (the birthplace of Sibelius) and Lahti, a winter sports centre while Jyväskla, which lies further north is renowned for its modern architecture. The eastern region of the Lakelands contains the vast Saimaa lake and a profusion of interconnected lakes with no fewer than 33,000 islets within them. It is possible to follow a network of waterways between the major towns such as Savonlinna, Mikkeli and Kuopio.

Main Tourist Offices
Savonlinna Tourist Service, Puistokatu 1, 57100 Savonlinna; tel 57 273 492/493; fax 514 449.
Lukiokatu 10, 95400 Tornio, Tampere; tel 689 40 048.
Mikkelin Matkallu Oy, Hallituskatu 3a, 50100 Mikkeli; tel 55 151 625.
Kupio Tourist Service, Haapaniemenkatu 17 70110 Kuopio; tel 71-182 584; fax 262 4004.

Bothnia

The west coast area lies on the gulf of the same name, across which lies Sweden. This is the main agricultural region whose coast has long, sandy stretches. The islands between Vaasa and Kokkola have old fishing villages and many coastal houses are of the traditional wooden type. There are Swedish-speaking Finns living in this region, mainly on the coast. Further north is the university town of Oulu which is also an important commercial centre. The inland town of, Seinäjoki has municipal buildings designed by the internationally renowned architect Alvar Aalto. Other main towns on the coast are Jakobstad and Raahe. There are ferry connections with Sweden from Vasa and Kokkola.

Main Tourist Offices
Kokkolan Matkailu Oy and Centre-Bothnia, Mannerheiminaukio, 67100 Kokkola; tel 68 311 902,828 9402.
Oulu Tourist Services Ltd. Torikatu 10, 90100 Oulu; tel 81 377 911; fax 377 873.
Vaasan matkailu-ja kongressitoimisto, Hovioikeudenpuisikko 11, PO Box 3, 65101 Vasa; tel 61 325 1145; fax 325 3620.

Eastern Finland

The eastern part of Finland lies between the lakelands and Lapland and and has characteristics of both at its southern and northern limits. It is a sparsely populated area of thick forests and clear lakes. The southern part, roughly the Joensuu-Ilomantsi district, is known as the cradle of Karelian and Orthodox culture whose influence was at its strongest at the turn of the century especially on literature. The best internationally known Finnish literary work, the Kalavela, a collection of epic folk poetry published in 1835 by Elias Lönnrot, was written after his travels, mainly in Karelia, to search for and record folklore. These traditions underpin rural values which are at the heart of most Finns' culture.

The region is also popular with Finns for spectacular hiking, shooting the rapids and winter sports. North from Kainuu and Kuusamo the character of the landscape becomes Lappish.

Main Tourist Office
North Karelian Tourist Office, Koskikatu 1, 80100 Joensuu; tel 73 167 5300; fax 123 933.

Lapland

There are no towns of any size in Lapland and it would be extremely difficult to live and work there, unless perhaps you are skilled with reindeer. However, the inspiring if desolate landscapes are attractive as a form of escapism, especially hiking trips where you are still likely to see the *Sami*, itinerant reindeer herders whose way of life has changed little with modern times. The region is characterised by rivers, swamps and some forested valleys. In the northernmost regions there is only tundra and scrubland. The four towns of the region are Rovaniemi, Kemijärvi, Tornio and Kemi. There are reckoned to be 200,000 people inhabiting this vast region of 100,000 square miles, which works out at two inhabitants per square mile. About 4,000 of these are Lapps and there are about 600 Skolt Lapps who belong to the Orthodox church. From September to January there are round-ups of the estimated half a million reindeer that roam freely, and reindeer driving competitions attract participants from all over the region.

Main Tourist Offices
Kauppakatu 22, 94100 Kemi; tel 698 199 465; fax 199 468.
Aallonkatu 1, 96200 Rovaniemi; tel 346 270; fax 347 351.

Residence & Entry Regulations

Current Position

Finland is one of the newest members of the European Union having joined on January 1st 1995. Finnish entry and residence regulations were changed as early as January 1994 when the European Economic Area (EEA), agreement came into effect. Under these regulations nationals of other EU countries and Liechtenstein do not need work permits. Furthermore, residence permits will be automatically given for stays of longer than three months. Such residence and entry regulations are common throughout the EU.

Nationals of other Nordic countries including Iceland are entitled to be treated exactly the same as Finnish citizens for however long they wish to remain in Finland.

Family members of EU or EEA citizens who are not themselves EEA or EU citizens will still have to comply with the visa requirements for non-EU/EEA nationals and will have no right of residence on their own account, but only if joining the EEA/EU national.

Passports and Identity Cards

EU and EEA citizens arriving in Finland need a valid passport or approved identity card. Finland recognises identity cards issued by the following nations:

Austria, Belgium, France, Germany, Italy, Liechtenstein, Luxembourg, the Netherlands and San Marino. At the time of going to press the British Visitor's passport was also recognised, but from June 1996 BVPs will no longer be issued.

Entry for EU Nationals

Nationals of Belgium, The Netherlands, Luxembourg, Germany, the UK, Austria, Ireland, Spain, Portugal, Greece and Italy can travel to Finland to look for work and then take up permanent residence; they do not have to seek any prior permission or obtain an entry visa. In other words, there is no difference at this stage whether someone is entering Finland as a tourist or a potential resident. Registration with the police or any other authority on arrival is not necessary.

Those who have a job to go to in Finland, or who intend to look for one on arrival, must apply for a residence permit within three months of entering Finland. The main point to note here is that only if you are intending to stay longer than three months should you apply for a residence permit.

Residence Permit

The Residence permit is granted by the local police authorities in the place of residence and is valid for up to five years if employment lasts longer than one year. After five years, renewal or permanent residence can be applied for. The renewal of a residence permit may be restricted if the applicant has been unemployed for more than one year before the first permit expired.

If the period of work is for less than one year then a residence permit will be granted for the period of employment only.

Work can be started before the permit has been obtained.

Although work permits are no longer required by EU citzens wishing to work in Finland they still need to obtain an employer's certificate before applying for the residence permit.

After receiving the residence permit you have to register (see below).

Entry for non-EU Nationals

Generally all non-EU nationals have to apply for a visa or residence permit at the Finnish Embassy or legation in their own country, before departing. Those planning to work or undertake some kind of training scheme will also need a work permit. If coming as a trainee on a recognised practical programme then a trainee work permit (valid for one to eighteen months) should be applied for.

Students. Students who have arrived on a visa to take an entrance examination which they subsequently pass, are given a residence permit for one academic year at a time by the local police authorities. They must be able to satisfy the authorities that they have funds or scholarships that will cover study and living expenses and are expected to deposit funds of FIM30,000 (US$ 5,000) in a Finnish bank. A similar deposit is expected at the beginning of each academic year. Sponsored/exchange students must show proof of acceptance. A student also has the right to work while studying and no permit is required.

Trainee Work Permit. Trainee Work Permits are granted to those coming to Finland to carry out practical training in their own professional or academic field. The main body authorised to issue trainee permits is The Centre for International Mobility (CIMA). Candidates must submit a written statement of employment from the prospective employer and a certificate signed and authorised by CIMO to the Finnish Embassy or Legation in their home country which will stamp the trainee work permit (Status B5) into the applicant's passport. After this, a residence permit will automatically be granted for the same period as the work placement.

Entering Finland to Start a Business

EU nationals who wish to carry out entrepreneurial activities or be self-employed in Finland must have a certificate of registration of a business or trade, or other suitable evidence of the type of business being carried out before applying for a residence permit.

Entering Finland with Retired Status

Those who are retired and receiving a pension from their own EU or EEA country are entitled to a Finnish residence permit if they have sufficient income to support themselves without resorting to Finnish social security. The same applies to the retiree's next of kin.

Registration

Non-EU nationals staying in Finland for longer than one month have to submit an official notification of new residence within three days of arrival. There are special forms for this available from caretakers and managers of apartment blocks, or from a post or registration office (*rekisteritoimisto*). Nationals of other Nordic countries have to sign a Joint Nordic Document of Moving.

In addition, anyone, regardless of nationality, who is staying in Finland for more than one year has not only to fill in the notification of new residence form, but also has to report to the local registration office in order to be included on the population register. This formality requires presentation of your passport (or national indentity card if applicable) and a completed registration form. The object of this exercise is that you will then receive a social security number (*sosiaaliturvatunnus*) known as *sotu* for short. You need this in order to be eligible for benefits (see *Daily Life* chapter).

Nationality & Citizenship Once in Finland

On expiry of the five year residence permit, an employee may apply for a further five-year renewal, or a permanent residence permit. An employee also becomes eligible for Finnish citizenship after five years.

Useful Addresses

Ministry of the Interior/Centre for Alien Affairs, Haapaniemenkatu 5, 00530 Helsinki; tel 90 160 2784; fax 90 160 2755. Any questions about residence permits can be addressed to the customer service of the above.

Ministry of Labour, Fabianinkatu 32, 00100 Helsinki; tel 90 18561; fax 90 1856 219. Contact for any questions concerning work permits: Chief Inspector Ms Arja Jussila.

Setting up Home

Foreigners living and working in Finland tend to be concentrated in the Helsinki metropolitan area where over a million inhabitants are based. The urban areas commenced their sprawl during the mass exodus from the countryside to the towns during the fifties and sixties. This caused an acute housing shortage which in some areas has never been adequately resolved, although since the 1992 relaxation of rent controls on the private sector, it has become easier to find rentable property in the last couple of years. However, ownership is more common in Finland than tenancy: seventy-five per cent of Finns are owner-occupiers making home ownership in Finland even more of a national pastime than in Britain and Finland is ranked sixth internationally in the league of owner occupiers as a percentage of the population. Home ownership is encouraged by the government through various schemes and subsidies (see below), and it is not unusual for Finns to buy their first home (or have their parents buy it), while they are still studying. Another reason for this apparent extravagance might be that there is a shortage of student accommodation and even when students attend university in their home town, they prefer to set up home independently. The pattern of home owning is therefore somewhat different in Finland than in other European countries. France, Belgium and Greece for instance have a much lower percentage of home ownership and in France it is not unusual for first time buyers to be in their thirties. Finland also has wide regional variations in availability of housing, rent levels and purchase prices of real estate.

How do the Finns Live?

According to the Finnish Housing Association, the standard of Finnish housing has improved dramatically in the last thirty years. In the early 1960s a staggering 65% of Finnish homes lacked an indoor lavatory, only a third were centrally heated and under half had a mains water supply. In the 1990s these amenities are standard in 95% of dwellings. Most of the improvements were brought about by new building. When an organised housing strategy was introduced about 30 years ago it was deliberate policy to avoid social segregation in residential areas. The result is that public and commercial housing has been integrated to the extent that in some cases the two types are to be found within the same building, but more usually in immediate proximity.

Most housing is built to high specifications. To withstand the winters, buildings need to be solid and insulated. Double-glazing and double doors are the norm. The entrance doors to public buildings seem to have been constructed with the biceps of Arnold Schwarzenegger in mind. In recent years all new houses have been given triple-glazing as part of the government's policy for the efficient use of energy. The traditional type of wooden house survives, especially in the countryside and when equipped with a porcelain, fuel burning, ceiling-high stove, indoor temperatures can be overwhelming.

According to received wisdom, the recent acquaintance of Finns with city life (most Finnish cities were still small towns in the 1920s) means that they are generally distrustful of metropolitan life. One commentator even goes so far as to say that 'a Finn's dream house is a lakeshore cottage in the middle of a town'. This conflict between city and rural ideals is apparently resolved by many Finns through posession of a 'summer cottage'. Not all Finns have one but they nearly all aspire to. A 'cottage' can be a simple shack minus even the basic facilities, or a more luxurious edifice built or bought in the countryside, preferably by a lake or on a Baltic or lakeland island. Those who can afford it buy the island too (there being thousands to choose from in the lakelands). Approximately 368,000 Finns have a holiday property in addition to their flat or house.

Rent or Buy

Rented accommodation in the public sector is still quite difficult to find in Finland. This is because Finnish Housing Policy of recent decades advocated the exercising of rigorous rent controls which benefited the tenant, at least initially, but which led to a shortage of rentable property as hard-pressed investors went after higher profits through other forms of investment. The policy therefore backfired dismally as the number of rentable homes in the commercial sector fell from 540,000 in 1970 to less than half that number by 1989. The social rentable housing however was augmented by almost 300,000 units during that period. The government, realising the full extent of the failure of the commercial rent controls began to introduce measures to deregulate the rent market from the end of the 1980s. By February 1992 all new leases were freed from rent control and the abolition of all controls in the public sector is the last remaining step to full deregulation. At present there are about 30,000 tenancies exempt from rent control and about 150,000-200,000 homes still subject to rent control under the state housing schemes.

The main type of tenancy agreement in the private sector is the fixed and long-term contract. This type of contract is for three or more years, the amount of the rent may be linked to an index without restrictions.

At the same time as giving the rental market this fillip, the government is having to reduce its input to the subsidised housing market and direct government loans for for new construction and basic repairs, are being cut and replaced with bank loans with government interest subsidies.

It is therefore difficult at this point to evaluate the effect that deregulation has had on the supply of private rental accommodation though it is true to say that in some areas it is more prolific than in others. Ways of tracking down possible accommodation include using an agency, scanning advertisements, or through word of mouth. Commercial rents are now generally high.

The decision to buy rather than rent a home will largely be dicated by the outcome of a comparison of the difficulties, expense and feasibility of these two alternatives. Buying a house therefore could be more of a necessity than a luxury if rentable accommodation is in short supply or wastefully expensive. A small consolation from the economic downturn of recent years is that the resulting high interest rates, have led to a glut of apartments on the market at somewhat lower prices than a few years ago though they are still not cheap by European standards. Another option in the rental market to bear in mind is social housing which is prevalent and usually of a high standard. In the European Union, applicants for social housing in one EU country are eligible for social housing in another, subject to the financial qualification rules of that country.

Right of Residence Apartments. A recent innovation which is in between renting and buying is the so-called right-of-residence-apartment whereby the occupier pays 10-15% of the value of the property plus monthly rent. This gives a high degree of security of tenure without the full expense of purchase. Further details are given below under *Types of Ownership*.

Buying real estate in Finland used to be very restricted for foreigners and obtaining permission from the Ministry of Housing was obligatory. Most of these restrictions have now been abolished. There are some remaining formalities however: if a foreigner wishes to acquire property situated in the Finnish border zone, or a protected area, or plans to use it as a holiday home, or for recreational purposes, then prior permission must be obtained from the County Government (*lääninhallitus*).

Useful Addresses
Estate Agents in Finland:

HK Property Advisors, Melkonkatu 16 A, 00210 Helsinki; tel 18031; fax 180 3227.
Helsingin Liiketeollinen Kiinteistönväliyys Oy; Mikonkatu 13A 16, 00100 Helsinki; tel 636 122; 631 751.
Huoneistomarkkinointi Oy, Mannerheimintie 4, 00100 Helsinki; tel 680851; fax 646 852.
Suomen SKV-Yrityspalvelu Oy, Sinimäentie 10C, 02630 Espoo; tel 502 3900; 502 3223.
The Finnish Real Estates Agents' Association, Kantelettarenkuja 3, 00420 Helsinki; tel 507 1533; fax 507 1257.

Housing Fund of the Republic of Finland
Over the last few years a reorganisation of housing finance and public management has been carried out under which the National Board of Housing (which was the body responsible for government financing of housing from 1966-1995), was replaced by the Housing Fund of the Republic of Finland (P.O. Box 100, 00521 Helsinki; tel 90-6 148 881; tel 90-1482 582). Part of the brief of the new HFRF is to liaise more with local authorities than the old NBH. Local authorities will therefore have a larger say in housing requirements (including the selection of those persons most in need) of public housing and they will be more influential in the decision as to the type of housing: rental or owner-occupied that may be needed, or indeed whether refurbishment of existing buildings is more appropriate for their area.

Henceforward there will be open competition for the production of new government subsidised building thus compelling high standards to satisfy the demands of the increasingly quality conscious consumer.

Judging by the stated aims of the the new HFRF, the emphasis in future housing programmes will be on refurbishment and repair of existing public housing (the majority of which is 20 years old) rather than promoting new construction as the priority. Another stated aim is to encourage owner-occupiers to renovate their homes by claiming the state subsidies on offer for some types of repair. Further details can be obtained from local authorities in the area of residence.

Main Types of Property Ownership
There are two main forms of property ownership in Finland. One is direct ownership which means that the owner has title to the property. Unlike in some European countries this form is not the most common form of ownership in Finland. The more usual alternative is owning shares in a housing company. There is a large disparity in the cost of stamp duty between the two forms at 6% for direct title ownership and 1.6% for real estate company shares.

Housing Companies. The first housing companies appeared in Finland in the late nineteenth century. As their number increased a regulatory law governing them was passed in 1926 which corresponded broadly to the Companies Act. A housing company is therefore also a joint-stock company whose shareholders are owners of property in a multi-household building held by the company. The shareholders have powers of decision which they can use depending on a majority vote being carried at shareholders' meetings.

The biggest obligation of a shareholder in a housing company is that of paying regular maintenance charges which are generally proportionate to the gross floor area of the property occupied. Should the shareholder (i.e. property-owner) default on the maintanance charges, the housing company, by majority decision, can elect to evict the defaulter from their property for a maximum of three years during which time they can rent the property out and recover the unpaid maintenance fees by such means. Needless to say, the property owner can rent out their own property as and when they please. Property-owners can also be evicted in a similar manner for anti-social behaviour that is considered by a majority vote of the shareholders to constitute a disturbance or nuisance to the neighbours.

While the cost of general exterior maintenance of the buildings and the building's structures, piping or electricity mains are payable by the shareholders collectively. The individual shareholder is fully entitled to alter the interior of their premises and make improvements (installing a sauna is a frequent improvement) without prior consultation with the company.

When selling shares (i.e. property) in a housing company property, the owner is not restricted unless there is a clause in the articles of association that allows for the company to have first option on them.

Right of Occupancy Housing. This system of housing people was introduced in Finland during the last few years and is likely to increase in popularity thus offering serious competition to the housing companies as the most popular form of housing as it basically gives what most Finns want, security of tenure. The occupier pays a regular charge which is not called rent (but amounts to virtually the same thing) which gives them the right of occupancy, but not proprietory rights which are retained by the owner.

ROO (Right Of Occupancy) is now common throughout the Nordic countries as well as being present in some other European states. There are however considerable variations in application procedures even within the same country. To try to avoid this happening in Finland, basic procedures were laid down in a law passed in 1990. The law presently restricts ROO to buildings for which state housing loans have been granted. The maximum loan limit is 90%. For the occupier, no more than 15% of the approved acquisition value of the building can be collected in residence payments. Any money accruing to the owner of the building must be reinvested in the building.

Prospective occupiers can apply for housing allowances on the same terms as those applying for rents. In addition prospective occupants can apply for a loan in order to pay the initial ROO payments and are entitled to the same tax deductions on interest as are granted to mortgage holders.

As ROO housing is essentially non-profit and self-perpetuating it does not appeal to speculators. Indeed the very restrictions imposed on eligibility for ownership are designed to preclude such occurences and ensure the continuity of an adequate stock of ROO accommodation. The restrictions stipulate that local authorities, municipal federations, government appointed corporation or a joint stock company created by any of these bodies are eligible to be owners.

Who is Eligible for ROO Housing

As ROO housing is intended for those aged 18 or over, unable to afford other housing. Eligibility is means tested. Neither the applicant, nor any member of their household may already be in possession of an owner-occupied dwelling. Applicants may stipulate the type of dwelling and the number of rooms required.

The application has to be approved by the local authority and is put on a waiting list which is dealt with chronologically rather than by a greatest need point system as in the UK. So far the residence charges for ROO housing have tended to be lower than rent payable for state-subsidised rentable property of the non-ROO type. An occupier can only be evicted in similar circumstances to those in housing company property (see above). Occupancy rights can be formally bequeathed to whomsoever the occupant wishes.

There are moves to make ROO housing ownable by special ROO housing associations on the same terms as the other owners of such housing (i.e. on a non-profit basis).

ROO housing systems operate in nearly all of Finland's large and medium-sized towns and a growing number of Finns are opting for this type of occupancy. Foreigners are also entitled to apply to the city authorities on the same terms as Finnish citizens.

Occupants' Democracy

Finland is different from many European countries in that most of the country's housing is public rather than private. There is therefore much more incentive for citizens to influence the handling of matters to do with public housing. Democracy is anyway considered a basic right of citizens in all matters in modern Finnish culture. Since the 1970s there has been an unofficial influence from tenants of government rental housing on the running of their own multi-occupied buildings. However not until 1991 was the absolute right to participate enshrined in a law that applies to all Arava (state-subsidised) housing. The aim of the 1991 law was to promote trust between the occupants and the landlords of rented building. It also helped to create a greater sense of responsibility amongst tenants towards the property they are living in. One of the important rights of occupants is to have open access to information about the workings of the building and to know how the level of their rents are determined. Occupants also have the right to form occupants committees which may elect a supervisor to oversee the administration and management of the building.

Other Ways of Obtaining a Home in Finland

There also exists in Finland a well organised DIY element which is more often found in the country than in urban areas. It is possible to buy or lease land, obtain finance (usually from a bank), commission plans, carry out direct purchasing, and organise with contractors the work of construction. In Finland as in other Nordic countries, the owner may well work on the building himself and call in professionals for the more specialised work. Even friends, neighbours and relatives may be called in to literally lend a hand. The existence of a DIY brigade has created a demand for 'house building kits' which can be bought ready made in separate units which can be assembled on the chosen site. Such a market may also offer an opening for those thinking of starting a business in Finland as the market for DIY house assembly kits and fittings is not by any means saturated. Holiday home kits may also be another possibility.

Finance

In Finland the majority of loans for property purchase are organised through banks (about 70%) and the rest through a variety of institutions including savings and cooperative banks, insurance companies and central and local government.

Useful Address (Mortgage Organisation)
Suomen Hypoteekkiyhdistys. Yrjönkatu 9, 00120 Helsinki; tel 90 647 401.

Utilities

Electricity

Electricity in Finland is cheaper than in most other European countries and is derived from a variety of sources including nuclear (29%), hydro (21%), coal, peat, solar and so on. Energy production is decentralised and there are about 370 power stations owned by 130 power companies or utilities. State-owned power companies represent about 40% of output, industrial companies a similar percentage, while municipal and private distribution companies account for the remaining 20%.

In addition the Finnish national grid is connected to those in neighbouring countries making it possible to even out the load amongst them. The effect of versatile production and integration of national grids is to keep electricity supplies low throughout most of Scandinavia.

Finland is a world leader in CHP (combined heat and power generation). Electricity prices for industry are even cheaper than for private consumers and industries and electricity utilities jointly own cogeneration plants where excess energy (including waste products that can be converted to energy) are channelled into the municipal district heating network. The by products of wood-processing are particularly useful for this.

Gas

Finland is not self sufficient in gas. A pipeline from the former Soviet Union brings natural gas to the Helsinki region and to the second city Tampere. There are plans to extend the pipeline to the west coast and even across the Baltic to Sweden.

Useful Addresses

The Association of Finnish Electric Utilities. POB 100, 00101 Helsinki; tel 408 188; fax 442 994.

Information Centre for Energy Efficiency, POB 402, 02151 Espoo; tel 456 6090; fax 456 7007.

Ministry of the Environment, POB 399, 00121 Helsinki; tel 19 911; fax 199 1499. Deals with energy use and the energy economy of buildings.

Removals

Importing a Car

Anyone who is taking up residency in Finland may import one motor vehicle, duty free, for private use, provided that he or she has owned it outside Finland, and been resident outside Finland for at least one year prior to importation. After the vehicle has been imported it may not be sold, hired out, or lent to anyone other than a family member (which includes couples living together but not married), until two years from the date of clearance have expired.

In the unfortunate event that the vehicle is damaged beyond repair before the two years are up, you may hand it over to your insurance company or sell it to a scrap dealer without paying duties and taxes provided that you have been granted tax relief.

Insurance. Third party motor insurance is compulsory in Finland. Claims are dealt with by the Finnish Motor Insurance Bureau (*Liikennevakuutusydistys*), Bulevardi 28, 001120 Helsinki 12; telephone 680401.

Useful Addresses
National Board of Customs, P.O. Box 512, 00101 Helsinki. Provides a leaflet in English, for immigrants on importing personal effects. The leaflet contains addresses of customs offices around Finland.

Importing Pets
Depending on the type of dog or cat or other pet you wish to take with you to Finland it is important to consider their likelihood of adapting successfully to the winter climate and new surroundings. Cats and dogs to be imported from the UK to Finland must be at least 10 weeks old prior to the date of entry. There is no requirement for an import permit or health certificate if they travel direct from the UK to Finland through any of the following countries: Sweden, Norway, Iceland or Ireland. Owners should however check with airlines and shipping companies as to whether they require a health certificate for animals being transported. If the animal is travelling overland through any other country not mentioned above, then a rabies vaccination certificate is required.

As regulations are subject to change it is advisable to check with the Ministry of Agriculture, Fisheries and Food, Animal Health section (tel 0181-330 4411; fax 0181-337 3640).

Daily Life

The Finnish Language

In Finland there is not a great incentive to learn Finnish as most Finns speak a little English and many can converse fluently in it. However, in order to integrate yourself to a greater degree, you should aspire to learn some Finnish not least because you will have greater access to Finnish culture. Unfortunately, Finnish is not for the faint-hearted as it is a difficult language to learn. Italian, French, Spanish and even Romanian share some similarities from Latin, but Finnish, like that other mysterious European language, Basque, is not related to any of these or even other Scandinavian ones. Instead it belongs to the Finno-Ugrian group of languages which includes Estonian and Lappish, and more distantly, Hungarian. One of the main characteristics of these languages is the number of cases (15 in Finnish) appearing as suffixes. Cases broadly equate with prepositions in other languages. However these are not the only Finnish suffixes. There is a whole range of them which alter the sound of the stem word to a complex degree. Articles do not exist and there is no grammatical distinction of gender e.g. the same word *hän* is used for he and she.

As regards pronunciation, Finnish is reliable in that every letter is always pronounced the same. Stress comes on the first syllable of words.

As in German, words can be strung together to form a complete word of unwieldy length which at first can be rather intimidating. After you have acquired a basic vocabulary you can usually recognise the constituent bits of long words. Finnish has a claim to fame in that it has the longest palindrome (a word that spells the same forwards and backwards), found in any language, *saippuakauppias*. Its use is fairly restricted however as it means soap salesman. Words likely to prove more useful in daily life are loanwords from languages that may be more familiar: *pankki* (bank), *sekki* (cheque) are fairly obvious, and *kauppa* (shop) is derived from the German *kaufen* (to buy).

As Swedish is Finland's second official language spoken by 6% of Finns, place names generally appear in both languages.

Sami and gypsies living in Finland have their own languages.

Learning Finnish

As you would expect, evening classes in Finnish are not commonplace nationally in the UK. The best source of information is probably the University of London's School of Slavonic and East European Studies (Senate House, Malet Street, London WC1E 7HU; tel 0171-637 4934; fax 0171-436 8916), which can provide a list of Finnish courses in the United Kingdom and in Finland.

Useful Addresses

Council for Instruction of Finnish for Foreigners, P.O. Box 293, Pohjoisranta 4A 4, Fin 00171 Helsinki; tel 90 134 171; fax 134 17374. Arranges summer courses in Finnish Language and Culture in Finland. Application forms from the above address.

Finnish Church Guild, tel 0171-237 7736; fax 0171-231 4261. The FCG is the
largest Anglo-Finnish organisation in the UK. As well as providing information
about affiliated courses around the country, private tuition and examinations,
it publishes a quarterly, bilingual newsletter *Horisontii* and an events calendar
twice a year. Annual membership of the Guild costs about £8.

Finnish Institute, 35-36 Eagle Street, London WC1R 4AJ; tel 0171-404 3309;
fax 0171-404 8893. The FI promotes educational, cultural, and economic
relations between Finland and the UK. Open weekdays Monday to Friday
10.00am-4.00pm.

Schools and Education

Pre-School

As more than three-quarters of mothers in Finland go to work, childcare for the
under-sevens is a priority. This area is under the control of the Ministry for
Social Affairs and Health who are responsible for providing municipal day-care
centres or registered child-minders. The former cover only about 66% of the
demand and in some cities there is an acute shortage of places which the
government is trying to ease by increasing availability to cover all five and six-
year olds. These two pre-school years are seen as an opportunity to prepare
children for proper school.

Interestingly 10% of training places for nursery school teachers are reserved
for men. The training lasts for three years which gives ample time for a thorough
theoretical training.

Junior and Secondary Schooling

In Finland schooling is compulsory for nine years from ages seven to sixteen.
The tenth year is optional. The educational system was reformed in the early
1970's when the basis of a comprehensive system aimed at reducing social and
regional inequalities was laid down. Before the 1970's secondary schools were
mostly fee-paying and private. Now most are run by the municipalities. The
range of compulsory subjects at junior level (forms 1-6), is an ambitious mixture
of the practical, the mind-stretching and the creative: mathematics, religious
knowledge, environmental studies, Finnish or Swedish (depending on mother
tongue), foreign languages (usually English), history, social studies, civics,
biology, geography, physical education, music, arts and handicrafts.

At senior level (forms 7-9) the same subjects are taught with the exception of
environmental studies. Compulsory subjects at senior level include chemistry
and physics, home economics and the second official language. At the senior
level optional subjects are available including economics, other foreign languages,
agriculture and computer studies.

Forms 10-12 (ages 17-19 years) are known as senior secondary school of which
there are two types in Finland: The three-year *lukio* which roughly corresponds
to a UK sixth form or a French baccalaureate class, i.e. the academic line, and
the more practical vocational schools. As in other countries the vocational
education has a tendency to become fragmented into diverse studies. Senior
secondary education is now modular-based with each course devised to last 38
study hours. Finnish students study Finnish, Swedish, 1-3 foreign languages,
maths, physics, chemistry, geography, biology, psychology, religious knowledge,
art or music and hygiene. Some of these are compulsory subjects, others optional.
Special *lukios* exist for the fostering of talent in music, art and physical education.

After three years the students sit a very competitive national matriculation exam, either in spring or autumn, to qualify for university entrance. There are usually some 30,000 qualified candidates for 18,000 university places, some of which are reserved. This results in a surplus of able candidates who have nevertheless failed to get to university, who then have to reappraise their options. Many take a vocational education or go to work.

The organisation of general education is the responsibility of the municipality. Teaching, materials and school meals are all free. Children who live more than 5kms from the school are provided with free transport. The state subsidises local authorities' education budgets by as much as is necessary to maintain them to the required standard. There is no limit to the state subsidy which can be 100%.

Current Trends in School Education. In the sparsely populated areas of Finland schools can be very small with only two or three teachers teaching classes in which the age difference can be as much as four years. There have been moves in recent years to reduce the class sizes generally and also to decentralise decision-making about education. Teachers and school boards have increasing freedom to run their local schools.

Higher Education
Finland's first university was the Royal Academy of Turku which was founded in 1640 at a time when Finland was part of Sweden. In 1828 the RA was transferred to the new capital Helsinki. Before Finnish independence in 1917, two other institutes of higher education were in existence and two additional universities were created immediately afterwards. Today there are seventeen universities and three academies of art with a total student enrolment of 80,000 of whom about 2,000 are international students from about 40 countries. Helsinki is the largest unversity (26,000 students), followed by Turku and Tampere (10,000 students each). The technology university in Espoo (near Helsinki) has 9,000 and Oulu has 8,000 and Jyväskylä has 7,000 students.

Vocational Institutions
For a vocational education students select a basic line from about 25 options of different trades and professions. Each is split into a year-long foundation phase which is identical for all students, after which, they specialise for 1-4 years. There are over 240 lines to choose from and an additional dozen or so advanced specialities. Those who complete the longest courses automatically have the option of continuing to university.

Finland has about 540 vocational institutions of various types. Fifty of these are Swedish-speaking. There are over twice as many students enrolled at vocational institutions as at universities. Nearly 50% of VIs are run by the state, 30% by the local authorities and the rest are private (either commercial enterprises or privately funded). At the time of going to press vocational education is being partly restructured. For instance there has been an experimental merging of some insitutions to form polytechnics (modelled on the German *Fachhochschule*) to award new types of professional degrees.

Student Grants and Loans
Students can apply for non-returnable state grants, or state-guaranteed low interest bank loans. Other state contributions to the cost of studying include subsidised hostels, health care and meals.

Useful Addresses
SAAKI, (Finnish Federation of Vocational Trainees), Siltasaarenkatu 3A, 00530 Helsinki; tel 90 772 1480.
National Union of Foreign Students' Organisations in Finland (NUFSOF), c/o

National Union of Finnish Students (SYL), Töölönkatu 15E, 00100 Helsinki; tel 90-492 522.

Scholarships, Grants & Exchange Programmes

There are various international, European and Finnish organisations which can offer the above to students from abroad.

Useful Addresses

Centre for International Mobility, (CIMO), P O Box 343, Hakaniemenkatu 2, 00531 Helsinki; tel 7747 7033.
The Finnish Academy, Hämeentie 158, 00550 Helsinki, tel 0 77 581.
COMETT, Infocentre Finland, Helsinki University of Technology, Dipoli, 02150 Espoo; tel 451 4020; fax 451 4042.
National Board of Education, Hakaniemenkatu 2, 00530 Helsinki; tel 774 775
FINNIDA, Finnish International Development Agency, Mannerheimintie 15C, 00100 Helsinki; tel 134 151.

Degrees

Until 1994, all Bachelor's or Master's degrees required about 5-7 years of study. However, last year (1994), three-year bachelor degrees in humanities and science subjects were introduced.

Government policy is to provide appropriately trained graduate researchers for the workplace particularly in science and technology subjects. This has been achieved by increasing the number of students in the sciences at the expense of the arts and social sciences.

Adult and Continuing Education

A parallel system of informal education exists alongside the full-time degree or diploma oriented education system. Originally conceived as a way of providing a general education and stimulating leisure time, adult education has steadily become more directed towards vocational training. Vocational education may involve training to upgrade skills, or training for a new vocation. Various organisations and associations run courses which are partly state-subsidised. For instance the national network of workers' institutes (established in 1899), nowadays has more than 600,000 students. They offer mainly evening classes in the traditional general and leisure subjects; also classes covering the senior secondary school syllabus (but usually without final certification), as well as vocational training.

The folk schools and academies (established 1899) which are mainly residential, have about 7,000 students a year and offer a similar mix of courses and vocational training.

Most universities have summer schools open to all. Only part of the tuition is at university level, the rest supplements vocational or upper secondary education.

International Schools

There are international, English, German, French, Russian and Jewish schools in Helsinki. Lessons are given partly in Finnish and partly in the language of the school. These schools are private, and charge fees for tuition.

Useful Addresses

Deutsche Schule, Malminkatu 14, 00100 Helsinki; tel 694 44 64; fax 694 6927.
English School, Mäntytie 14, 00270 Helsinki; tel 477 1123.

Helsingin ranskalais-suomalainen koulu, (French-Finnish School of Helsinki), Laivurinkatu 3, 00150 Helsinki; tel 634 116; fax 634 437.
Suomalais-Venäläinen koulu, (Finnish-Russian School), Kaarelankuja 2, 00430 Helsinki; tel 535 940.

Media & Communications

Newspapers

The Finnish press made its debut with the publication of a newspaper in Turku in 1771. A few magazines also appeared about the same time. The first regular newspaper was not published until 1809 when Finland was an autonomous Russian Grand Duchy. In the 1820s more newspapers appeared, but in Swedish. They included the oldest newspaper still being published today *Ab Underrättelser*, founded in 1824. The oldest Finnish-language journal is *Uusi Suomi* founded in 1847.

Today there are 103 Finnish newspapers with a combined circulation of 3.28 million, or 660 copies per 1000 inhabitants. These UNESCO statistics show Finns to be the world's third largest consumers of newsprint. There are about ten leading newspapers none of which is truly a national newspaper except perhaps *Helsingin Sanomat* which has a wide distribution. The daily *Uusi Suomi* has a page summarising the news in English. In descending order of circulation the main papers are: *Helsingin Sanomat* (482,944), *Ilta-Sanomat* (218 642), *Aamulehti* (144,567), *Turun Sanomat* (134,705), *Maaseudun Tuelvaisuus* (122 343), *Iltalehti* (113,544), *Kaleva* (96,955), *Savon Sanomat* (90,609), *Kauppalehti* (84,068) and *Keskisuomalainen* (81,852).

The press receives state subsidies most of which go to the politically-affiliated papers.

Overseas newspapers including US and British ones, can be bought at the *Academic Bookstore* in Helsinki (Pohjoisesplanadi 39).

Magazines

It is not possible to state the exact number of magazines in Finland because of the tradition of leafletting and private publishing that goes on there. The Post Office has over 1,000 publications on its delivery list. Many magazines are reviews and trade and professional journals. The leading magazines are a mixture of general interest, women's and cultural and political reviews.

Television & Radio

The Finnish Broadcasting Company (Oy Yleisradio Ab) known as YLE was established in 1926 and the Radio Act was passed in 1927 to regulate broadcasting of which it had a virtual monopoly until the 1950's. YLE's radio output consists of the usual array of programmes plus one unique claim to fame: *Nuntii Latini* (News in Latin) launched in 1989. It is a five-minute summary of worldwide events broadcast every Friday on international shortwave. Details of broadcasting times and wavelengths for radio programmes broadcasted internationally can be obtained from YLE Radio Finland (Box 78, 00024 Yleisradio, Finland).

In 1956, when television came on the scene, Helsinki Tesvisio and Tampere Tamvisio were granted broadcasting licences for television programmes. In 1957, a third company MTV came into being and linked up with YLE which subsequently took over the Tesvisio and Tamvisio which became TV2. However, although YLE and MTV work together they are entirely separate organisations. A third channel, TV3 started transmitting in 1986 and is a joint venture between

YLE, MTV and Oy Nokia Ab. English Sky Channel and French ECS channel are available via satellite and cable. Since 1988, Swedish programmes have been available on TV4 which is aimed at Swedish subsribers in Finland and can only be received in the coastal zone where most of them live. Many English-language channels and the French TV5 are relayed by satellite and can be received by those with the appropriate equipment. The cable company HTV has over 100,000 subscribers in the Helsinki area. Almost half the programmes shown on the three main Finnish channels are home grown. The most popular of these are Finnish films and serials.

Post and Telephone

Telephone

Most telecommunications are run by the state-owned post and telecommunications company (Finnish P & T Telecom). There are sixty regional telecommunications offices which perform the same functions nationwide under government supervision. The privately owned HTC (Helsinki Telephone Company) serves the Helsinki metropolitan area. About 60 out of every 100 inhabitants is on the telephone.

As regards mobile telephones Finland's Nokia company is one of the world's leading producers of mobile phones and Finland has the third highest number of mobile telephones per head in the world at about 10% of the population. There are five public mobile telephone networks. The Nordic Mobile Telephone System (NMT 450 and NMT 900) covers the whole of Scandinavia. NMT 900 is also the lowest priced mobile network in Europe providing roaming to Dutch, Swiss and Estonian (Tallinn) networks as well as to the rest of Scandinavia. Two pan-European GSM mobile networks have been running since 1991. The ARP network, running since 1971 is countrywide.

Finnish telecommunications are state of the art so it comes as no surprise that nearly half the population of the Helsinki metropolitan area works with information technology linked to the telephone system.

The Helsinki telephone directory has a page of instructions in English. The area code for Helsinki metropolitan area is 90. Codes for other areas are given in the telephone directory. For direct dial international calls 990 is the international access code, followed by the country code, the area code and the subscriber's number.

Calls can be made from telephone booths with FIM1 or FIM5 coins. Many public telephones now use disposable cards. Colourfully designed phonecards (*tele puhelukortti*) of FIM30, 50 and 100 values, are sold by Tele shops, post offices and other outlets such as bus stations in the vicinity of public telephones. If using a credit card to phone, the minimum charge is FIM5 and the call is automatically disconnected when the charge reaches FIM100.

Local calls are cheaper from 5pm to 7am and at weekends. Call rates to other parts of Finland are reduced from 5pm-9pm and at weekends. The cheapest rate is from 9pm to 8am every day.

Cars and Motoring

Foreigners may drive in Finland using their national driving licence for one year. After six months they become eligible to apply for a Finnish licence. The initial point of contact for this is the local police station.

Finland has an excellent road network of over 45,000kms and congestion problems are almost unknown. There are no toll roads. Snow is a problem away from the main population centres, especially when it melts.

The Road Administration has masterminded a road weather service supplying road users with weather forecasts complete with radar and satellite images. Elk and reindeer sometimes wander on to the highways and the former can cause considerable vehicular damage (not to mention their own demise), if collided with. Any collision, including those with elk and reindeer, should be reported to the police. Speed limits are 80kph except where indicated otherwise, and 100kph on motorways.

Accidents and Breakdowns. The countrywide number for the police is 10022 and for ambulance 112.

Parking. In Helsinki and major towns parking is controlled by meters from 8am to 5pm Monday to Saturday. *Pysäköiminen kielletty* means no parking.

Petrol. Petrol stations are open generally 7am to 9pm, six days a week. They generally also open on Sundays in holiday areas during summer only. Petrol prices are approximately FIM5 per litre.

Regulations. As with other Scandinavian countries, motorists and motorcyclists are required to drive with headlights any time of day or night outside built-up areas and regardless of weather conditions.

Special winter tyres are compulsory from November to March.

Road Directions. *aja hitaasti* (slow); *kelirikko* (frost damage); *keskusta* (town centre) *irtokiviä* (loose stones); *liukasta* (slippery surface); *lossi* (ferry); *räjäytystyö sulje radiolähetin* (danger, explosives, switch off your radio), *tietyö* (road works).

Touring Club. Autoliitto, Hämeentie 105A, 00550 Helsinki; 774761.

Finnish Motor Insurer's Bureau, Bulevardi 28, 00120 Helsinki; tel 90/680401.

Transport

Air. Internal flights are operated by Finnair, whose head office is at Mannerheimintie 102, 00250 Helsinki (tel 818 81). There are more than 20 domestic airports and the flights are among the cheapest in Europe. There are discounts on certain routes at weekends. For the over 65s and young people aged 12-23 there is a 50% discount (with some restrictions). Buses to Helsinki-Vantaa airport from the city take about 30 minutes. For airport and flight information dial 9700 8100.

Rail. Finland has 6000kms (3,700 miles) of rail network. The railways are run by Finnish state railways (*Valtionrautatiet*), P.O. Box 488, 00101 Helsinki (information 7071). Seat reservations are required for Express (EP) trains. There are reductions for groups of three or more and for children under 12 years.

Bus. There is a network of long distance buses, 300 of which depart from Helsinki daily with connections to all parts of the country. The majority are in the hands of *Oy Matkahuolto Ab* bus company. Bus fares are cheaper than second class rail fares. Rural areas are often served by post buses.

Useful Addresses

Oy Matkahuolto Ab, Simonkatu 3, PL 709 00100 Helsinki 100 (tel 9600 7090 or 9600 4000 for enquiries and 642 744 for complaints and lost property).
Helsinki Coach Station, Simonkatu; tel 642744. For information on coach timetables, dial 9600 4000.

Boat. Apart from the ferry traffic criss-crossing between Finland and Sweden and further afield, there is an abundance of steamers and motor boats, on the lakelands of Finland.

One of the most popular, and cheapest ferry routes (if you can stand the drunken Finnish company) is between Helsinki and Talinn, the Estonian capital. Finns use these trips to indulge in alcohol both internally and to bring back duty frees and the ferries, operated by several companies, are almost literally awash with the stuff. The trip however can cost as little as £4. Tallin is a starting off point for the rail trip (1,300 miles) to St. Petersburg. At the time of going to press tickets for the sleeper could cost at little as £2.

Within Finnish waters, main routes include those between Hämeenlinna and Tampere, Tampere and Virrat and various routes on the Saimaa Lake. The lakes of Päijänne and Inari also have regular services as does lake Pielinen. Car ferries and overnight lake steamers with cabins also exist. However, most of the lake services are aimed at holidaymakers and therefore progress at a leisurely pace and are not particularly economical.

City Transport. In the larger towns and cities urban transport is excellent and integrated. In Helsinki for instance tickets for the bus, tram, suburban rail lines and ferries to the Suomenlinna Islands are all linked to a common fare system. Multi-trip tickets (10 rides) can be bought in advance and work out slightly cheaper. There are various cheap deals including renewable 30-day season tickets.

After midnight you may have to resort to taxis (*taksi*). Fares are generally more expensive in towns than in the country. The basic fare is about FIM12 and extra kms at FIM6 each. Higher charges are made in the evenings (6pm-10pm; Saturdays from 2pm) and the highest charges are from 10pm to 6am.

Banks and Finance

The Bank of Finland (founded 1811) is the central bank that regulates bank rates and currency. Its activities are supervised by parliament. The Finnish currency, the *markka* (plural *markkaa*) was devalued in 1993 which reduced its value by over a third and made Finland much better value for foreigners. Officially, Finland now rates itself as on a par with Germany as far as prices are concerned (which still makes it pretty expensive).

At the time of writing Finnish banking is being revolutionised after the government's approval of the selling off of the national chain of savings banks to four big, rival Finnish banks the private Kansallis and Union Bank of Finland, and the Post Office Bank and Central Co-operative Bank. Savings banks have suffered badly in the recessional crisis and the central institution is now under government control.

Banking Services. There are no restrictions on foreigners opening bank accounts in Finland. Bank cards that accompany a current account can be used in almost all the many automatic cash machines (*pikapankki*) countrywide. There is also no charge for paying bills via a cash machine. If however you pay these by bank transfer the charge is FIM5-10. When arranging a transfer you must produce proof of identity.

Banking hours are generally Monday-Friday from 9am or 9.15am to 4pm or 4.15pm and closed on Saturdays. There are some regional variations.

Money. Finland's national currency is the *markka* made up of 100 *penniä*. Coins come in denominations of 10, 50, FIM1, FIM5 and FIM 10. Notes come in FIM20/50/100/500/1000.

Taxation

In common with other Scandinavians, Finns have long been subject to swingeing personal taxation. However in January 1993 there was a major reform of the tax system beginning with personal and corporate tax rates which have been lowered (though they are still high by most other EU country's standards). Phase two of the reforms beginning January 1994 with the introduction of full value-added tax (*liikevaihtovero*) is aimed at gradually broadening the tax base. The main personal taxes are national income tax (*valtionvero*), municipal income tax (*kunnallisvero*) and net wealth tax (*varallisuusvero*). Other taxes include inheritance and gift tax, witholding tax and stamp duty. Indirect taxes include VAT (generally at 22%), and excise duty (*valmistevero*).

Taxation for Foreigners and Trainees. There are some allowances made for foreigners working as trainees on an approved scheme organised by CIMO (see *Education* above); if they work for fewer than six months, they pay a special reduced rate of taxation known as *lähdevero*. Anyone working in Finland for up to 100 days and actually resident for less than six months has a tax threshold of FIM3000 up to which no tax is paid. Earnings above this are taxed at the reduced rate of 35%. Anyone working in Finland for 6-18 months pays income tax at the normal rate.

Tax Administration. Taxation for individuals relates to the calendar year. Tax returns must be filed by 31 January of the following year. If the individual has a professional income the deadline for filing is extended to 1 March. If the individual has a business income and their financial period ends between 1 January and 1 October/2 October and 31 December then the filing date is 1 January and 1 April respectively. For details of tax on businesses see *Starting a Business.*

The ministry of finance bases the final assessment for tax on the returns which are normally dealt with by October of the year following the tax year. Taxpayers receive a final tax bill. If the tax paid exceeds the final assessment the difference is refunded in December. If the individual needs to pay more tax then it normally has to be paid in three tranches in December and the following two months.

Health Care & Hospitals

The Finnish health care system is of a high standard. There is a public and private sector. The public one is financed by the government and the municipalities. The private sector is also open to all citizens and is partly subsidised but is much more expensive than the public sector.

Health Care Centres. The public health care centres (*terveyskeskus*) provide local medical services including anti-natal and postnatal clinical services and pre-school health care. All newborn citizens in Finland are issued with a healthcard which is kept up-to-date throughout their school years. Apart from centres offering valuable services including those for expectant mothers, and mothers and infants, there are private centres (*lääkäriasema*) where authorised doctors practise medicine in parallel with their hospital duties. Some health centres have wards for the chronically sick.

Health centres are also responsible for providing the local ambulance service. Health centre fees vary in different localities. The charge may be FIM100 for the first visit, or FIM50 for the first three visits in a given year. After the initial fee, appointments are free of charge.

It is the responsibility of employers to provide occupational health care for employees under a special law aimed at protecting employees' health at work. Regular inspections of workplaces by official inspectors are an important aspect of occupational health care.

Students. Students in higher education have their own health care scheme which does not however exclude them from using the public and private systems. The Finnish Student Health Service FSHS (Ylioppilaiden terveydenhoitosäätiö, YTHS), has a student health care centre in every university town open to all student union members. Most basic services are free but for specialist ones e.g. psychologist, there is a small fee of FIM5-20.

Hospitals

Finland has 21 hospital districts and the municipal governments within each district are responsible of the upkeep of their central (i.e. general) hospital(s). The state pays a contribution to the costs depending on the means of the district. To supplement the main hospitals there are smaller local hospitals which are required to provide treatment in three specialist fields. Supplementary hospitals are maintained by the local authorities and they are established on a voluntary basis.

Other types of hospitals for specialist functions include those catering for the mentally sick, the military and penal hospitals.

The total number of hospitals in Finland is 430 which provide 13 beds per 1000 inhabitants.

Private hospitals are rare in Finland where the local communities have become the traditional providers of healthcare.

Social Security

Finland's social security system is excellent, especially pre-natal, post natal and childhood services, but it has not reached the same level of munificence as that of its Scandinavian neighbours. The system is financed from taxes and from contributions from insured people and employers and it consumes about 18.5% of the budget. It encompasses five areas of requirement: health insurance and maternity, pensions, unemployment security, workers' compensation and occupational disease insurance and subsistance benefits.

Health Insurance

All Finnish workers contribute to the health insurance scheme administered by the National Pensions Institution which is open to all residents of Finland. Health Insurance contributions entitle you to medical examination, laboratory and x-ray facilities and subsidised physiotherapy. As in most countries there is a charge for prescriptions except in the case of the chronically sick for whom they are free.

Hospital patients are required to pay running costs of hospital treatment and travel expenses. However above a certain minimum, these are refunded. The cost of private medical consultation and attention is also partly subsidised but is much more expensive to the patient.

The dental treatment scheme provides free dental treatment up to the age of 17. After this, there are reductions in the cost of some dental treatments if you are a member of the state health insurance scheme.

In order to make use of Finland's health insurance scheme, the resident has to obtain a sickness insurance card from the local social insurance office (*Kansaneläkelaitos*) known as KELA for short.

British nationals not eligible for the Finnish health insurance scheme should obtain form E111, the entitlement to reciprocal medical care (see section on E111 in *Denmark*)

Benefits

Unemployment Benefit. Most workers belong to voluntary unemployment benefit schemes run by the trades unions. Eligibility for unemployment benefit is restricted to those who have been subscribing to a fund for a minimum of six months. There is an upper limit on annual benefits payable and also for those paid within a three-year period. The employer and the state fund the major part of the unemployment benefit while the employee contribution is much less.

Anyone not covered by an unemployment fund will have their unemployment benefit paid by the state. The benefit is aimed at covering only the basic needs.

Child Benefit. The parents of all children under 17 are entitled to family allowances. Children under 3yrs command an increased benefit. Munipalities run day-care centres for pre-school aged children of working parents. Such parents receive a monthly allowance. Despite the obligation imposed on municipal authorities by the government to provide day care facilities for all pre-school children this has so far not been achieved although there is considerable variation among the municipalities.

For single mothers, i.e. those receiving no financial support from the father, the state pays a maintenance benefit.

Further information on the Finnish Social Security System can be obtained from the Finnish Embassy or legation in your own country or from the Ministry of Foreign Affairs (Kanavakatu 3C, 00160 Helsinki).

Social Life

As with other Nordics, Finns have a reputation for reticence and a disinclination to make small talk. Often this is ascribed to the Finns' modesty about speaking a foreign language in case they make mistakes. There are reckoned to be some regional character differences: for instance the inhabitants of Karelia and Savo are considered jollier and keener on socialising than those from Häme and the southwest. Life in Finland tends to operate at a relaxed pace and Finns place a lot of emphasis on comfort. This was not always the case: their not-too-distant forbears rated determination and fortitude against adversity (summed up by the word *sisu*) as the most important characteristic of the Finns.

The Finns are great coffee drinkers and virtually any event that can be, is celebrated with a gathering for cakes and coffee. Another good way to socialise with Finns is to practise a sport. Sports are probably the Finns' most common pastime whether it is skiing or ice hockey, swimming, walking, cycling or jogging and so on. However, this does not stop Finland having the highest rate of heart attacks among males in the European Union.

Finns also have the Scandinavian bent towards melancholia, particularly in winter when many of them are inclined to drink to excess. However, younger Finns are tending more to treat drinking as a pleasure rather than as an alcoholic marathon. Drinking and dancing the tango and foxtrot are the traditional Finnish methods of warding off winter blues. In summer, Finns are generally more optimistic and expansive and most take a month's holiday in the country. Many have summer cottages near the lakes, others take their camping gear and move round the country. Such times are good opportunities to meet Finns in their natural surroundings. Increasingly though Finns are taking holidays in the southern European countries.

It is probably a cliché, though one reiterated by the Finns themselves, that they are at their most relaxed in that great Finnish invention (later adopted by other Scandinavians), the sauna. Along with the clothes goes the reserve it seems. Interestingly the sauna was not always a place for washing and cleansing by steam, but a kind of community medical centre where children were born and the sick cared for.

Most flats in Finland have their own sauna. Ideally it should be near a lake for the essential cold plunge afterwards. In the countryside virtually every property has an adjoining sauna and the whole family go together. Sooner or later, the foreign resident will be invited to sweat out grime and cares and beat him or herself (or someone else), with a bunch of fragrant birch twigs.

Manners and Customs. When dealing with Finns remember that they like to be addressed, at least initially, by their professional titles such as Director, Doctor, Professor etc.

Food and Drink

Finnish dietary staples are filling and insulating ones. A typical Finnish breakfast is porridge, dark Finnish rye bread, eggs, ham and so on. Lunch is regarded as the main meal of the day; expect heavy soups, and stews and lots of fish dishes in typical restaurants though imported burger houses and pizzerias have long since made their mark and Russian restaurants are a feature of Helsinki. Restaurants are better value since the maarka lost a third of its value. Typical ingredients of home cooking are meat or fish, potatoes, vegetables and dairy produce. In addition there is a host of regional dishes. In the north, reindeer meat is a speciality sometimes meat and fish are mixed as in *Vorschmack* (peppered beef and herring), or the Finnish version of *en croute Kalakukko* (fish baked in black bread) which is from eastern Finland.

Seasonal fruits like wild strawberries, blueberries and the slightly later lingonberries and cranberries are delicacies and the rarer cloudberries and artic brambleberries are used to flavour vodkas.

The traditional liquid accompaniment to a meal, is most likely to be the nonalcoholic milk or sourmilk (even for adults), though beer is also very popular.

Alcohol. It is a myth that all Finns are alcoholics, though they do tend to overimbibe at weekends. Average yearly consumption is only 0.01% higher than in the UK. Beer is served in *tuoppi* glasses which are 30% bigger than a pint. Homegrown spirits include Finlandia and Koskenkorva vodkas.

Crime and Police

For those concerned about prodigious crime rates in their home countries, Finland can be a pleasant surprise. Rates of crime are still comparatively low everywhere, including in Helsinki, though a brochure aimed at foreign students and trainees does give a brief caution about not wandering around Helsinki railway station at night. This is however countered with the reassuring comment, 'You do not need to panic about your handbag or wallet'.

The police are more guardians of the peace than trouble-shooters and the only dealings most foreigners are likely to have with them are mundane administrative matters such as renewing residence permits. The majority of incidents dealt with by the police are domestic disputes, public drunkeness or traffic accidents. One of the busiest times of the week for the mobile police in Helsinki is Friday night.

Local police are divided into 246 districts of which 26 are police departments and 220 are rural police districts. A police department is headed by a commissioner and a rural police district by a sheriff (a title that goes back to medieval times). A re-organisation of the police is currently underway aimed at radically reducing the number of police districts by 1995.

The entire police administration in Finland employs 11,854 people of whom about 8,500 are police officers. Of these 7,380 are local police, 710 mobile police, about 230 Central Criminal Police and 100 Security Police. Only about 350 police officers are female.

Helsinki has its own police department which is bigger than any other. Its 1,600 officers are divided among the three areas which make up the city.

It remains to be seen how high unemployment, (higher now than for decades) will affect the behaviour of Finns. In neighbouring Sweden where circumstances are similar the crime rate has soared in recent years. Most pundits' predictions do not include any dire warnings of general social and moral instability and have put their faith in the Finns' ability to keep their feet firmly on the ground. However crime statistics show that the crime rate has shot up substantially over the past few years and that it outstrips the increase in police strength. Drugs and connected firearms offences are one of problems on the increase.

The emergency number for the police is 10022.

Public Holidays

1 January — New Year's Day
6 January — Epiphany
March/April — Good Friday
March/April — Easter
March/April — Easter Monday
1 May — May Day
May — Ascension Day
May — Whitsun/Pentecost
June — Midsummer Eve and Day
November — All Saints Day
6 December — Independence/National Day
December 24 & 25 — Christmas Eve, Christmas Day
December 26 — Boxing Day

The holidays where no exact date is given vary from year to year.

Retirement

Finland is not a country that most people would consider retiring to unless they had some prior connections there. These days it is increasingly likely that Finns will emulate other northern Europeans, by retiring to Mediterranean countries where they can enjoy sunshine all year round. The only advantage of retiring in Finland would be the high level of general amenities, the relatively low pollution and the good welfare provisions for the elderly provided by the state. Probably the main disadvantage, from the point of view of retirees is the long winter and the cold. A cold that Peter Ackroyd, the travel writer described as 'an elemental cold, a cold which invades the body and leaves it stunned'.

Municipalities are responsible for the care of the aged at local level. Many different services are provided at a nominal cost and they include daily help with domestic chores including cooking, cleaning and shopping. There are community centres for the elderly which function as information bases as well as centres for social activities. Some centres are attached to homes for the elderly. The emphasis in housing for the elderly is to create an environment where they can be as independent as possible. Many are housed in service flats and houses where home helps and home nursing services provide the essential back up. Other services provided by the state include bathing, pedicure, hairdressing and a clothes service.

Residence and Entry

It is possible to enter Finland as a retiree with funds to support yourself, or preretirement and then to work in Finland and retire there. After three months you are required to register and obtain a residence permit which is automatic in the case of EU and EEA citizens.

For further details, see chapter on *Residence and Entry Regulations*.

The Right to Remain

Once you have entered Finland and registered you have the right to remain indefinitely on a renewable residence permit. After a permanent stay of two years it is possible to apply for a permanent residence permit. After five years you become eligible to apply for citizenship.

Finnish Pensions

Foreigners employed in Finland are obliged to make compulsory contributions to a pension scheme also contributed to by employers. The flat-rate pension in 1989 was about FIM 6000 monthly comprised of a basic amount of FIM365 plus an increment of FIM1704 and finally a housing allowance of FIM761 (maximum). Everyone gets the basic amount, but the amount of the basic amount increment varies depending on the individual's circumstances. Those receiving other pensions such as an earnings related pension will receive a reduced increment.

Earnings Related Pensions. The system of earnings related pensions was introduced in Finland in 1963 and has been introduced in stages which will continue
taking effect until 2002. Earnings-related pensions are proportional to total
earnings and length of service and accumulate at the rate of 1.5% of pay annually.
A person who has worked for the full forty years will receive the full 60%.
pension subject to certain limits. Pensions are in fact considered taxable income.
Only those receiving the minimum flat-rate and earnings related pension are
entitled to tax exemption on their pensions.

There are certain fields of employment which have their own separate pension
arrangements and systems, notably employees in the public sector, the church
and maritime jobs.

Earnings related pensions are managed by insurance companies and pension
funds and foundations and are co-ordinated by the Central Pension Security
Institution whose ultimate controller is the Ministry of Social Affairs and Health
(Snellmaninkatu 4-6, POB 267, 00170 Helsinki; fax 650 442, 16057 63.

SECTION II

Working in Finland

Employment
Permanent Work
Temporary Work
Business and Industry Report
Starting a Business

Employment

The Employment Scene

As with most Western economies, Finland's was smitten by a steep recession at the beginning of the 1990s. This setback followed a period of unprecedented expansion in the 1980s when the economy was growing at 10% a year for several years and unemployment was at an all time low of 3.5%, Finland experienced (and to some extent is still experiencing) its worst slump for 60 years. In Finland's case, this has been exacerbated and prolonged by the loss of one of its main export markets following the collapse of the Soviet Union. Now with unemployment of at 17.9% (October 1994) it compares with Ireland (18.4%) and Spain (21.5%) both consistently notorious as having the highest unemployment in the EU. The outlook may appear bleak, especially for those seeking jobs there however, Finland's recent inclusion in the European Union is helping to produce a fresh ripple of optimism throughout industry in Finland and the economy has begun to recover, albeit slowly and unemployment is already declining. However, even the most optimistic forecasters do not expect Finnish unemployment to fall below 15% by the end of the decade.

Finland's recovery is export driven and she is well aware of the need to recruit foreign talent particularly in the area of international marketing where the Finns could benefit from improving their technique. This process of closer economic ties to Europe will lead to an expansion in relations with the European Union and beyond. An increasing number of foreign companies are expected to set up in Finland in order to use the country as a springboard to the east and from them will arise increasing employment opportunities for both Finns and foreigners. Finland is also very active in promoting international student exchanges and in hosting work training schemes (covered later in this chapter) which are an excellent way to gain an introduction to the country. At a higher level, there are openings for academics including linguists and scientists.

If you go to Finland to look for temporary work, you will however find it more difficult than in other countries: for instance, in Belgium and the Netherlands there are hundreds of temporary work agencies and in France there is a lot of casual farm and harvest work so short-term work is relatively abundant. The situation is somewhat different in Finland where commercial employment agencies are embryonic and casual work is considerably harder to find than in countries with larger populations, a less harsh winter climate with more year round agriculture and a bigger tourist industry, all of which are the usual mainstays for temporary workers. In addition, the prohibitive cost of living in Finland means that finding somewhere cheap to stay, while looking around for a job is well nigh impossible. Making sure you have somewhere to stay in advance, perhaps through friends or relatives working there or with contacts is therefore a virtual necessity.

A couple of factors which may inadvertently aid the foreign job seeker is that the benefit system in Finland is generous enough to make it not worth the while of locals to take the most menial and casual work when they can receive government support by way of benefits while waiting for something more permanent which is suited to their skills. A modest number of unskilled jobs are therefore available for foreigners in hotels and to a lesser extent on farms. The Finnish government has organised an array of courses for the newly and long-term unemployed to update their skills at technical colleges. A high level of training is very much the norm in Finland as is job mobility. Finns tend to move from job to job gaining experience, rather than spend years with the same company. Otherwise, the fact that Finns are apparently emigrating at the current rate of about 10,000 per year, may open up further possibilities for jobs. The cause of this continuing exodus is attributed to the climate and the state of uncertainty in Finland itself. Many young Finns are keenly European in outlook and there has been a tendency for many of them to spend time gaining experience abroad. Once their country has asserted itself on the European scene, fewer may be inclined to leave for long periods as by then, Finland will have become sufficiently Europeanised to satisfy their interests and ambitions.

An inherent disadvantage of Finland's permanent job scene is that there is not the diversity of fields that you might expect to find, compared with other industrially developed countries. Finland concentrated on its two main industries, forestry and heavy engineering (which are still the main industries), for many years and the creation of new areas of enterprise expertise came later than in many other European countries. Engineers, which Finland churns out of its universities in thousands, are overly abundant for the jobs available, so prospects are not good for foreign engineers unless their technical skills are outstanding. Tourism, technology, language services and international marketing are some of the areas where foreigners with the appropriate qualifications and experience have reasonable prospects for finding work.

The need to reduce the high number of long-term unemployed in Finland has led to the labour market being reorganised with new flexibility including time off for training schemes aimed at improving and updating skills for those still in work as well as those out of work. The result is that Finland has a perpetual supply of trained and skilled workers waiting to step in once there are jobs available. Foreigners will therefore be at a disadvantage, unless they are on special training shemes, or are prepared to do very unskilled menial jobs, or have some very specific skill which is in demand. In other words foreigners will have a hard job convincing Finnish employers that they should employ them rather than a Finn, whatever any EU directive says about equal consideration for jobs for all EU citizens in any EU nation.

Sources of Jobs

Depending on your trade or profession, it may be advantageous to go to Finland in person to look for work especially if you are from another EU or EEA nation. You can arm yourself with a stock of cv's and photo-copies of your qualifications, references etc.

Newspapers

British and International
If you are looking for work before you go and you have experience and qualifications for teaching English, then you may find suitable adverts in the Times Educational Supplement (published Fridays), the education pages of the Tuesday edition of the *Guardian* and the professional paper the *EFL Gazette*

all of which have carried adverts from Finnish English language schools in the past.

The European newspaper, published weekly on Thursdays has a jobs wanted section on the *Careers* page where anyone looking for a job can advertise free. *The European* estimates their circulation in Finland to be 1,640 per week, so this is just about worth a try.

Useful Addresses

EFL Gazette, 10 Wrights Lane, London W8 6TA; tel 0171-938 1819.
The European, Orbit House, 5 New Fetter Lane, Holborn Circus, London EC4 1AP; tel 0171-822 2002.

For details of other magazines, journals and directories, particularly those of professional associations, please see the *Newspapers* section in *Denmark*.

Finnish Newspapers
Advertising in some Finnish newspapers has produced results in many cases. One of the best newspapers for this is *Helsingin Sanomat*, a daily newspaper with the widest area of readership in Finland which is published every day including Sundays.

Useful Addresses
Some regional newspapers are:

Aamulehti adverts in the Tampere daily *Aamulehti* can be booked through the London office at 70 Campden Hill Court, Campden Hill Road, London W8 7HL; tel 0171-937 4732. In Helsinki: PL 327, 33101 Tampere; tel 931-666 111; fax 666 259.
Demari, Paasivuorenkatu 3, 00530 Helsinki; tel 701 041; fax 753 4688.
Ilta-Sanomat, Korkeavuorenkatu 34, 00130 Helsinki; tel 1221; fax 122 3419.
Kansan Tahto, PL 61, 90101 Oulu; tel 981-371 722; fax 981-311 6457.
Kaleva, Ahjotie 1, 90101 Oulu; tel 981-5377 111; fax 981-537 7195.
Kauppalehti, PL 189, 00101 Helsinki; tel 50 781; fax 563 0001. (Financial and business).
Turun Sanomat, Kauppiaskatu 5, 20100 Turku; tel 921-693 311; fax 921-693 274.
Helsingin Sanomat. Ludviginkatu 6-8, 00130 Helsinki; tel 10 90 1221. If calling from the UK to place an advert dial 00 358 0 1221.

The UK Employment Service
Any office of the UK National Employment Service can be used to access the Overseas Placing Unit (OPU) in Sheffield which handles the processing of vacancies within the EU. They also produce a series of booklets covering each member state's immigration laws, health care system and advice on how to best find work. Although vacancies in Finland are likely to be few, it costs nothing to register and so is worth trying. You should fill in form ES13, one copy in English and another in Finnish though if this is not possible, you can complete both copies in English.

Comparability of Qualifications. If you are not sure how your qualifications compare with those in Finland, for instance hotel and catering and motor trade qualifications. You can consult the Comparability Coordinator. If you want to compare your educational qualifications check with the British Council via the local jobcentre

Euro-Advisors. In order to provide help to those seeking work abroad, there are a number of Euro-advisors based at the OPU in Sheffield and several UK jobcentres.

Claiming UK Unemployment Benefit While Looking for Work Abroad. Provided that you have been registered unemployed for a minimum of four weeks you can arrange to have your benefit paid abroad while you look for work. For further details and an application form (known as UBL 22) ask at your local benefit office.

Useful Addresses
Comparability Coordinator Employment Dept., Qualifications and Standards Branch (QSI), Room E454, Moorfoot, Sheffield SP1 4PQ; tel 0114 2594144.
Overseas Placings Employment. Employment Service (0PS 5), c/o Moorfoot, Sheffield SP1 4PQ.
DSS Overseas Branch, Benton Park Road, Newcastle-upon-Tyne, NE98 4YX.

UK Recruitment Agencies
There are some agencies in the UK which specialise in finding overseas jobs for clients or which recruit for corporate clients. Generally speaking such agencies deal with a specific sector, for instance, electronics, secretarial, accountancy and so on, and will only consider job applicants with the appropriate qualifications.

Final year university students can contact CV Database which will match them up with graduate recruiters. The *CEPEC Recruitment Guide* (latest edition 1995) is available from reference libraries or direct from The Centre for Professional Employment Counselling (67 Jermyn Street, London SW1Y 6NY; tel 0171-930 0322) lists about 550 recruitment agencies, a few of which have contacts in Finland.

Useful Addresses
Berndtson International, 6 Westminster Palace Gardens, Artillery Row, London SW1P IRL; tel 0171-222 5555; fax 0171 222 5180. One of the few recruiters that encourages speculative application and keeps its own register. Office in Helsinki: tel 0-607 300.
CV Database Ltd: World Trade Centre, International House, St. Katherine's Way, London E1 9UN.
Dennis & Gemmill Ltd. 2 The Courtyard, Smith Street, London SW3 4EE; tel 0171-730 7138; fax 0171-730 6983. Takes speculative applications. Helsinki office: George Ramsay Oy; tel 64 29 44.
Egon Zehnder International Ltd. Devonshire House, Mayfair Place, London W1X 5FH; tel 0171-493 3882; fax 0171-629 9552. Accepts speculative applications. Helsinki office: Mikonkatu 13A, 00100 Helsinki; tel 65 8911; fax 65 71 75.
EPC European Personnel Counsellors Has various UK specialist offices and Helsinki contact: Oy Rbaron AB, Ulla Petagavaara, Korkeavuorenkatua 1B11, 00170; tel 637 622.
Heidrick & Struggle. London office: tel 0171-491 3124; In Helsinki: Heidrick & Struggle, Erottajankatu 11A, 00130 Helsinki.
P E International plc, Park House, Wick Road, Egham, Surrey TW20 OHW; tel 01784-434411; fax 01784 437828. Has branch in Finland: Mec-Rastor, Kimmeltie 1, Espoo; tel 80 469 71.
Scientific Resources Ltd. King's Court, Kirkwood Road, Cambridge CB4 2PF; tel 01223-420129; fax 01223-424281. Helsinki contact: Scientific Generics, Ryytimaatie 5, 00320 Helsinki 32; tel 57 8577; fax 57 0869.

Finnish State Employment Offices

The Finnish state employment offices are known as *työvoimatoimistot* of which there is one in every town and several in Helsinki. The *Helsingin Työvoimatoimisto* (Employment Office of Helskinki) can be reached on tel 0-7021 and fax 0 7022260. Employment offices are generally open from 9am to 4pm; some from 8am to 3pm. At the time of going to press virtually all employment offices in Finland were state ones though there are plans to establish private services which might lead to more job openings or even create business opportunities for foreign businesses willing to open branches in Finland. For further information on regional employment services in Finland, contact the Ministry of Labour (POB 524, 00101 Helsinki; tel 0-18 561; fax 0-173 6340).

Types of Work

Executive Recruitment

The best possibilities are in marketing, finance, accountancy, general management, linguistic services, training, and development of new technology. By joining the EU Finland has ended an era of isolation from mainstream European trade and is in need of individuals who can provide skills which will aid communication and liaison with other European countries. For some executive jobs, a knowlege of Finnish would not be essential initially.

Teaching

There are sometimes opportunities for school and university teachers in Finland. At the time of going to press the Central Bureau for Educational Visits and Exchanges (Seymour Mews House, Seymour Mews, London W1H 9PE; tel 0171-486 5101) had no corresponding organisation in Finland through which teacher exchanges could be arranged. However if the individual teacher concerned were to find their own partner in Finland with whom to do an exchange, the Central Bureau would be willing to assist them with the rest of the process. According to a spokesperson at the Central Bureau, the setting up of an official teacher exchange organisation in Finland is imminent now that Finland is part of the European Union. On the assisant scheme, (also organised by the Central Bureau), whereby students work as unqualified assistants to teachers of English in foreign schools, the programme sent one participant to work in Finland in 1993.

British teachers could also consider applying to the schools in Finland where some programmes are taught in English. These include the English School and the International School in Helsinki, both of which have kindergartens attached. In addition certain mainstream Finnish state comprehenensive and upper secondary schools and vocational institutes have been teaching some subjects in a variety of languages including English since 1991. In 1992 there were comprehensive school classes in English at Helsinki, Espoo, Tampere, Turku, Oulu, Jyväskylä, Kirkkonummi Kuopio, Lappeenreanta, Lahti, Taruma, Rovaniemi and Vaasa state schools. The Espoo-Vantaa Technical College and Vaasa Technical College also teach some programmes in English.

Translating and Interpreting

Translators convert written documents into their mother tongue, and therefore have to be bi-lingual. Most translators tend to specialise for instance in technical or legal material. It is therefore useful for translators to have worked in scientific or other fields before adopting a a career as an interpreter. Apart from a degree in modern languages, further training at an institute for professional linguists or at university will almost certainly be necessary.

Interpreters have to have the ability to switch effortlessly between languages and so interpreting is often more difficult than translating, especially when simultaneously interpreting (while the speaker is speaking). In consecutive interpreting, the interpreter interprets during the pauses made by the speaker. That growing tower of babel, The European Commission in Brussels employs an army of interpreters. In Finland there is likely to be more demand for translators than interpreters.

Further information on careers in interpreting and translating is available from:

Institute of Linguistics: 24a Highbury Grove, London N5 2EA; tel 0171-359 7445.
Institute of Translation and Interpreting: 318a Finchley Road, London NW3 5HT; tel 0170-713 7600.

Short-Term Work

Au Pair Work and Family Stays
This is an option for both young men and women. Until Finland became a full EU member in 1995, the entry of foreign au pairs was severely restricted by the need to obtain a prior work permit. With the removal of this obstacle, au pair agencies outside Finland are now free to set up contacts there. At the time of going to press there were only a few which had done so. Another apparently proven method of obtaining au pair work is by advertising in a Finnish newspaper (see above). You can do this in English, or find someone to translate your advert into Finnish or Swedish. *Helsingin Sanomat* (the Helsinki daily paper) advertises a few domestic situations most days. One former au pair also recommends putting up advertisment flyers in places where they are likely to catch the eye of busy parents, such as at playgroups in affluent city suburbs. You should stress the fact that you are an English-speaker as most Finnish parents are keen to have their offspring proficient in English. Pocket money generally works out at FIM 1,000-2,000 monthly. The Finnish Youth Cooperation Alliance, Allianssi, is a non-profit youth exchange organisation which deals with small numbers of placements with Finnish families for six to 12 months. The pocket money is FIM 1,100 for about 30 hours work a week.

Useful Addresses
Allianssi, Olympiastadion, Eteläkaarre 00250 Helsinki; tel 348 24312; fax 491290. Finds placements for foreign au pairs in Finland.
CIMO, The Centre for International Mobility, POB 343, 00531 Helsinki, tel 774 77033/fax 774 77064. Part of Finland's international trainee exchange organisation organises a Family Programme whereby you can stay with a Finnish family for one to three months in summer or up to 12 months beginning any time of year. Participants are expected to help families with their English as well as housework, gardening and looking after children. There are also openings for those with farming experience. The Family Programme is open to 18 to 23-year-olds who can speak English, German or French.

Teaching English
Swedish is Finland's other language, but English follows a close third. Despite the prevalence of English teaching as part of the national school curriculum, there is still an increasing requirement for special English language tuition in a variety of establishments including private kindergartens, vocational colleges,

business schools, folk schools and universities. There are over 20 private English language schools in Helsinki alone.

The so-called *Native Teacher* programme run by CIMO (see below) enables native speakers of English (also German and French) to teach their mother tongue. This can be just in a private family, but also in kindergartens, schools and even in private companies whose employees are taking an English course. The position normally depends on the previous working experience of the applicant. The age limits for applicants are 18 to 30.

It can also be profitable to advertise yourself as a freelance teacher of English. The going rate for private lessons is up to FIM 120 (about £15 per hour).

Useful Organisations

British Council, Hakaniemenkatu 2, 00530 Helsinki; tel 070-18731; fax 018725. Can provide a list of private schools in Helsinki only. The British council runs its own schools and offers one or two-year contracts. Perks include a tax free salary and help with airfares and relocation costs. Anyone applying for work with the BC must normally have the RSA/Cambridge/Trinity Diploma. Preference is given to expatriates already on the spot such as spouses of those with jobs in Finland. The BC may occasionally employ those with just the RSA Certificate, but do not count on it.

Federation of Finnish-British Societies, Puistokatu 1b A, 00140 Helsinki. There are at least a dozen Finnish-British Societies around Finland which employ teaching staff. The largest one Helsinki (see above address) takes on a number of experienced teachers and less experienced graduates as teaching staff. The other Societies around Finland also employ teachers though to a lesser extent than the main branch in Helsinki. Contracts are generally for nine months and airfares are paid for. Applications should arrive by the end of February and interviews (in London) take place in April. Accommodation can also be arranged.

Linguarama, Oceanic House, 85 High Street, Alton, Hants GU34 1LG. Linguarama is a commercial organisation which advertises 'Language Training for Business'. They offer graduates with a TEFL certificate and six months basic experience a short training course that qualifies them to teach in Linguarama's own centres including in Helsinki and occasionally other Finnish towns.

Richard Lewis Communications, Itätuulenkuja 10b, 02100 Espoo; tel 0455 4811 is a British-based organisation that specialises in providing language training for business people and professionals. Their UK address is 107, High Street, Winchester SO23 9AH; tel 01962-868888.

Trainee Schemes

CIMO (Finnish Trainee Placement Programme)

It is possible to arrange a trainee post in Finland through CIMO, Finland's International Trainee Exchange Programme (POB 343, 00531 Helsinki; tel 0-7061) through which the Finnish Ministry of Education actively encourages trainees to come to Finland for short-term paid work. Trainees from abroad receive the statutory minimum trainee wage of about FIM3300 net for agriculture and about FIM4000-5000 net per month for other types of work.

There is a wide range of work categories covered by this programme which includes all of those types mentioned below. In order to qualify for the CIMO programme, you must have be at least a year into undergraduate studies, preferably with an additional year of related experience, and be aged 18 to 30.

CIMO Contact Organisations Abroad
You can either contact CIMO direct or apply through an organisation in your own country. Some of the main contacts are listed below:

Canada Canadian Federation of Student Services, SWAP, 243 College Street, 5th Floor, Toronto, Ontario M5T 2Y1. Also: Youth and Personalities Exchange, International Higher Education, External Affairs and International Trade, Canada, 125 Sussex Drive, Ottawa, Ontario K1A OG2.

UK: Central Bureau for Educational Visits and Exchanges, Vocational & Technical Education Department, Seymour Mews House, Seymour Mews, London W1H 9PE.

United States of America
Association for International Practical Training, 10 Corporate Center, Suite 250, 10400 Little Patuxent Parkway, Columbia, Maryland 21044-3510. (Hotel/Culinary applicants).

The American-Scandinavian Foundation, Exchange Division, 725 Park Avenue, New York, NY 10021 (technology, horticulture and forestry students).

Also: InterExchange Inc, Job Program, 161 Sixth Avenue, Suite 902, New York NY 10013.

Future Farmers of America, National FFA Center, 5632 Mt Vernon, Memorila Highway, Alexandria, Virginia 223309-3600. (Farming students).

IAESTE (International Association for the Exchange of Students for Technical Experience) based in the UK at the Central Bureau for Educational Visits and Exchanges in London (see above address) is a worldwide organisation. This is one of the best known organisations for trainees looking for posts in industry. Those in Finland can range from working on the factory floor to helping with research and development. Students should apply for work in the area for which their studies are appropriate.

Some IAESTE Contact Addresses Abroad
Canada. IESTE Canada, POB 1473 Kingston, Ontario K7L 5C7, Canada. Visiting Address: room 110, St. Lawrence Building, Queen's University, Kingston, Ontario; tel 613-549-2243; fax 613-545-6869.

United States of America IAESTE US, c/o The Association for International Practical Training, 10400 Little Pautext Parkway, Suite 250, Columbia, Maryland 21044-3510; tel 410-997-3068; fax 410-992-3924.

Types of Jobs Available
EU nationals in particular should note that they can access the following jobs in Finland, such as those below by contacting organisations in their own countries, by contacting Finnish employers direct or by applying on the spot in Finland, as appropriate.

Agriculture, Forestry, Horticulture. These programmes can involve arduous physical, hands on experience but may also involve working in a specialist institute, for instance in an enviromental protection department of a large company. Farming proper in Finland requires an appreciation of the problems of agriculture in the Arctic where the winters last longer, and while other European farms are spring planting, Finnish ones are under a metre of snow in temperatures of −20°C. It is therefore no wonder that Finnish farm prices are twice as high as the rest of Europe. Despite the hardships and the fact that only 8% of Finns are engaged in agriculture, they are an influential minority in the Centre Party. You need two years practical experience to get on the International Farm Experience programme which. Farming jobs for three to twelve months can also be arranged through the International Farm Experience programme in the UK (YFC Centre, National Agricultural Centre, Stoneleigh Park, Kenilworth, Warwickshire CV8 2LG; tel 01203-696584; fax 01203-696559).

It is also possible to get casual work in horticultural nurseries by contacting them direct or visiting in person. There are quite a few in the Helsinki area.

Hotels, Catering and Tourism. It is possible to get a hotel job by writing directly to some of Finland's hundreds of hotels, especially those in tourist resorts like Hämeenlinna. A list of hotels can be obtained through the Finnish tourist office in your own country. The only hotel it would not be advisable to apply to is the Artic Hall Hotel at Jukkasjärvi which is a giant igloo built in December; in March it melts. Smart international hotel chains like Intercontinental of which there is one in Helsinki, may prefer to take trainees through CIMO as they will consider them more motivated. Those studying tourism or related subjects can work in travel agencies and Finnish offical tourist offices. Trainee chefs, waiters, bar and housekeeping staff are also eligible to go through CIMO.

One hotel that advertises for kitchen and waiting staff in Britain, is the *Hotel Ruotsinsalmi* (Kirkkokatu 14, Kotka 10). A charge of £35 per month for board and lodging is deducted if needed. The only snag is that a knowledge of Swedish is required and if possible Finnish as well.

Social & Voluntary Work. There is plenty of scope for voluntary work in Finland. There are traineeships in old people's homes, in youth work and on summer camps with young Finns or a more international participation.

As well as applying through CIMO there are some international voluntary work camp organisations in Finland:

Allianssi, Olympidstadion, Eteläkaarre 00250 Helsinki. Arranges international workcamps in Finland.
KVT, Raulhanasema, Veturitori, 00520 Helsinki, runs summer work camps. In the UK you should apply through International Voluntary Service (IVS, Old Hall, East Bergholt, Colchester, Essex C07 6TQ; and in Leeds at 188 Roundhay Road LS8 5PL).
Valamo Monastery 79850 Uusi-Valamo, takes volunteers all year round to help in the gardens, kitchens and other household departments of the monastery. A full day's work is expected in return for keep. English and German are spoken as well as Finnish. A great way to get away from the rat race and especially interesting for anyone wanting to learn more about Eastern Orthodox religion.

Aspects of Employment

Salaries
It may come as a surprise that Scandinavian salaries are some way behind Germany and Switzerland and that Finns are generally lower paid than other Scandinavians. However, Finns are better paid generally than the French, Italians and Britons (except at top executive level) and even North American salaries are slightly lower. Typical salaries are FIM 20,000 per month (about £30,000 per annum) base salary before commission for a sales manager, FIM 14,000 (about £21,000 per annum) for an office manager, FIM 8,770 (about £13,000 per annum) for a secretary. In 1991 the average Finnish income was FIM81,789 (about £10,220). There is a statutory minimum rate of pay for men and women in manufacturing of about FIM54 and FIM 42 respectively per hour. There is a minimum statutory wage for industrial trainees which varies between FIM3000-5000 depending on the category of work.

The cost of living however, is reckoned to be higher than the UK. Taxation, after substantial reductions across the board during the recession is likely to increase once the recovery is underway.

Salaries are negotiated by collective bargaining agreements between the trade unions and the employers' federations. In order to combat inflation Finland has imposed strict restraints on wage levels which increased only by about two per cent in 1994. The salaries of managerial and professional staff are usually negotiated directly by the employee and employer and often individual contracts drawn up.

Table of Monthly Earnings in FIM/£'s (Private Sector) 1991

Advisor for a government subsidised organisation	7,039	(£879)
Agent	16,354	(£2,044)
Clerical Worker	8,704	(£1,088)
Book-keeper	8,607	(£1,075)
Caretaker	7,536	(£942)
Car Dealer	11,386	(£1,423)
Day Care Asst. (Govt. subsidised organisation)	6,370	(£796)
Industrial Foreman	10,977	(£1,374)
Administrator	14,199	(£1,774)
Waiter	7,940	(£992))
Secretary of an Organisation (full-time)	13,699	(£1,712)
Secretary	8,723	(£1,090)
Service Station Attendant	6,762	(£845)
Shop Assisant (foods)	6,423	(£802)
Shopkeeper	9,360	(£1,170)
Stock Clerk	6,543	(£817)
Travel agent employee	7,711	(£963)

Table of Monthly Earnings in FIM/£'s (Public Sector) 1991

Bus/Tram Driver	9,592	(£1,199)
Teacher (comprehensive school)	10,885	(£1,360)
Cleaner	6,519	(£814)
Cook	7,426	(£928)
Electrician	9,703	(£1,202)
Engineer	13,316	(£1,664)
Laboratory Technician/assistant	7,701	(£962)
Assistant Librarian	9,126	(£1,140)
Nurse	10,200	(£1,275)
Nursery-school teacher	8,142	(£1,017)
Office Worker	7,109	(£888)
Physician in a health centre	20,786	(£2,600)
Police Officer	14,286	(£1,785)
Social Worker	8,129	(£1,016)

Fringe Benefits and Perks

Apart from bonuses paid to executive staff, the only perk widespread in Finland is a payment of an additional 50% of the regular salary during the employee's holiday time. Some employers also provide or subsidise, meals and transport and occasionally housing.

Working Hours, Overtime and Holidays

The law governing working hours states that a regular working week consists of 40 hours a week, eight hours a day. As in other northern European countries lunch breaks are not usually longer than one hour. The normal working day begins at 8.30am and ends at 5pm but with flexible working hours many jobs can be arranged around other commitments. The recession has caused Finnish employers to be more adaptable and schemes for jobs sharing and allowing employees sabbaticals to enrol on a study year or further their skills with additional training have been introduced. This is to create opportunities for those entering the job market for the first time who would otherwise be severely disadvantaged by the current state of very high unemployment in Finland.

The normal annual holiday allowance in addition to public holidays, is five weeks, one week of which must be taken during winter.

Overtime is normally restricted to a maximum of 200 hours per year on weekdays and 120 hours for weekends. Legislation also governs the payment for overtime: for the first two hours on weekdays and Saturdays the rate is a minumum premium of 50%. The rate for more than two hours on a weekday and Sunday work is at least 100%. The Labour Council may allow up to a 50% increase in overtime subject to special terms of negotiation.

The recession has caused employers to lobby for a reduction in overtime rates.

Trade Unions
Finland has a high level of union membership in the main industries. This ranges from about 65% in the services sector to nearly 95% in the metal and paper industries. It is not compulsory to belong to a union but the unions are important in the area of collective bargaining and the major ones set the pattern for wage increases nationally. For the last four years, wage hikes have been almost non-existent.

Employment Contracts
As in other countries a written contract of employment is not essential. If there is no written contract the national labour laws govern the terms of dismissal. Employers may therefore consider a written contract desirable, depending on the type of employment. Some employers insist on a trial period of about three to four months before offering a more permanent contract.

Termination of a Contract
Theoretically employers and employees have equal rights to terminate employment contracts. However, in practice is is more difficult for an employer to terminate a contract than an employee. As an employee you cannot be dismissed except in exceptional circumstances such as *force majeure* or severe misconduct. Employees cannot be dismissed for illness, pregnancy, religious, political or other beliefs, or trade union activity. If there is a reduction in the volume of work the employer has to try to find other work for employees.

Dismissal periods are laid down in collective bargaining agreements or specific employment contracts. If there is no contract then the dismissal time may be based on the length of service, but must be a minimum of two months.

If an employee wishes to terminate a contract a minimum of one month's notice must be given.

For fuller details of the terms of dismissal see *Employing Staff* in the chapter on starting a business.

Maternity Benefits, Parental Leave & Employment Rights
Parents are entitled to maternity, paternity or parents' leave from work when their child is born. Allowances are paid at the rate of 80% of pay. The mother also gets a maternity benefit in cash, or in the form of a maternity pack of baby items which is valued at twice the amount of the cash benefit.

A summary of maternity/paternity benefits available to parents are:

1. Maternity benefit
2. A child allowance (paid from 0-17 years).
3. Maternity, paternity and parents' allowance (0-9 months)
4. Child home care allowance (1-3 years)
5. Child day care (1-6 years) and day care for school children (7-10 years)
6. Leave of absence to look after children at home 1-3 years
7. Partial leave of absence (shorter working hours) 1-4 years.

Child Care. There is a choice of possibilities from the above. Children under three can have a place in a communal day centre or the parents can have an allowance for the child to be cared for at home after the end of their maternity/paternity allowance. In some cases the parents' choice may be dictated by the circumstances in their area as there may be a shortage of municipal, pre-school day care places locally. Parents of children who are sick can apply for compensation for loss of earnings if they stay at home to look after them.

Women at Work
Europe seems to lag behind Scandinavia when it comes to equal opportunities for women at work. However by the high standards of Scandinavia generally opportunities for women in Finland are not considered the best — Sweden is generally considered the pinnacle of sexual equality in this respect. Nonetheless, career opportunities for women are improving helped by a significant female presence (38%) in the Finnish parliament and a few top industrial jobs. It is tempting to attribute this partly to the high rate of heart attacks amongst Finnish males, which makes women seem a better bet when it comes to coping with stressful jobs, and even creates opportunities (such as those in politics), for them. However such a simplistic view ignores the fact that although Finnish society tends towards accepting women as equal at work there is still some way to go. For example, in 1992 the average monthly earnings for regular work for men was FIM10,322 and for women FIM8450. Of the really top jobs in Finland, few are held by women except, notably, the high profile governorship of the Bank of Finland.

Women have very good conditions for work generally and having a family is compatible with developing career prospects where desired, thanks to generous maternity and paternity leave, child allowances and state and commercial child day care provisions (see above).

Income Security
Most income security comes from employee and employer contributions to statutory insurance which covers sickness, accident, pension and unemployment insurance. As in most European countries, the bulk of contributions is borne by the employer. The types of income security available are:

Sickness Insurance. Patients and those convalescing from illness or injury are entitled to a daily allowance calculated at 80% of average earnings.

Industrial Accidents. Employees' contributions cover accidents at work, occupational diseases and accidents while commuting to or from work. Intangibles may also be taken into account. Compensation at the rate of 80% of earnings is paid, as well as the cost of treatment, rehabilitation and so on. In the event of a fatal accident survivors' pensions where appropriate as well as funeral expenses are paid.

Unemployment Security. Employees who are members of a trade union are paid from union funds, a daily allowance that is usually 60% of normal income up to a period of two years. After that the unemployed person receives a flat-rate unemployment allowance from the state as do employees who are not affiliated to a trade union.

An income allowance is paid to those whose income is not sufficient to cover daily outgoings. The amount is tailored to need. It is basic living allowance designed to prevent extreme hardship. It is paid by the local authorities.

Long-term unemployed people over 60 can claim an unemployment pension.

Finnish Pensions

There are several pension categories in Finland: Old-age pension, Unemployment Pension, Invalidity Pension and so on. An individual may receive more than one of these. The average old-age, invalidity and unemployment pension received in 1991 was FIM1417 (about £177) per month.

The retirement ages in Finland are 65 or 63 for the private and public sectors respectively. Increased unemployment has caused the government to consider financial incentives for early retirement which is becoming more common in Finland. Further details of Finnish pensions can be found in the *Retirement* chapter.

Business and Industry Report

Finland, like other parts of Scandinavia is primarily industrially developed in the south. In Finland's case most of the industry is in the highly developed south west of the country while the paper industries are in the southeast in the lakeland. Climatic conditions dictate that the density of population decreases as you travel northwards towards the uplands and tundra which being environmentally severe are largely bereft of human inhabitants except for the estimated 4,000 Lapps. It is therefore not surprising that the main industries are situated where most of the inhabitants are. The middle of the country and upper third are areas dominated by the forestry industry and agriculture and are where urban centres are smaller than those of the south. The upper third of the country is also an area where there are so-called extractive industries, principally mining.

The gap between the prosperity of the south and the under-developed north is understandably marked. The Finnish regional development fund finances or subsidises industries which provide substitutes for imports and others such as fishing, tourism and fur-farming in the Nordkalotten (the academic term for the the far north of all the Scandinavian countries).

The Forestry Industry. Forestry is one of Finland's primary industries along with metals. Most of the large production plants are concentrated in southern Finland on lakes and rivers as huge amounts of water are needed to generate energy for many of the processes involved in turning timber to pulp and paper. The majority of Finnish plants are large integrated enterprises which produce pulp, paper, packaging and a variety of chemicals.

Directory of Major Employers

The following are the top nineteen companies in Finland (list supplied by the Finnish Trade Centre in the UK — tel 0171-747 3000) listed in order of net sales:

Neste, Keilaniemi, 02151 Espoo; tel 0-4501; fax 0-4504 447. Mainly oil, also chemicals and plastics. Over 13,000 employees.

Repola, P.O.B. 203, Snellmaninkatu 13, 00170 Helsinki; tel 0-182851; fax 0-630807. Mainly wood and machinery, but very diversified. Over 27,000 employees.

Kymmene Oy, Kymmene Corporation; POB 1079, Mikonkatu 15A, 00101 Helsinki; tel 0-131411; fax 0-653 884. Chemicals, plastics, forestry, metals. About 17,000 employees.

Enso-Gutzeit Oy, P.O.B. 309, Kanavaranta 1, 00101 Helsinki; tel 0-16 291; fax 0-16291 471. Forestry, chemicals, plastics. Over 14,000 employees.

Metsäliitto-Yhtymä, Revontulentie 6, 02100 Espoo; tel 0-46 941; fax 0-4551 276. Mainly forestry. Over 13,000 employees.

Kone Corporation, P.O.B. 8, Munkkiniemen puistotie 25, 00331 Helsinki; tel 0-4751; fax 0-7454 375. Metals, lifts and metal instruments. Over 20,000 employees.

Valmet Corporation, P.O.B. 27, Panuntie 6, 00621 Helsinki; tel 0-777 051; fax 0-77705 580. Metals. About 16,000 employees.

Kesko Oy, Satamakatu 3, 00161 Helsinki; tel 0-1981; fax 0-655 473. Wholesale and retail trade. Over 6,000 employees.

Nokia, P.O.B. 226, Eteläesplanadi 12, 00101 Helsinki; tel 0-18 071; fax 0-656 388. Telecommunications, paper, rubber tyres, electronics. Over 25,000 employees.

Outokumpu Oy, P.O.B. 280, Länsituulentie 7A, 02101 Espoo; tel 0-4 211; fax 0-4312 888. Metals. Over 17,000 employees.

Kemira Oy, P.O.B. 330, Porkkalankatu 3, 00101 Helsinki; tel 0-13 211; fax 0-6946 167. Over 11,000 employees.

Tuko Oy, Valimotie 17, 00380 Helsinki; tel 0-6191; fax 0-6196 157. Consumer goods, wholesale and retail. Over 5,000 employees.

A Ahlström Corporation. P.O.B. 18, 48601 Karhula; tel 52-291 111; fax 52-63 958. Metals. Over 12,000 employees.

Suomen Osuuskauppojen. Keskuskunta SOK. Fleminginkatu 34; 00511 Helsinki; tel 0-1881; fax 0-1882 332. Consumer goods, wholesale and retail. Over 5,000 employees.

Metra Oy Ab. P.O.B. 230, John Stenberginranta 2; 00101 Helsinki; tel 0-70 951; fax 0-762278. Paper, machinery. Over 15,000 employees.

Rautaruukki Oy. P.O.B. 217, Kiilakiventie 1, 90101 Oulu; tel 81-327 711; fax 81-327 506. Metals. Over 9,000 employees.

Valio Ltd. P.O.B. 390, Maijeritie 6, 00370 Helsinki; tel 0-50 661; fax 0-50662 417. Consumer goods, wholesale. Over 3,000 employees.

Huhtamäki Oy. Eteläranta 8, 00130 Helsinki; tel 0-7088 100; fax 0-660 622. Foods, food processing. About 10,000 employees.

Imatran Voima Oy. Malminkatu 16, 00019 IVO; tel 0-85 611; fax 0-6946 654. Energy. About 5,500 employees.

International and British Companies in Finland
A list can be supplied by the British Embassy in Helsinki; tel +358 0-661 293.

Accountancy
Arthur Anderson Kihlman Oy, Kansakoulukuja 1A, 00100 Helsinki; tel 0 693 6331; fax 0 693 63350.

BDO Finland Oy Kansakoulukuja 1A, 00100 Helsinki; tel 0 693 6351; fax 0-694 3276.

Coopers & Lybrand Oy (c/o) Salmi, Virkkunen & Helenius Oy (see below).

Deloitte Touche Tohnmatsu International Tilintarkastus Oy Hietale, Paul and Tuominen Kaisaniemenkatu 4A, 00100 Helsinki; tel 0-624 733; 0-624 860.

Ernst and Young National Office, Kaivokatu 8, 00100 Helsinki; tel 0-172771; fax 0-6221323. (plus 12 offices in main Finnish towns).

Grant Thornton International Oy Tilintarkastustoimisto Revico Revisionsbyrå Ab, Thurmaninpuistotie 8, 02700 Kaunianinen; tel 0 5052166; fax 0-5052172.

KPMG Wideri Oy Ab, Pl 1037, 00101 Helsinki; tel 0-693 931; fax 0-693 9399.

Midsnell International. Tilintarkastusoimisto Kalevi Ariluoma Oy, Keskustie 4, 01900 Nurmijärvi; tel 0-209 595; 0-209 715.

Price Waterhouse Oy, Vattutniementranta 2, 00210 Helsinki; tel 0-673 011; 0-674 118.

Russell Bedford International, Tilintarkastustoimisto Selinheimo Ky, Peltolantie 21, 01300 Vantaa; tel 0-857 3711; fax 857 3755.

Salmi, Virkkunen & Helenius Oy, Box 1015 (Keskuskatu 3), Helsinki; tel 0-658 044; fax 0-174 102. Parent Company of Coopers and Lybrand in Finland.

Starting a Business

Business Background

Finland was slower than other Scandinavian countries to develop industrially and the process only really began after World War Two. Thus ensued several decades when the forestry and metal industries were the backbone of the economy. Over the last twenty years Finland has grown into a world leader in telecommunications (Nokia is the second largest telecommunications company in the world). Also very developed are the freight transport and consumer durables industries. Companies such as Oy Sisu-Auto Ab which makes trucks and port tractors, and the Repola Corporation which manufactures paper for magazines and newspapers worldwide, are multi nationals. The Metra company meanwhile is a world leader in diesel engines. Chemicals and pharmaceuticals are industries that have been added in recent years as have oil refining and fertiliser production. Meanwhile Finland continues to be only second to Canada in the world for the production of pulp and paper.

Finnish design has also attracted a worldwide market in functional objects such as, scissors, cutlery and furniture, and decorative ones such as glass, not to mention textiles. Leading companies include Marimekko textiles, Iittala glass and Arabia ceramics.

For many years Finland maintained restrictions on foreign companies part-owning or buying up Finnish ones. In 1989 the government took the first positive steps towards dismantling the legal restrictions against foreign investment in Finnish companies. These were finally lifted on 1 January 1993 in preparation for Finland's entry into the European Union. Transfers of shares of Finland's largest companies, which in practice affects about 100 enterprises, are still subject to government monitoring until the end of 1995. This does not however apply to newly established companies.

The status of foreign-owned businesses in Finland is the same as that of home-grown ones. The government offers subsidies for starting up businesses in development areas. Freight subsidies and special financing deals are also available. Subsidies are available on a countrywide basis for various purposes including: research and development, export promotion and machinery and equipment purchases.

As Finland has only recently opened up fully to foreign investment, there are considerable commercial possibilities awaiting companies and individuals with enough foresight to exploit them. These include access to the emerging economies of the Baltic Republics and Russia with which Finland has long established links. At the time of going to press, St Petersburg and Estonia are the most lucrative potential markets. In addition there is a surge of tourist interest in these areas with the concomitant requirements for services to take care of them.

With one of the highest jobless rates in Europe, there is no shortage of labour available in Finland. Far from resigning itself to permanent high unemployment, Finland is currently making huge investments in training schemes for its human resources aimed at producing individuals whose skills are tailored to the requirements of industry, particularly in the area of new technology. Finland's advanced technology industries include dental, medical and automotive equipment. Finland also has the largest technical research facility in Scandinavia, VTT (see *Useful Addresses* below), whose main laboratories are within Helsinki University campus.

The transport infrastructure has been planned to facilitate human movement and cargo delivery. Over 80% of all cargo to and from Finland passes through one of Finland's 20 highly automated ports.

While there are several good reasons for considering running a business in Finland, the current state of the economy is not one of them. Consumer spending in the home market is down and export markets are picking up only slowly. The number of bankruptcies amongst businesses more than tripled from 2,122 in 1985 to 7,349 in 1992. Despite the disastrous recession and the the sluggish progress of recovery so far, there is however some cause for optimism especially now that Finland is in the fold of the European Union which will undoubtedly generate a spate of international cooperation and interest in Finland. Also, at the time of going to press Finnish interest rates were at their lowest level for decades which is encouraging to foreign investors. Something to watch out for however is the government's planned clawback of its recent generous tax cuts once the economy gets going again.

Procedures Involved in Buying or Starting a New Business

The Ministry of Trade and Industry in Finland provides help and advice on setting up a business in Finland. There is also an Investment in Finland Bureau, set up in 1992 to promote inward investment and to push Finland as a major gateway to the Baltic and Eastern European markets.

Investment Incentives

Foreign companies are eligible for government incentives on the same basis as Finnish companies. There are special incentives for so-called development regions or 'structural adjustment areas' which include most of northern and central Finland. Investments likely to attract government support include manufacturing, tourism and business services.

The government is currently planning a complete overhaul of the incentives system. However, at the time of going to press incentives included:

Business Subsidies. Granted by the Ministry of Trade and Industry and its regional offices. Business subsidies take the form of regional investment aid, aid for small businesses or development subsidies for SMEs (small and medium-sized companies). The level of subsidy varies from 20-40% depending on the category of the region where the investment is taking place.

Subsidies for SMEs. There is a special investment and start-up package for small companies with no more than 50 employees and an annual turnover not exceeding FIM 30 million.

For SMEs with no more than 250 employees and a turnover not exceeding FIM 120 million there is a development subsidy for improving competitiveness in the international marketplace.

A special interest subsidy is offered to SMEs nationwide until the end of 1995.

Other Incentives. Tax reliefs are provided by the local tax authorities in development regions. These include a refund of the stamp duty (usually at 4 to 6%)

on the purchase of industrial real estate for starting or expanding business operations.

Transportation subsidies are provided by the Ministry of Trade and Industry for firms in development regions. The Ministry also provides grants for the promotion of exports covering up to 50% of the cost of market research, brochures and sales costs during the start-up period, and it will give grants for attending trade fares abroad.

Useful Addresses

Department of Trade and Industry (DTI), Finnish Desk, Kingsgate House, 66-74 Victoria Street, London SW1E 6SW; tel 0171-215 5000; fax 0171-931 0397. Mainly helps British companies planning export drives to Europe but may be useful source of contacts in Finland.

Finnish Foreign Trade Association: POB 908, 00101 Helsinki; tel 0-69591; fax 0-6940028.

Investment in Finland Bureau, Arkadiankatu 2, P O B 908, 00101 Helsinki; tel 0 695 9285; fax 0 694 7934.

Ministry of Trade & Industry, Commission for Foreign Investment: Aleksanterin- katu 10, 00170 Helsinki 17, Finland; tel 0 1601; fax 0 1603666.

Regional Development Fund of Finland Ltd (KERA) POB 1127, 70101 Kuopio; tel 71 160111; fax 71 124437. Provides funds for start-up and development, investment in fixed assets and operating capital. Grants soft, long short-term loans and guarantees. A subsection of KERA, Start Fund of KERA, provides financing for high-tech industries.

Technology Development Centre of Finland (TEKES) POB 69, 00101 Helsinki; tel 0693691; fax 0 6949196. Provides grants and loans as high as 50% for research and technical development. Also credits for as much as 75% of salaries, raw materials, machinery, subcontracting, travel and patents.

VTT Technical Research Centre of Finland, Vuorimiehentie 5, 02150 Espoo; tel 4561; fax 456 7011. Deals with among other things technological and related economic research and development and international cooperation.

Grants Controlled by the European Commission

There are hundreds of business grant regimes which are overseen by the European Commission. A useful comprehensive listing of them is contained in *The European Grants Directory.* Private and public sector grants, grants for voluntary organisations and individuals are all available. The directory is published annu- ally by European Consultancy Services (01482-651695) and costs £15 including postage.

Business Structures and Registration

There are several business forms which are recognised in Finland:

Limited Company. (*Osakeyhtiö,* or *oy*). An *oy* is the type of business entity most found in Finland. It is the only corporate form in which capital is divided into shares and liability is assumed by the company itself. The Limited Companies Act (*osakeyhtiölaki*) of 29 September 1978, is in the process of overhaul at the time of going to press, and the new version will allow both private and public limited companies. As in Denmark, where this distinction already exists, the main difference between public and private companies is the amount of share capital needed: FIM 50,000 for a private company; FIM500,000 for a public company.

Under the new law, a limited company will be considered a private limited liability company unless the shareholders elect to adopt the public limited company form. If there is a change to a public form, the articles of the company will have to be amended and the company must have evidence of a share capital of not less than FIM500,000. The company will be deemed to have become a public company only after its articles of association have been recorded in the trade register.

Partnerships. Partnerships are the most usual form adopted by small entities, and there are two main kinds: the general (denoted by *ay*) and limited (called *ky*). In a general partnership, the partners are jointly and severally liable for the obligations of the partnership. In a limited partnership, at least one of the partners has unlimited liability.

There is the minimum of formalities for creating this type of business. The parties involved enter into a partnership agreement and register it with the Trade Registry and the tax authorities.

There are no minimum capital requirements for partnerships and the partners may be individuals or companies.

Financial Registry of Partnerships. Partnerships and other unincorporated entities must file a financial statement with the trade registry if two of the following three requirements are satisfied during the previous accounting period:

1. Turnover exceeds FIM 20 million
2. The balance sheet total (amount equal to total assets) exceeds FIM10 million.
3. The total of employees exceeds 50.

Joint Venture. Joint ventures, otherwise known as 'silent partnerships' are when one partner (a company or an individual) runs the partnership's business affairs on behalf of the other partners. Limited companies with shares owned by the partners also adopt the joint venture system.

Sole Proprietor Status
The most appropriate form for individual entrepreneurs is usually sole proprietorship which must be registered with the trade registry. A sole proprietor has unlimited personal liability for company debts. For accountancy purposes, sole proprietorships are treated the same as partnerships.

Branches of Foreign Companies
An application to start a branch of a foreign company must be submitted to the local administration office in Finland. The application should comprise a copy of the trade registry document from the company's own country and an officially certified Finnish translation. Also a document confirming the company's decision by the board of directors to establish a branch in Finland; also a Finnish translation. The documents will be forwarded to the trade registry. The application to the trade registry must be signed by the person who is going to be in charge of the branch in Finland. He or she must be resident in Finland.

Accounting requirements are the same as for domestic corporations, but there is no requirement for an external audit. If the branch's turnover exceeds FIM10 million, the branch has to file financial statements with the trade registry within six months of the of the end of the tax year.

Registering a New Company

There are certain formalities involved in establishing a new company in Finland. These are normally handled by lawyers, accountants or commercial banks providing a complete formation package. A draft of the articles of incorporation of the company have to be submitted to the Trade Registry which must be notified about the proposed registration of a new company. The registration must be submitted within six months of the establishing a corporation, otherwise its incorporation will be deemed to have lapsed. The registrar is responsible for gazetting the formation of a new company in the *Virallinen Lehti* (Official Gazette).

The company officially becomes an entity at the first share issue.

It usually takes about three months to complete all the formalities needed to form a corporation.

Cost of Starting a New Company

Apart from the minimum share capital needed to start a public or private company (see above), there are normally advisor's fees which are generally low (about FIM 5,000-10,000), as are registration fees. At present the fee for registration is FIM1,400. An amendment notice costs FIM280. It is also possible to obtain 'off the shelf' companies for less.

Ideas for New Businesses

Most countries are keen to encourage inward investment and Finland is no exception. Business people will find that there are many incentives for business start-ups or for investing in Finnish businesses. Finland is also very keen to promote Finnish products abroad, so any foreigner with language and proven international marketing skills would have an excellent chance of talking themselves into a job. The types of business which could be started in Finland with a reasonable prospect of doing well would be private employment agencies (as yet virtually unknown there), language services agencies (translating, interpreting etc.) and language schools.

Running a Business

Employing Staff

Contracts. Managerial and professional staff are normally provided with individual contracts whereas other types of staff are protected by a barrage of regulations enshrined in the Employment Contract Law and the Work Safety Law. Wage rates and conditions are to a large extent governed by collective bargaining agreements.

Trade Unions. Trade Unions are particularly strong in the metal and paper industries where 95% of employees in these sectors are signed up members. It is less in the services sector where it is about 60%. Trade unions are important for their function in the collective bargaining process.

Wages and Salaries. Minimum wages are usually fixed by agreement between managment and unions. The average worker's hourly wage is about FIM 55 for men and FIM43 for women. Industrial workers' are paid about one fifth less than those in Norway and Sweden and about the equivalent of France, Italy, the US, Canada and Japan.

Social Security Contributions. Other expenses which accrue largely to the expense of the employer are the compulsory social security contributions for pensions, sickness and disability, occupational accident and unemployment insurance. The employer pays about 75% of the total cost of these contributions.

Contributions do not normally have to be paid for foreign employees staying in Finland for less than one year.

Termination of Employment. In theory employers and employees have equal rights to terminate employment contracts. However, the termination of employment by the employer is hedged about with restrictions. For instance employees may only be dismissed for exeptional reasons. Employees may not be sacked for illness or pregnancy, religious or political or any other beliefs, or for taking part in a strike or other union activity. If there is a temporary reduction in the volume of work, the employer is bound to try to find other work for the employee.

Periods of notice required for both parties are usually defined by the collective bargaining agreements. If this is not the case the length of time varies according to length of employment. The minimum is two months' notice if terminated by the employer and one month if the employee resigns.

If the employee is deemed to have been unlawfully dismissed the employer has to pay a financial penalty equivalent to three to 20 months' wages. This is likely to increase under imminent labour reforms.

Taxation

The principal taxes affecting businesses in Finland are corporation tax and VAT, though they are also liable for capital gains tax and stamp duties in certain circumstances. In a sole proprietorship, personal income tax is payable. Finland carried out a major tax reform which took effect in January 1993. Among innovations designed to bring Finland into line with other EU countries, the corporation tax basic rate was lowered to 25%. The tax year for companies depends on the financial period of the company concerned. If the company's financial period ends between 1 January and 1 October, the tax return must be filed by 1 January of the following year. Alternatively companies whose financial period ends between 2 October and 31 December must file tax returns by 1 April of the following year.

For limited companies, partnerships and the self-employed the tax is usually paid in 11 advance instalments based on an estimate made by the local tax office. Late payment incurs a penalty of 1% per month.

Final assessments of tax returns are usually completed by October of the year following the tax year. If the tax office calculates that an overpayment has been made, the difference is refunded, usually by December. If the reverse is the case and the tax office has underestimated, then any addition tax due has to be paid in December. If the owed amount is considerable, it may be divided into three instalments due in consecutive months.

Tax Audits. The tax authorities have authority to examine the books of any company. Large companies are subject to regular audits, about every five years, but there are not enough resources to give small companies the same treatment.

Tax on Partnerships. For tax purposes a partnership's income is calculated in the same way as a company's taxable income and then allocated among the partners. An individual's share of the partnership income is divided into capital income and earned income. Capital income is usually calculated at 15% of the partnership's net assets. The remainder is regarded as earned income. The division of income is not applicable to corporate partners.

VAT. VAT is levied at 22% on most goods and services sold by businesses. The

VAT system changed at the beginning of 1994 when the right to deduct VAT was expanded.

Capital Gains Tax. Capital gains is tougher on companies than on individuals. Where companies have assets such as real estate or shares which are not reported to the tax authorities as business assets, they may not claim indexation in calculating the gain as an individual would be allowed to do. For instance they must base their calculations on the purchase price, whereas an individual can usually deduct 30% or sometimes 50% of the sales price before calculating the gain.

Stamp Duty. Businesses are also liable for stamp duties: on transfers of shares (1.6%). However, stamp duties are not levied on transactions on the stock exchange or so-called OTC (over-the-counter) dealings. Loans from banks or other financial institutions are liable for a 1.5% stamp duty on the amount borrowed and if the loan is raised abroad then there is a 0.5% loan tax.

Other stamp duties for which businesses may be liable is a 4-6% rate on transfers of real estate.

Accountancy and Auditing Requirements

Finland passed a new Accounting Act in December 1992 to comply with the EU's company law directives:

A company must present financial statements annually within three months of the end of the accounting year and these must be presented for adoption to a general shareholders' meeting to be held no later than six months after the end of the accounting year. Within two months of the financial statements being adopted, companies should file with the Trade Registry a certified copy of their statutory accounts, including consolidated accounts with an auditor's report. All of these are then made available for public inspection.

Limited liability companies and co-operatives may be exempted from this obligation if two of the following conditions are satisfied during the preceding accounting year.

1. Turnover does not exceed FIM four million.
2. Total assets on the balance sheet are under FIM two million.
3. The average employee total is under ten.

Appointing Auditors

Limited liability companies must appoint a at least one indpendent auditor who must be Finnish, or a permanent resident of Finland. If there is more than one auditor only one need be Finnish. If the company is a large one then one of the auditors must be authorised or working for a company authorised by the Central Chamber of Commerce. A large company for this purpose is defined as one which:

1. Is listed on the stock exchange
2. Whose share capital and restricted reserves exceed FIM two million.
3. Whose average number of employees exceeds 500 during the previous two accountancy years.

If the company fulfils only number two above, it is sufficient for the auditor to be authorised at local level by the chamber of commerce.

Useful Addresses

Central Chamber of Commerce, Fabiankatu 14B, 00100 Helsinki; tel 650133.
Oy Ernst & Young Ab, National Office, Kaivokatu 8, 00100 Helsinki; tel 172771; fax 6221223. Main Finnish branch of a worldwide chartered accountants Ernst and Young providing full business service including public accounting,

tax and management consulting. Other Finnish branches in: Jyväskylä, Kajaani, Kotka, Kuopio, Mariehamn, Lahti, Oulu, Rauma and Rovaniemi. Publishes a series of country profiles including *Doing Business in Finland*.

Finnish Association for Accounting Firms, Salomonkatu 17A, 00100 Helsinki; tel 694 4077; fax 694 9596.

Finnish Employers' Confederation (STK). Eteläranta 10, 00130 Helsinki; tel 17281.

Finnish Institute of Authorised Public Accountants, Fredrikinkatu 61A, 39, 00100 Helsinki; tel 694 2255; fax 693 1567.

National Board of Patents and Registration (Trade Registry), Albertinkatu 25, 00181 Helsinki; tel 6939500; 6939511.

National Association of Insurance Companies, Bulevardi 28, 00180 Helsinki; tel 680401.

Patents, Trademarks & Copyrights

Finland has amended its laws on the above to bring registration of intellectual property in Finland into line with other EU countries. Asserting a right over a patent, design or trademark normally entails registering with the National Board of Patents and Registration.

Patents. The application for a patent must be in Finnish or Swedish and submitted by a resident of Finland, or a company registered in Finland. The patent takes effect from the date of the register of the application and is in force for 20 years. The actual issuing process can however take up to five years for a foreign patent

It is important to note that having a patent in force in Finland, cannot prohibit the import of the patented product from EU or EEA countries into Finland, if the patentee has sold the product abroad. This applies equally to the import of designs and other intellectual property registered in Finland (see *miscellaneous* below).

Trademarks. The registration of a trade mark is similar to a patent except that it is in force for ten years and can be renewed for further ten year periods. The fee is FIM870 (renewal FIM930).

The definition of a trademark is:

1. A device
2. One or more letters, words or numbers
3. A distinctive arrangement of goods or packaging

Once a trademark has been registered, the owner has the exclusive right to use it as a distinguishing symbol for their goods or packaging. It is possible to still have the sole right to a trademark even without registering, if it has an established reputation and has become generally associated by the business community or customers in Finland with a particular owner's goods. This is known as a broadly recognised trademark.

Copyright. The copyright act is for creative literary or artistic work. The categories included are: written or spoken fictional or descriptive renderings and may be musical, dramatic or cinematographic, fine art, architectural, artistic handicraft or industrial art or design. The copyright entitles the owner to the exlusive right to control the work by producing copies and making the work available to others.

A copyright on any of the above remains in force for fifty years after the death of its creator.

Since 1991 computer programmes have come under the copyright act as they are considered literary works.

Miscellaneous Intellectual Property. Designs can also be registered for five years and renewed twice for a total of fifteen years. Utility models, covered by a law of 1992 is for technical solutions which are not sufficiently unique to warrant a patent but which involve progressive inventive processes. Methods and chemical products cannot however be protected. Utility models are protected for four years from the date of application and are renewable for another four years.

When naming your company or product or setting up a foreign company in Finland you should check that the words in the title or product name do not mean anything laughable or worse in Finnish. Conversely some words are acceptable in Finnish that are not in English. You cannot however call your company Bonk Business Inc. as this firm already exists in Helsinki. Bonk means a mechanical noise in Finnish.

Iceland

Living and Working in Iceland

General Introduction
Residence and Entry Regulations
Setting up Home
Daily Life
Employment
Temporary Work
Business and Industry Report
Starting a Business

General Introduction

Destination Iceland

Iceland's position in Europe is an anomaly in every sense. Although classed as a Scandinavian country, Iceland's nearest neighbour is Greenland. It is Europe's second largest island but the total population is smaller than than of Luxembourg. To many Europeans Iceland is best known for its canned fish and woollen sweaters and few would be able to think of an Icelandic place name other than the capital Reykjavík. Yet all this is starting to change as more and more people are turning to Iceland as Europe's last wilderness. If you want to have a real change of scene yet still have access to European culture and amenities Iceland might be the place for you.

The description of Iceland as the 'land of ice and fire' has become a little hackneyed, but it does suggest some of the dramatic natural landscape of Iceland. Nature has a very powerful presence in Iceland and set against this harsh if beautiful natural world and even harsher climate is a land steeped in myth, legend and folklore. A rock is never just a rock in Iceland — it is a troll caught out after sunrise. Even the most educated and sophisticated Icelanders can profess a belief in the 'little people'.

Iceland was officially discovered by Norwegian explorers around AD 860 although it was almost certainly occupied by a small number of Irish monks prior to that. Five years after the discovery Hrafna Flóki successfully spent a winter there and named it Iceland. In AD 870 Ingólfur Arnarson became the first successful settler. A steady stream of Norwegians followed and appropriated the land and Iceland became Europe's only medieval commonwealth. The Alþing or national assembly was established in AD 930. It flourished until 1281 when a new legal code transferred absolute powers to the Norwegian king. The unification of Norway and Denmark in the 14th century further reduced Icelandic autonomy and Iceland eventually came under Danish rule. Iceland gained independence from Denmark in 1944 but there are still close links between the two countries. Today the tolerated invaders are the US military forces based at Keflavík Airport and kept there because of Iceland's geographic and strategic importance.

Political & Economic Structure

The key to Iceland's political and economic structure can be traced in both Iceland's special geographical position as a northern island nation and in its history of invasion and domination by other Scandinavian countries.

Government

Iceland's parliament, the Alþing is one of the world's oldest legislative assemblies which dates back to AD 930. Today Iceland is a multi-party democratic republic. The constitution, adopted by referendum in 1944 following independence from

Denmark, invests the highest judicial authority in a seven member, supreme court.

The titular head of the Alþing is the President who is democratically elected every four years. In 1980 Iceland elected the first ever woman president in the world, Mrs. Viglis Finbógadottir. She has remained in office since then. The main legislative powers rest with the prime minister who is accountable to the Alþing. The 63 members of the Alþing are elected from eight electoral districts and serve a four-year term of office. Despite its tiny population Iceland has seven main political parties including a Woman's Party which has 8% of the votes. The conservative Independence party is currently in power and holds 38.6% of the votes.

Economy

Iceland operates on a mainly free market economy. It has one of the highest per captita incomes in the world and the gross national product (GNP) is increasing more rapidly than the population.

Iceland is the world's fifth largest fishing nation. The mainstay of the economy is the fishing industry which accounts for betweeen 70 and 80% of the nation's exports and employs about one sixth of the population. Only a very small part of the country is cultivated (about 1%) and farming is organised on a regional cooperative basis. The main farming activity is sheep (there are more sheep than humans in Iceland) and lamb is the main agricultural export followed by cheese. The country also exports about 1,000 of the unique native breed of Icelandic pony (*equus Scandinavicus*) per year.

In the southwest of Iceland around Hveragerði are geothermally heated greenhouses which produce locally grown fruit and vegetables for the home market. Iceland is able to produce hydroelectric power well in excess of her domestic needs and is encouraging foreign development. Both Norway and Switzerland have established processing plants on the island.

Main manufacturing sources other than the fish industry are aluminium, ferrosilicon and woollen goods. With decline in the fishing industry due to over fishing and problems with over production in farming, Iceland is increasingly capitalising on its unique natural landscape by turning to tourism. This is a boom area in Iceland which increased by 21% in 1994.

Iceland's major imports include construction materials, mineral fuels and transport equipment and the main importers are Britain, Germany and Denmark. Her principal export markets are the United States, Germany and Britain. Despite having only a tiny population Iceland can boast an international airline (Icelandair), two international shipping lines, and has been a member of the World Bank and International Monetary Fund since 1945.

Geographical Information

Iceland occupies a total area of 39,756 square miles/103,000 square km. It has more than 3700 miles/5 960 km of rugged coastline and measures about 300 miles/483 km from east to west and 190 miles/306 km from north to south. Its nearest European neighbour is Scotland — 500/803 km miles southeast. The Icelandic mainland lies just beneath the Arctic Circle in mid-Atlantic although the island of Grímsey off the north coast actually straddles the Circle.

Geologically, Iceland is a relative newcomer and lies on the mid-Atlantic ridge between the European and American continental plates which are pulling the country apart. There is no imminent danger — the process has been going on for 25 million years — but it has resulted in a volcanic zone from the central north to the south and west. Geographically, Iceland is as varied as it is spectacular and seems to be made of the stuff of geography text books: volcanoes, glaciers, geysers, lava fields, fertile flood plains and barren deserts are just some of the natural features of Iceland. Inevitably, it is a huge draw for natural scientists.

Iceland has a population of just over 250,000 which is increasing by about 1½% annually. 83% of the population live in communities of over 1,000 people and about 150,000 people live in Reykjavík and its suburbs which means that many parts of Iceland are very sparsely populated. Most of the population outside Reykjavík lives in the south west between Reykjavík and Vík. The Icelandic interior is virtually uninhabited. All towns are built around the ring road which circles the island.

Climate
There's a popular saying in Iceland: 'If you don't like the weather wait a minute — it'll probably get worse'. No one goes to Iceland for a sun tan. Extreme changeability and harsh conditions characterise the Icelandic climate. Summer is a brief affair which begins in June and is all but finished by the end of August. The few bright summer days are heavily interspersed with wet and windy ones and the sunniest place is the north east around Mývatn and Akureyri. The deserted interior is prone to blizzards and violent snowstorms even in summer. It could, however, be worse. Iceland lies in the path Gulf Stream and has relatively mild temperatures for such a northern situation. The average July temperature is 11 ° Centigrade/ 52 ° Fahrenheit and January 0 ° Centigrade/ 31 ° Fahrenheit. The mildness is undermined by the relentless Arctic winds which can add a chill edge to even a mild day. Rainfall varies considerably from about 160 inches/ 4,100 mm in the southeast to 16 inches/400 mm around Akureyri in the northeast.

Midnight Sun and Northern Lights
In summer Iceland experiences very long hours of daylight. Only the island of Grímsey which lies on the Arctic circle actually experiences the midnight sun but between May and early August nowhere can be described as truly dark. Conversely, midwinters have only a few hours of daylight which may appear between 11am and be gone by 3pm. At Easter hours of night and day are about even. The northern lights (a.k.a. aurora borealis), is a phenomenon which can be seen from early September but the best viewing times are March and October. The lights come in many shapes and sizes but are frequently seen as a shimmering curtain of light across the sky on a clear night. The aurora is usually green but can be red and yellow too.

Regional Guide

As a large country with a sparse population, Iceland can be divided into the following large regions:

Reykjavík and the Reykjanes Peninsula
Reykjavík is the world's most northerly capital and also one of its newest. 100 years ago most Icelanders worked and lived on farms but today 150,000 people, more than half the population, live in Reykjavík. The city's origins however, date back to the late ninth century when the country's first settler, Ingólfur

Arnarson, named it 'Smokey Bay', mistakenly thinking that steam rising from hot springs was caused by fire. In the mid-18th century Skúli Magnússon, regarded as Reykjavík's modern founder, established local industries of tanning, weaving and wool dyeing to stimulate trade. The city flourished over the next century as a fishing centre.

Although the most visited place in Iceland, Reykjavík is probably its least representative. With many centres of culture, museums, cafés, theatres and restaurants and and active night life (mainly on Friday nights) the atmosphere is distinctly cosmopolitan. Despite the rapid spread of suburban apartment blocks, central Reykjavík is attractive and atmospheric.

Reykjanes Peninsula
This is usually the first part of Iceland that visitors are exposed to on landing at Keflavík airport. It is a bleak lava field just west of Reykjavík which can leave the uninitiated with the impression that they have landed on the moon. Its main attraction is the geothermally heated Blue Lagoon bathing place which is reputed to have miraculous curative powers for skin disease.

South
From Reykjavík along the south coast to Vík is the most densely populated part of Iceland. Even so, populations are based in small towns which are miles apart and usually comprise only one main street and a few amenities. The main towns are: Hveragerði, Selfoss, Hella and Hvolsvöllur. The landscape is of fertile floodplains reaching down to the sea and the area is well populated by sheep and Icelandic horses. This is the area of the geothermally heated greenhouses. Carrying on from Vík takes you past the magnificent Vatnajökull glacier — the third largest in the world — and the beautiful Skaftafell nature reserve to the fishing port town of Höfn in the south east. Below Vík are the Vestmannaeyjar islands of which only Heimaey is inhabited. In 1963 the island of Surtsey was born when a volcano erupted out of the sea. It is the world's youngest island.

East
Eastern Iceland is very sparsely populated — even by Icelandic standards. The largest town is Egilsstaðir. Apart from rugged coastline small farming communities and fjords it contains Iceland's largest forest.

North
The ring road by-passes the coastal region of the north east and crosses the deserted interior towards Lake Mývatn ('Midge Lake') and Akureyri. Lake Mývatn is a national conservation area and one of Iceland's most popular tourist spots, enjoying some of the finest weather in Iceland. Akureyri, west of Mývatn is Iceland's second town with a population of 14,000. It has most of the amenities of Reykjavík and a rather better climate. West of Akureyri is very scarcely populated.

Westfjords and the West
The Westfjords are a rugged expanse of peninsula on the north west tip of Iceland. This consists of rocky plains, small lakes and the glacier at Drangajökull. It is a very windy and inhospitable landscape with a small fishing population. The west coast of Iceland from Reykjavik to the Westfjords was the setting for the *Laxedaela* and *Egills* sagas. Although attractive and rich in history the area is notorious for cold west Atlantic weather.

The Interior

The Icelandic interior contains Europe's only desert. This barren wilderness of mainly grey lava fields, interspersed with volcanos and ice peaks, can only safely be seen by guided tours or robust, four wheel drive vehicles. There are no proper roads — just dirt tracks — few bridges and only primitive accommodation. Perhaps its qualities can best be conveyed by the fact that the first lunar astronauts trained for their moon landing here.

Residence and Entry Regulations

The Current Position

There are currently about 5,000 foreign nationals living in Iceland, the bulk of whom are from the Scandinavian countries. There are about 400 UK nationals living and working in Iceland. From 1 January 1994 Iceland and other members of the European Economic Area agreed to form a joint labour market. Effectively this means that citizens of member states are no longer required to have obtained an offer of work and a work permit before entering the country and can enter the country with the intention of looking for work.

Requirements for EEA Citizens

Although Iceland is not a member of the EU it is a member of the EEA and anyone from another member country can enter Iceland and stay for three months and apply for permanent residence.

Residence Permit

Anyone staying in Iceland for over six months needs to have legal domicile in Iceland. This also applies to any foreign national working in Iceland even though they may be staying for less than six months. In practice this means that you or your employer should contact the municipal authorities who will inform the Statistical Bureau of Iceland. The Bureau will issue you with an identity card and identification number and the date of issue. You will need to provide a photo for your identity card.

Entering to Work

All foreigners who remain in Iceland to work need to have an identity card with a photograph and an identification number obtained from the Statistical Bureau of Iceland. You will also need to obtain a personal tax card from the Directorate of Internal Revenue which will state your exemption allowance. You are obliged to file an income tax return before leaving the country.

Entering to Start a Business

The rules on foreign direct investment in Iceland were simplified and liberalised in 1991 but several restrictions still apply see the chapter *Starting a Business*. Every new company in Iceland must obtain an identification number from the Statistical Bureau. The current fee is 5,000 ISK. Companies must also obtain a VAT number from the tax authorities. Most companies will also need to obtain a trading licence before beginning operations.

Useful Addresses

Directorate of Internal Revenue: Laugavegur 166,150 Reykjavík; tel 1-5631100.
Statistical Bureau of Iceland: Skuggasund 3, 150 Reykjavík; tel 1-5609800.

Non-EEA Nationals
Regulations for citizens of non EEA countries are considerably more strict. To enter Iceland as a visitor a valid passport is required and some countries require visas. Before entering Iceland to work, a non EEA national should already have been offered a job and a work contract. Non EEA nationals are not permitted to begin work unless a work permit has been granted to their prospective employer by the Ministry of Social Affairs. Initially this is often be a temporary permit which does not specify the name of the individual concerned and a full permit will be given on arrival in the country. Residence and work permits are usually granted for the same length of time and the length of a work permit will never normally exceed the length of a permit to stay. Permits are usually granted for a few months and are rarely extended beyond a year. If you need to extend your residence or work permit you should apply before it expires.

Useful Addresses
Icelandic Embassy: 1 Eaton Terrace, London SW1W 8EY; tel 0171-730 51312.
British Embassy: Laufasvegur 49, Reykjavík; tel 1-15883-4.
USA Embassy: Laufasvegur 21, Reykjavík; tel 1-5529100.
The Immigration Office: Hverfisgata 115, 150 Reykjavík; tel 1-5699000.
Ministry of Social Affairs: Directorate of Labour, Hafnarhusi,Tryggvagata, 150 Reykjavík; tel 1-5609100.
Confederation of Icelandic Employers: Garðastraeti 41, 101 Reykjavík; tel 1-5623000.
Directorate of Internal Revenue: Laugavegur 166, 150 Reykjavík; tel 1-5631100.
Statistical Bureau of Iceland: Skuggasund 3, 150 Reykjavík; tel 1-5609800.

Setting Up Home

Moving to Iceland is not a particularly common occurrence and information and agencies geared to this are fairly scarce. some employers will have accommodation at their disposal or will help you to find it. For those obtaining a work permit prior to arrival in Iceland (i.e. non EEA nationals), the employer must convince the authorities that suitable accommodation has been found for their employee for the duration of their contract of engagement (if the prospective employee does not procure accommodation for him/herself). Until 1 January 1994 all foreign nationals employed in Iceland had to satisfy this criterion. Providing or helping to find accommodation for foreign workers is common practice. If you are working in fish processing firms accommodation is usually provided free or at a nominal rent and with agricultural work it is usual to live as family with the employer.

How Do Icelanders Live

88% of Icelanders own their own homes. The standard of living is generally very high and Icelandic society is highly materialistic. One in two people own a car, almost every household has the latest consumer durables and Iceland holds the world record on video and telephone ownership per capita.

Generally, you can buy anything in Iceland that can be bought in the rest of Europe — but at many times the cost. As an island nation heavily dependent on imports, the cost of living is one of the highest in the world and food in particular is very highly priced. Standard fare in Iceland is lamb and fish; delicacies which you might encounter on Icelandic menus are: ram's testicles, sheep's face and shark's innards. Most Icelanders cope with the hefty cost of living by working very hard; many have more than one job, leaving them perhaps less time than they would like to enjoy the consumer durables they are working so hard for. Apartment blocks are common in the Reykjavík suburbs but wide open spaces allow for houses to be fairly sizeable. 86% of Icelandic housing enjoys geothermal heating and hot water. Most Icelanders are broad minded and liberal — in Iceland about 30% of children are born out of wedlock — and the prevailing ethos seems to be one of live and let live.

Finance

If you are intending to live in Iceland you will find it difficult to raise money from a British bank for buying property. However, Icelandic banks perform the usual functions of any other European bank and can help you to arrange a mortgage. For further details contact: Central Bank of Iceland (Kalkofnsvegi 1, 150 Reykjavík; tel 1-5699600.)

Purchasing Property

Property is purchased through estate agents in Iceland. Many of them advertise through national papers. The principal estate agent is Felag Island Stokaupmanna (Husi Verslunarinnar, 103 Reykjavík).

Renting Property

With the majority of Icelanders owning their own homes,there is little accommodation available for rent in Iceland and when available it is very expensive. One letting agency in Reykjavik may be able to help: Leigjendasamtokim (Hverfisgotu 8–10, 101 Reykjavík; tel 2-5532666).

Removals

Inevitably moving is expensive and the cost of buying items in Iceland very high. If you can reduce your items to the contents of a car you can take the ferry from Scotland (but only in summer). Alternatively, you can send freight and cars by sea via Eimskip, the Icelandic Steamship Company (Pósthússtraeti 2, 101 Reykjavík; tel 1-5697100, fax 1-5697179.).

Pets can be imported to Iceland provided that you comply with the terms of the import permit issued by the Icelandic Ministry of Agriculture. Note that it is forbidden to keep dogs in Reykjavík.

Useful addresses
Scotpac International Moving: Security House, Abbey Wharf Industrial Estate, Kingsbridge Road, Barking, Essex IG11 OBT; tel 0181-591 3388, fax 0181-594 4571.

Ministry of Agriculture: Animal Health Division, Hook Rise, South, Tolworth, Surbiton, Surrey KT6 7NF; tel 0181-330 4411 gives advice on importing pets.

Daily Life

Iceland may be categorised as part of Europe but that does not prevent it from being something of a culture shock to outsiders. What follows is a guide through some of the quirks of living in mid north Atlantic.

The Language

The language spoken by present day Icelanders is essentially the same as Old Norse of the ancient Vikings. Linguistic purity is preserved by a refusal to incorporate foreign terms for new technology — computer for example is *tolva* which translates as number prophetess. Icelandic is not particularly user-friendly, having a complicated grammar and difficult pronunciation but English is spoken almost nationwide and is the second language taught in schools after Danish. There is therefore little problem for foreigners with a good knowledge of English in communicating with Icelanders. Anyone planning a long stay in Iceland should make an effort to learn the language but there are currently very few Icelandic language or phrase books. For language courses in Iceland contact:

Mímir School of Languages: Ananaust 15, Reykjavík; tel 1-5510004-2 or 1-5521655.

The Icelandic Correspondence College: Hlemmur 5, PO Box 5144, 125 Reykjavík, Iceland; tel 1-5629750.

Icelandic for Beginners (tape & book) c/o *Dick Phillips:* Whitehall House, Nenthead, Alston, Cumbria, CA9 3PS; tel 01434-381440.

Schools and Education

Iceland has 100% literacy. Education is compulsory until the age of 16 when students can enrol at four-year academic colleges. On successful graduation they are entitled to apply to the University of Iceland, founded in Reykjavík in 1911. Nearly all Icelandic schools from primary to university are free.

The only English speaking school in Iceland is *The American Embassy School* (c/o The American Embassy, Laufásvegur 21, Reykjavik; tel 5643237/5518209, fax 5643237).

Media and Communications

Newspapers/Books

There are five daily newspapers in Iceland — all of them in Icelandic — the most popular of which is *Morgunbladid*. The only English language newspaper is the monthly *News from Iceland*, and there are two quarterly magazines — *Iceland Review* and *Iceland Business*. If you are interested in subscribing to any of them write to: Iceland Review (Höfðabakki 9, 112 Reykjavik, Iceland; tel 1-5675700, fax 1-5674066). English newspapers can be bought in Reykjavík. Icelanders are great readers and the country publishes the world's greatest number of books per capita in the world. Books in the English language are readily available in Reykjavík. Iceland has produced one literature Nobel Laureate — Halldór Laxness who was born in Reykjavík in 1902 and won the Nobel Prize in 1955.

Television/Radio

Icelandic television has two channels — the state-run Channel One and the commercial Channel Two. Both show a high proportion of English language programmes. There are a variety of competing Icelandic radio stations. Between June and August there is an English newscast daily at 8.55 am or telephone 91-5693690 for an around the clock recorded version.

Telephone/Post

The code for Iceland when calling from abroad or sending faxes is: 00 354 followed by the area code. The code for Reykjavík is 1 when dialling from abroad and 41 from within Iceland. Note that all Reykjavík numbers have seven digits (as given in this book) from 1 June 1995. Individuals are listed by their first names in an Icelandic telephone directory and sometimes their profession is listed too. Dial 03 for information on telephone numbers and addresses anywhere in the country. To call a mobile phone in Iceland dial 985 for anywhere in the country and 85 from overseas. Post services are generally good.

Transport

Cars

The only main road in Iceland is the Route 1 which is the 1,402 km ring road which circles the island. In many places this degenerates into an unpaved, bumpy track and it is no wonder that well-built four wheel drive autos are the norm in Iceland. Driving in the interior in anything less robust than a landrover would be severely tempting fate. The Icelandic Tourist Board (172 Tottenham Court Road, London W1P 9LG; tel 0171-388 7550) publishes a free leaflet *How to Drive in the Interior*. Petrol stations are dotted fairly frequently around the ring road but there are none in the interior. Most overland transport grinds to a halt in winter. Vehicles can be imported via ferry from Europe, including Scotland.

Public Transport

There is no railway system in Iceland. There is a fairly good daily bus service around the country in summer but this service is reduced from autumn to spring. Reykjavík is served by a good network of buses. Domestic flights are a common means of travel in Iceland and the domestic airline *Flugleidir* offers an efficient if expensive alternative to the ring road. Iceland is easily accessible by air. The national airline, Icelandair (0171-388 5599 — same address as the tourist board above) has daily flights from London. You can sail to eastern Iceland by ferry from Scotland between May and September.

Banks and Finance

Banks are only found in sizeable towns. There are three commercial banks in Iceland including the Central Bank of Iceland ((Kalkofnsvegi 1, 150 Reykjavík; tel 1 5699600) and 33 savings banks which perform all the usual banking functions. Banking hours are 9.15am-4pm Monday to Friday. Most major credit cards are accepted in Iceland.

Taxation

Income tax is deducted at source and there is only one income tax bracket. National income tax in Iceland is currently about 34.3%. Non-residents working temporarily in Iceland (for 183 days or less) are subject to tax on some of their income but may be entitled to a refund at the end of their stay. Those working in Iceland on a longer term basis may find that they are liable for the Municipal Income tax (currently about 7%) and may be expected to contribute to the Construction Fund for the Elderly. This is currently fixed at ISK 3,915. The standard rate of VAT is 24.5% with few exceptions. For further details consult the booklets *Taxes in Iceland — An Overview* and *Value added tax in Iceland — An Overview* available from the Directorate of Internal Revenue: (Laugavegur 166, 105 Reykjavík; tel 1-5631100, fax 1-5624440, or from embassies.

Health Insurance and Social Security

On 1 January 1994 the European Free Trade Association, of which Iceland is a member, joined with the European Community to form the European Economic Area. The social security, health care rights and benefits of nationals of these countries are essentially the same as those of the EU. For medical care you will need to obtain an E111 form available from any post office. British residents in Iceland are entitled to receive health care on the same terms as Icelandic nationals. The number of in-patient beds in Iceland is relatively high at 3,985 and in-patient hospital services are provided free of charge but you may have to pay a small fee for ambulances, doctors and dental treatment. See *Starting a Business* for social security and unemployment benefits. For further details consult the leaflet *SA 24 Social Security Agreement between United Kingdom and Iceland* and *SA 29 Your Social Security Insurance, Benefits and Health Care Rights in the European Community* available from The Overseas Benefits Directorate (Department of Social Security, Newcastle upon Tyne, NE98 1YX) or write to The State Social Security Institution (Laugavegi 114, Reykjavík,Iceland).

Crime and the Police

Despite the Viking traits associated with Iceland, crimes of rape and pillage are very rare there. Overall crime rates are exceptionally low and most consist of driving offences.

Religion

97% of Icelanders belong to the Lutheran church but few people actively attend church. There is quite a strong new age and pagan revival movement in Iceland.

Social Life

Like their Scandinavian cousins, the Icelanders are easy going if not particularly out going. Once the ice is broken, however, you will find that many a dour exterior hides a wry sense of humour. Despite their geographical isolation and cultural uniqueness, most Icelanders take an active interest in worldwide current affairs and enjoy an exchange of views and discussion with foreigners and most Icelanders are hospitable. There are very few class barriers in Iceland and everyone from the President downwards is addressed by their first name. Only about 10% of Icelanders have surnames; the rest use patronyms ie instead of a surname the first name of the father is used with *son* or *dóttir* to denote son or daughter. Inevitably, in such a small community, most Icelanders are related to each other in one form or another and genealogy seems to be a national passion. It is customary to shake hands on greeting and leaving and if you are invited to an Icelander's home remove your shoes.

Entertainment and Culture

In Iceland, nightlife really only exists in Reykjavík where most bars, cafés and restaurants are found. Extortionate food and drink prices make eating out a luxury. Reykjavík has a surprisingly active art life with galleries and exhibitions of local painters and sculptors. Sports such as golf, skiing, fishing and riding are popular in Iceland and swimming in geothermally heated swimming pools is almost a national pastime. Long winter nights may account for the fact that one in ten Icelanders will write and publish their own book.

Public Holidays

Independence Day is celebrated on 17 June

Verslunarmannahelgi: this is the first weekend of August which is celebrated as a long weekend (including Monday) throughout Iceland.

Réttadgur: this takes place in September and is an annual celebration at the close of sheep rounding, followed by singing, dancing and general festivities.

Employment

The Employment Scene
Until recent years Iceland enjoyed 100% employment but economic setbacks now mean that unemployment stands at a record level of about 4.5%. The fishing industry in particular has been hard hit and as this is traditionally the business which engages the greatest numbers of foreigners opportunities for non-nationals have inevitably diminished. Employment prospects are further diminished by the fact that many Icelanders are now taking on two or even three jobs themselves to make ends meet. Unless you are looking for casual/seasonal or unskilled work you will find the language something of a barrier to your chances of getting long term work. See chapter two *Residence and Entry Regulations.*

Despite current difficulties, Iceland's membership of the EEA has left the country optimistic about its economic future and there is a general tendency in Iceland to view the present situation as a temporary trough.

Sources of Jobs

Newspapers
The most up to date sources of information on work available are Iceland's five daily newspapers but unless you can read Icelandic these will be of limited use.

Professional Associations
You will need to have certification to work in specialised fields such as civil engineering and architecture and this has to be validated in Iceland. Professional associations may not be able to provide you with any direct help in finding work but can supply additional information.

Useful Addresses
Iceland Chamber of Commerce: Hús verslunarinnar, Kringlan 7, 103 Reykjavík; tel 1-5886666.
The Trade Council of Iceland: Hallveigarstígur 1, 101 Reykjavík, Iceland; tel 1-5517272.
Association of Icelandic Importers, Exporters and Wholesale Merchants: Húsi Verslunarinnar, 103 Reykjavík, Iceland; tel 1-5888910.
Federation of Icelandic Industries: Hallaveveigarstígur 1, 101 Reykjavík; tel 1-5699500.

Au Pair Work
Au pairs are not widely used in Iceland but one Danish Agency claims to be able to make placements there (see useful addresses). Being an au pair might be one way of solving the problem of the heavy cost of living as you should receive free food and accommodation.

The Fishing Industry
About 11% of the working population is currently employed directly in the fishing industry. Fishing is a seasonal industry with peak periods being February to May and September to November. Traditionally, men go to sea and do the heavy lifting and women work in the processing factories. Working on trawlers is popular because of the high wages (upwards of £3,000 a month) and in the current economic climate there is very stiff competition. You have no chance of being taken on unless there is no Icelander to do the job which it is very likely there will be.

Fish processing work used to be a popular option for those wanting to work abroad. Contracts were issued for six to eight months and included return flights. These are much less available now. The work takes place in fishing villages around Iceland in the dark winter months. Processing involves all aspects of fish packaging from cleaning and weighing to packing in cold and inevitably smelly conditions. Pay is piecework and although you will usually be provided with accommodation the high cost of living can rapidly eat into your wages.

Farms and Agriculture
The majority of farms in Iceland are small family affairs. Nonetheless, some do take on workers for a limited period, offering food and accommodation in return for work. The greenhouses around Hverageröi and Eden in the south east also sometimes employ casual workers. If you ride horses and are around in September you could volunteer to help with the annual sheep round-up for which you will probably be given board and lodging. Another possible opening for horse riders is working on the growing number of horse riding centres throughout the country. You could try contacting Icelandic Farm Holidays (Baendahöllin, v/Hagatorg, 107 Reykjavík; tel 1-5623640) who can provide details of farms offering trekking and riding.

Tourism
This is a relatively new growth area in Iceland but is developing rapidly. There may well be a demand for workers in related areas eg in horse riding centres in the future. The author managed to earn several nights' free accommodation in Iceland by rendering a guesthouse's brochure into coherent English.

Voluntary Work
Language would be a considerable barrier in the social work sector but a number of conservation projects use volunteers during the summer.

Useful Addresses
The Municipal Employment Office: Borgatúni 1, Alafoss, 121 Reykjavík; tel 1-5666300.

Au Pairs
Exis-Europair: Skeldevigvej 12, 6310 Broager, Denmark; tel 74 44 22 33.

Fishing
Icecon: Skúlagata 51, PO Box 5138, 125 Reykjavík; tel 1-5622911.
The Union of Icelandic Fish Producers: Adalstraeti 6, 101 Reykjavík; tel 1-5511480.

Farming and agriculture
Samband of Iceland: Samband House, Kirkjusandur, 105 Reykjavík; tel 1-5698100.

Iceland Agricultural Information Service: Hagatorg 1,107 Reykjavík; tel 1-5630332.
Icelandic Dairies Association: Bitruháls 2, 110 Reykjavík; tel 1-5691600.

Conservation
Icelandic Nature Conservation Volunteers: SJA PO Box 8468, 128 Reykjavík.
International Development Unit of the British Trust for Conservation Volunteers: 36 St Mary's Street, Wallingford Oxfordshire OX10 OEU; tel 01491-839766.

Nordic House
If you have any Scandinavian blood in you, you could try contacting Nordic House (Saemundargata, Reykjavík, Iceland; tel 1-5517030), which arranges work programmes for nationals from Scandinavian countries and may be able to help anyway

Aspects of Employment

Salaries
The legal minimum wage in Iceland is currently about 250 Icelandic krona per hour but this is subject to change. Men and women are paid at the same rate for the same work and skilled persons receive 20-30% more than unskilled workers. Wages are paid on an hourly basis for the first three months and then on a weekly or monthly basis. Incentive systems, bonus payments and piecework are practised in some industries so there can be considerable supplements for experienced workers. Excess payments above wage tariffs are also available in Iceland. Fishermen are given a minimum wage guarantee but also enjoy a percentage of the share of the catch. Foreign nationals can transfer up to 40% of their total wages into foreign currency during the first two years of working in Iceland. After that the same rules apply as for Icelandic citizens.

Working Conditions
The average working week is 40 hours spread over five days. In practice many Icelanders work much longer than this to make ends meet. Overtime is frequently worked in the fish processing industry. The minimum holiday allowance is 24 working days after a year's service. Workers have the right to two paid days leave for every month of work.

Trade Unions
Whilst the majority of the workforce belong to trade unions or employer organisations strikes are rare and major manufacturing industries have remained unaffected by them. Union membership costs between 0.8 and 2% of wages and foreign nationals are advised to contact the shop steward or trade union office on starting work.

Women at Work
A tradition of holding the fort whilst the men are away at sea has produced a strong race of women who are frequently compared to the mythological Valkyrie, the handmaidens of Odin who selected heroes to be slain in battle. Iceland has the first ever democratically elected woman president and the first ever Women's Party in the world and, as you would expect, Iceland has a good record on women's rights. Women are well represented in all sectors of society and seven out of ten women have jobs.

Business and Industry Report

Iceland has very few natural resources and is heavily reliant on imports for its largely consumerist society. What follows is a round up of some of the major industries:

Fishing and the Fish Industry

Iceland is the world's fifth largest fishing nation and exports 97% of its catch in the form of frozen, canned and salted fish and as seafood products like cod liver oil. This amounts to about 80% of the country's total exports and accounts for about one quarter of the gross national product. Capelin and cod comprise the bulk of the catches. About 11% of the workforce is employed in fishing or fish processing.

The industry has been affected adversely in recent years by over fishing and declining fish stocks in the northern seas which have led to a vessel quota system being introduced. Whilst the cost of buying the right to catch has risen in recent years, a fleet's total quota for cod has been cut by 40%. Nonetheless, Iceland expects the fishing industry to benefit considerably by the substantial reductions on tariffs and removal of trade barriers following membership of the EEA. Iceland will also stand to gain a more fluid access to Japanese and US seafood and fishing technology markets.

Farming

About 5% of Icelanders are employed in agriculture. With only 1% of Iceland being used for cultivation and a further 20% for grazing, huge tracts of Iceland are wasteland. Sheep form the bulk of the livestock at 487,000 and lamb is the main agricultural export. There are currently about 4,000 working farms in Iceland but many of them are feeling the economic pinch — overproduction of lamb and milk has led to the imposition of a quota system and small farms in particular are ceasing to be viable. Many farmers are diversifying into the fish (river) and fur (fox and mink) markets. In this age of environmental awareness, Iceland is hoping to cash in on the fact that the majority of its agriculture is organic and produced in an almost pollution free environment. Market gardening in the southwest provides Iceland with locally grown fruit and vegetables.

Tourism

With a recent increase of 21.3%, tourism is a rare boom area in Iceland. In regularly efficient fashion the Icelanders are preparing to market their natural resources of spectacular scenery and an unspoiled environment to visitors in search of something different. Many farmers are taking advantage of the growth in tourism by offering farmhouse accommodation — there are currently 131 farms offering accommodation throughout the country. They are also offering walking, fishing, horse riding and other tourist related activities. Tourism is Iceland's third-largest currency-earning industry.

Manufacturing

About 12% of the population work in manufacturing. Iceland has been driven by economic necessity to diversify into different manufacturing areas and as well as woollen goods has begun to export natural resources of spring water, lava, and pumice for the building industries. The power-intensive industries of aluminium, ferrosilicon and diatomite account for 15% of the national exports. Iceland has developed and manufactured equipment for the fishing industry which has proved popular with overseas buyers.

Power Resources

Iceland currently obtains 85% of its power from hydroelectric and geothermal sources and over 90% of economically feasible energy is still unharnessed. Iceland is actively seeking overseas environmentally aware investors and currently both Norway and Switzerland have established energy processing plants on the island. For further details contact the Icelandic Energy Marketing Unit (Háaleitisbraut 68,103 Reykjavik, Iceland; tel 1-5600700, fax 1-5686085).

Conferences

Reykjavík is equidistant from Moscow and Washington — a fact that was made much of when Ronald Reagan and Mikhail Gorbachev met there for a summit meeting which was to have important reverberations for East-West relations. For once, Iceland's geographical position was working to the country's advantage and Iceland has been trying to promote itself as a conference centre ever since. Many major companies are now taking advantage of Iceland's unusual and attractive location and Iceland's key hotels all offer conference facilities. The main company dealing in conferences is Iceland Incentives inc (Hamraborg 1-3, 200 Kópavogur; tel 1-5541400, fax 1-5541472).

Starting a Business

As a relative newcomer to the European economic arena, facilities for starting a business in Iceland are less developed than in other EU countries. Nonetheless, as Iceland becomes increasingly active in the worldwide network of business and trade and increases participation in the global business sector it is expected that opportunities for investments and trade with Iceland will increase. In response to this, the publishers Iceland Review launched the quarterly English language magazine *Business Iceland* in January 1994 which provides excellent coverage of the state of the business art in Iceland. To subscribe contact Iceland Business (Höfðabakki 9, 112 Reykjavík, Iceland; tel 1-5675700, fax 1-5674066).

Procedures Involved in Buying or Starting a New Business

Every new company in Iceland must obtain an identification number from the Statistical Bureau. The current fee is ISK 5,000. Companies must also obtain a VAT number from the tax authorities. Most companies will also need to obtain a trading licence before beginning operations.

Useful Addresses
Directorate of Internal Revenue: Laugavegur 166, 150 Reykjavík; tel 1-5631100.
Statistical Bureau of Iceland: Skuggasund 3, 150 Reykjavík; tel 1-5609800.

Foreign Investments
Since 1991 the rules on foreign direct investment in Iceland have been both liberalised and simplified. Non-residents can make portfolio investments in quoted stocks and bonds and there are no restrictions on money transfers in relation to such investments.

Iceland's membership of the EEA means that the flow of goods, capital, services and the labour force are now much freer than they were previously although some restrictions still apply: foreigners cannot invest in the fishing, fish processing or energy sectors and foreign investment in banking is currently limited to 25%, whilst investment in aviation is limited to 49%. If total foreign investment in any sector of the economy exceeds 25% of the total investment in that sector a licence is required. This also applies if an investment exceeds ISK 250 million. There are no restrictions on buying into the transport, retail, oil or industrial industries other than those laid down in general or sector-specific legislation. All monetary caps were dissolved on 1 January 1995 and as of this date capital movements to and from Iceland are unrestricted. Drawbacks for foreign investors include the small home market and the distance from major export markets.

Business Structures
There are four basic types of companies in Iceland: joint stock-owned companies, cooperative societies, partnerships and personal firms. There are also branches of foreign companies. Joint-stock companies must have at least two founders. The minimum authorised capital is ISK 400,000, half of which must be paid in at the time of registration. The registration fee is ISK 100,000. Cooperative societies must be registered with the Registry of Cooperative Societies and partnerships and personal firms must be registered with the local sheriff. All must obtain an ID number and a VAT number. Branches of foreign companies must be registered with the Company Register (for joint-stock companies) or the local sheriff (other kinds of companies). The registration fee is ISK 50,000.

Finance
There are a number of financial institutions in Iceland offering financial backing. The Islandsbanki Group offers a full range of commercial bank services to private, institutional and corporate customers both domestically and internationally. The Industrial Loan Fund (*Iðnlanasjoður*) is an independent establishment operating as an investment loan bank. It is the biggest provider of credit to the Icelandic industrial sector. The Icelandic Industrial Development Fund (Iðnþrounarsjodður) grants medium and long-term investment loans to companies of all kinds and sizes.

Useful Addresses
The Central Bank of Iceland: Kalkofnsvegur 1, 150 Reykjavík; tel 1-5676666, fax 1-5621802.

The Industrial Development Fund: Kalkofnsvegur 1, Reykjavík; tel 1-5699990, fax 1-5629992.

The Industrial Loan Fund: Armúli 13a, 155 Reykjavík; tel 1-5680400, fax 1-5680950.

Islandsbaki: International Department, Armúli 7, 155 Reykjavík; tel 1-5608500, fax 1-5687784.

Investment Incentives
Icelandic law does not provide for any particular tax incentives for foreign businesses.

Ideas for New Businesses
Iceland's manufacturing base is small and the country is heavily dependent on imports. Clothing, cosmetics and food are some of the main imports. The Department of Trade and Industry identifies the following as promising sectors for foreign trade: clothing and textiles, food, insurance, tourism, construction and telecommunications.

Running A Business

The labour force is well-educated, skilled and the majority speak excellent English. Icelandic workers are entitled to terms and wages arranged by collective agreement of the organisation regardless of sex, race, nationality or length of service. Individual agreements made by workers and employers which grant less favourable remuneration or worse conditions are invalid.

Under Icelandic law, an employer can stop work and payment to workers for an unspecified period under special circumstances (e.g. when raw material is unavailable but without breaking off the contract of engagement). This rule applies particularly to the fishing industry but a special provision in the wages and terms agreements means that an employee who has served uninterruptedly for three months will be paid a fixed engagement agreement. Notice to end a fixed employment agreement is four weeks by both parties.

The average working day is eight hours but overtime is frequent. Under law, every worker is entitled to a minimum of ten hours rest in every 24-hour period. This can be abridged to eight hours if an exemption is granted by the Administration of Occupational Health and Safety.

Workers are entitled to two days paid leave for each month worked. So the minimum holiday period for a year's work is 24 working days. Normally the holiday entitlement is taken in one lump between 2 May and 15 September. The minimum, vacation allowance is 10.17% of the wages.

To qualify for unemployment benefit an employee should be resident in Iceland and have worked at least 425 hours and have made obligatory insurance payments. Allowances are calculated on the wages of an eight hour day for the common labourer. Unemployment insurance is financed by the employer and the Treasury. Self-employed individuals who become unable to continue their business operations, are unemployed and seeking employment can receive unemployment benefit.

Sickness and Accident benefits are paid at a variable rate, depending on length of service. The minimum entitlement for the employee is two days unabridged wages in respect of each month of work. If an employee is still unable to work they can claim from the State Social Security Institute.

Contribution to an annuity fund is compulsory. The fund pays old-age pensions, invalidity benefits and sometimes spouse and children's annuity, according to the terms of the fund. Wage earners contribute 4% of their earnings and employers 6%.

Taxation

For purposes of taxation, corporations, cooperatives and partnerships which are chartered in Iceland or whose management is located in Iceland are regarded as residents of Iceland. The taxable base for all resident corporations is the net income. Non-resident corporations are subject to income tax on their net taxable income from Icelandic sources and are also subject to taxation on their net worth if their assets are used to earn taxable income in Iceland. Rates for state net worth tax are the same as those of resident companies. The recent income tax rate for corporations was 33% and 41% for partnerships. The Icelandic tax year corresponds to the calendar year and corporate tax returns with supporting documentation must be sent to the tax authorities before 31 May of the assessment year. There are no general provisions for group taxation on groups of companies under Icelandic law. Municipal tax is only levied on the income of individuals.

All businesses trading in taxable goods are subject to VAT, of which the general rate is 24.5%. Non-residents without a fixed place of business in Iceland should appoint a local representative. Enterprises whose annual turnover is less than ISK 185,200 or whose sole business is the sale of VAT exempt goods may qualify for VAT exemption.

For further details consult the booklets *Taxes in Iceland — An Overview* and *Value added tax in Iceland — An Overview* available from the Directorate of Internal Revenue (Laugavegur 166, 105 Reykjavík; tel 1-5631100, fax 1-5624440), or from the Embassy.

Accountancy and Legal Advice
Anyone intending to do business in Iceland should seek specialist accountancy and legal advice from firms with branches in Iceland. The acountancy firm Ernst and Young have a branch in Reykjavik. Contact: Endurskodun Radgjöf HF (Ernst and Young, Skeifan 11A, PO Box 8693, 108 Reykjavik; tel 1-5685511, fax 1-5689585). The following English-speaking law firms deal with acquisition of commercial property and commercial law:

Tryggvason and Jónsson: Tjarnargata 10d, PO Box 1067, 121 Reykjavkík; tel 1-5517752, fax 1-5637019.

Sigurdur Georgsson: Lágmúli 7, 5H, 108 Reykjavík; tel 1-5532110, fax 1-5678720.

T S Gunnarsson: Armuli 17, PO Box 8807, 128 Reykjavík; 1-5681588, fax 1-5681151.

Useful Addresses
Jordan and Sons Ltd: 21 St Thomas Street, Bristol, BS1 6JS; tel 0117-9230600, fax 0117-9230063, offers help and advice to individuals setting up in business abroad.

Icelandic Chamber of Commerce: Hús verslunárinnar, Kringlan 7,103 Reykjavík; tel 1-5676666, fax 1-5686564.

Trade Council of Iceland: Hallveigarstígur 1, 101 Reykjavík; tel 1-5517272, 1-5517222.

Norway

SECTION I

Living in Norway

General Introduction
Residence and Entry Regulations
Setting Up Home
Daily Life
Retirement

General Introduction

Destination Norway

Set on the edge of the North Sea and the Arctic Ocean, Norway often seems to be more of a European outpost than a fully paid up European country. This is hardly surprising — geographically Norway is separated from mainland Europe by a narrow strip of water, it lies in northerly latitudes and its most southern tip barely reaches down as far as the far north of Scotland. Politically and economically too, Norway has retained a certain independence from Europe and this was particularly apparent in the November 1994 referendum when a narrow majority opted to stay out of the European Union despite the fact that Norway joined the European Economic Area in January of the same year.

Reasons for voting against joining the European Union tended to have a more idealistic basis than an economic one. Norwegians see themselves as a unique country which does not relish being told what to do by the bureaucrats of Brussels. Centuries of domination by Denmark and later Sweden have left the Norwegians wary of outside interference in their country and there is also a strong sense of the need to preserve national identity and culture. Much of the opposition came from Norway's traditional farming and fishing communities who were anxious to protect their livelihood. Even though the fishing and farming contribution to the economy is relatively small there was a lot of support throughout the country for protecting the traditional rights of the small individual. As the country itself is rich in oil and gas resources Norway is in a position to stay self-sufficient for the time being and can exist quite easily without the financial backing of the EU.

However, it would be a mistake to see Norway as an isolationist country that is constantly casting suspicious glances over its shoulder. Norway is a highly developed nation with enlightened socialist leanings and an excellent welfare state. The small population of 4.3 million Norwegians have enjoyed a disproportionate amount of national wealth thanks to discoveries of oil and gas resources in the second part of the twentieth century. Norway is over 1,000 miles/1,600 km long but twentieth century communications have meant that a country which was once divided by mountains into isolated, tiny farming communities is now a highly-organised, fully modernised, efficient European state whose inhabitants enjoy one of the highest standards of living in the world.

Even so, Norway and the Norwegian way of life remain largely unknown to many outsiders. If pressed on what they know about Norway, some might mention the dramatist Ibsen or the composer Grieg, others the painter Munch or the famous explorers Amundsen and Heyerdahl. A few might know Norway as the home of the Nobel Peace Prize giving ceremony (although Nobel himself was Swedish), and others might recall beautiful fjords, the stomach churning height of the ski jump at Holmenkollen or Winter Olympics at Lillehammer. But overall Norway tends to be something of an unknown quantity to many Europeans. In some ways this adds to Norway's attractions — with all its modern amenities, Norway can seem like a home from home whilst being somewhere entirely different. If you would enjoy a change of scene yet want to go somewhere highly civilised, Norway might be worth considering.

Pros and Cons of Moving to Norway

Historically the Norwegians have earned a reputation for being less than welcoming to foreign workers and there has been a general ban on immigration to Norway since 1975. Until Norway's membership of the European Economic Area (EEA) in January 1994 gaining a work or residence permit in Norway was very difficult (although exceptions were made for specialist skilled workers for the oil and gas industry) and this situation still holds for non-EEA nationals.

Yet Norwegians are far from being insular and narrow-minded towards foreigners *per se*. Few European nations are as generous, welcoming and friendly although the Norwegians are usually rather less effusive when showing it than their southern European counterparts. Reasons for keeping a fairly closed door policy are more likely to lie in history and economics rather than mere insularity. Until the second half of the present century life in Norway was a hard battle to gain a subsistence level of existence from poor unyielding soil and a valley in Norway could rarely support more than one or two farming families. Like their Viking ancestors, many Norwegians turned west in search of opportunity and wealth, and the 19th century saw a mass emigration of over 750,000 Norwegians to America. In present day Norway there is a strong environmental awareness and concern about overcrowding and encroachment on the country's beautiful green spaces.

One of the main drawbacks which immediately strikes foreigners who take up work in Norway is the hefty cost of living. There are many reasons for this — heavy farming subsidies, high taxes and the cost of importing being a few. Whilst wages are correspondingly good generally, opportunities for saving in Norway are diminished by high costs — food and drink in particular are very expensive. Set against this is a country with excellent social and welfare services, a very low crime rate and some of the most stunning scenery in Europe. English is widely and excellently spoken throughout Norway and amongst all sectors of the population with the possible exception of the elderly. However, not being able to speak Norwegian could adversely affect your job prospects. Whilst the rules of the European Economic Area grant the right to all member nationals to look for work in all member countries, this does not affect the individual employer's right to hire or not to hire.

Norway is considerably less geared towards employing foreigners than mainstream Europe and finding work and accommodation can be more of a struggle than in other parts of Europe. There are opportunities, however, and the North Sea oil fields off Norway's western coast have provided wealth and work opportunities for the British, Americans and French in particular. The Norwegians claim to have a special affection for the British although they are less than happy about pollution, specifically the acid rain, which blows over from Britain. This is quite a sore point — in 1987 when the then British Prime Minister Margaret Thatcher visited Oslo the police had to mobilise the riot squad for the first time ever because of protesters about acid rain.

Norwegians are great lovers of folklore and nature and the 4.3 million population has a lot of it to enjoy. Of all the Scandinavian countries, Norway has the most glorious scenery which is ever changing and always stunning. Sports and the Great Outdoors are very important in Norway and this holds true all year round. Set against the natural beauty assets of Norway is the fact that the country is in a relatively northern position which can lead to dark, snow-laden winters.

Below is a summary of the main pros and cons of moving to Norway:

Pros: Strong economy.
Excellent social security system.
High standard of living.
English widely spoken.
Friendly, helpful people.
Glorious scenery.
Open Access to the job market for EEA nationals.

Cons: Very high cost of living.
Not as geared to employing and housing foreigners as the rest of Europe.
Very long distances to travel between places.
Long, dark and cold winters.
High taxes.
Difficult for nationals of non-EEA countries to get work.

Political and Economic Structure

Until the discovery of North Sea oil in the 1960s both weather and terrain have had a powerful influence on Norway's development as a nation. As an outpost on the northern North sea, Norway has played a relatively low-key role in international affairs and only truly emerged onto the European scene in the second half of this century.

Recorded history of Norway begins only in about 800 AD but the Norwegians are probably the oldest nation in Europe whose ancestors descend from a race whose origins predate classical Greece. Until about 500 BC most Norwegians were migratory hunters but a deteriorating climate led to the development of settled communal farming. From this, small communities emerged which were democratic in nature and by the eighth century, Norway comprised a number of small independent kingdoms which were isolated from each other by the mountainous terrain. Mercantile attractions to the west led to the Norwegian Vikings pillaging their way across Britain and Ireland in the eighth century and moving further west into Iceland.

Christianity was brought to Norway in the 12th century although early paganism lingered until after the Reformation. The Hanseatic League was formed during the Middle Ages and in Norway operated principally from the harbour of the then capital, Bergen. The League was a chain of European and Baltic cities with shared trading agreements — an early forerunner of the European Community. Squabbles over succession to the Norwegian throne were a constant feature of medieval Norway and the arrival of the Black Death in 1349 devastated Norwegian farming communities and decimated the nobility. A period of comparative stability was brought to Norway and all Scandinavia when Norway, Sweden and Denmark were united in 1397 by Magareta, widow of King Håkon of Denmark who persuaded Norway and Sweden to hand over their crowns to her five-year-old nephew Erik.

The union was beset by difficulties and Norway came increasingly under Danish influence and in 1536 was relegated to a humble Danish province. The union with Denmark survived until 1814 when, following the defeat of Denmark in the Napoleonic Wars, Norway became united with Sweden. Initially this was an uneasy alliance, with Norway subservient to Sweden. The 19th century saw a period of domestic reform and economic growth in Norway, the country prospered and by the late 19th century it had the third largest merchant navy. Overpopulation in rural areas lead to widespread emigration to America.

The tide of nationalism of the late 19th century swept through Norway and in 1905 a plebiscite voted overwhelmingly for dissolution of the union. Norway was declared an independent monarchy and in 1905 Håkon VII was elected to the throne as the titular head of state.

Although Norway remained neutral in World War I the economy was crippled by a rise in state expenditure and soaring inflation at the end of the war. Unemployment and industrial disputes led to the rise of the Norwegian Labour Party which came to power in the 1920s and has remained a powerful political force in Norwegian affairs to the present. Norway wanted to remain neutral throughout World War II but Nazi invasion, aided and abetted by the treachery of Defence Minister Vidkun Quisling, brought Norway under Nazi Occupation. King Håkon abdicated and fled to Britain where he worked with the Norwegian exile movement. With the surrender of Germany in May 1945, he returned with his son Crown Prince Olav to tumultuous reception which sealed the popularity of the monarchy in Norway.

After the war, Norway had to face the devastating effects of the Nazi's retreating scorched-earth policy which had burned and rased many towns and villages in northern Norway. A programme of rebuilding began, industry was expanded and modernised and the standard of living rose faster than in most other European countries. The drilling in the North Sea oil fields in the 1970s led Norway into a period of unprecedented prosperity and the Socialist government introduced a comprehensive social welfare programme and reinvested wealth from the oil fields into the welfare state. Post-war Norwegian socialism has been mainly middle-of-the-road creating an equal society from which everyone can benefit.

Economy

Norway operates as a free-market economy. Over 95% of industrial companies have less than 100 employees but these account for half of the industrial labour force and for more than half of production. Foreign companies account for about 10% of production. Only a few larger industries are state owned but Government businesses account for nearly half of the GDP. The largest company in Norway, Statoil, is 100% state owned and Nordsk Hydro is 51% state owned. Agriculture is strongly subsidised, fishing is to a lesser extent and the government actively participates in the oil industry. Norway is particularly rich in natural resources of which the most important are oil, gas, hydroelectric power, metals, forestry and fish. Hydroelectric power from Norway's numerous natural water sources forms the basis of much of the electricity which powers Norwegian industry. In 1993 foreign sales accounted for an impressive 43% of the GDP.

Only about 3.5% of Norway's elongated landmass is cultivated. Most farms are small family affairs with less than 1% having more than 125 acres. The main agricultural product is livestock. The country has over three million hens, just over a million sheep and nearly a million cattle. The majority of agricultural land (56%) is used for mowing and pasture lands and the principal crops are grain, peas, oil seed, potatoes and root crops. The most fertile food growing area is in the south. Given the inauspicious climate and poor growing conditions it is remarkable that, Norway is self-sufficient in livestock products and produces an impressive 59% of its own food. This is done mainly by huge subsidies — 10% of the national budget goes on farming subsidies and much of this is spent on small farms which are not economically viable.

About one third of Norway consists of forests which provide the basis of the wood processing industry. Wood is a small but important export commodity in Norway and about 22.9% of the land area in use in Norway is productive forest area. Half of Norwegian farms depend on forestry as a second source of income.

The paper and pulp industry, of which the forests form the basis, has been a growth export area for Norway.

Fishing plays a similar role for farmers as forestry. Only half of Norway's fishermen claim fishing as their sole occupation and many farmers fish as a seasonal occupation. With an extensive coastline and multiple varieties of North Sea fish, fish is staple fare in Norway with cod being the most prolific catch. Only about one third of the haul is for human consumption with the rest being processed as fish meal and oil. Fish and fish related products account for over 14% of traditional commodity exports per year.

The shipping industry has traditionally played an important part in the Norwegian economy. After considerable set-backs, bankruptcies and closures in the late 1980s the shipping market in Norway has taken an upward turn and Norway now has one of the world's largest merchant fleets. Norwegian shipping giants Kvaerner have become the world's third largest ship owners.

The Norwegian economy experienced huge growth following the discovery of the Ekofisk oil and gas fields in 1969. North Sea Oil brought considerable wealth to Norway's 4.3 million population. In the 1970s oil and gas became the most important exports and by the 1980s rivalled the total value of traditional commercial exports. Money from the oil and gas fields was injected into Norway's declining industry, into the welfare, education and the transport systems leading to a consequent increase in the standard of living. Like Britain, Norway was hit hard by the 1986 oil crisis and experienced 6% unemployment and many bankruptcies. One of the problems facing the Norwegian economy is the need to promote and develop the traditional commodity exports and knowledge-based industries to prevent overdependence on the oil reserves. The government has responded by instituting a queue system for oil and gas developments. 64,000 Norwegians still work in the oil sector.

An offshoot of the oil and gas industries has been a boost in the engineering industry. About one third of manufacturing is the production of equipment for the petroleum industry. Electrical equipment, electronics and telecommunications also play a significant part in the Norwegian economy.

Norway spends more money per capita on foreign aid than any other country. Unemployment in Norway is currently about 7% (including people on job creation schemes), relatively high for a Scandinavian country, but the country has a shortage of specialised workers and, particularly in the oil industry, is dependent on expertise from abroad. Inflation is relatively low at less than 2% and has remained fairly stable.

Government

Norway has a constitutional monarchy and a multiparty political system. The parliament or *Storting* has 165 members who sit in two chambers — the *Odelsting* and the *Lagting*. Members are democratically elected every four years and the Prime Minister and State Council are nominally selected by the monarch with the approval of the *Storting*.

The monarch's role is as symbolic head of state and the current king, King Harald V has reigned since 1991. The role is an exclusively male affair as the constitution allows succession only through the male line. Generally the Norwegian monarchy is low key and popular with pomp and ceremony being kept to a minimum.

The Norwegian constitution was drafted in 1814 when Norway and Denmark dissolved a 434-year-old union. Eclectic in nature, the constitution draws on British political traditions, the US constitution and the notions of Liberty, Equality, Fraternity, embodied in the ideals of the French revolution. Amendments can be made to the constitution by a two thirds majority in the *Storting*.

Candidates for the *Storting* are nominated from each of Norway's 19 counties or *fylker* and the number of candidates representing each *fylke* depends on the size of its population. From before World War II to the mid 1960s Norwegian politics have been dominated by the *Norske Arbeiderpartiet (DNA)* Labour party. This was followed by a series of coalition governments in which no single party held a majority. In the present *Storting* (1993-1997) the Labour Party holds the majority of seats with 67, followed by The Centre Party (32),The Conservative Party (28), The Socialist Left (13), The Christian Democrats (13), The Progress Party (10), The Red Electoral Alliance (1) and The Liberal Party (1).

The Grand Lady of Norwegian Satespersonship is the highly popular Labour Prime Minister, Mrs Gro Harlem Brundtland, who was Norway's first Norwegian woman prime minister.

Norway is a member of NATO, the Council of Europe and the European Free Trade Area. In a 1972 referendum Norway voted against joining the European Community, opposition coming largely from among farmers and fishermen who feared the loss of subsidies, but there was also opposition from young urban professionals who saw joining as a threat to national identity. The result was Norway opposed joining by 52.5% The country reconsidered membership in the autumn of 1994. The referendum then produced an almost identical narrow majority against joining (52.2%) as the 1972 one. Even the fact that the Swedes decided to join the EU had no impact on the attitude of the Norwegians towards membership. Euroscepticiscm and a traditional independence, as well as a sense of security from the reserves of the North Sea oil and gas were the main reasons behind Norway's opting out, but many industrialists have expressed concern about the future implications for Norway's activities in the commercial world. In addition to this Norway will have limited bargaining power in seeking concessions from the European Union and there are fears that the country may suffer from isolation over international issues of trade and the environment.

Geographical Information

Area

Norway occupies a total area of 150,000 sq miles/386,958 sq km including Spitzbergen (Svalberd), the remote northern islands which lie 400 miles (640 km) north of the mainland. Norway is approximately the size of the United Kingdom or the former west Germany and comprises an elongated, thin landmass resembling a tadpole in shape with the broader southern tip as the head. At over 1,000 miles/1,600 km long, the country would reach Rome if it was pivoted on Oslo and is so long that the weather maps on the nation's TV screens divide the country in two. In places however, it is less than five miles wide. Western Norway has a jagged, fjord indented coastline which measures 4,300 miles/2,650 km (excluding the fjords) and is studded with about 50,000 tiny islands. The country stretches from latitude 57° 57'N at Kristiansand to 71° 11'N at the North Cape and about half of the country lies above the Arctic Circle.

Norway is a neighbour of Sweden (they share a 1,000 mile/1, 619 km border) and Finland in the North. Norway's non-Scandinavian neighbour, the former Soviet Union, shares the Spitzbergen islands with Norway in a fairly easy relationship.

About two thirds of Norway's terrain is mountainous — the average elevation is 1,600 feet compared with an average of 1,000 feet for Europe as a whole. Traditionally this has made transport and communication difficult and accounts for the fact that even today many farms are isolated in valleys. The Hardanger plateau in Southern Norway is Europe's largest mountain plateau covering 4,600 square miles/11,900 square km. Large areas of Norway are covered in forest but the soil is poor agricultural land.

Population

Norway is the fifth largest country in Europe but has the second lowest population density after Iceland. With just over 4.3 million inhabitants Norway has approximately 34 inhabitants per square mile/13 per square km. About 473,000 people (11% of the total population) live in Oslo. Other main cities' estimated populations are: Bergen 218,000, Trondheim 140,000 and Stavanger 101,000. The majority of the population lives in the south and the far north is very thinly populated. Low birth rates have reduced population growth but an increasing proportion of the population is elderly because of low death rates and high longevity.

The north of Norway is home to 90% of the 20,000 Lapps or Sami population of Norway. The Lapps form an ethnic minority whose culture and language differ widely from the rest of Norway. There are very few truly nomadic reindeer herders left amongst the Lapps and only about 2,000 of them live on the Finnmark Plateau. Despite this the Lapps have clung fiercely to their own identity and in 1989 were granted their own parliament the *Sametinget*.

Norway has historically operated a fairly open door policy towards refugees and visitors to Norway are often surprised that this land of mainly blond, blue-eyed people has a surprising multi-cultural mix of races and religions. Although it has had a particularly good record on granting refuge to refugees, Norway is currently operating a very strict immigration policy.

Climate

As you would expect, Norway is not the best place to go for a sun tan — its northerly position militates against that — nonetheless, it is a mistake to lump the whole of Norway together as a cold northern country. Its length means that there is considerable variation in climate. Norway is warmer than its northern position should warrant owing to the benevolent effect of the Gulf Stream which means that the fjords do not, as a rule, freeze over even in the far North. The west coast experiences an average annual temperature of 7°C/45°F and the Lofoten Islands which fall inside the Arctic Circle experience well above average winter temperatures for the latitude because of warm southerly air currents.

The west coast of Norway experiences frequent gales and weather changes because of North Atlantic cyclones. It has fairly cool summers, mild winters and up to 80 inches/2030 mm of rain. Eastern Norway is more sheltered because of the mountains and summers are relatively warm whilst winters are cold. Average rainfall for the east is less than 30 inches a year. In the far north, winters are long, snowy, cold and dark and summers are brief, bright and surprisingly warm. Temperatures around Oslo are mild thanks to the Gulf Stream but it can be dark and bleak in winter. Average temperatures in the main cities are: Oslo 5.9°C, Bergen 7.8° C, Trondheim 5.2°C, Bodø 4.6°C, Tromsø 2.9°C.

There is usually plenty of snow throughout the country in winter and skiing is as much a means of local transport as it is a sport. It is sometimes joked that Norwegians are born wearing skis and the oldest pair of skis found in Norway dates back 2,600 years. Generally the road transport is good even in winter — centuries of bad weather have taught the Norwegians a thing or two about keeping the roads open; but inevitably some of the minor roads may be closed.

Midnight Sun and Northern Lights

With so much of the country within the Arctic Circle, northern Norway experiences a considerable amount of midnight sun. From 13 May to 29 July the midnight sun is visible from the North Cape (Nordkapp). The further south you go, the less it is experienced but generally summers in Norway have very long hours of daylight and in winter correspondingly long hours of night. Adjusting to these extremities takes time and even Norwegians experience difficulty sleeping in the long summer nights. Long hours of darkness in winter can lead to seasonal depression although reflections from the snow can make things lighter than they normally would be.

The northern lights (a.k.a. aurora borealis), can be seen in the north in winter. Viewing is often better just below the Arctic Circle than above it. The lights appear as shimmering colours of light in a clear night sky. The usual colour is green but they can be red and yellow too.

The following table gives average monthly temperatures and precipitation throughout the year (courtesy of Statistics Norway, the Royal Ministry of Foreign Affairs, Norway):

Average Temperatures Degrees Centigrade

Month	Oslo	Bergen	Trondheim	Tromsø
January	−4.7	1.5	−3.1	−3.5
February	−4.0	1.3	2.6	−4.0
March	−0.5	3.1	0.4	−2.7
April	4.8	5.8	3.5	0.3
May	10.7	10.2	8.2	4.1
June	14.7	12.6	11.6	8.8
July	17.3	15.0	14.7	12.4
August	15.9	14.7	13.6	11.0
September	11.3	12.0	9.8	7.2
October	5.9	8.3	5.4	3.0
November	−1.1	5.5	1.8	−0.1
December	−2.0	3.3	−0.7	−1.9

Average Rainfall in mm
Month Oslo Bergen Trondheim Tromsø
January 49 193 57 96
June 71 135 68 59

For more immediate information about the weather in Norway contact the Norwegian Weather Bureau (*Meterologisk Insitut, Klima-avdelingen*, Niels Henriks Abels Vei 40, 0371 Oslo; tel 22 96 30 00).

Regional Guide

Norway is a large country with a small population. The mountainous terrain which divides region from region can account for the fact that neighbours in the next valley may speak a different dialect and will be regarded as slightly foreign. In the past, rural families tended to be isolated and self-sufficient, cut off in a valley whose soil was not good enough to support more than one or two farms. Today Norwegians still appreciate having plenty of space and towns tend to be small and are spread out throughout the country. In the north the Sami people do not acknowledge national boundaries and move freely between Norway, Sweden, Finland and the former Soviet Union.

Norway is arguably the most attractive of the Scandinavian countries and after Iceland the most spectacular. Lakes, valleys, mountains, forests and fjords often feature within the same breathtaking panorama.

The country can be divided into the following regions:

Østlandet (Eastern Norway)

Øtlandet contains more than half of Norway's population most of whom live in the capital city of Oslo. Oslo itself is vast, comprising 454 square kilometres of which only a small proportion is city, the rest being taken up with areas of forest, beach and water. Oslo is bounded on the east by Oslomarka — an area of seven adjoining forests which is larger than greater London. The land extending south eastwards towards the Swedish border is relatively fertile lowland which is intensely cultivated for cereal grains. Forests in this area form a significant proportion of farm acreage and the region has just over half of Norway's total forest resources and fully cultivated land. The southern coastline of the Øtlandet which faces across to Denmark is densely populated with small towns and coastal villages, the most significant of which is the city of Kristiansand on the southern tip of Norway.

Vestlandet (Western Norway) and the Fjord Country

The narrow coastal zone of south western Norway is characterised by a jagged coastline of fjords cutting into the mountainous region of the main land. It contains Norway's two major cities of Stavanger and Bergen. The Jaeren Plain south of Stavanger is exceptionally fertile because of mild winters and long growing seasons. Stavanger itself is a major industrial centre built on a fjord. Once predominantly known for its fish canning industry, Stavanger became wealthy on the oil riches of the North Sea and was in danger of becoming the Dallas of Norway but it has remained an attractive well-preserved city thanks to money being invested in restoration as well as in local industry and social services. Stavanger marks the beginning of the Fjord Country which stretches north to the great Hardanger Fjord, encompassing Bergen, the Fjord capital, past the Sognfjord and Nordfjord to the less well known Geirangerfjord. Bergen, about 100 miles north of Stavanger is the former capital of Norway and is a beautiful city built on seven hills around a harbour. Once a major trading centre for northern Europe, Bergen operated as the hub of the German Hanseatic League. Today it is the most cosmopolitan town of Norway although many Norwegians feel that the Bergenese suffer from an inflated sense of their own importance and have never quite resigned themselves to the fact that Bergen is no longer the capital city. Further north from Bergen in the Sunnmore District with Ålesund at its centre is a major engineering area. Many large smelting plants are built on the Vestlandet fjords taking advantage of the hydroelectric resources of the area. This is also the centre for Norway's furniture industry.

Trondelag, Nordland and Troms

Standing just above the western fjords, Trondelag and Nordland are two long thin counties. Trondelag in the south represents the last contact with the gentler forested regions of the south and leads into Nordland where the Arctic Circle and the wilderness begin. The major town of Trondelag is Trondheim in the south, an attractive medieval town, which is Norway's third city and former home to the early Norse parliament. The major attraction today is the *Nidaros Domkirke*, a medieval cathedral and Scandinavia's largest surviving medieval building. South east of Trondheim is the marvellously preserved eighteenth century mining town of Røros. Northern Trondelag is scenic but thinly populated and leads into Nordland. At Mo-i-Rana just before the Arctic Circle is an enormous steel plant. From here towns are few and far between and the railway runs out at Fauske. To the northwest are the Lofoten Islands — a string of mountainous islands which are famous for their bird life. Adjacent to the Lofoten

Islands on the mainland is Narvik an important iron-ore town with an impressive, if not particularly attractive, industrial complex. During the war Narvik was heavily bombed by the Germans and many British soldiers lost their lives here. From Narvik the population becomes even more sparse and the only major town is Tromsø in the county of Troms. Variously called the Gateway to the Arctic and the Paris of the North, Tromsø is a large fishing town with four filleting factories, several museums and the world's most northern university and cathedral. From Tromsø it is possible to fly to Spitzbergen.

The Far North

Finnmark is Norway's most northerly county and its largest. Although it covers 15% of the entire country it is inhabited by just under 2% of the population. Despite being on the same latitude as Alaska and Siberia, Finnmark is easily accessible by car, public transport and domestic planes. Many of the towns, villages and farms of the region were burned by the German scorched earth policy at the end of World War II and were rapidly rebuilt and consequently look and are architecturally uninspiring. The biggest town is Alta with a population of 14,000 but the main attraction of Finnmark is the landmark of North Cape. Just South of Alta is Kautokeino, home to the largest Lapp community in the country. Between mid May and the end of July, Finnmark experiences up to 24 hours of daylight and between the end of November to the end of January it is in almost constant darkness. The landscape is a vast, sparsely populated wilderness of mountain ranges, fells and wild windswept coastline.

Spitsbergen

Spitsbergen, or Svalbard as it is known in Norway, consists of two main islands and many smaller islands 400 miles/640 km north of the mainland. It is just 600 miles/960km south of the North Pole and is surrounded by pack ice throughout the winter. The islands are rich in coal and have been mined since about 1900. Sovereignty over Spitzbergen was granted to Norway after World War I but Norway currently shares the islands with Russia. Spitzbergen is also home to the polar bear.

Residence and Entry Regulations

The Current Position

Since joining the European Economic Area Norway has been bound by the agreement of 1 January 1994 which states that all nationals of the European Union (EU) and the European Free Trade Area (EFTA) states have the right to live and work in any of the member countries. Citizens of member countries (Austria, Belgium, Denmark, Finland, Germany, Greece, Iceland, Ireland, Italy, Luxembourg, the Netherlands, Norway, Portugal, Spain, Sweden and the United Kingdom) are allowed to enter Norway with the intention of looking for work and do not need to secure a work permit before entering the country.

Since 1975 Norway has imposed a ban on immigration because of the rapid rise in foreign immigration figures preceding this year. Until its membership of the EEA, Norway operated extremely tight controls on foreigners wanting to work and live in Norway but all this is now set to change as Norway is coming to terms with the EEA agreement. There are currently nearly 200,000 foreigners living and working in Norway. The majority are Europeans (about 100,000) and the bulk of these are from other parts of Scandinavia. In principle, members of EEA states now have the same rights as Norwegian nationals as regards employment, wages and working conditions. Exceptions to this rule apply to certain public sector jobs such as police work.

Requirements for British Citizens

British citizens can enter Norway and stay for up to three months but if you are going with the intention of looking for work or to take up permanent residence you need to register with the police. Visas are not required for British Citizens entering Norway.

Entering To Work — EEA Members

Any EEA national can stay in Norway for up to three months to look for work but must be able to fully support themselves financially during this time. Given the high cost of living in Norway this is not something which should be entered into lightly and requires thought and forward planning.

If you do not find work within the three month period but would like to extend your stay in Norway you should report to the local police before the three month period expires. You may be expected to provide proof that you can continue to support yourself and the Norwegian authorities reserve the right to ask you to leave the country if you do not satisfy this condition. If you take up temporary or short-term work and your total stay in Norway does not exceed three months you will not need to apply for a residence permit and nor do you have to report to the police.

Residence Permit

Whilst work permits are no longer required for EEA nationals who live and work in Norway, residence permits are required for stays of more than three months. You can start work in Norway before you have obtained a formal residence permit. A residence permit is usually valid for up to five years but may be extended if the grounds on which it was granted still apply or can be shortened if you are not intending to stay for the whole period. For students a residence permit is usually granted for one year at a time and is renewable. When you find work you must apply for a residence permit. To do this go to the nearest police station and present your passport, two photographs, and a document of Confirmation of Employment (*ansettelsesbevis*) which your employer should provide or you can get one from the police station. You will be given an application form with instructions specifying the required documents. When your application has been processed you will be notified of the outcome by the police. If you apply through an embassy the procedure is the same but your application will be dealt with by the Directorate of Immigration (*Utlendingsdirektoratet*).

If you have a firm offer of employment which extends beyond three months before you arrive in Norway you can apply for a residence permit when you arrive. Again, you will need to go to your nearest local police station and present your passport, two photos and confirmation of employment.

You can also apply for a residence permit prior to departure for Norway — application forms can be obtained from embassies. If you already have a residence permit before arriving in Norway you should report to the local police within seven days of arriving. Family members of EEA nationals working in Norway are entitled to residence permits even if they themselves are not EEA nationals.

Commuting

If you work in Norway but are permanently domiciled in another EEA country and return to your country of origin once a week you will not be required to have a residence permit. You will, however, have to report to the local police within a week of the day your work in Norway started. If you spend a number of weeks working in Norway followed by a number of weeks in your home country you will still need a residence permit.

Residence in Norway

Any EEA national can live in Norway provided they can support themselves regardless of whether they work or not. This also applies to students and retired people. You must apply for a residence permit (see above) within three months of your arrival and you must provide additional proof that you are able to support yourself financially and that you have sufficient health insurance. You can also apply for a residence permit via your nearest embassy.

Entering to Start a Business

EEA Citizens have the right to establish or purchase businesses in Norway and professionals such as doctors, architects etc have the right to set up practice (for validation of professional qualifications see the *Employment* Chapter). In most cases a government permit is required and the enterprise should be registered. To register you should contact the Register of Business Enterprises (*Foretaksregisteret*). For further details see the chapter *Starting a Business*.

Self-Employment

EEA nationals have the right to acquire or establish a business in Norway on a self-employed basis but must comply with the usual regulations for setting up a business. See *Starting a Business*.

Providing a service

It is not necessary to start a business in Norway if you are intending to offer professional services such as those of a lawyer or architect but you must be prepared to submit details about the type of service you are offering, the length of time you are offering them for and provide proof that you will be receiving sufficient payment to support yourself whilst in Norway.

Unemployment Benefit

If you have been registered as unemployed in your home country for at least four weeks before coming to Norway you will be entitled to have your benefit paid to you in Norway. It should be borne in mind however that the cost of living is very high and you may not be able to live on the benefit of your home country.

Non-EEA nationals

Those seeking work in Norway from countries other than those of the European Economic Area will still have to face Norway's stringent laws on working and living in Norway. Normally you will need to have a firm offer of a job and a work permit before coming to Norway and it is forbidden to come to Norway with the intention of looking for work. The time required to process an application (usually done through the embassy) is about three months. Usually the work permit will limit you to working for a specific person or company, for a specific length of time and at a specific place. The employer must arrange or provide suitable accommodation and the employee must be physically fit and literate in their own native language. In the case of specialist skilled workers, particularly in the technical field, it may be possible to get a work permit whilst working within Norway and you should consult your prospective employer and nearest embassy.

Foreign nationals who are required to have a visa to enter Norway and who are granted a residence permit have the right to leave and return to Norway within the time for which the permit is valid.

If there is doubt about your eligibility for a residence permit your case will be dealt with by the Directorate of Immigration (*Utlendingsdirektoratet*), not the police.

If a residence permit is not granted, applicants may appeal in writing to the local police or the foreign Ministry. The appeal will be forwarded to the Ministry of Justice via the Directorate of Immigration.

Part-time Work

Usually to be classed as employed you will need to work at least half of a full-time position. If you work part-time you must be able to prove that you are earning enough to support yourself in Norway.

Nordic Nationals

Under the terms laid down by the Nordic Council, founded in 1952 all Nordic citizens (Norway, Sweden, Denmark, the Faroes, Iceland and Greenland) are granted the freedom to travel without passports and work without work permits in other Nordic countries.

Useful Addresses

The Norwegian Embassy: 25 Belgrave Square, London, SW1X 8QD; tel 0171-235 7151, fax 0171-245 6993.

The British Embassy: Thomas Heftyes gate 8, 0244 Oslo; 22 55 24 00, fax 22 55 10 41.

Utlendingsdirektoratet (Directorate of Immigration): Postboks 8180 Dep., N-0032 Oslo; tel 67 53 08 90.

Foretaksregisteret (The Register of Business Enterprises): Postboks 1400, N-8901 Brønnøysund; tel 75 02 20 22.

The Ministry of Industry and Energy: Postboks 8148 Dep, N-0033 Oslo; tel 22 34 90 90.

Setting Up Home

Moving to Norway is not so common an occurrence as moving to other parts of Europe — most notably the Mediterranean — and information on how to go about it is consequently thinner on the ground. Inevitably in such a long country, experiencing a variety of climatic and geographical features, it is hard to be too specific about how Norwegians live so what follows is a generalized picture.

How Do the Norwegians Live?

According to the United Nations Norwegians enjoy the highest quality of life in Europe and one of the highest per capita incomes. Thanks largely to the oil and gas reserves of the west coast a high standard of living is enjoyed by all sectors of society — the advanced social welfare system ensures this. Even small farms which would normally be struggling to survive make a decent living because of state subsidies. Society is largely consumerist with most households possessing the latest state of the art technology. Satellite and cable TV are available in many parts of the country and the video is transforming viewing habits in the north of Norway. Many Norwegians own two homes, one of which is the holiday hut or *hytte* which is often larger than the actual permanent home and used as a retreat where the Norwegians can get back to nature. Space is in large supply in Norway. The largest concentration of the population, 11%, live in and around Oslo, whilst the rest is divided over a broad region. The most thinly populated area is Finnmark in the North with 1.8% of the population. Whilst there are inevitably a number of cramped apartment blocks in Oslo, housing generally is spacious. The majority of Norwegians own their own home and the average number of persons per household is 2.4. Norway has a near 50% divorce rate and there are a striking number of single home-occupiers. First time young Norwegian buyers receive heavily subsidised home loans and it is not unusual for Norwegians to build their own homes.

Accommodation

Many of the more casual, seasonal or voluntary jobs will provide their own accommodation — this is the norm in farm work, hotel work and au pair work. Workers recruited by recruitment agencies for engineering and technical work will usually have access to a Norwegian representative at the place of work who will put them in touch with landlords. In sectors where a large number of foreign workers are employed simply asking around will usually produce something. Some recruitment agencies may expect you to stay in a hotel for an initial one or two nights until accommodation is arranged and you may be expected to pay for this yourself. Other professional posts such as lecturing in Norwegian colleges, or scientific and research work for the oil industry will often either come with accommodation or your employer will often help you to find it. If you receive a firm offer of employment before going to Norway your future employer will probably be the best source of help and you should raise the matter with him/her at the earliest opportunity if the matter has not already been raised. If you find work whilst in Norway, your best source of finding accommodation will undoubtedly be your work colleagues. Norwegians generally are exceptionally helpful and will probably go out of their way to point you in the right direction so don't be afraid to ask. Staying at the nearest Youth Hostel or Seamen's Mission could be a good interim measure whilst you are looking as they are a relatively cheap option.

Renting

Property in Norway is usually rented for one or two years and is generally fully furnished. Rent is usually paid one month in advance. National and regional papers carry accommodation adverts; look under *Til Leie* for renting. Most estate agents in Norway rent as well as sell property. If you are moving into rented accommodation make sure there is a written contract signed by both parties.

Buying Property

Foreigners wanting to buy property in Norway must apply for a concession when acquiring real property. The exception to this, however, is that foreign citizens who are permanently domiciled in Norway can buy property concession free. Residence of more than six months in Norway is regarded as permanent domicile. The purchase of property entails a registration fee of 2.5% of the property price and an official stamp duty payment. Norwegian mortgages are arranged in similar ways to British mortgages and you will need to apply through the Norwegian banks.

Houses for sale are advertised extensively in the national and local press. Look under *Til Salgs* (for sale). A flat is indicated by the word *Leilighet* and a family house by *Enebolig*. Housing is quite difficult to obtain and even Norwegians may have to wait months to find a place but estate agents will usually succeed in finding you at least a rented home within 30 days. Inevitably there are regional variations in availability and prices but average costs for the mid 1990s in Oslo are:

Detached Houses: 1,253,000 NOK
Semi-detached and street houses: 818,600 NOK
Apartment flats: 510,000 NOK

Norwegian property is sometimes advertised in the property section of the British papers such as *The European* and you may occasionally find that one of Norway's thousands of tiny islands on the west coast comes up for sale. A one and three quarter acre island with two houses was advertised recently for $900,000 with fishing rights thrown in.

Estate Agents

You will almost certainly need to deal with a Norwegian estate agent when buying property as you are highly unlikely to find a British agent who deals with Norway. For details of Norwegian estate agents contact the *Norwegian Association of Real Estate Agents (NEF)* (Inkognitogaten 12, 0258 Oslo; tel 22 44 79 53, fax 22 55 31 06). The Association has ten local associations covering the whole country and a total of 450 members and 150 student members. Choosing to use the services of a member of the association has several benefits. Members of the association must have passed the appropriate estate agents exams in Norway and are bound by ethical and professional codes. The Association can provide a leaflet *Information to Consumers* written in English from the above address. A new act relating to estate agency practice in Norway came into force in April 1990. According to the Act only authorised estate agents or advocates can deal in the selling of property and estate agents are bound to safeguard the interests of both the buyer and the seller by providing advice and information that is of importance to the implementation of the transaction before the completion of the transaction. When buying a flat the prospective purchaser should be provided with written information about the rules, regulations, budgets, accounts etc of the relevant housing company. Estate Agents who fail to carry out the assignment in accordance with the law will be liable for any costs incurred by the buyer as a result.

Legal Advice
You should certainly seek proper legal advice before embarking on a property purchase abroad and preferably with a lawyer who is familiar with Norwegian law. See under useful addresses for Norwegian law firms which are English speaking and deal with conveyancing and property purchase.

Useful Addresses
Engelschiøon & Co ANS: Akersgaten 65B, Postboks 8333 Hammersborg, Oslo 0129; tel 22 36 36 30, fax 22 36 36 80.
De Besche & Co: Tordenskioldsgaten 4, Postboks 1424 Vika, 0115 Oslo; tel 22 20 60 90, fax 22 33 40 00.

Utilities
Norwegian homes have all the usual modern conveniences — and often a sauna too. Despite having some of the world's biggest oil and gas reserves, Norway itself has always had relatively cheap electricity from the thousands of waterfalls and watercourses in its mountainous terrain. Hydro-thermal energy accounts for nearly 60% of domestic energy consumption compared with 35% for oil and gas. All Norwegian homes are well-insulated against the elements and another common source of heating in Norway is the traditional log fire. The Norwegians recognise that chopping wood is an effective way of staying warm. The electricity supply in Norway is 220 volts AC. Most plugs have two small round pins. In this green conscious country, waste is usually kept to a minimum and what can be recycled usually is. Rubbish disposal is a municipal concern.

Removals
Moving anywhere holds inherent trauma but this is particularly the case when moving overseas. It is inevitably an expensive process and you should carefully consider what is essential and what is not. Buying household items in Norway is likely to be more expensive than buying at home. Choose a removals company which is experienced in international removals. The British Association of Removers can provide a leaflet of hints for anyone planning to move overseas. Send an SAE to the address below:

Useful Addresses
Scotpac International Moving: Security House, Abbey Wharf Industrial Estate, Kingsbridge Road, Barking, Essex IG11 0BT; tel 0181-591 3388, fax 0181-594 4571.
Allied Pickfords: 492 Great Cambridge Road, Enfield, Middlesex EN1 3SA; tel 0181-367 0045, fax 0181-367 8445.
Gauntlett International Ltd: Gauntlett House, Catteshall Road, Godalming, Surrey GU7 1NH; tel 01483-428982.
The British Association of Removers: 3 Churchill Court, 58 Station Road, North Harrow, Middlesex HA2 7SA; tel 0181-861 3331.

Importing Cars

Regulations regarding importation of cars depend on your length of stay and whether you intend to take up permanent residence in Norway. The Norwegian Directorate of Customs and Excise provide the English language leaflet RG-0195 which gives a detailed breakdown of the legal position regarding the importation and use of foreign-registered cars to Norway and RG-1093 which gives information on the duties and taxes payable on the importation of motor vehicles. Both are available from embassies (see also under *Cars and Motoring* in the *Daily Life* chapter).

Importing Pets

To import cats and dogs to Norway you should acquire an import permit. An application form can be obtained from the Norwegian Ministry of Agriculture (see below). To get a permit you must comply with the health conditions laid down by the Ministry of Agriculture which will basically want to know that your pet is healthy and has been properly vaccinated. For further details contact the British Ministry of Agriculture (see below).

Useful Addresses

Ministry of Agriculture, Fisheries and Food: Animal Health (International Trade) Division B, Hook Rise South, Tolworth, Surbiton, Surrey KT6 7NF; tel 0181-330 4411.

The Royal Ministry of Agriculture: Division of Veterinary Services, Akersgaten 42, Postboks 8007 Dep, 0030 Oslo; tel 22 34 90 90.

The Norwegian Embassy: 25 Belgrave Square, London SW1X 8QD; tel 0171 235 7151, fax 0171-245 6993.

Daily Life

Moving to Norway involves getting to grips with the day to day realities that influence life for the Norwegians. Whilst you will find most Norwegians helpful above and beyond the call of duty when asked, you will still have to deal with the frustrations as well as the excitement of coping with a new way of life. What follows is a run-down some of the basic facets of daily life which should help make your transition to a foreign country and culture smoother.

The Language

Most Norwegians have an extraordinary capacity for speaking foreign languages. As a tiny nation of only 4.3 million the Norwegians have learned that if they want to be heard in the world they have to speak a language it understands and in practice this is English. English is mandatory in schools but many Norwegians will study French and German too and can switch from one language to another with seeming effortlessness. English is widely spoken in business, service industries and by everyone from the king to the cashiers. The pervasiveness of the British and American media in Norway mean that most Norwegians will hear English every day of their lives and many are keen to practise what they have learned on a native speaker so don't be afraid to initiate a conversation in English.

The Norwegian language is a Germanic language. Mountainous divisions in the country mean that there are many dialects in Norway. Until about 1850 the official language was *Riksmål* — this was a written language which was heavily influenced by Danish and resulted from the 434 year union of the two nations. After 1850 *Landsmål* or Country Language was created mainly out of rural dialects. After many disputes, a compromise was drawn in which both languages received equal status under the new names of *Bokmål* or Book Language for written Norwegian and *Nynorsk* or New Norwegian for spoken language. In the spirit of national feeling of the 19th century it was decided to replace the Danish influence on the Norwegian language by three principle means: 1) Danish words were exchanged for corresponding Norwegian dialect words 2) Danish soft consonants were replaced by Norwegian hard ones and 3) Norwegian syntax replaced Danish syntax.

The differences between *Bokmål* and *Nynorsk* are not very significant and *Bokmål* is usually the taught language-about 83% of school children use *Bokmål* as the main language in schools. Most newspapers and three-quarters of the programmes of the Norwegian Broadcasting Corporation are standardized in *Bokmål* and 90% of all business publications are written in Bokmål. *Nynorsk* is heavily influenced by the Old Norse of the Vikings and is based on rural culture. *Nynorsk* has suffered from 20th century urbanisation but interestingly about 15% of the country's fiction writers use *Nynorsk*. They are principally to be found in the west of Norway.

The Sami or Laplanders in the north have retained their own language and in recent times have had active encouragement from the Norwegian government. The Sami language is used and taught in Sami primary schools and the Universities of Oslo and Tromsø make provision for courses to be taught in the Sami language. There is a *Sami* teacher training college at Alta.

Language Study

Books and cassettes on the Norwegian language are widely available and you may be able to borrow them from your local library. Norwegian is sometimes available through evening classes at local colleges of further education. Norwegian language courses can be arranged through The Berlitz School of Languages, and Linguarama and both have regional offices. If you want to learn Norwegian whilst in Norway you can contact the local adult education organisation *Friundervisningen* who provide details of courses for foreigners wanting to learn the language.

Useful Addresses

The Berlitz School of Languages: 79 Wells Street, London W1A 3BZ; tel 0171-580 6482.

Linguarama: Queen's House, 8 Queen Street, London EC4N 1SP; tel 0171 236 1992, fax 0171-236 7206.

Friundervisningen i Oslo: Torggata 7, 0105, Oslo; tel 22 42 44 90, fax 22 42 01 28.

Schools and Higher Education

Nine years of basic education is compulsory for all of Norway's school children from the age of seven years to sixteen and there is an optional tenth year. In 1997 compulsory schooling will begin from the age of 6. Children attend a primary school from the age of seven to thirteen and lower secondary school for the next three. After completing primary and lower secondary schools, students can attend the three-year upper secondary schools for ages 16-19 and are then eligible to take examinations leading to university entrance. Compulsory subjects include Norwegian, English, maths, religion, music, PE and science. In higher grades, students have the option of taking further arts and languages courses and vocational courses such as office skills and seamanship. Most Norwegian schools are free. The country currently has four universities: Oslo (founded in 1811), Bergen (1946), Trondheim (1968) and the world's most northern university at Tromsø (1968). Just over half of students going on to further education attend vocational colleges and several thousand go to Folk High Schools. These are boarding colleges which offer 17-year-olds from rural backgrounds a one year training course. All students are eligible for a government loan. For further information contact: The Royal Ministry of Church Affairs, Education and Research (Akersgaten 42, Postboks 8119 Dep, 0030 Oslo; tel 22 34 90 90).

International Education

Norway has a surprising number of international schools and classes most of which offer a choice of British style education and the International Baccalaureate (an international curriculum and university entrance examination). The cosmopolitanism of education is a legacy of the offshore oil industry which led to increasing numbers of foreigners (principally English, American and French) taking up work and residency in Norway following the oil discoveries. The majority of schools are, understandably, on the west coast and both Stavanger and Bergen have English, French and American schools. The American school in Stavanger accepts Norwegian students. Foreign children who have lived in Norway for more than three months must attend school.

Useful Addresses

The European Council of International Schools: 21 Lavant Street, Petersfield, Hants GU32 3EL; tel 01730-268244 or 263131, fax 01730 267941.

International Schools

The American School: Gamle Ringeriksvei 53, 1340 Bekkestua; tel 67 53 23 03.

The British International School: PO Box 7531, Skillebekk 0205, Oslo 2; tel 22 44 49 16, fax 22 55 11 35. (Language of instruction is English. Accepts boys and girls age 3-18. Offers UK and International Baccalaureate).

The International School of Bergen: PO Box 3268, Slettebakken, Bergen 5022; tel 55 28 77 16, fax 55 27 14 88 (Language of instruction is English. Accepts boys and girls ages 3-16. Offers an international education).

Skagerak Gymnas: PO Box 1545, Framnes 3206, Sandefjord; tel 33 44 60 20, fax 33 46 93 63. (Language of instruction is English. Accepts boys and girls from the age of 16. Offers the Norwegian national curriculum and the International Baccalaureate).

The International School of Stavanger: Treskeiveien 3, 4042 Hafrsfjord, Stavanger; tel 51 55 91 00, fax 51 55 29 62 (The language of instruction is English. Accepts boys and girls aged 3-18. Offers US, UK and international education).

Stavanger British School: Gauselbakken 107, N-4032 Gausel, Stavanger; tel 45 75 55 99, fax 45 71 51 6 (the language of instruction is English. Accepts boys and girls aged 3-13. Offers UK and Common Entrance examinations).

Birralee International School: Bispegate 9C, Trondheim 7013; tel 73 52 16 44, fax 73 52 03 75 (The language of instruction is English. Accepts boys and girls aged 4-13. Offers a UK curriculum).

Media and Communications

Newspapers and Magazines

About 84% of the adult population read a daily newspaper — a slightly higher percentage than those watching TV. The Norwegians are avid news followers and over 150 national and regional papers are produced daily in Norway. The daily newspaper circulation is a staggering 2,900,000. Many papers are kept going by government subsidies, state advertising and loans and many of the smaller papers are the mouthpieces of political parties. The bigger city based papers are more independent and the daily independent *Verdens Gang* claims the highest figure circulation with over 366,000 on week days. It is followed by the liberal paper *Dagbladet* with a week day circulation of 221,000. A wide variety of popular, special interest and professional journals are published in Norway. Most large *Narvesen* (kiosks) sell English language newspapers and the main public library (Deichmanske Bibliotek, Henrik Ibsens gate 1, Oslo) has a selection of international papers and periodicals in its reading room.

Useful Addresses

Verdens Gang A/S: Akersgaten 34, N-0180 Oslo 3; tel 22 11 40 40, fax 22 42 66 89.

UK editorial Craven House, 34 Foubert's Place, London W1V 2BH; tel 0171-434 9963, fax 0171-434 1514.

Dagbladet: Akersgaten 49, N-0107, Oslo 1; tel 22 20 20 9.
   UK editorial: 11 Marlborough Street, London W5 5NY; tel 0181-567 8373.
Arbeiderbladet: PO Box 1183, Sentrum, N-0107, Oslo 1; tel 22 65 00 00, fax 22
   64 92 82.
Dagens Naeringlsiv: Stenersgaten 1a, Oslo City N-0107, Oslo 1; tel 22 17 83 00,
   fax 22 17 73 10.

Books
In Oslo English language books are available and can be bought from: *Erik Qvist*
(Drammsveien 16, Oslo) and *Tanum Karl Johan* (Karl Johansgate 43, Oslo).

Television and Radio
The television network has expanded over the past few years to come in line
with Europe. As well as the state channels NRK and TV2 there is the satellite
TV Norge and Norway also receives TV3, a channel which is common to
Denmark, Sweden and Norway. Norway imports a significant amount of English
and American TV so even if you are several hundred miles inside the Arctic
Circle you may still find your favourite programme showing on television.
Satellite and cable TV are available in parts of Norway. In summer English is
broadcast on the radio on 106.8 FM. You can tune into the English speaking
NATO station all year round on 105.5 FM.

Post
The main post office is at Dronningensgate 15, Oslo and is open Monday to
Friday 8am-8pm and Saturday 9am-3pm. The general opening times of other
post offices are 8am-5.30 pm Monday to Friday and 9am-1pm on Saturdays.
Stamps are also available from kiosks and stationers.

Telephones
The cheapest calling times in Norway are outside business hours in the early to
late evening: 5-8pm. In Oslo you can telephone from the Central Station or
phone booths within the city but the best place is from the main telegraph office
at Kongensgate 21 (entrance on Prinsensgate) from where you can also send
telegrams, faxes and telexes. At the present time a local call costs a minimum
of 2 NOK. Rates vary according to distance and time of day. A useful feature
of the Norwegian telephone directory is a page of English instructions listed in
the index. Calls from outside and inside a region normally have eight digits.
Norway uses the international access code of 00, bringing it into line with the
movement for a single European code. Dialling codes are subject to change but
at the present time to call Norway dial: 00 47 followed by an eight digit number.
To call the UK from Norway dial 00 44 followed by the area code and number.
All telephone books list country codes. From Norway for the United States and
Canada dial 1, and for Australia 61. For operator assisted calls dial 117 for
national calls and 115 for international calls. All operators speak good English.
For information for Norway and the rest of Scandinavia call 180 and for other
international telephone numbers telephone 181
   The area code for Oslo is 22. For emergency services dial:

Police 112;   Fire 110;   Ambulance 113.

All these are free of charge. For local emergency numbers outside of Oslo dial
the operator on 0180.

Cars and Motoring

Roads

The principle road in Norway is the E6 Arctic Highway which runs from the southern tip on the Norway/Sweden border, north through Oslo and up through the northern towns of Trondheim, Mo-i-Rana, Narvik, Alta and up to Kirkenes on the Russian border. The E6 has branches off to most main towns north of Oslo including Ålesund, Kristiansund, Tromsø and Hammerfest. In the more populous south there is a reasonably good network of major and minor roads and the principal towns of the southern tip of Norway are served by the E18. The further north you go the fewer the roads, reflecting both the increasingly wild terrain and the small population. There are only two main routes from Norway into Sweden in the north-the E75 at Trondheim and Route 70 just after Narvik. Given the harsh climate, major roads are well maintained in Norway and of the 50,000 miles of road in Norway about two-thirds are hard-surfaced. Cars in Norway have studded tyres in the winter months and most cars carry snow chains, particularly when passing through mountainous terrain. The further north you go the less traffic there is and it is possible to drive for many miles on empty roads. Away from the major routes, roads often run through tunnels. There are many sharp twists through the mountains and there may only be guard rails as a safety precaution. Roads along the west coast frequently run into ferry stops for which a charge is levied. Norwegian roads are well signposted with information, directions and distances. Some roads in mountainous areas can be closed for the whole or part of winter. Petrol stations are frequent and those marked *Kort* operate for 24 hours. At 24-hour stations there is a slot to insert an oil company credit card or bank card directly into the pump. Diesel and unleaded petrol are widely available.

Driving Regulations

Driving is on the right and the important rule when driving in Norway is always yield to the vehicle approaching from the right. Drivers of right hand cars should adjust their headlights so that they sweep to the right. Dipped headlights should be used at all times and seat belts are mandatory in both the front and back of cars.

Speed limits are 30 mph (50kph) in built up towns and cities and 18 mph (30 kph) in residential areas. On major motorways the maximum speed limit is 55 mph (90kph) and on other highways the speed limit is 50 mph (80 kph). Speed limits are very strongly enforced and most roads are monitored. Along main roads there are periodic warning signs of *Automatisk Trafikkontroll* (Automatic Traffic Monitoring).

Regulations concerning drink driving in Norway are some of the strictest in Europe. The allowable alcohol limit is a blood alcohol percentage of 0.05% which is the equivalent of half a litre of low alcohol beer. On Friday and Saturday night routine road checks are common and if you are stopped you may have to take a breathalyser test. If the result is positive you will be required to give a blood sample. Punishment is severe; you could lose your licence on the spot and foreigners are no exception to this. Fines of over 10,000 NOK are levied and in some cases drink driving can lead to imprisonment. In practice most Norwegians don't drink and drive at all.

Breakdowns and Accidents

The British motoring organisations The RAC and The AA both offer a service covering breakdowns and accidents for motorists driving abroad. Two motoring organisations in Norway, the KNA and the NAF can advise you on all aspects of motoring and breakdowns in Norway (see useful addresses). If you are involved in an accident where there are no injuries telephone 23 20 85 or 42 94 00 from any location for breakdown assistance. In the case of minor accidents it is not usually necessary to call the police but you are legally obliged to exchange names and addresses with the other driver involved. For a real emergency call the police (112) or ambulance (113).

Driving Licences
To drive abroad you will need an international driving permit. In Britain this can be obtained through the AA (Automobile Association) by holders of a full British licence. You should provide your driving licence, a passport sized photo signed on the back and the appropriate fee. You can also apply through the Driver and Vehicle Licensing Centre (see useful addresses). Other nationals who do not have a British driving licence should make applications to the country of issue.

Exporting a Vehicle
Vehicles kept or used in Britain are registered at the Driver and Vehicle Licensing Centre for the Department of Transport. If you intend to take your car abroad for more than 12 months it is regarded as a permanent export. Before you go you should complete the form V5 registration document (available from your local vehicle registration office) to show your intended date of export. This form should be returned either to the vehicle registration office or to the DVLC at Swansea. You will then receive the V561 Certificate of Export. Allow at least a month for processing.

If you do not intend to keep your vehicle out of the country for more than 12 months you should take a V5 registration document with you (available from the DVLC or your local vehicle registration office). When it has been checked that you are the owner of the car you will be issued with a Certificate of Registration (V3790 which will cover you whilst you are driving abroad.

If you are expecting to have to relicense your vehicle before you return to Britain you should apply by post on form V10 (available at post offices and vehicle registration offices) before you go. Send it to a head post office in Britain at least six weeks before the new licence should start. You will need to give both your British address and foreign address on the V10.

Note: a foreign MOT is not acceptable for a British vehicle licence application. You must fix a plate on the back of your vehicle indicating nationality e.g. GB for Britain.

Most major shipping lines to Norway allow passengers to bring their cars.

All vehicles registered abroad must carry international liability insurance and an accident report form. These are available from motoring associations. Collision insurance is also recommended.

Useful Addresses
The Automobile Association: Head Office, Norfolk House, Priestley Road, Basingstoke, Hampshire RG24 9NY Tel 01256-20123, fax 01256-493389.

The Royal Automobile Club: PO Box 700 Spectrum, Bond Street, Bristol BS99 1RB; tel 0117-9232340.

DVLC (The Driver and Vehicle Licensing Centre): The Exports Section, Swansea, SA 99 1BL; tel 01792-783100.

Kongelig Norsk Automobilklub (KNA, Royal Norwegian Automobile Club): Parkveien 68, Oslo 2; Tel 22 56 26 90.

Norges Automobil Forbund (NAF, Norwegian Automobile Association): Storgate 2-6, Oslo 1; tel 22 33 70 80.

Transport

Air

There are regular daily flights to Norway from most major airports in Europe. Norway has international airports at Oslo Fornebu, Bergen, Stavanger, Kristiansand and Trondheim. A new Airport is scheduled to open at Gardermoen 25 miles/40 km from Oslo in 1998. The main Norwegian Airline is the Scandinavian SAS. In 1994, British Midlands launched a daily scheduled service from Heathrow to Bergen and the Norwegian airline Braathens (which boasts a 93% on-time record) offers daily scheduled flights from Gatwick to Oslo and Bergen.

Large, thinly populated distances make domestic flights a convenient form of travel in Norway, particularly in the north. Journeys which can take several days by road can be completed in hours by plane. The main domestic air companies in Norway are Braathens, NorskAir and Widerøe. The biggest is Braathens SAFE (standing surprisingly for the South Asian and Far Eastern routes of the parent shipping company) which operates 240 internal departures daily and serves domestic airports throughout the country, including Spitzbergen.

Useful Addresses

SAS: Ruseløkkveien 6, Oslo 3; tel 22 42 99 70.
Braathens SAFE AS: Ruseløkkveien 26, Oslo 2; tel 22 41 10 20.
NorskAir Gardermoen: tel 06 97 82 20.
Widerøe Flyveselskap AS: Mustadsveien 1, Oslo 2; tel 22 55 59 60.

Trains

The Norwegian State Railway System (NSB) operates five main lines from Oslo S (Central) Station and 2,600 miles of railway track. The northern line runs up the country, through Trondheim and reaches its most northern point at Fauske with a short western run to Bodø. There are two southern lines, one covers the south coast to Stavanger and the other runs through Gothenburg and is the main connecting route with continental Europe. The western line takes a particularly scenic route from Oslo to Bergen. The eastern line runs through Kongsvinger to Stockholm in Sweden. From Trondheim you can take a ticket to Hell (literally) and carry on eastwards into central Sweden. You can also take a train south from Narvik on Sweden's Ofot line which takes you to Sweden's north east coastline.

Norwegian trains are punctual, clean, comfortable and costly. Most offer special compartments for the disabled and for families with young children. You can buy first or second class tickets and sleeping compartments consist of one, two and three bunk cabins. On long journeys seat and sleeper reservations are compulsory.

Although Norwegian State Railways do not claim leaves on the line as an excuse for lateness they do occasionally have problems with wild elks wandering onto the line — over 500 elks are killed by trains each year and with each elk weighing an average of 120 stones they can cause substantial delays.

Useful Addresses

NSB: Jernbanetorget 1, Oslo Tel 22 36 37 80.
Norwegian State Railways: 21-24 Cockspur Street, London SW1 5DA; tel 0171-930 6666.

Buses Trams and the Underground

Nearly every sizable settlement in Norway is served by bus and where a rail route runs out a bus route begins. This is particularly important in northern

Norway where the railway ends at Fauske. Several bus routes are operated by the Norwegian State Railway (address above). The buses travel as far north as North Cape and up to Kirkenes on the Russian border. Long distance buses are only slightly cheaper than trains.

Oslo has a comprehensive tram and bus service which is efficient and clean. You can find details at every stop and information on public transport is also available from Oslo S Station. There is a skeleton night service. Oslo is also served by an Underground — the *T-bane*. Its eight lines cover Oslo and go out to quite distant suburbs. The station entrances are marked by *T*. For details contact the tourist information in Oslo S station.

Boat

To get to Norway by sea, there is a twice weekly sailing from Newcastle to Bergen in winter and a sailing three times a week from May to mid-September operated by Colour Line. Scandinavian Seaways run a longer route from Harwich via Esbjerg in Denmark from where you take the train to Norway. See a travel agent for details.

In Norway the proximity of the sea and the coastline eaten into by Fjords means that ferries form a significant part of the transport system. Ferries often provide short cuts and help avoid many extra road miles. In busy areas near Oslo ferries are also widely used by commuters in particular on the Oslofjord where the Horten-Moss ferry carries regular commuters between Vestfold and Østfold.

Norway's most famous boat trip is done by the Coastal Express or *Hurtigrute* which takes six days to travel from Bergen to Kirkenes and takes in 36 stops en route. Although the *Hurtigrute* is very expensive and tends to be a tourist's pleasure trip in summer, it sails throughout the year and is used by local people as a ferry service.

Banks and Finance

The central bank of Norway — Norges Bank, was founded in 1816. Today it primarily serves as the government's executive agency for credit and foreign exchange policy. Commercial banks are set up as limited companies and were originally directed by the government to deal with national and corporate matters whilst the savings banks were directed to deal with local matters. In practice there is not a great deal of difference between the two and whilst commercial banks offer long-term loans they can also do short-term loans such as overdrafts. Most savings banks are local banks. Originally they acted as a banking facility for the municipality and for arranging individual mortgages but today they offer the same services as commercial banks. Foreign banks were allowed to establish branches in Norway for the first time in 1984.

Bank opening times are Monday to Friday only between 8.15am-3.30 pm (Thursdays until 5pm) and they are closed on Saturdays. Cash points are spreading throughout Norway and like the banks will accept most major international credit cards.

Currency

The Norwegian currency is the Krone (literally translated means Crown). The plural is Kroner. It is usually written NOK although this rarely appears on price tags and Kr is used. One Krone contains 100 øre with denominations of ten or fifty øre. In practice øres are almost worthless. Kroner come in notes of 50, 100,

500 and 1000. At the current time the exchange rate is 10 NOK to £1 and 7 NOK to $1 but this is obviously subject to fluctuation.

Taxation

Taxes in Norway are generally higher than in other European countries because of the high costs of financing welfare arrangements, social services and state subsidies. Taxes are levied at national, county (*fylke*) and local authority (*Kommune*) level. Both individuals and corporations are subject to tax. Income tax is paid directly as a percentage of individual income and is deducted at source by the employer. Norway also operates a wealth tax (ie tax on commodities such as cars) which ranges upwards from 2.3% on capital wealth. Norway has a double taxation agreement with all EEA countries to prevent individual liability for paying taxes in two countries at the same time. Individuals should discuss their tax and national insurance contributions directly with the employer before accepting work. When you start work you will be issued with a tax deduction card; failure to produce a tax deduction card means that you will be taxed the maximum amount which is currently 50% of your earnings. Income taxes on individuals on net ordinary income are currently 28%. Of this, 21% consists of municipal tax and 7% is county tax. For further details see *Starting a Business* or contact the Inland Revenue (see useful addresses).

VAT (known as MVA, or MOMS throughout Scandinavia) is 22% on all services and purchases with the exception of books. It will normally be included in the price of goods. The Central Office for Foreign Tax Affairs (see address below) provides a *Guide for Foreign Employers and Employees* which deals with the tax situation in detail.

Useful Addresses
Inland Revenue: EC Unit Room S20, Somerset House, London WC2R 1LB.
Oslo Ligningskontor: Hagegaten 22-23, N-0653 Oslo.
Central Office for Foreign Tax Affairs: Prinsens vei 1, N-4300 Sandnes; tel 51 67 80 88.

Health Insurance and Hospitals

A well developed system of health and welfare programmes in Norway means that there is a very high standard of public health. Membership of a national health insurance scheme is compulsory for all people resident in Norway regardless of nationality if they intend to reside or have resided in Norway for 12 months or more. Employees of Norwegian companies are members of the National Insurance System even if they intend to live in Norway for less than one year. The obligation to be insured starts from the time of arrival in Norway. This ensures free medical care in hospital, compensations for doctor's fees, free medicine and a compensation allowance for lost earnings. Salaried employees must join an additional scheme which secures cash benefits during pregnancy or illness and this scheme is optional for the self-employed. Most hospitals are in the ownership of the state, the county or the municipality and the majority of Norwegian doctors work in the hospitals. Maternal and child health care are well developed and school health services are compulsory. Other features of the Norwegian health care system include free family counselling, and free dental care for 90% of children aged between seven and 15. In some areas dental care extends from the age of three to 20. In Norway the state pays a family allowance for all children up to the age of 16.

Since Norway joined the European Economic Area on 1 January 1994 she has had reciprocal agreements with other member countries on social security, insurance benefits and health care rights. Effectively the rules of the agreement are the same as those of the European Community regulations on social security and therefore EEA national should receive the same health care arrangements as Norwegians when in Norway. Any employed person and their dependent family members are normally entitled to sickness benefits from the employed person's country of employment.

In Norway most medicines and prescriptions are paid for by the individual. You can choose your own doctor (most will speak good English) but there is a small fee if the doctor works in the municipality scheme and slightly more if he/ she works outside it. Admittance to hospital is usually arranged by a doctor. If you are unemployed and looking for work in Norway you should take the form E111 which enables you to receive urgent medical treatment free of charge. It is available from most post offices or Department of Social Security offices. For further details about your health rights in Norway contact: *Statens Helsetilsyn* (Calmeyers Gate 1, N-0183 Oslo; tel 22 34 90 90).

Private Medical Insurance

If you are working for a British employer a variety of international health insurance policies are available in Britain and have the additional advantage of being valid throughout Europe. BUPA (British United Provident Association; International Centre, Imperial House, 40-42 Queens Road, Brighton BN1 3WU; tel 01273-23563) or PPP (Private Patients Plan; Philips House, Crescent Road, Tunbridge Wells, Kent TN1 2PL; tel 01892-512345) both offer such packages.

If you are intending to move to Norway permanently you should register your change of address with the Overseas Branch of the Department of Social Security (Longbenton, Newcastle upon Tyne, NE98 1YX).

For a detailed account of benefits consult the leaflets: SA 16 *Social Security Agreement between United Kingdom and Norway* and SA 29 *Your Social Security insurance, benefits and health care rights in the European Community*. Both are available from the Benefits Agency (Overseas Benefits Directorate, Department of Social Security, Longbenton, Newcastle upon Tyne, NE98 1YX) or from your local post office, unemployment office or job centre.

Private doctors are listed in the phone book under *Leger*, the word *lækjarvak* indicates doctor on duty.

To make an appointment with a doctor in Oslo dial 22 20 10 90.

Emergencies and Chemists

For medical emergencies dial 113 in Oslo. In other parts of the country dial the operator on 0180 and ask for the local emergency medical help (*Nødhjelp*).

For chemists look for the word *Apotek*. Most large cities have all-night pharmacies. In Oslo you will find one opposite the Oslo S central station: Jernbanetorgets 4b; tel 22 41 24 82; in Bergen it is Apotek Nordstjernen near the bus station; tel 05 31 68 84; in Stavanger you can phone a 24-hour pharmacy service on 04 52 01 28 and in Trondheim it's at St Olav's Apotek, Kjøpmannsgate 65; tel 07 52 31 22. In some cities there is a rotating system of 24-hour pharmacies in which case the schedule will be displayed on the chemist's door. Emergency dental treatment is available in Oslo outside office hours from Oslo Kommunale Tannlegevakt (Tøyen Senter, Kolstadgata 18; tel 22 67 48 46).

Useful Addresses
Department of Health: Health Services Division, Alexander Fleming House, Elephant and Castle, London SE1 6BY.
The Royal Ministry of Social Affairs: Grubbegt. 10, Postboks 8011 Dep, 0030 Oslo; tel 22 34 90 90.

Social Security and Unemployment Benefit

The Norwegian social security system is funded by contributions from employers, employees or self-employed workers, the government and municipalities. Employers contribute about 16.7% of an employees gross salary. The employee's contribution is up to 7.8%. Self-employed individuals contribute 10.7% of their business income and 7.8% of their personal income. People under 16 and pensioners contribute 3% of their income.

The Norwegian social security system provides financial security for the persons covered by the system in areas of pensions, disability allowances, occupational injury, medical treatment, sickness benefits, maternity allowance, single parent support and unemployment benefit. Non-residents are insured if working for a Norwegian employer and are covered from the moment of starting work regardless of the period of employment. Non-resident employees working on the Norwegian continental shelf are only insured for occupational injury. Those working on ships operating beyond the territorial borders (7-8 km or 4.2-4.8 miles from shore) are not covered by the Norwegian Social Security Act.

Foreigners working in Norway may be exempt from the Norwegian social security system if they are working for their home country employer in which case they may pay into the social security system of their normal country of residence. This agreement means that employees are not obliged to pay social security contributions to each country.

Unemployment
If you become unemployed in Norway register with the nearest jobcentre (*Arbeidsformidling*) who will advise you on where and how to claim benefits. All EEA nationals will receive social security benefits on the same basis as Norwegian nationals if they are employed or self-employed in Norway. Any social security you have obtained in an EEA country can be transferred to Norway.

If you have been registered unemployed in your home country for at least four weeks before you go to Norway unemployment benefit to which you are entitled can be paid to you from your home country. Pick up the form E303 from the DSS before you leave for Norway and hand it in to your nearest jobcentre in Norway as soon as possible. This secures payment of your unemployment benefit whilst you are in Norway but you should bear in mind that you may not be able to live on unemployment benefit in a country as expensive as Norway.

Useful Addresses
Rikstrygdeverket (National Insurance Administration): Drammensveien 60, N-0241 Oslo; tel 22 92 70 00.
Arbeidsdirektorated (Directorate of Labour): Postboks 8127 dep, N-0032 Oslo; tel 22 94 24 00.

The Royal Ministry of Social Affairs: Grubbegt. 10, Postboks 8011 Dep, 0030
Oslo; tel 22 34 90 90.
Department of Social Security: Overseas Branch, Longbenton, Newcastle upon
Tyne, NE98 1YX.

Local Government

Norway is divided into 19 regions of local administration of which Oslo og
Akershus forms one (the others are: Østfold, Hedmark, Oppland, Buskerud,
Vestfold, Telemark, Aust-Agder, Vest-Agder, Rogaland, Hordaland, Sogne og
Fjordane, Møre og Romsdal, Sør-Trøndelag, Nord-Trøndelag, Nordland, Troms,
Finnmark and Svalbard). The regions, or *fylker*, are divided into rural and urban
municipalities. Councils are elected every four years, two years after the *Storting*
elections, and tend to reflect the political divisions of the *Storting*. Each council
elects a board of aldermen and a mayor. The governing bodies of towns also
often employ councillors for local affairs such as finance, schools, social welfare
and housing. Norwegians pay direct taxes to local as well as central government.
Delegates for the *fylker* councils are elected by the municipalities but *fylke*
governors are elected by the Cabinet.

Crime and the Police

Crime Rates are very low in Norway and most law breaking tends to be driving
offences. The streets of major cities are very safe compared with the rest of
Europe and the main form of harassment is likely to be from drunks hustling
for cigarettes although Vigeland Park in Oslo has a reputation for drug dealing
and theft. Serious crime is very rare and even very small children are left to
play outside by parents. Violence on TV and in cartoons is carefully monitored.
Crime against foreigners is infrequent and more likely to come from other
foreigners. The further north you go the lower the crime rate gets and it is not
unusual for people to leave their cars and houses with all their possessions
unlocked for long periods. Generally the police are friendly, approachable and
helpful. A police officer has the power to stop and search if he/she has reasonable
grounds for suspicion. A person can be detained for up to 24 hours without
charge but has a statutory right to see a solicitor. Drug violations carry very
strict penalities. Drug dealing carries a maximum penalty of 21 years imprisonment — the same as for premeditated murder. In emergencies dial 112 for the
police in Oslo and 0180 for local emergency numbers outside of Oslo.

The Legal System

Norwegian law is largely the product of the interaction of customary law and
general civil law. In the courts, precedent is not binding except in decisions of
the Supreme Court. Civil cases must, in most cases, be submitted to conciliation
councils first and many issues are settled without the need for formal legal
action. Appeals can be made against the decision of conciliation councils to the
courts and there is also a formal system of courts of appeal. The final arbiter of
legal decisions is the Supreme Court. Citizens' rights are upheld by an
ombudsman who can act as an intermediary on their behalf in matters of public
administration.

Foreign judgements cannot be enforced in Norway by action on the judgement
but where the foreign court was deemed to be competent, the Norwegian court

will base its decisions on the foreign judgement. In 1961 Great Britain and Norway agreed a convention which gave reciprocal recognition and enforcement of judgments in civil cases. This does not apply to family law, for decisions in the proceedings of the recovery of taxes, fines or other penalties.

For further details about the Norwegian legal system contact: *Den Norske Advokaftorening:* (Kristian Augustsgate 9, 0164 Oslo 1), or contact the local district governor (*Fylkesmann*). In Oslo this is at: *Fylkesmannen i Oslo og Akershus:* (Postboks 8111 Dep, 0032 Oslo; tel 22 42 90 85, fax 22 42 21 22).

Religion

88% of Norwegians belong to the Evangelical Lutheran church. Whilst almost every village is graced by the distinctive white Lutheran chapel, active church attendance, particularly by the young, is low. There are many churches in Oslo including the American Lutheran Church which holds services in English, as does the Anglican Episcopalian Church of St Edmund's. Norway has a surprising mix of religious minorities which includes: Quakers, Jews, Baptists, Pentecostalists, Methodists, Catholics and, because of Asian immigration, Buddhists and Muslims.

Social Life

The Norwegians

Despite the reputation for Nordic reserve, Norwegians are usually exceptionally friendly and helpful when approached. Whilst they do not as a rule make the first move, any move on your part is likely to be very well received. Norwegians can show exceptional hospitality to foreigners way above and beyond the call of good manners. Don't be deceived by the serious exterior — whilst they don't go in for slapstick much, Norwegians often have a very dry sense of humour. Norwegians generally are gentle and pleasant but they are also tend to be very independent in their views. Centuries of domination by Denmark have left Norway fiercely patriotic — criticise Norway to a Norwegian at your own peril.

Manners and Customs

Handshaking is the norm when meeting strangers in Norway but even casual acquaintances usually shake hands on meeting and parting. In Norway it is customary to introduce yourself by your full name. Norwegians set great store by politeness although this tends to be more out of pleasantness than formality. If you are invited to someone's home, a gift of flowers or chocolates is always acceptable. When drinking a toast or to someone's health (*skåling*) there is a delicate ritual of eye contact. Eye contact is made before drinking, then say *Skål* (cheers), chink glasses look each other in the eye again and drink it. How this works in large gatherings is hard to imagine.

Culture

Given its tiny population and the historically agricultural leanings, Norway has made a significant national and international cultural contribution. The 19th century in particular saw a blossoming of culture and talent in Norway and the end of the century produced such famous names as the dramatist Henrik Ibsen, the novelist and nobel laureate Knut Hamsun, the expressionist painter Edvard Munch and the composer Edvard Grieg.

Norway has a powerful folk art culture based around isolated farming communities and this is particularly apparent in the works of Grieg, most notably his suite for Peer Gynt, the text of which was written by Ibsen. National romanticism (sometimes referred to as Viking romanticism) went hand in hand with Norway's cultural revival at the turn of the 19th century when thoughts were turning towards independence from Sweden. Although the Vikings are universally known for their rape and pillage culture, their skills and craftsmanship in jewellery, boat building and exploration are revered by modern Norwegians. Heavy-timbered houses with the traditional turf roofs are highly prized and protected as are handcrafted objects and furniture made from wood in local forests. Wooden objects are often decorated by the distinctive *rosemaling* or rose painting which features prominently in Norwegian folk art. The earliest surviving examples of the *rosemaling* art date back to the 1700s but it may well predate this by many centuries. The remote separate valleys often reveal a distinct local artistic style. The tradition of woodcarving survives into the present with modern day *hytter* or wooden holiday homes exhibiting intricate carving on the exterior. Many Norwegians wear the national costume (the *bunad*) not just for fancy dress but as formal attire for events like weddings making the *bunad* is one of the most frequently worn national costumes in Europe.

The Great Outdoors

Exploring the wilds is a national pastime in Norway which is hardly surprising in a nation which produced some of the world's most famous explorers. Amongst the earlier ones were Garðar Svarsson who discovered Iceland in the late 9th century and Leif Eriksson who in about 1000 AD was the first European to set foot on the American continent and of course the Vikings made tours of a sort. More recently in the 19th and 20th centuries Norway has produced the polar explorers Roald Amundsen and Fridtjof Nansen and the nautical explorer Thor Heyerdahl. Whilst most modern Norwegians do their exploring on a more modest domestic scale, the Great Outdoors have a tremendous hold on the Norwegian national character. Enshrined in Norwegian Law is the public's right of way law which guarantees the individual right to cross land regardless of ownership. Even though there is no concept of trespass in Norway (or perhaps because of it) Norwegians respect and protect the land and the whole country is imbued with a strong ecological sense.

With vast tracts of Norway being wild, unspoilt and indescribably beautiful it is hardly surprising that one in four Norwegians lists outdoor recreation as their favourite pastime. Walking, mountain climbing and cross country skiing are some of the favourites and are enjoyed by all sectors of the population from king to commoner. One quarter of the population own a *hytte*, a wooden holiday home which, ideally, is situated in a remote valley, space being highly valued in Norway. Many Norwegians also own their own boats. Sailing is a favourite summer pastime and both the late King Olav V and present King Harald V hold Olympic medals for sailing. Messing about on the fjord may be an atavistic yearning for the Viking sea-going era but the boat was also a common feature of daily life for remote rural communities for fishing and crossing the local water source. Sport is also very popular and there are indoor and outdoor facilities nationwide. Cycling, canoeing, fishing, golf, horse riding, rafting skating and skiing are all popular.

Entertainment

Hardly surprisingly, the majority of Norway's night life is in Oslo. Cities outside of Oslo are relatively small and quiet by European standards which makes the northern City of Tromsø claim to be the Paris of the North seem unduly pretentious. Although Oslo has tended to have a fairly low profile, the late 1980s saw Oslo blossom as a cosmopolitan city thanks to injections of cash from the oil boom. Money has been invested in the arts and Oslo has a thriving cultural life, many museums, a national theatre, 30 cinema screens and an active music life. Clubs and concerts are hosts to international and mainstream music makers. Bands can be seen at the Drammen Stadium and a new arena, the Forum, is being built near the central station to provide multicultural activities. It is advisable to book cinema places on Sunday night as this is the most popular time for cinema going.

Some clubs have a minimum age of 21 or 23 and in some it is as high as 26. There are bars, clubs and cafés throughout Oslo which range from the homely to the upmarket. The tourist information centre produces the *Oslo Guide* and *What's On in Oslo* which gives a run-down of what's available and it is advisable to consult listings in the paper as venues can open and close down fairly quickly.

Food and Drink

Food in Norway has traditionally been regarded more as a source of human fuel than as a source of titillation for the palate. Home made Norwegian food still tends to reflect this and is simple and filling. Norway's is a largely carnivorous society and vegetarians may need to be particularly inventive when creating dishes other than those which are cheese based. Typical Norwegian fare includes: *kjøttkaker* (meat cakes), *medisterkaker* (pork sausage patties) and *reinsdyrkaker* (reindeer meatballs). Lamb is also popular but inevitably the mainstay of the Norwegian diet is fish served in many varieties. Some fish dishes are an acquired taste, in particular *rakfisk* (fermented trout) which even native Norwegians may find hard to stomach. Food is easy to come by throughout the country, including the far North but is generally very expensive — a result of hefty government subsidies which encourage farmers to produce home grown fare in less than auspicious circumstances. Typically, Norwegians eat a large breakfast, of bread, herrings, cold meat and cheese, a simple lunch of open sandwiches and a hot meal at dinner. Dinner is eaten relatively early between four and six pm. Norwegians are great coffee drinkers and it is usual to serve coffee whenever people meet. You may also be bombarded with pastries — if you must refuse do so politely.

Attitudes to alcohol are fairly ambivalent in Norway. You can sometimes get the impression that the country is split between hardline would-be prohibitioners and potential candidates for Alcoholics Anonymous. Beer is sold in most grocery stores but the import of wines and spirits is a state monopoly and alcohol is sold in the chain of Vinmonopolet shops. Laws regarding the sale of alcohol are decided at the *Kommune*, or town and local council levels and the availability of alcohol varies considerably throughout the country. Alcohol is widely available in Oslo and can be sold in some places into the early hours of the morning. Generally, the Vinmonopol is open from 10am-5pm Monday to Friday and from 9am-1pm on Saturdays. There is a widespread ban on drinking on Sundays. Home-distilling from sugar and potatoes is illicit though the law is not always strictly observed. Alcohol is prohibitively expensive — about 40 NOK for half a litre of beer.

Eating and drinking out in Oslo (and all of Norway effectively) is a very expensive affair. International cuisine tends to be restricted to the restaurants of Oslo and the major cities.

Shopping

Most shops are open 9am-5pm on weekdays although on Thursdays there is usually an extended opening time until 7 or 8 pm. Large shopping centres, kiosks and supermarkets also often have extended opening times. Private offices are open from 8am-4pm Monday to Friday and public offices from 8am-3.15 pm (in summer they close slightly earlier at 3pm). There is a range of typical Norwegian crafts for sale in almost every city and they include woollen knitwear, (classic designs are snowflakes and reindeer), textiles, candlesticks, wooden ornaments and useful kitchen objects. Norwegian jewellery is distinctive — often made of silver and tending to favour Viking designs. Antique Norwegian rustic items may not be exported.

Public Holidays

Everything closes on the following days:

1 January — New Year's Day
Easter — Maundy Thursday, Good Friday, Easter Monday
1 May — Labour Day
17 May — Independence or Constitution Day
Ascension Day
Whit Monday
23 June — Midsummer Eve (Sankt Hans ie Saint John) is a nationwide
    celebration with dancing and beach bonfires throughout the country
25 December — Christmas Day
26 December — Boxing Day

Retirement

Unless you have some prior connection with Norway it will probably not spring to mind as the ideal retirement spot. Anyone considering the leap of moving to Norway needs to think carefully through the implications of living on a pension, and therefore probably on a reduced income, in a country where the basic cost of living is exceptionally high. As long as you are active and able to drive you should not experience any mobility problems but bear in mind that significant areas of Norway are covered in snow in winter and roads can become impassable. Most of the southern cities also experience some snow in winter and retirement age might not be quite the best time to take up skiing.

Set against this is the fact that most Norwegians speak excellent English (although if you are planning to retire there it's a good idea to acquire as much Norwegian as you can before taking up retirement). Health provision in Norway is excellent and elderly people are not treated as second class citizens or as a 'poor investment' by the health services. The average number of patients per doctor is just over 300. Norway enjoys some of the highest longevity rates in the world and elderly people tend to remain active. The environment in Norway should be excellent given the ecological consciousness of the nation but this is marred by acid rain from other countries (principally Britain) and the industrial effluent from the neighbouring former Soviet Union in the east. Before taking up permanent residence in Norway it is advisable to spend a trial period there, preferably including winter.

Residence Requirements

You can stay in Norway without working but you must be able to provide documents that you are receiving sufficient financial help to support yourself in the form of regular payments. Evidence that you have sufficient means can be provided in the form of bank account statements. The amount you receive must be at least the equivalent of a basic state pension in Norway — currently 59,868 NOK per annum. You will also need to provide evidence of medical insurance from either your own country or prove that you have taken out sufficient medical insurance for the duration of your stay in Norway.

Pensions

Since joining the European Economic Area, Norway has come into line with the rest of the EU as regards social security, insurance benefits and health care rights of nationals of the countries involved. If you are entitled to a state pension before leaving Britain you should be able to have it paid to you in Norway but it will remain at British pension payment level. If you move to Norway before retirement age and are still paying national insurance contributions to Britain you will qualify for a British state pension. If you are working for a Norwegian company or employer and have made a sufficient contribution to the Norwegian social security system you will be entitled to a Norwegian pension. Norway introduced a 'people's pension' in 1967 to help ensure that retired people enjoyed a standard of living reasonably close to the one they had enjoyed during their working life. The basic pension is adjusted every year regardless of income paid in premiums. Individual pensions vary according to pension earning time and individual income. The normal age for the old-age pension in Norway is 67. For further details on obtaining a pension when retiring in Norway contact the Department of Social Security (Overseas Branch, Newcastle upon Tyne, England NE98 1YX). For details of the Norwegian National Insurance scheme contact the Rikstrydeverket (Drammensveien 60, Oslo 2) or The Royal Ministry of Social Affairs (Grubbegt. 10, Postboks 8011 Dep, 0030 Oslo). If you work in two or more EEA countries you can combine state pension contributions paid to both countries to qualify for a state pension. The nearest embassy should also be able to offer help and advice. Further details are given in the DSS leaflet SA29: *Your Social Security insurance, benefits and health care rights in the European Community* and SA16: *Social Security Agreement between United Kingdom and Norway*, both obtainable from the DSS.

Health
All employees of Norwegian firms automatically contribute to the national health insurance scheme. Nationals of the states of the European Economic Area are entitled to receive reciprocal health care arrangements in Norway (see *Health* in the *Daily Life* chapter).

Offshore Banking
Retired British citizens moving to a foreign country may find it worthwhile to consider investing capital in offshore banking which offers a tax free investment opportunity. A basic minimum is usually required to open a deposit account (rarely less than £500). Interest can usually be paid monthly or annually.

Useful Addresses
Nationwide Overseas Ltd: PO Box 217, Market Street, Douglas, Isle of Man tel 01624-606095 fax 01624-663495.
Albany International Assurance Ltd: St Mary's, The Parade, Castletown, Isle of Man; tel 01624-823262, fax 01624-822560.

Entertainment and English Language Clubs
British television and satellite and cable TV are widely available in Norway. The English language NATO station is available all year round on 105.5 FM in Norway and English is available throughout the summer on 106.8 FM. You can also tune into the BBC radio World Service. For frequencies and times contact London Calling (PO Box 76, Bush House, London WC2 4PH). Both the Embassy and the British Council should be able to provide you with information about expatriate communities and clubs.

Useful Addresses
The British Council: Fridtjos Nansens Plass 5, 0160 Oslo; tel 22 42 68 48.
The British Embassy: Thomas Heftyes gate 8, 0244 Oslo; tel 22 55 24 00.

Wills
It is highly advisable to draw up a will before moving to a foreign country and to take expert legal advice. You should also seek legal advice on wills in Norway. The English-speaking law firms below deal with wills and probate.

Useful Addresses

Engelschiøon & Co ANS: Akersgaten 65B, Postboks 8333 Hammersborg, Oslo 0129; tel 22 36 36 30, fax 22 36 36 80.

De Besche & Co: Tordenskioldsgaten 4, Postboks 1424 Vika, 0115 Oslo; tel 22 20 60 90, fax 22 33 40 00.

Death

If you are considering staying permanently abroad, it is advisable to make funeral wishes known in advance as in the event of death, relatives may not be on the spot to deal with the situation. Having a body shipped home for burial is very expensive and arrangements should be made in advance. The nearest British Embassy should be able to help with arrangements.

SECTION II

Working in Norway

Employment
Permanent and Temporary Work
Starting a Business

Employment

The Employment Scene

At a first glance the employment scene in Norway looks promising. Inflation currently stands at a mere 1.3%, interest rates are the lowest in Europe and the budget deficit is 3% of the GDP. Unemployment is relatively high at 7% but Norway is still dependent on specialist skills from abroad that cannot be supplied by the home labour market. Furthermore, Norway it is predicted that Norway is set to become the world's second largest oil producer after Saudi Arabia. All of these factors would seem to offer good prospects for the foreign worker.

Despite its economic strength, Norway's decision in 1994 not to join the European Union has caused some consternation amongst business officials. Following Norway's rejection of EU membership, the Norwegian Confederation of Business and Industry warned that the vote might lead to the loss of as many as 100,000 jobs in the next four years. Many Norwegian industrialists have viewed Norway's decision to go it alone, despite the fact that Sweden and Finland have both joined, with dismay and have warned that many manufacturers may consider moving to lower-cost countries in the EU. In voting against the EU, Norway has placed its faith in its natural resources of gas and oil to see it through. Whilst Norway is still riding a roller coaster as far as the North Sea oil and gas reserves are concerned the economy is inevitably subject to fluctuations in oil prices. Whilst for the moment things are looking good, the possible long-term effects of the vote against the European Union need to be borne in mind by those comtemplating Norway's future as a provider of jobs.

One third of Norway's population is employed in community, social and personal services. Nearly 19% work in mining, industry and electricity and water utilities. The retail trade and hotel and restaurant industry account for 17.6%, agriculture 5.3%, financing, real estate and business services 7.3%, building construction 7.8% and transport, storage and communications 8.4%. The fishing industry employs just under 1% of the population and forestry 3%. Between 1987 and 1992, employment vacancies fell by nearly 50% from 12,400 to 6,422 and the current rate of unemployment is expected to continue to fall.

UK citizens can undertake both full-time and part-time work in Norway providing that the part-time work is sufficient to provide their living expenses. Short-term jobs are often available because the Norwegians do not want to do them — this is particularly true of low paid work such as farming. Whilst there is no minimum wage in Norway, wages are usually considerably higher than normal for Europe although the high Norwegian taxes and cost of living mean that what looks like well remunerated employment may not be quite as profitable as you thought.

Residence and Work Regulations

Nationals of the European Economic Area do not need to obtain a work permit to work in Norway and can stay in Norway for up to three months to look for work. For further details on work and residence regulations see Chapter Two, *Residence and Entry Regulations*.

Skills and Qualifications

To pursue professional careers abroad, authorisation, official approval or licences are often required. Since joining the European Economic Area, Norway has come into line with the European Union regulations with regard to reciprocal recognition of professional qualifications. If you have had a professional training you would not therefore, normally, need to undergo supplementary training or examinations before taking up a professional career in Norway. Examples of professional careers might be medicine, nursing, dentistry, veterinary, law etc. There are fewer regulated professions in Norway than in the UK and each profession has its own national association. For an exhaustive list of transferable professional qualifications contact the European Division of the Department of Trade and Industry (Ashdown House, 6th floor, 123 Victoria Street, London SW1E 6RB; tel 0171-231 5000) who also publish the booklet *Europe Open for Professions*. For details of comparability of academic qualifications in Norway contact NAIC (The National Academic Information Centre: International Education Services, University of Oslo, Postboks 1081 Blindern, N-0313 Oslo; tel 22 85 88 50). You can also get information on comparisons between British and Norwegian Qualifications by contacting the Norwegian Central Government Educational Offices (*Statens Utdanningskontorer*; tel Oslo 22 92 77 00), or through The Royal Ministry of Church Affairs, Education and Research (Akersgaten 42, Postboks 8119 Dep, 0032 Oslo; tel 22 34 90 90). Professional Associations at home should also be able to provide this information. For the comparability of vocational qualifications such as catering, construction and agriculture contact the Comparability Coordinator at the Employment Department (TS1E 1, Moorfoot, Room E603, Sheffield S1 4PQ; tel 0114-259 4144). Anyone wanting to work on the Norwegian oil rigs (even if it is only as a refurbisher) will need to have an Offshore Safety Certificate. Those awarded by the Robert Gordon University (Aberdeen AB9 2PG) meet with Norwegian requirements and are the equivalent of the Norwegian *Leiro* offshore certificate.

Sources of Jobs

Newspapers and Directories

Jobs in Norway are occasionally advertised in the UK press. *Overseas Jobs Express* (available by subscription only from Premier House, Shoreham Airport, BN43 5FF; tel 01273-440220, fax 01273-440229) occasionally has adverts for jobs in Norway — for example the shipping and oil companies sometimes recruit workers in engineering, design and construction for the off-shore petroleum industry. On Fridays *The Guardian* advertises European appointments and these are sometimes included in the Saturday Careers section of the Saturday edition. *The Times* and *The Independent* also carry European advertising. Recent adverts for Norway have included researchers in the chemical and petroleum industry for major oil companies. *The Guardian* Education Section on Tuesday lists jobs abroad for English teachers, as do the professional papers *The Times Educational Supplement* and The Times Higher Educational Supplement, both of which include adverts for teaching at tertiary level. Norway's English language colleges sometimes advertise there too. Casual and summer jobs can be found in the publications *Work Your Way Around the World, The Au Pair and Nanny's Guide to Working Abroad, Summer Jobs Abroad* and *Teaching English Abroad* all available from Vacation Work Publications (9 Park End Street, Oxford OX1 1HJ; tel 01865-241978, fax 01865-790885). Of the international papers, *The European* and *The International Herald Tribune* carry advertisements for posts abroad.

Advertising in Newspapers

You could try placing your own advertisement in one of the Norwegian dailies such as *Dagbladet*. Contact the UK advertisement rep: Frank L. Crane Ltd; tel 0171-837 3330 or *Verdens Gang:* (UK advertisement representative Oliver Smith and Partners Ltd; 0171-978 1440) or *Aftenposten:* (contact Powers Overseas Ltd 46 Keys Place, Dolphin Square, London SW1V 3NA; tel 0171-834 5566).

Norwegian Newspapers

If you can read Norwegian consult the daily national and regional papers which carry adverts for jobs. The major source for jobs is the daily Aftenposten. You can subscribe to it by contacting Aftenposten (Postboks 1178 Sentrum, 0107 Oslo; tel 22 11 50 40, fax 22 86 40 39). Regional papers which advertise jobs are *Bergens Tidende* in Bergen, *Adresseavisen* in Trondheim and *Stavanger Aftenblad* in Stavanger. Vacancies for engineers, teachers, lawyers and other professionals are advertised in *Norsk Lysinblad* (Postboks 177, 8501, Narvik). You can take out a subscription for 160 NOK per quarter. The *Teknisk Ukeblad* (Postboks 2476 Solli, 0202, Oslo 2) is a weekly for engineers and other technical staff where you can place an advertisement. *Benn's Media Europe*, available from most main reference libraries, has an exhaustive list of Norwegian newspapers, magazines and trade journals. Your local newsagent may be able to order the main Norwegian newspapers for you.

Writing

Another possible source of finding work is by direct written application to organisations. This is particularly true for casual and unskilled work where there may be a seasonal need — the ski resorts in winter for example or the youth hostels and hotels in summer. For lists of resorts and hotels contact the Norwegian Tourist Office (Charles House 5-11 Lower Regent Street, London SW1Y 4LR) enclosing an sae. For addresses of major Norwegian companies see the end of this chapter or consult *Kompass* available in most main libraries.

Professional Journals and Magazines

If you have a profession you should check your professional paper or magazine for possible jobs abroad. *Benn's Media Directory* for the UK and for Europe provides a comprehensive list of trade publications in Norway and can be found in most main reference libraries.

Professional Associations

Many major professional associations have contacts with other similar associations throughout Europe and the rest of the world. Even though they may not be able to provide direct help in finding work abroad, they may be able to provide you with contacts and with information about working overseas. In Norway you can contact the Norwegian Federation of Trade Unions: *Landsorganisasjonen i Norge (LO):* (Youngs gate 11, 0181 Oslo; tel 22 40 10 50, fax 22 40 17 43). The directory of *Trade associations and Professional Bodies* in the UK is available at most main reference libraries. Below is a list of some of the major professional associations.

Useful Addresses

The Biochemical Society: 7 Warwick Court, Holborn London WC1R 5EL.
The British Computer Society: 13 Mansfield Street, London W1M 0BQ.
The British Medical Association: BMA House, Tavistock Square, London WC1H 9JP.
The Chartered Institute of Bankers: 10 Lombard Street, London EC3Y 9ASD.

The Chartered Institue of Building Services Engineers: Delta House, 222 Balham High Road, London SW7.

The Chartered Institute of Building: Englemere Kings Ride, Ascot, Berks SL5 8BJ.

The Institute of Actuaries: Napier House, 4 Worcester Street, Gloucester Green, Oxford OX1 2AW.

The Institute of Chartered Accountants: Chartered Accountants' Hall, Moorgate Place, London EC2P 2BJ.

The Institute of Chartered Foresters: 22 Walker Street, Edinburgh EH3 7HR.

The Institute of Chartered Secretaries and Administrators: 16 Park Crescent, London W1N 4AH.

The Institute of Chartered Ship Brokers: 24 St Mary Ave, London EC3A 8DE.

The Institute of Civil Engineers: 1-7 Great George Street, London SW1P 3AA.

The Institute of Electrical Engineers: Michael Faraday House, Six Hills Way, Stevenage, Herts SG1 2AY.

The Institute of Gas Engineers: 17 Grosvenor Crescent, London SW1X 7ES.

The Institute of Marine Engineers: The Memorial Building, 76 Mark Lane, London EC3R 7JN.

The Institute of Mining and Metallurgy: 44 Portland Place, London W1N.

The Royal College of Nursing: Henrietta Place, 20 Cavendish Square, London W1M 0AB.

The Registrar and Chief Executive, United Kingdom Central Council for Nursing, Midwifery and Health Visiting: 23 Portland Place, London W1N 3AF.

The Royal College of Veterinary Surgeons: 32 Belgrave Square, London SW1X 8QP.

The Royal Institute of British Architects: 66 Portland Place, London W1N 4AD.

The Royal Pharmaceutical Society of Great Britain: 1 Lambeth High Street, London SE1 7JN.

Employment Organisations

The Norwegian State Employment Service (*Arbeidsformidlingen*)

The Arbeidsformidlingen has a European division which can provide useful information for foreigners looking for work in Norway. They produce the leaflet *Looking for Work in Norway*, available on request from Europa-Service (Postboks 420 Sentrum, 0103 Oslo; tel 22 42 41 41, fax 22 42 44 38). The visiting address is Europa Service, Øvre Slottsgate 11, 0101 Oslo; tel 22 42 41 41, fax 22 42 44 38. If you are looking for temporary work, an agency operates from the same organisation. You can phone them on 22 42 60 00, fax 22 42 10 08. The Employment Service also operates a Green Line (the *Grønne Linje*) which is a free telephone service providing information on vacancies throughout Norway (telephone 80 03 31 66). Another source of job information is the Job Automat which is a computer terminal where job seekers can look at vacancies themselves. Job centres and some libraries have job automats.

To find the address of your nearest job centre in Norway look under *Arbeidskontor* in the Yellow Pages (*gule sider*). There are over 150 jobcentres in Norway which all provide free advice on regulations for EEA nationals seeking work, working and living conditions in Norway, job vacancies and unemployment benefit and you will be allowed to use the telephone to ring an employer free of charge and use a typewriter. In principle all job vacancies advertised in Norway are registered on the employment services data base. The opening hours are 9am-3pm.

Norwegian Temporary Employment Agencies

Private temping agencies are listed in the Norwegian Yellow Pages under *Vikarutleie* and several cities have temping agencies such as Manpower, Norsk

Personnel and Top Temp. The main jobs offered are secretarial, accountancy and switchboard operators. All charge a fee for their services.

Job Organisations in the UK

Jobcentres in the UK can also offer advice and information on Norway. They should be able to put you in touch with Euroadvisors who are trained to deal with enquiries about working in the EEA and have computer contact with Norwegian labour market information. The Employment Service Overseas Placing Unit (Courtwood House, Silver Street Head, Sheffield S1 2DD; tel 0114-2596051, fax 0114-2596040) produce a useful fact sheet *Working in Norway*. You could also try contacting the Federation of Recruitment and Employment Services (FRES, 36-38 Mortimer Street, London W1N 7RB; tel 0171-323 4300, fax 0171-255 2878) which is a trade association of professional UK agencies licensed by the Employment Department and can place people abroad. Recruitment services specialising in technical personnel for the oil, gas and petrochemical industry are:

Dowell Schlumberger: Marble Arch House, 66-68 Seymour Street, London W1H 5AF.

(US address: International Services, C/O Dowell Schlumberger Inc, PO Box 4378, Houston, Texas).

Overseas Technical Services Ltd: First Floor, 100 College Road, Harrow HA1 1BQ.

Recruitment Services Ltd: Penthouse Suite, Worthing House, 2-6 South Street, Worthing, West Sussex BN11 3AE.

Shell International Petroleum Co Ltd: Shell Centre, London SE1 7NA.

Technical, Engineering, Administrative and Management Personnel (TEAM): TEAM House, Macklin Avenue, Cowpen Industrial Estate, Billingham, Cleveland TS23 4BZ.

Kvaerner Professional Services Ltd: Raglan House, 8-24 Stoke Road, Slough, Berkshire SL2 5AG.

Permanent Work

Nursing

The International Council of Nurses' Nursing Abroad scheme enables nurses who are members of the Royal College of Nursing to work in Norway. Contact the Royal College of Nursing (20 Cavendish Square, London W1M 0AB).

Teaching and Lecturing

Teaching English as a foreign language has become a passport to earning your way around the world but whether it will be your ticket to living and working in Norway is by no means certain. The Norwegian population generally has a very high level of English competence and whether dealing with manual workers or high fliers you will probably find you have no problem in making yourself understood. Consequently, the demand for English teachers in Norway is not particularly high and the outlook for TEFL teachers is not very promising. The stalwart of English teachers abroad, the British Council, has no overseas teaching sector for Norway. Adverts in the UK press for teachers in Norway are relatively rare although there are occasionally adverts in the *Times Educational Supplement* for teachers in Norway's English Language schools and colleges. Those wanting to teach in Norway will almost certainly have to have a degree (preferably English or foreign languages) *and* teaching qualifications — the minimum would be the Royal Society of Arts Preparatory Certificate in Teaching English as a

Foreign Language, although most schools would prefer the Diploma or a PGCE (Post Graduate Certificate in Education). Business experience or a knowledge of business English would be advantageous. Some schools will also expect you to have a reasonable level of competency in Norwegian and may choose to interview you in Norwegian. You could try writing directly to schools enclosing photocopies of your qualifications. Some language schools conduct interviews over the telephone. Full-time teaching jobs are hard to find and the majority of schools employ teachers on a part-time basis. You will usually be expected to arrange your own accommodation although if you ask for assistance in finding somewhere to live the school will probably try to help you. Basic hourly rates are about 100 NOK although you could expect to be paid more for teaching business English. The Folk Universities of Norway often hire native speakers to teach English and have branches in Stavanger, Kristiansand, Hamar and Skien.

International schools where teaching is done in English may also hire teachers whose discipline is not the English language.

Some Norwegians also study English at night school and you may be able to find work in one of the Norwegian voluntary adult education schemes (see address below).

The Norwegian Ministry of Church Affairs, Education and Research produce the useful leaflet: *Information for Foreign Teachers Seeking Positions in the Norwegian School System*, available free on request.

Specialists in English Language or literature (i.e. with postgraduate education up to doctorate level) could approach the English faculties of Norwegian Universities as posts are sometimes advertised in *The Times Higher Education Supplement* or *The Times Educational Supplement*. The New Red Cross Nordic United World College in Norway (which opened in 1995) has advertised for teachers in many disciplines (languages, history, geography, the sciences, art and design, economics and environmental science) in *The Times Educational Supplement*. The language of instruction is English.

Business specialists could approach The Norwegian School of Management (the NSM) which offers an 11 month MBA course and an MSC for students with a business background, both taught in English. The NSM is an amalgamation of four Norwegian business schools in Norway-the Norwegian School of Marketing, the Oslo School of Marketing, the Oslo Business School and the Norwegian School of Management-and is the nation's largest business school and the second-biggest educational establishment in Europe. It has over 15,000 students (including foreign students) and a faculty of 230. The NSM is Norway's only private business school and is not dependent on government budgets and regulations.

Useful Addresses

The Norwegian Ministry of Church Affairs, Education and Research: Postboks 8119, Dep 0032, Oslo 1; tel 22 34 90 90.

Folkeuniversitetet: Torggata 7, Postboks 496 Sentrum, 0105 Oslo; tel 22 42 44 90, fax 22 42 01 28.

Folkeuniversitetet Rogaland: Kongsgaten 58, 4012 Stavanger; tel 04 52 85 75, fax 53 48 56.

Kommunike Sprakinstitutt: Seilduksgaten 4, 0553 Oslo 5; tel 22 71 94 04, fax 22 71 82 11.

The European Council of International Schools: 21 Lavant Street, Petersfield, Hants GU32 3EL; tel 01730-268244 or 263131, fax 01730 267941.

Tertiary Education Colleges

The Red Cross Nordic United World College: Postboks 98, N-6810 Dale, Fjaler, fax 57 73 66 85.

The Norwegian School of Management: Sandvika, Oslo; tel 67 57 05 00, fax 67 67 05 70.

Voluntary Teaching Organisations
Friundervisning i Oslo: Postboks 496 Sentrum, 0105, Oslo 1.
Arveidernes Opplysningsforbund: Postboks 8703 Youngstorget, 0028 Oslo 1.

For a list of International Schools in Norway see *Schools and Education* in the *Daily Life* chapter.

Oil, Gas and Technical

Norway is among the world's major producers of oil and gas. The Norwegian oil industry is based in Stavanger and foreign nationals have traditionally filled many technical posts as Norway has a shortage of skilled engineers and technicians in this field. Rewards are high but so are standards and only workers with the appropriate skills will be employed. Oil and gas companies need a wide variety of engineers and support staff. Those wanting to work on the oil rigs should have taken an offshore survival course (see *Skills and Qualifications*) and many UK companies will require at least two years' experience on the North Sea rigs before considering workers for overseas assignments. The preferred age is often between 21 and 28.

Norwegian heavy technology plant giants Kvaerner have diversified into many main areas of the Norwegian technical and petrochemical fields and are a major recruiter of overseas foreign workers. Kvaerner offer contracts from between two weeks and four years. A married worker is entitled to return flight to their home every two weeks and an accommodation allowance. A single worker receives less but is allowed some expenses. Workers should be prepared to pay for the first one or two nights in Norway in a hotel but should contact the Norwegian representative at the work site to arrange local accommodation. In practice many workers arrange this through word of mouth with colleagues. Most landlords will expect a month's rent in advance and advances can be paid by the company towards this. Wages are paid monthly. On contract work there are no paid holidays and most workers take holidays at the end of their contract. Wages are good — workers are given a net deal and typically a draughtsman can earn £11 per hour take home pay. Skilled engineers can earn as much as £40 per hour after tax.

For further information on the oil and gas industry consult *The Oil and Gas International Yearbook* available from most public libraries. Details of production and exploration licences in the Norwegian sector of the North Sea can be found in *The UK Offshore Oil and Gas Yearbook*. Contact the personnel departments of major national and multinational oil and construction companies for details on recruitment for Norway.

Useful Addresses

Engineering and Construction Companies:
Kvaerner Professional Services Ltd: Raglan House, 8-24 Stoke Road, Slough, Berkshire Sl2 5AG; tel 01753-824621.
W S Atkins Group Consultants: Woodcote Grove, Ashley Road, Epsom, Surrey KT18 5BW.
Kennedy and Donkin: Westbrook Mills, Godalming, Surrey GU7 2AZ.
Mott MacDonald Ltd, Demeter House, Station Road, Cambridge CB1 2RS.

Recruitment Consultants
Dowell Schlumberger: Marble Arch House, 66-68 Seymour Street, London W1H 5AF.

(US address International Services, C/O *Dowell Schlumberger Inc:* PO Box 4378, Houston, Texas).
Overseas Technical Services Ltd: First Floor, 100 College Road, Harrow HA1 1BQ.
Recruitment Services Ltd: Penthouse Suite, Worthing House, 2-6 South Street, Worthing, West Sussex BN11 3AE.
Shell International Petroleum Co Ltd: Shell Centre, London SE1 7NA.
Technical, Engineering, Administrative and Management Personnel (TEAM): TEAM House, Macklin Avenue, Cowpen Industrial Estate, Billingham, Cleveland TS23 4BZ.

British Oil Companies in Norway
BP Norge AS: Arbiensgate 11, 0203 Oslo 2.
BP Petroleum Development Ltd: Forusbeen 35, Postboks 197, 4033 Forus.
Castrol Norge AS: Drammensveien 97, 0205 Oslo 2.
ICI Norge AS, Drammensveien 126, 0277 Oslo 2.
Mobil Exploration Norway: Postboks 501, 4001 Stavanger.
Norsk Shell AS: Postboks 50, Manglerud 0612, Oslo 6.
Schlumberger Norge AS: Gamle Forus vei 49, Postboks 233, 4033 Forus.

Temporary Work

Farming

Norwegian farms are mainly small, family run affairs and there is considerable seasonal demand for extra labour. Work is varied and can range from haymaking, tending livestock, picking fruit and vegetables, driving tractors, milking, painting fences, maintenance and house work. Under Norwegian law all foreigners working on farms with domestic animals in Norway must go through a disinfection of both themselves and their clothes — you will be given further details on applying although it is apparently a fairly harmless procedure. Foreign workers usually live with the family who will probably speak good English. Farms are situated throughout Norway and whilst most people don't go to work on a farm for the night life, it should be borne in mind that farms in the north tend to be a long way from the nearest town and you may have to be inventive at providing your own entertainment when you are not working. Most people experience the Norwegians as friendly, laid back and very hospitable and you will probably be treated as if you were one of the family. An average working day might be from 8 am to 4 pm although bear in mind that some farmers may want you to do more, especially when harvesting or haymaking and work can be quite physically demanding. There are two main agencies which can offer placements on Norwegian farms: Atlantis Youth Exchange (Rolf Hofmosgate 18, N-0655 Oslo; tel 22 67 0043, fax 22 68 68 08) operates a working guest programme where you will receive pocket money and board and lodging. Agricultural experience is preferred but is not essential. The International Farm Experience programme (YFC Centre, National Agricultural Centre, Stoneleigh Park, Kenilworth, Warwickshire CV8 2LG; tel 01203-696584, fax 01203-696559) is part of the National Federation of Young Farmers Club and offers placements of three to twelve months at any time of the year. To be offered a place on the programme you must have at least two years farming experience (one of these could be at an agricultural college), be aged 18-28, have a valid driving licence and intend to take up a career in agriculture or horticulture. Participants usually live and work with a farming family although for horticultural placements which involve working in nurseries alternative accommodation will be found for you. As far as possible individual interests and requirements are matched with the work and the purpose of the programme is to enable participants to broaden their knowledge of farming methods abroad. Work is paid but wages are often only sufficient to cover costs and you will be taxed at local rate. Accommodation and food are free. There is a registration fee of £85 and you will need to make your own travel and insurance arrangements. The average working week is about 40 hours.

Casual farm labour in Norway is generally employed for fruit picking. The majority of harvesters are foreign — a reflection on the comparatively low wages which are paid for piece work. You could try contacting farms around Drammen in early July for the season. Beyond Trondheim the harvest is from mid-July to August. Crops include strawberries, raspberries, blueberries and potatoes and other vegetables. For accommodation you will probably have to take your own tent though you may see other Europeans, mainly Poles who make for the Norwegian harvests and camp in their cars.

The Skiing Industry

Ask a Norwegian if he's a skier and he'll probably tell you 'No, I'm a bank manager/teacher/farmer...'. To most Norwegians skiing is almost as natural as breathing and hardly worth a mention unless you are one of the country's possessors of Winter Olympic medals. The saying goes that Norwegians are born with skis on and this slight exaggeration implies, not without justification that they are on skis almost as soon as they can stand upright. Norwegian ski resorts are comparatively uncommercialised and the ratio of skiers to ski slopes is much lower than in the central European Alps. The scenery is spectacular and there are plenty of opportunities for cross country skiing. Qualified ski instructors can try contacting Norwegian winter skiing resorts prior to the season. Although there is no shortage of Norwegian instructors, many resorts also employ English-speaking ones too. If you simply want to go to Norway for the marvellous skiing facilities and to support yourself whilst you take advantage of them you could approach the peripheral parts of the ski industry such as shops and hotels. Norwegian ski resorts may be far less congested than those of the Alps, but there are still work opportunities in the skiing season and foreigners have found work in bars, hotels and cafeterias and also in snow clearing and D-Jing. If you get work you will probably find that it is only sufficient to cover your living costs and to enable you to ski through the season. Relaxed laws for EEA nationals wanting to work in Norway mean that you can now go over and look for work on the spot but you may be deterred by the hight cost of living if you will have to find and pay for your own accommodation. You could try fixing up work in advance by writing to resorts, outlining your skills. The main skiing resorts are: Oppdal, Trysil, Geilo, Voss, Gausdal and of course Lillehammer which was home to the 1994 Winter Olympics. For a comprehensive list of Norwegian ski resorts contact the Norwegian National Tourist Office (5-11 Lower Regent Street, London SW1Y 4LX). For further details on working in the skiing industry consult the book *Working in Ski Resorts* (Vacation Work Publications, 9 Work End Street, Oxford OX1 1HJ; tel 01865-241978, fax 01865-790885).

Travel and Tourism

Tourism is a boom area and one of Norway's biggest earners. About 90,000 people are employed in the tourist industry and this figure looks set to increase. Although you can go to Norway and look for work it is better to try to arrange something in advance to save time, money and possible disappointment. You can obtain a list of Norwegian hotels from the Norwegian tourist Office (see above address). The majority of hotels are based in the south and around the beach resorts of the south coast and on the fjords. The net monthly wage for an unskilled worker is about 7,000 NOK after deductions for board and lodging. Unless you have a particular skill or are able to speak the language you are unlikely to get anything more lucrative. The big advantage of hotel work is that food and accommodation will be provided. Several Norwegian youth hostels also employ unskilled domestic staff, providing board and lodging but little more than pocket money. Contact the headquarters at: *Norske Vandrerhjem:* (Dronningens Gate 26, 0154 Oslo; tel 22 42 14 10).

Au Pairs

The demand for au pairs in Norway is not huge but there are opportunities, particularly in the larger cities of Oslo and Bergen. The other cities of southern Norway are also worth trying to locate jobs in. Preference is given to au pairs who are prepared to work for ten months or more, although some families will accept au pairs for shorter stays during the summer. Conditions laid down for au pairs by the Council of Europe are strictly observed in Norway and you will not normally be expected to work more than six hours a day. Usually you will live with the family. Most Norwegian families are very friendly and welcoming and will probably speak excellent English. The typical age for this kind of work is 18-30. Boys are also eligible for this type of work. Board, lodging and pocket money are provided. On the Atlantis Youth exchange programme this is currently 2,300 NOK per month but is, unfortunately, subject to a 30% tax deduction. To apply you should provide two references and a medical certificate obtained within the previous three months. Apply up to three months in advance. For further details on au pair work in Norway and a list of agencies consult *The Au Pair and Nanny's Guide to Working Abroad* (Vacation Work Publications, 9 Park End Street, Oxford OX1 1HJ; tel 01865-241978, fax 01865-790885).

Useful Addresses

Helping Hands Au Pair and Domestic Agency: 39 Rutland Avenue, Thorpe Bay, Essex Southend-on-Sea SS1 2XJ; tel 01702-602067.
Euro-Pair Agency: 28 Derwent Avenue, Pinner, Middlesex HA5 4QJ; tel 0181-421 2100, fax 0181-428 6416.

In Norway
Norsk Personnel AS: Postboks 202, N-1301 Sandvika; tel 67 54 57 90.
ASSE Norge: Kirkveien 64B, N-0364 Oslo; tel 22 46 73 40, fax 22 46 87 90.
Norintres Aupair Bureau: Nordnesveien 30 A, N-5005, Bergen; tel 55 23 08 46, fax 55 23 08 46.
Atlantis Youth Exchange: Rolf Hofmosgate 18, 0655 Oslo, Norway; 22 67 00 43, fax 22 68 68 08.

Voluntary Work

There are a few opportunities for voluntary work in Norway. The Nansen International Centre which is south of Oslo needs volunteers to work with emotionally disturbed teenagers on a renovated farm. Volunteers help with all day to day aspects of running the farm including cooking, looking after the animals and cleaning. They should be prepared to help motivate young people and encourage them to participate in the centre's activities. There are opportunities for sports and excursions. Applicants should be 22 or over, possess a full driving licence, have had previous experience of working with children and be prepared to work hard and show initiative. The normal length of stay is one year but there is a special six week summer programme. Volunteers receive full board and lodging and 500 NOK per week. Apply to the director before April for the summer project.

International Dugnad is the Norwegian branch of the Civil Service International which promotes international peace through work projects. Volunteers should be 18 or over and be prepared to work a 35-40 hour week. Work camps take place between June and September and participants stay for two to four weeks. Food, accommodation and insurance are included but you will have to provide your own transport and there are no wages. Work could be on farms or in the community and is usually manual in nature.

The Atlantis Youth Exchange is a non-profit making foundation for international youth exchange. Each year about 500 people aged between 18-30 participate in the Working Guest Programme which places them with Norwegian farming families. Participants live as part of the family and help with work on the farm and in the house. Average work times are about 35 hours a week with one and a half days off. The minimum stay is four weeks and the maximum three months. Board, lodging and 500 NOK per week pocket money are provided. You will have to pay your own travel expenses and there is a registration fee of 830 NOK. Most of this will be refunded if you are not placed. Applicants should apply at least three months in advance and will need to produce two passport photos, a medical certificate and the registration fee. Some families will accept two people who apply together. UK applicants should apply through Concordia Youth Service Volunteers (address below).

The British Trust for Conservation Volunteers arranges working holidays for two weeks in the summer in conjunction with the Norwegian Nansen society. Work involves construction of footpaths, conservation of old buildings and aspects of countryside maintenance. Volunteers should be aged over 18. Transport, board and lodging will be provided in Norway but you will have to provide your own fares and there is a cost of £165 for the holiday. No wages are paid.

Useful Addresses

Nansen International Centre: Barnegården Breivold, Nesset, 1400 Ski, Norway; tel 09 94 67 91.
International Dugnad: Langes Gate 6, 0165 Oslo 1.
The Atlantis Youth Exchange: Rolf Hofmosgate 18, 0655 Oslo; tel 22 67 00 43.
Concordia Youth Services Volunteers: Recruitment Secretary, 8 Brunswick Place, Hove, Sussex BN3 1ET; tel 01273-772086.
The British Trust for Conservation Volunteers: Room 1WH, 36 St Mary's Street, Wallingford, Oxfordshire OX10 0EU; tel 01491-839766.

Aspects of Employment

The Norwegian labour force generally is of a high quality, literate and hard working. There is no shortage of unskilled and management level personnel but there is, however, an overall shortage of skilled workers particularly engineers and specialized personnel for the oil sector. Turnover rates in industry are generally quite low. Absenteeism for unskilled labour averages at 11% for women and 16.5% for men. The labour force comprises about 65% of the total population.

Salaries

Surprisingly for a socialist country there is no national minimum wage in Norway. Base wages are fixed in collective bargaining agreements. In practice, a wage would rarely be less than the equivalent of £5 per hour. Wages in Norway are high relative to the rest of western Europe but highly educated professionals are on a comparable level. Payment for overtime is at an agreed rate of between

50%-100%. Most employers will provide group insurance benefits, a subsidised canteen and some employees receive a company car. Payment is usually made directly into a current account.

Working Conditions

The Working Environment Act legislates on employment conditions and regulates employees' rights and duties and employers' obligations. Because of the Act employees have more say about their working environment and have increased protection against dismissal. The average working week in Norway is 40 hours although administrative jobs tend to be 37.5 hours per week. Shift workers have slightly shorter working weeks. The hours are usually worked over a five day period. Overtime is limited by Norwegian law but a temporary exemption can be granted by the *Arbeidsdirektoratet* (Labour Directorate). All employees are entitled to four weeks plus one day of holidays each year and ten days of legal holidays. Employees aged over 60 are entitled to five weeks holiday. Employees can take three consecutive weeks of holidays during the summer vacation. Workers receive 10.2% of their total compensation, paid to them for the rest of the year. Short-term contract foreign employees, particularly in the oil and gas fields, may not receive paid holiday as part of the contract and many choose to wait until the end of the contract before taking holidays.

Dismissals and Discrimination

Employment can be terminated because of a company's situation e.g. reduced production levels or because of an employee's behaviour e.g. gross misconduct, incompetence etc. Between two and six months notice are required depending on the length of service. The notice period with full pay usually eliminates the need for severance payments. Employees have the right to contest dismissals but in practice this rarely happens. If you feel that you are being unfairly treated at work you can contact the local office of the the Directorate of Labour Inspection (*Arbeidstilsynet*) who will treat your case with confidentiality.

Social Security

The 1966 Social Security Act in Norway requires everyone who works or resides in Norway to contribute to the social security programme. Contributions range from 0-7.9% of gross income. Foreigners are exempt from paying social security contributions if they are covered by a social security system in their home country and/or are a member of a country with which Norway has signed a social security agreement.

Trade Unions

The majority of workplaces in Norway have one or more trade unions. The relationship between unions and employers is generally good with unions taking an active part in company decisions. Most companies with between 50 and 200 employees have one third labour representation on the board of directors. Although this is not compulsory, employees are entitled to request it. Companies with more than 200 employees elect a corporate assembly with a minimum of 12 members, the majority of whom are chosen at the annual shareholders meeting and the rest by fellow employees. The corporate assembly is the final decision making body and elects the board of directors. Assembly meetings are held twice a year and decisions are made about major investments, modernisation and other issues affecting the labour force. Shop stewards are often part of committees for the hiring of workers so that unions are often involved in the hiring and laying off of workers.

Membership of a trade union is voluntary and the annual monthly membership fee is about 1% of the gross pay. Most trade unions provide collective insurance coverage. Unions are organised according to trade or craft under the umbrella of the Norwegian Confederation of Trade Unions (LO). Negotiations on working conditions and wages are usually conducted on an industry wide basis between the Confederation of Norwegian Business and Industry and the LO. If agreement cannot be reached the matter is usually referred to arbitration.

Women at Work

Norway claims to provide equal rights for workers regardless of gender, race, colour or religion. Norway's record generally on women's rights is good and this applies to the work place. Norwegian women are entitled to ten months maternity leave on full pay. European regulations state that the minimum allowance should be 14 weeks. Inevitably the rich pickings for manual and technical labour in the oil and gas fields of the North Sea, still tend to be a male preserve.

The Norwegian Regional Development Fund (*Distriktenes Utbyggingsfond*) makes relatively high grants for projects which are aimed at employing women, particularly in business and industry and has special incentives for training women in these area.

Etiquette in the Workplace

Norwegians like state-of-the-art business frills and mobile phones, business cards and electronic diaries are prevalent.

Beyond the frills they can be disarmingly honest — the used car salesman pitch is rare in Norway and you will probably be told of a product's shortcomings before getting down to the business of fixing a deal. It can be quite a relief not to have to work it out for yourself but the honesty can take a bit of getting used to.

Business matters are conducted along proper channels in Norway but the atmosphere will probably be pleasantly relaxed even though the compulsive hand-shaking can seem rather formal. Norwegians dress for business occasions as much anywhere else although there is a tendency towards more casual dress in summer to take account of the better weather. Most people take their holidays from mid-June to the beginning of August so this is not the best time to do business. Liquid lunches are rare in Norwegian business and work circles and given the very high price of alcohol this is probably a blessing. The working day tends to end by about 4pm but this can be earlier in the dark winter months.

Business and Industry Report

Owing to geographical factors, Norway was industrialised comparatively late by European standards. Historically, Norway has always been an agrarian country and until fairly recently the economy was dependent on farming and fishing. The influence of both these areas still exerts a powerful influence on the Norwegian economy even though their input into the national revenue is now relatively small. Norway's decision not to join the European Union came largely from the fishing and farming communities. The roots of Norway's opposition to Brussels lie in Norway's vision of itself as an independent and self-sufficient community rooted in the soil and its own national heritage.

During the post war years Norway experienced a marked development in manufacturing, industries and exports and now ranks as one of the world's most modern and advanced nations whose products have won acceptance abroad particularly amongst highly developed industrial countries. The range of Norwegian manufacturing is wide for such a small nation and includes raw materials, semi-finished products, consumer goods and industry goods. Norway is particularly noted for its advanced technology and for its electrochemical and electrometallurgical industry. Norway is the largest producer of aluminium in Western Europe and the world's largest exporter after Canada. The discovery of oil and gas in the 1970s has transformed Norway into one of the world's richest nations and the oil and gas industry on the Norwegian Continental shelf is highly developed. Off-shoots of the oil and gas industry have been the production of equipment for the oil industry and the development of oil technology and a large petrochemical industry has also been created. Traditional commodity exports (engineering, metals, fish and fish products, chemical products, pulp and paper, and other manufactured goods) accounted for 113 billion NOK in 1993. Norway needs to promote strong growth in traditional commodity exports to reduce over dependency on the oil revenues which are subject to fluctuation and eventual depletion.

Norway is heavily dependent on foreign trade. Approximately 44% of the GNP comes from exports whilst imports account for 37%. Main imports include oil rigs, airplanes, ships, motor vehicles, metal ores, industrial material and equipment, clothing iron and steel, office machines and petroleum related products. Major exports include natural gas, petroleum and petroleum-related products, fish, ships and oil platforms. Norway's main trading partners are the United States, the UK, Sweden, Denmark, Germany, France and the Netherlands.

Shipping

Shipping has been a traditional mainstay of the Norwegian economy. Until 1973, Norwegian ships carried up to 10% of the world's tonnage and accounted for one third of the country's foreign currency earnings. However shipping crises in the 1980s, high costs and strict personnel regulations led to many ship owners registering their ships abroad in order to stay competitive. Economic depression at the end of the 1980s and increased competition from low-cost Far-Eastern companies lead to empty order books and closed ship yards in Norway as elsewhere in the world. Shipping, is, however a cyclical business and although the shipping sector of the Norwegian economy has been reduced, it is expected to increase its impact on the economy in years to come. The introduction of the Norwegian International Ship Register in 1987 has helped revitalise shipping operations and there has been a consequent increase in export revenues. Gross shipping freights accounted for 46 billion NOK of the 90 billion NOK earned abroad in the Norwegian service sector in 1993. Norway currently commands the third largest merchant fleet in the world (including Norwegian ships under foreign flags). The biggest success story is the rise of the ship building division of Kvaerner, Norway's heavy technology plant, who have risen to become one of the world's top three shipbuilders (the others are Japan's Mitsubishi and South Korea's Hyundai) with profits of over 1 billion NOK ($145 million). Kvaerner employs a total of 23,400 workers, a 60% increase in the workforce from 1989 and has bought up many of Europe's ailing ship yards including yards in Scotland eastern Germany and Finland.

Fishing

Norway's extensive coastline and poor soil mean that fishing has traditionally played an important role in the Norwegian economy. Today, however, it contributes only about 1% of the GDP. Of the country's 26,700 fishermen, only about half list fishing as their sole occupation and the fishing industry forms the basis for a large and increasing fish processing industry which offers seasonal employment to many farmers. The last few years have seen more and more resources being diverted from the traditional fisheries to fish farming with bred salmon and trout figuring increasingly on the export list. Like most western fishing nations, Norway has had to contend with the problem of depleted fishing resources but Norwegian stocks have recovered to some extent and from the early 1990s Norway increased its cod quota. Unlike in the rest of the European Union where trawlers are banned from returning to port with undersized fish, Norwegian fishermen have to register the entire catch thus facilitating closer supervision of quotas and fish stocks. Management of fishing stocks in the Barents sea around the Norwegian and Russian controlled Svalberd Islands is negotiated biannually with Russia. About two thirds of the Norwegian catch goes into fish meal and oil but some is processed for human consumption in freezing plants. Fish offal is used to feed the mink on Norway's fur farms. A key Norwegian export is salted fish sold mainly to Greece, Spain and Portugal. Fishing accounts for 14% of Norway's non-petroleum export earnings and a large percent of the exports is in the form of raw fish to the European Union which is then processed in a third country to avoid heavy duties. Norway was intending to sell more processed fish to the European Union if they had become a member state but now this is not set to happen. Opinion on membership was sharply divided in the fishing industry with many fishermen fearing that Norwegian membership would mean ceding control over territorial waters to the EU's Common Fisheries Policy (CFP). Others were hoping for increased profits that would have come with the abolition of tariffs of up to 20% which are currently imposed on Norwegian fish products. Norway's leading fish products manufacturer the Frionor Group were largely in favour of membership. Frioner has a current turnover of 2 billion NOK and sells about 23% of its production to the European Union.

Oil and Gas

The petroleum industry in Norway is relatively young but it has been enormously successful. Norway proclaimed sovereignty over the Norwegian Continental Shelf in 1963 when the first oil and gas licences for exploration were allocated. In 1969, after four years of exploratory drilling, the first commercially important discovery of petroleum was made at the Ekofisk field. The first submarine pipeline was put into operation in 1975 when petroleum was first exported. By 1980 the export of oil and gas had come to rival the combined value of traditional commodity exports. In 1980 drilling began north of the 62nd parallel and in 1981 the first discoveries were made outside the coast of Norway. By 1987 seventeen fields were in production on the Norwegian Continental Shelf. Most of the reserves of the Norwegian Continental Shelf are in the North Sea (south of the 62nd parallel) where there are an estimated 4.2 billion ton oil equivalents (toe). Of the reserves, about 63% is gas and 37% oil.

Norway now produces as much oil as Venezuela, more than Nigeria and twice as much as Indonesia and it has the biggest export of oil and gas in western Europe. Oil and gas exports account for one third of total foreign sales. Oil export is expected to peak in the mid 1990s at around 2.3 million barrels a day and it is predicted that this level of production should be maintained for about another 40 years. The oil services sector is a major employer, employing 64,000 Norwegians. The oil service is also heavily dependent on overseas expertise to fill in the lack of skilled manpower in Norway and is a major employer of overseas labour. Economists are predicting that oil revenues should remain buoyant in the 1990s. About 88% of the oil and gas is exported.

Although Norway has vast reserves of natural gas, selling it abroad is more of a problem than selling oil. 60% of Norway's domestic energy comes form hydrothermal sources of the multitudinous waterfalls and water sources and there is little need for gas in Norway although the country is now considering the possibility of using its own most abundant resource itself. The first gas-powered station is expected to be in operation by the end of the century and gas production is expected to last for another 100 years.

Whilst the oil and gas discoveries have given a massive boost to the Norwegian economy, making it one of the world's richest nations, it has left Norway highly vulnerable to oil price swings. Norway experienced its deepest depression since the 1930s when oil prices slumped in 1986 fro $40 to $10 a barrel, directly causing a reduction of 7% in the GDP. Whilst there is a general awareness of the dangers of over dependence on off-shore energy Norway has so far been slow to implement any effective measures to protect the economy in the face of oil slumps and there is of course the eventual prospect of depletion of the energy reserves.

Mining, Minerals and Chemicals

Norway has a few ores, principally pyrites (giving copper and sulphur) and iron ore, small amounts of zinc, copper and lead are mined. In southwestern Norway is Europe's largest deposit of ilmenite (titanium). Huge quantities of electric power are supplied by rivers and as well as supplying domestic need, electricity from hydroelectric power also fuels industry. Half of Norway's hydroelectricity is used by the electrochemical and electrometallurgical plants which make Norway the world's largest exporter of iron-based alloys and metals combined. Norway is also a major exporter of aluminum, nickel, copper and zinc. The plant at Herøya is the world's second largest producer of magnesium. Other industries include silica, graphite and quartz. Chemical exports accounted for 13 per cent of traditional (i.e. non oil and gas) exports. Norway's biggest international industrial group, Norsk Hydro, centres some of its main activity on key industrial materials with an energy base and has more than 40 sections based throughout western Europe. They have recently opened a new materials section of the Norsk Hydro research centre which employs materials scientists.

Farming and Forestry

About 5% of Norway's total area is agricultural land and there has been a decline in the number of farms since the Second World War. Farms are generally small and isolated. Only about one third of the farms have more than 25 acres (ten hectares) and less than 1% have more than 125 acres. Farm labour is scarce and most farmers do the work themselves whilst taking on seasonal temporary labour. Farms are usually highly mechanised and fertilised and the total output is relatively high. Livestock is the main agricultural produce particularly sheep, milk cows, goats, pigs and hens, making the country more than self-sufficient in animal products. A major agricultural import is cereal crops. Farms are heavily subsidised by the government.

Forestry has formed a traditional role in the Norwegian economy and forms the basis for the wood processing industry. Exports of pulp and paper amount to about 5.6% of traditional commodity exports.

Manufacturing

Many Norwegian industries provide products used in gas and oil exploration, development and production. The decline in the shipping industry saw a move away from ship building to the production of sophisticated equipment for off-shore exploration and Norway has become a leader in the technology of off-shore exploration products. About one third of the employment in manufacturing is in the engineering industry. Norwegian civil engineers claim to be some of the best in the world and they have achieved some outstanding results in the transportation system with the unpromising material of Norwegian terrain in terms of road building and surfacing, tunnelling and bridge building. Electrical equipment is a major Norwegian industry and electronics for computers and telecommunications is a growth industry. A large part of the manufacturing industry is developed around raw materials like wood and mining extracts which are mainly intended for the export market. Other areas of manufacture are iron, steel, ferro-alloys and aluminium, industrial chemicals (fertilisers and artificial fibres) and paper products.

Manufactured Goods
Manufactured goods other than fish, chemicals and engineering account for about 11% of the traditional commodity exports. This area includes building, furniture and clothes.

Tourism
Tourism is a boom industry in Norway and its revenue (14 billion NOK in 1993) equals that of the fisheries and fish farming industry combined whilst employing nearly four times as many people (an estimated 90,000). Norway has experienced a rise of 30% in commercial guest nights between 1990 and 1993. Foreign nationals formed 45% of the total tourist numbers. Norway sells itself on its healthy natural image and since 1989 has emphasised its clean air and eco-friendliness. The tourist industry has quadrupled its marketing and image building budget to promote the traditional attractions of fjords and mountains. Paradoxically whilst Norway has been promoting an image of a country living in harmony with nature its tourist industry has been under a silent boycott from international animal rights activists because of the Norwegian whale killing reputation. Nonetheless Norway has been cashing in on the natural attractions of whales by offering 'whale safaris'. The unofficial boycotts are estimated to have cost the Norwegian tourist industry a minimum of 10 million NOK ($1.4 million) a year but tourism still accounts for 2.5% of the GNP and the figure is expected to rise.

The heavy cost of living ensures that Norway is unlikely to become an attraction for the masses but prices over the past few years have been relatively stable whilst costs in other parts of Europe have increased and there is now more of a parity in costs than there has been previously.

Regional Employment Guide

Inevitably, employment in Norway is influenced by the regional variations in population. The majority of the population live in the south with Oslo, Bergen, Trondheim and Stavanger forming the major urban areas. Most industry in Norway has developed along the coastline which has historically supplied the hydroelectric power needed for Norwegian industry. The fjords of Vestlandet are home to the majority of Norway's smelting plants which were built here to capitalise on the great resources of hydroelectic power in the region. The interior and in particular the vast plains of Finnmark have very little industry but industry is spread throughout the long Norwegian coastline up to Narvik, which is a major iron ore centre, and further north the city of Tromsø has a large fish processing industry. Central Norway around the Trondheim Fjord forms the heart of Norway's agricultural region, being amongst the more fertile areas of Norway. This area also contains a large percentage of Norway's mining and forestry industry. The inland fjords of the Hardanger district are more sheltered and are the home of the fruit growing regions, specialising in apples and cherries. The Sunnmøre district north of Bergen has many engineering firms and contains the bulk of the Norwegian furniture industry, centred on the industrial town of Ålesund. The oil and gas industries operate primarily from the south east coast of Norway and the hub of the off-shore mining activity is Stavanger. Stavanger is also an expanding industrial centre and is historically linked to the canning and fishing industries. Whilst fishing is carried out throughout the Norwegian coastline, it tends to predominate around the cities of Molde and Kristiansund. The shipping industry is based mainly around the larger port towns of the southern tip of Norway. The south coast forms the heart of the tourist industry with the majority of hotels being in southern coastal towns.

Directory of Major Employers

For an exhaustive list of Norwegian companies consult *Kompass Produkter* which should be available from your local library. It is produced in association with the Norwegian Trade Council and provides information on all major companies and manufacturers in Norway in Norwegian, German, French, English and Spanish. Its fellow publication *Kompass Firma Informasjoner* gives further details of individual companies. The Norwegian Trade Council can also provide this and additional information. The UK Norway Trade Council is at Charles House (5-11 Regent Street, London SW1Y 4LR; tel 0171-973 0188, fax 0171-973 01 89). The US Norway Trade Council is at 88 Third Avenue, 23rd Floor, New York, NY 10022, USA; tel 1-212 421 92 10; fax 1-212 838 03 74. Or contact the headquarters in Norway (Drammensveien 40, N-0243 Oslo; tel 22 92 63 00; fax 22 92 64 00). For financial information from the largest Norwegian companies consult *Norges Største Bedrifter*. It is available in most main libraries and is published by Økonomisk Literatur AS (Lørenveien 68, Postboks 315, Økern, 0511 Oslo; tel 22 63 51 00, fax 22 63 10 84).

Norwegian Banks
Bankenes Betallingssentral AS: Postboks 81 Kaldbakken, 0902 Oslo; tel 02 89 89 89, fax 02 21 24 24.
Den Norske Bank (DNB) Fonds, AS: Postboks 399, Sentrum, 0103 Oslo; tel 22 94 88 50.
Finans A/S: Postboks 2536 Solli, 0202 Oslo; tel 02 55 74 24, fax 02 34 66 51.
Industri and Skipsbanken A/S: Bradbenken 1, 5003 Bergen; tel 05 31 90 70, fax 05 31 99 10.
Kreditkassen (Christiania Bank og Kreditkasse): Middelthunsgate 17, N0368 Oslo 3; tel 22 48 44 81, fax 22 48 49 43.
Sparenbanken Møre: Postboks 121, 6001 Ålesund; tel 07 18 90 00, fax 07 12 98 85.
Sparebanken Kredittselskapp A/S: Postboks 8283 Hammersborg, 0129 Oslo; tel 02 20 24 34, fax 02 20 74 58.

Building and Construction
Drillcon Contracting avd. Norge: Elgveien 6, 1640 Rå de; tle 09 28 55 44, fax 09 28 50 32.
Eeg-Henriksen Anlegg AS: Postboks 745 Sentrum, 0104 Oslo; tel 02 20 81 35, fax 02 11 28 60.
Selvaagbygg AS: Postboks 100 Vineren, 0319 Oslo; tel 02 41 36 90, fax 02 49 45 20.
Statoil: Postboks 300, 4001 Stavanger; tel 04 80 80 80, fax 04 8-70 42.

Chemical Engineering

BASF Norge AS: Postboks 311, 1370 Asker; tel 02 90 46 60, fax 02 90 47 55.
Henkel Nopco AS: Postboks 2040 Strømsø, 3003 Drammen; tel 03 88 03 80, fax 03 88 02 45.
Norsk Hydro AS: Bygdøy allé 2, 0240 Oslo; tel 02 43 21 00, fax 02 43 27 25.

Computer Software
ComIT AS: Postboks 1854 Lade, 7002 Trondheim; tel 07 92 18 44, fax 07 92 25 11.
Control Data AS: Postboks 112 Refstad, 0513 Oslo; tel 02 15 14 00, fax 02 15 98 21.
IBM: Postboks 500, 1411 Kolbotn; tel 02 99 80 00, fax 02 99 93 33.
Computer Associates Norway AS: Postboks 244, 2001 Lillestrøm; tel 06 80 00, fax 06 80 07 11.
Electronic Data Systems AS: 2001 Lillestrøm, tel 06 81 18 00,fax 06 81 58 79.
NCR Norge AS: Postboks 24 Grefsen, 0486 Oslo; tel 02 95 36 00, fax 02 95 36 01.
Scandinavian Software Norge AS: Postboks 115, 5062 Bønes; tel 05 12 15 10, fax 05 12 59 20.

Computer Hardware
G & L Beijers Electronics AS: Postboks 487 Brakerøya, 3002 Drammen; tel 03 89 42 70, fax 03 89 51 01.
Hitachi Data Systems AS: 1324 Lysaker; tel 02 12 53 70, fax 02 12 53 75.
IBM: Postboks 500, 1411 Kolbotn; tel 02 99 80 00, fax 02 99 93 33.
Control Data AS: Postboks 112 Refstad, 0513 Oslo; tel 02 15 14 00, fax 02 15 98 21.
NCR Norge AS: Postboks 24 Grefsen, 0486 Oslo; tel 02 95 36 00, fax 02 95 36 01.
3M Norge AS: Postboks 100, 2013 Skjelten; tel 06 84 75 00, fax 06 84 17 88.
Universal Communications AS: Postboks 3644, 3007 Drammen; tel 03 20 33 00, fax 03 20 31 10.

Fish Processing
Frioner AS: Postboks 195, 1324 Lysaker; tel 02 1 30 10, fax 02 12 30 10.
Norfood Group AS: Kai 16, Brattøra,7010 Trondheim; tel 07 51 29 99, fax 07 52 22 47.
Nordica Foods AS: Øtrem, 6013 Ålesund,; tel 07 13 05 76, fax 07 13 05 76.
Northern Seafoods AS: Postboks 303, 3430 Myre; tel 08 83 41 77, fax 07 31 54 38.

Insurance Companies
Norsk Hydro AS: Bygdøy allé 2, 0240 Oslo; tel 02 43 21 00, fax 02 43 27 25.
Thomas Howell Group Norway AS: Ankerveien 209, 1343 Eiksmarka; tel 02 24 96 05, fax 02 24 92 97.
Vital Forsikring AS: Folke Bernadottesvei 40, 5020 Bergen; tel 05 17 80 90.

Legal Firms
De Besche & Co: Tordenskioldsgaten 4, Postboks 1424 Vika, 0115 Oslo; tel 22 20 60 90, fax 22 33 40 00.
Engelschiøn & Co: Akersgaten 65 B, Postboks 8333, Hammersborg, Oslo 0129; tel 22 36 36 30.
A G Kvamme: Strandgaten 18, Postboks Box 509, Bergen 5001; tel 05 31 70 31; fax 05 32 84 35.
Hjort, Eriksrud & Co: Akersgaten 20, Postboks 471 Sentrum, Oslo N-0105; tel 22 42 31 00, fax 22 41 24 36.

Media and Newspapers
Aftenpost: Schibsted Group, Akersgaten 51,N-0180 Oslo 1; tel 02 86 30 00, fax 02 42 08 93.
Dagbaldet AS: Akersgaten 49, N-0107 Oslo 1; tel 02 20 20 9.

VG Verdens-Gang AS: Akersgaten 34, N-0180 Oslo 1, tel 22 11 0 40, fax 22 42 66 894.

Oil Gas and Petrochemical Companies

Mobil Oil AS: Postboks 64 62 Etterstad, 0605 Oslo; tel 02 57 52 00, fax 02 57 52 52.

Norsk Hydro AS: Bygdøy allé 2, 0240 Oslo; 02 43 21 00, fax 02 43 27 25.

Norsk Texaco AS: Postboks 7000 Homansbyen, 0306 Oslo; 02 95 73 00, fax 02 69 95 18.

Statoil: Postboks 300, 4001 Stavanger; 04 80 80 80, fax 04 80 70 42.

Statoil Norge AS: Postboks 1176 Sentrum, 0107 Oslo; tel 02 96 20 00, fax 02 69 32 00.

For further addresses of British and American companies see under working section.

Off-shore Oil Field Equipment

G & L Beijer Electronics AS: Postboks 487 Brakerøya, 3002 Drammen; tel 03 89 42 70, fax 03 89 51 01.

Fjord Instruments (Schlumberger) AS: Kvassnesveien, 5100 Isdalstø; tel 05 35 11 80, fax 05 35 13 37.

Marstrand & Astrup AS: Postboks 355, 1301 Sandvika; tel 02 54 17 93, fax 02 54 78 40.

Norsk Pumpeindustri AS: Postboks 173 Økern, 0509 Oslo; tel 02 64 25 30, fax 02 64 06 45.

Midco Norway AS: Postboks 688, 4300 Sandnes; tel 04 66 50 74, fax 04 66 73 22.

Paul Munroe (PM) Engineering Norway AS: Veritasveien 1, 1322 Høvik; tel 02 51 71 30, fax 02 51 71 31.

Norsk Hydro AS: Bygdøy allé 2, 0240 Oslo; tel 02 43 21 00, fax 02 43 27 25.

NSC (Norsk Subsea Cable) AS: Postboks 369, 30001 Drammen; tel 03 80 93 00, fax 03 81 83 20.

Turoteknikk AS: Postboks 225, 1301 Sandvika; tel 02 54 72 25, fax 02 54 40 77.

Starting a Business

The Norwegian economy is heavily dependent on international trade and has a favourable attitude towards foreign investment in most sectors. There are relatively few investment restrictions and investment is particularly encouraged in projects that help to develop the oil and gas resources and in areas of high technology. Cooperative ventures between national and international partners are also encouraged and since 1988 foreign investors can own up to one third of the capital share of a Norwegian industrial firm and up to 25% of the largest commercial banks.

Currently there are about 2,200 businesses with foreign ownership in Norway (i.e. foreign investors have more than 20% of the capital) and these account for about 100,000 jobs. About half of foreign investment has traditionally been in manufacturing, with the majority of foreign owned companies being in the machinery, equipment and metal fabrication sectors. 3.5% of manufacturing enterprises have foreign ownership whilst in the wholesale trade the figure is about 7%. The major foreign investors in Norwegian industry come from the UK, the USA, Sweden, Germany and Switzerland.

Foreign investment is prohibited in the following: government monopolies, the armaments industry and basic utilities. It is relatively difficult for foreign companies to obtain permission to drill for oil and preference will be given to subsidiaries of foreign firms established in Norway. Foreign companies which have set up new industrial ventures or formed joint ones with Norwegian firms will have greater bargaining power in this area.

For anyone considering doing or setting up a business in Norway there are a number of advantages. Economically, inflation is relatively low at below 2% and has remained stable. The economy is powerful and Norway has vast natural resources to boost it, although it should be borne in mind that swings in the oil prices can have a significant effect on the Norwegian economy. Norway is an advanced industrial nation with an excellent communication and transport infrastructure. The workforce is well-educated although there is a shortage of skilled workers, particularly in engineering and technology. Many Norwegians speak several languages with comparative ease and English is widely used. Disadvantages for those wanting to do business in Norway are the general high costs. Additionally, unemployment has been relatively high in Norway in recent years and currently stands at around 7%.

Norway's dependence on foreign trade means that the country is well clued up to the needs of foreign businesses and information and advice are widely available.

Procedures Involved in Buying or Starting a New Business

Anyone contemplating starting a business in Norway should seek appropriate advice from the relevant sources. To establish a business in Norway, a foreign investor must obtain the relevant permits from the Ministry of Industry. Permits are usually readily granted. All business permits must include a clause which states that Norwegian labour and materials will be given preferential treatment but where there is a shortage of Norwegian skilled labour, foreign skilled labour may be used.

Where appropriate, a building permit must be obtained from the local authorities and permission must be obtained for altering or expanding premises when the development costs 25 NOK million or requires 100 man years or 100 employees. All new businesses should be registered at the Register of Business Enterprises (*Foretaksregisteret*) and firms must also register with the tax and social security offices.

Useful Addresses

The Ministry of Industry and Energy: Postboks 8148 Dep, N-003 Oslo; tel 22 34 90 90.

The Register of Business Enterprises (Foretaksregisteret): Postboks 1400, N-8901 Brønnøysund; tel 75 02 20 22.

The Directorate of Taxes (Skattedirektoratet): Postboks 6300 Etterstad, N-0603 Oslo; tel 22 07 70 99.

The Ministry of Foreign Affairs: 7 Juni Plass 1, Postboks 8114 Dep, 0032 Oslo; tel 22 34 36 00.

The Ministry of Social Affairs: Grubbegt. 10, Postboks 8011 Dep, 0030 Oslo; tel 22 34 90 90.

Sources of Help

The Norwegian Government is particularly open to foreign investment and a number of sources can provide useful information for the prospective entrepreneur. From 1995 the Norwegian Industrial and Regional Development Fund will provide an English brochure *Establishing Business in Norway.* The Central Office for Foreign Tax Affairs in Norway provides the very detailed *Guide for Foreign Employers and Employees* in Norwegian and English outlining tax legislation and providing examples in both English and Norwegian of forms that you will be required to fill in when doing business in Norway. The Office also welcomes further enquiries and may initiate a personal discussion with you to discuss your individual requirements. Details on Norwegian business can be obtained from the Norwegian Trade Council which is the national service organisation for all exporters of goods and services. The Council prepares market surveys with information about customs and import regulations, sales channels, current profit rates etc. The Trade Council is particularly involved in assisting in setting up trade links between Norwegian exporters and foreign firms and has 32 missions in 29 countries and has close links with the Norwegian Chamber of Commerce. The Norwegian Trade Council publishes the magazine *Norway Exports* in English French, and German to inform foreign countries about Norwegian trade. The Christiania Bank provide a brochure *Establishing Business in Norway* and the Accountancy firm Ernst and Young also provide a booklet *Doing Business in Norway.* For current economic information on Norway, Barclays Bank can provide a detailed country account of current economic trends and the medium-term outlook in Norway and the Christiania Bank prepare a monthly publication *Economic Review* on the state of the Norwegian economy and on Norwegian international trade. *Economic Review* is available on subscription (see under useful addresses).

Useful Addresses

The Norwegian Industrial and Regional Development Fund (Statens noerings og distriktsuvikingsfond): Postboks 448 Sentrum, 0104 Oslo, tel 22 00 25 00, fax 22 42 96 11.

The Central Office for Foreign Tax Affairs (Sentralskattekontoret for Uten-landssaker): Prinsens Vei 1, N-4300 Sandnes; tel 51 67 80 88, fax 51 67 85 59.

The Norwegian Trade Council: Drammensveien 40, N-0243 Oslo; tel 22 92 63 00, fax 22 92 64 00.

The Norwegian Trade Council (UK): Charles House, 5-11 Lower Regent Street, London SW1Y 4LR; tel 0171-973 0188, fax 0171-973 0189.

The Norwegian Trade Council (US): 800 Third Avenue, 23rd Floor, New York, NY 10022, USA,; tel 1 212 421 92 10; fax 1 212 838 03 74.

Christiania Bank: Middellthunsgate 17, N-0368 Oslo 3; tel 22 48 44 81, fax 22 48 49 43.

Christiania Bank: Economic Review, Macroeconomics, Postboks 1166 Sentrum, 0107 Oslo; tel 22 48 50 00, fax 22 56 80 85.

Ernst and Young: Stenersgaten 10, 0184 Oslo; tel 22 86 27 00; fax 22 17 05 77.

Ernst and Young USA: 787 Seventh Avenue. New York, NY 10019 USA.

The Norwegian Chamber of Commerce: Drammensveien 30, Postboks 2483, 0202 Oslo; tel 22 55 82 20.

Barclays Bank PLC: The Librarian, Economics Department, PO Box 12, 1 Wimborne Road, Poole, Dorset BH15 2BB.

Raising Finance

If you are intending to reside in Norway you will find that British banks will not usually lend money for you to set up a business in Norway. Norwegian Banks will lend money to foreign businesses in the form of short or medium term credit. For long-term credit you will normally have to apply to a commercial bank or to private investors. For all types of loans you will usually have to submit a detailed business plan with your loan application, including details of the business, the intended market and available collateral. You will also need to provide a loan repayment schedule with cash flow projections. Some lenders will also require audited financial statements. Foreign companies or their Norwegian subsidiaries have full access to the Norwegian capital market. The Norwegian Bank of Industry (AS Den Norske Industribank) has a branch in London and grants mortgages and loans to small and medium-sized industrial companies. Loans for investment are granted for up to 40% of the investment. The bank favours the establishment of new businesses or the upgrading of existing industry. Other major commercial banks are Den Norske Bank, Kommunalbanken, the Chrisiania Bank (has a branch in London) and the Nordic Investment Bank. For a list of addresses of Norwegian Banks see under *Directory of Major Employers.* For more details on corporate banking in Norway contact Barclays Bank PLC (see under useful addresses).

Useful Addresses

Barclays Bank PLC: Europe Line, European Corporate Group, Nordic Team, 5th Floor, Murray House, 1 Royal Mint Court, London EC3N 4HH; tel 0171-3488 1144.

Christiania Bank og Kreditkasse: Lloyds Chambers, 6th Floor, 1 Portsoken Street, London E1 8RU; tel 0171-702 1390, fax 0171-481 1860.

Kreditkassen (Christiania Bank og Kreditkasse): Middelthunsgate 17, N0368 Oslo 3; tel 22 48 44 81, fax 22 48 49 43.

Investment Incentives
The principal body for Government incentives is the Regional Development Fund (*Distriktenes Utbyggingsfond*) which gives loans, guarantees, grants and free advice to foreign companies investing in Norway.

Loans: may be given if all other means of financing have been exhausted. Loans are provided for investment in equipment, machinery and buildings although construction loans must be obtained from other credit institutions. Interest is charged at the prevailing rate and the period of repayment of loans on buildings does not usually exceed 25 years. In most cases repayment of the loan does not begin for one to three years and in some cases other terms can be negotiated.

Investment Grants: These are usually given with the intention of developing economic activity in business and of increasing employment in areas with unemployment problems and low economic activity. Grants are not normally made for public administration, retail trade, agriculture and fishing. The largest grants are awarded for the establishment of a new business enterprise, the relocation, expansion or restructuring of an existing enterprise or for upgrading existing technology within an enterprise. Relatively high rates of grants are paid to projects aimed at employing women.

Grants for the Development of Business and Industry: These are grants to encourage the development of new businesses and to strengthen existing ones. Grants may cover as much as 50% of the cost of the projects and projects in northern Norway attract the highest amount. Each case will be considered on its merit. Again, projects which increase the employment of women can lead to higher grants. Special regional support programmes include: applied information technology, marine biotechnology and management, organisation and administration.

Location Advice: The Regional Development Fund can advise on the location of establishing a business enterprise and has location registers for most of the country's municipalities. Information includes the availability of premises, manpower, communications and housing. For further details contact: The Norwegian Industrial and Regional Development Fund (Postboks 488 Sentrum, 0104 Oslo; tel 22 00 25 00, fax 22 42 96 11).

Other sources of finance are the Norwegian Industrial Fund (*Industrifondet*) which grants loans to research and development for the Norwegian manufacturing industry and ordinary loans for manufacturing. The fund can also provide some grants for product development.

The Small Business Fund (*Småbedriftsfondet*) is a government owned credit institution which provides loans to companies outside the geographic range of the Regional Development Fund.

The Industrial Estates Corporation (*SIVA*) is a government owned corporation which purchases industrial buildings for lease to companies. *SIVA* owns the land and constructs the industrial buildings as well as footing the bill for the cost of infrastructural investments. Businesses may rent or purchase the premises from the Corporation.

For details of these schemes contact the Norwegian Trade Council (see above address).

Business Structures
There are three main types of companies in Norway:

— The Corporation where the liability of its members is limited to the extent of their share ownership.

— The Limited Partnership where at least one partner has overall liability for the debts of the partnership and where one partner is liable for a specified limited amount.
— The General Partnership where each partner in the company is personally liable for debts incurred by the firm to the extent of his/her private assets.

All new companies must be listed in the Register of Companies *Foretaksregisteret* (Postboks 1400, N-8901 Brønnøysund; tel 75 02 20 22) for which there is a registration fee and a filing fee for subsequent amendments to the original registration. The time required for processing a registration application is usually two weeks.

Corporations: To establish a corporation in Norway a minimum share capital of 50,000 NOK is required. 50% must be paid on registration and the rest should be paid within a year. Corporations are obliged to set aside a minimum of 10% of the annual income in a statutory reserve fund until it reaches 20% of share capital. Corporations should have at least one founder. The founder may be foreign but should be resident in Norway and have lived there during the two preceding years (exceptions may be made to this stipulation by the Ministry of Industry). Corporations may be 100% owned by foreigners. If the share capital exceeds 1 million NOK the board of directors must have a minimum of three members. If the company has a corporate assembly there must be at least five members on the board of directors. Details of board members, share capital and company intentions should be disclosed in the official gazette.

Common and preferred shares are both permitted with each share carrying one vote; resolutions may be passed by a majority of those present at shareholder meetings. Normally a company cannot own its own shares.

Branches: A branch of a foreign company is treated as a Norwegian corporation and is subject to the same tax requirements. The foreign company remains liable for the branch's debts and the branch must be registered in the Register of Companies (see above). To register a branch, the foreign company must indicate its type of business, share capital and share of distribution and provide proof that it is legally registered in its own country. A branch must have its own board of directors who have the same liability to a third party as the directors of Norwegian companies.

Exporters

The Norwegian desk of the Department of Trade and Industry Europe Branch in London (DTI 1 19 Victoria Street, London SW1H 0ET; tel 0171-215 5103, fax 0171-215 5611) provide help and information for prospective exporters to Norway. Services include market reports, on specific companies, import procedures and details of tariff rates. The DTI also provide a number of useful publications for individuals setting up businesses abroad.

Ideas for New Businesses

The British Department of Trade and Industry has identified the following areas as providing opportunities for British firms: offshore engineering for companies with experience of the UK Continental Shelf (although competition is fierce); the construction industry due to the building of the Gardermoen airport which includes an associated rail link and the construction of a major new university hospital at Gaustad. The demand for advanced capital equipment and for consumer goods such as home textiles and clothing is continuing to rise (very little clothing is produced in Norway and British fashion tends to be highly regarded) and concern over enviromental issues and pollution in Norway make it a very open market for manufactured, environmentally friendly goods.

Running a Business

Employing Staff

Contracts: Employment contracts should be written and drawn up according to Norwegian employment legislation. However, employees may not usually be dismissed without at least one month's notice unless there is a collective agreement or other written agreement stating otherwise. Managerial posts often require three months notice but the notification period can be longer. The two main reasons for dismissal must be plausible and relate to the circumstances of the company or to the behaviour of the employee.

Recruitment: In Norway wage earners are normally recruited through labour exchanges and salaried personnel and managers through the media.

Wages and Salaries: Surprisingly for a socialist country there is no national minimum wage in Norway. Base wages are fixed in collective bargaining agreements. In practice, a wage would rarely be less than the equivalent of £5 per hour. Wages are usually paid monthly into a bank account. Payment for overtime is at an agreed rate of between 50%-100%.

Paid Holidays: All employees are entitled to four weeks plus one day of holidays each year and ten days of legal holidays. Employees aged over 60 are entitled to five weeks holiday. Employees can take three consecutive weeks of holidays during the summer vacation.

Labour Relations: Most companies with between 50 and 200 employees have one third labour representation on the board of directors. Although this is not compulsory, employees are entitled to request it. Companies with more than 200 employees elect a corporate assembly with a minimum of 12 members, the majority of whom are chosen at the annual shareholders meeting and the rest by fellow employees. The corporate assembly is the final decision making body and elects the board of directors. Assembly meetings are held twice a year and decisions are made about major investments, modernization and other issues affecting the labour force. Shop stewards are often part of committees for the hiring of workers so that unions are often involved in the hiring and laying off of workers.

Social Security Contributions: Employers are obliged to pay employees for the first 14 days of sickness and must contribute 16.7% of the employee's gross salary and benefits in social insurance contributions. In less industrialised areas such as the north this may be less. Employees normally contribute 7.8% whilst self-employed individuals contribute 10.7% of their personal income. The employer's contribution is levied on all salaries and benefits which are required to be reported to the tax authorities. Generally, a foreign employer must pay the social security contribution for employees working in Norway or on the Norwegian Continental Shelf. The system covers all areas of basic need including sickness, unemployment and maternity benefit, disability and pensions. Norway operates a totalisation agreement whereby foreigners living in Norway may be fully or partially exempt from social security contributions if they work in Norway for three years or less and are still working for an employer from their home country. In this case they would be making contributions to the social security system of their home country.

For further details see *Aspects of Employment*.

Taxation

Norwegian regulations on tax are multiple and detailed and anyone considering working or doing business in Norway should try to familiarise themselves with them. For a very detailed overview consult the *Guide for Foreign Employers and Employees*, published by the Central Office for Foreign Tax affairs (Prinsens Vei 1, N-4300 Sandnes, Norway; tel 51 67 80 88, fax 51 67 85 59) available free in English. International accountants Ernst and Young publish the booklet *Doing Business in Norway* which has useful information on tax matters for foreigners (available from Ernst and Young Publications Department: Melrose House, 42 Dingwall Road, Croydon, Surrey CR0 2NE; tel 0171-928 2000). What follows is a brief overview of the Norwegian tax situation.

Employers are required to withhold taxes from salaries paid to employees. Both self-employed people and employees are obliged to make advance tax payments during the income year. Employees are issued with a tax deduction card from their local assessment office. If this card is not presented or is not issued the employer is obliged to withhold 50% of the employee's gross salary and should deposit the amount withheld with the tax authorities.

Resident Corporations: Resident companies are subject to taxes on worldwide income, excluding net income derived from property abroad. The corporate tax rate is 28% of which 21% is municipal tax and 7% is county tax. Corporation taxes are payable during the year after the income year. The Foreign Tax Affairs central office can make an estimated preliminary tax based on information from the company's previous year's income, which is paid in two instalments on 15 February and 15 April. The remainder is paid in instalments on the 15 September and the 15 November. The amount of the last two payments is based on the actual tax liability according to the tax payer's return. Interest charges are levied if half of the total tax is not paid before 1 May.

Non-Resident Companies: Non-resident companies are taxed on income which can be attributed to Norwegian business activity. Usually non-resident companies are subject only to corporate tax if they trade in Norway through a branch firm. The branch will normally be taxed at the going corporate rate.

Partnerships and Joint Ventures: Partnerships, limited partnerships and joint ventures are taxed on a parity level with companies and corporations.

Self-employed: Income from self-employment is subject to the ordinary income tax (business income) at 28% and personal income tax up to 13%. Personal income includes income from personal services, pensions, self-employment income and shareholder income. Additionally, employee social security contributions are computed according to personal income. Self-employed individuals receive an estimate of taxes to be paid during the income year from the assessment office. Estimated taxes are paid in equal instalments on the 15th of March, May, September and November.

Indirect Taxes

VAT: (known as MVA or MOMS throughout Scandinavia) is 22% on all services and purchases with the exception of books and it will normally be included in the price of goods. Real properties are not classified as *Goods* for VAT purposes. The company will have to collect VAT on all sales and deduct VAT paid on purchases. Services exempt from VAT include the renting of property, passenger transport, banking, finance, insurance, education, the health service, legal advice and auditing. There is no VAT on levied exports or in the purchase of services or goods used in the sea areas outside Norwegian territorial waters. All enterprises selling goods and services subject to VAT whose taxable income exceeds a certain limit must be registered with the VAT register which is done through the county tax office where the enterprise has its permanent place of business. Foreigners doing trade or business who have no permanent establishment or residence in Norway are obliged to be registered by a representative in the VAT register. Every VAT period (two calendar months) a sales and turnover return must be submitted to the County Tax Office within one month and ten days at the end of each period.

Investment Tax: This is a one off tax levied on the acquisition of durable items of business equipment and supplies. The normal rate is 7%. Manufacturing and Mining industries are exempt.

Stamp Duty: This is levied on registration of documents which transfer the ownership of real estate. The rate is 2.5% of the transfer price. No stamp duty is paid on mergers.

Legal Advice

Anyone contemplating doing business in Norway should seek proper legal advice both for purchasing and setting up a business. You should use lawyers who are familiar with Norwegian law. The following lawyers speak English and deal in most areas of business law: Engelschiøon & Co ANS (Akersgaten 65B, Postboks 8333, Hammersborg, Oslo 0129; tel 22 36 36 30, fax 22 36 36 80) and De Besche & Co (Tordenskioldsgaten 4, Postboks 1424 Vika, 0115 Oslo; tel 22 20 60 90, fax 22 33 40 00).

Accountancy and Auditing Advice

Financial statements must be presented annually in accordance with Norwegian law and should contain the necessary information for evaluating a company's financial position. A company should retain accounting records for up to ten years after closure. Accounts may be kept abroad if most business is conducted out of Norway. All companies should keep the following records: a cash journal for receipts; a separate journal for all other entries; ledgers for accounts which are payable and accounts which are receivable; a general ledger; a bound register which includes the balance sheets, income statements the director's and auditor's reports and consolidated group accounts where applicable. Annual accounts should include: a director's report (if the company has a board of directors); a balance sheet; an income statement; notes for the financial statement; a cash flow analysis (for companies valued at more than 10 million NOK).

Auditing Requirements. All companies (including limited companies, general partnerships and limited partnerships) must appoint an independent auditor. Self-employed individuals with a turnover of less than 2 million NOK are exempt from this requirement. To be appointed as an independent auditor in Norway the accountant must be either a Registered Auditor or a State Authorised Public Accountant. The Auditor's Report should be free of any restrictions imposed by the company. The accountancy and management consultant firm Ernst and Young has over twenty offices throughout Norway and provide a brochure *Doing Business in Norway*.

Useful Addresses

Ernst and Young Chartered Accountants: Apex Plaza, Forbury Road, Reading RG2 1YE; tel 01734-500611, fax 01734-507744 and Stenersgaten 10, N-0184 Oslo, Norway;tel 22 86 27 00, fax 22 17 05 77.

Sweden

SECTION I

Living in Sweden

General Introduction
Residence and Entry Regulations
Setting Up Home
Daily Life
Retirement

General Introduction

Destination Sweden

Mention Sweden and the following tend to spring to mind — pine trees, saunas, wooden houses, Abba and au pairs. Sweden conjures up images of a squeaky clean environment of wide open spaces, glittering lakes, mysterious forests and a pine fresh atmosphere. At a first glance there is something almost disarmingly pure about Sweden; this is a country which has stayed neutral for nearly two hundred years, is the birthplace of the founder of the Nobel Peace Prize, promotes one of the most advanced 'cradle to grave' welfare states and has an environment as fresh as its numerous pine trees. A less superficial look at Sweden, however, reveals some contradictions in all this: despite Swedish neutrality the country earns a disproportionate amount of money manufacturing arms to subsidise the welfare state, the founder of the Nobel Peace Prize, Alfred Nobel, was also the inventor of dynamite (which like nuclear power is a double-edged sword). In fact the home of good clean living uses more nuclear energy per capita than almost any other country and the nation which provided the model welfare state has some of the highest suicide, deliquency and alcoholic rates per capita in the world.

Contradictions tend to be a feature of Swedish life but this does not detract from the enchanting beauty of the country and the enlightened social concern. Despite being geographically rather removed from the rest of western Europe, Sweden has made a significant contribution to the diplomacy for world peace, to the arts and not least to safer motoring in the form of Volvos and Saabs. In recent years Sweden has experienced some of its worst economic difficulties with unemployment levels rising as high as 14%. Whilst the welfare state has cushioned some of the burden, the country has had to tighten its purse strings considerably. Set against this is Sweden's membership of the European Union. The former red tape difficulties of obtaining work and residence permits have been dismantled and this is a time of exciting opportunity for Europeans seeking work in Sweden.

Pros and Cons of Moving to Sweden

Although, not considered part of mainstream (i.e. EU) Europe until recently, Sweden is certainly more highly advanced industrially and socially than many nations and Swedes enjoy a very high standard of living. Despite the country's nonpareil welfare state and social equality there is a downside. Funding the 'Swedish Model' costs an arm and a leg in taxes and welfare contributions and the general cost of living generally ranks as one of the highest in the EU.

Those going to Sweden for the first time are often amazed at the spaciousness of the country. Cities are small and towns and villages are spread out thinly across a land dominated by pine trees and lakes. Whilst the country is undoubtedly beautiful the predominance of trees and lakes can become rather tedious and outside the main cities most entertainment is of the home-made variety.

As a northern country Sweden experiences very long hours of daylight in Summer and very long nights in winter (within the Arctic Circle daylight hours in winter can be reduced to three per day and are accompanied by extremely low temperatures. Set against this is the beautiful light and shade on the forests and lakes in summer. The coastline has numerous beaches and small islands and these are pleasant to visit on the long summer days when temperatures can be surprisingly warm.

Opinions on the Swedish character tend to be divided and the Swedes themselves are fiercely opposed to national stereotyping but generally, like their Nordic counterparts, Swedish people are reserved and it usually takes a few drinks to bring some of them out of themselves. Perhaps it is the long dark winters which contribute to the heavy alcohol consumption and a tendency towards melancholia. Nonetheless, many Swedes have a very dry sense of humour and are helpful and friendly when approached and the majority speak excellent English.

Pros: Beautiful Country.
Excellent Welfare State.
High Standard of Living.
Small population.
Most people speak English.

Cons: Not as geared to employing and housing foreigners as the rest of the EU.
Long hours of cold and darkness in winter.
Limited entertainment resources.
High cost of living.
High unemployment levels.

Political and Economic Structure

In modern history Sweden has played a relatively low-key position in European economic and political affairs and until fairly recently has been happy to take a back seat. Since 1814 Sweden has remained staunchly neutral (including during both World Wars) and, in common with the other Nordic countries, (except Denmark), has stayed out of the European Community. In the 1990s. However, much of this is liable to change as Sweden becomes increasingly integrated into the economic and political arena of western Europe.

Sweden has one of Europe's longest recorded histories. Nomadic herders probably first roamed across Sweden in about 6000 BC and by 3000 BC had begun creating settlements. The early Swedish settlers were keen traders in fur and amber but trade was disrupted by a deteriorating climate around the time of the birth of Christ. The sixth century saw the rise of the small kingdom tribe of the *Svear* which gave Sweden its present day name of Sverige. The eighth century marks the beginning of the Viking era and there is some evidence to suggest that the Swedish Vikings were amongst the first to begin raids, turning eastwards towards the Baltic and on towards the Byzantine Empire. The era marked the heyday of paganism and nine human sacrifices were offered annually at Uppsala north of Stockholm. The Vikings established a parliament or *Thing* which operated in each province and was elected by free men. Christianity was slow to establish a foothold in Sweden although in 1008 King Olof Skättonung was converted and by 1130 Uppsala had changed from being a pagan site of worship to a centre for Christianity.

The Middle Ages saw conflict waged between a succession of rulers but Sweden enjoyed a measure of stability and progress under the rule of Magnus Ladulås. Swedish trade flourished under the German Hanseatic League and a trading centre was established at Visby on the Swedish island of Gotland. The Black

Death arrived in 1350 and wiped out about one third of the population but Sweden enjoyed a brief period of stability when Norway, Denmark and Sweden were united at Kalmer in 1397 under Erik of Pomerania. The Kalmar Union was a troubled one and Sweden seceded in 1523 when Gustav Ericsson founded the Swedish Vasa dynasty. The 17th century saw Sweden's age of greatness and the rise of the great Swedish king Gustavus Adolphus when Sweden was a military force to be reckoned with. Denmark waged war on Sweden in the hope of resurrecting the Kalmar Union, but was defeated by Sweden in the Thirty Years War. In 1660 at the Peace of Copenhagen the present day boundaries between Denmark and Sweden were agreed.

Following the Napoleonic Wars in 1814 Sweden attacked Denmark forcing her to surrender Norway from Danish rule and by the Treaty of Kiel in 1814 a union was established between Norway and Sweden which lasted until 1905.

Industrialisation was slow to take root in Sweden in the 19th century and poor rural areas saw mass migration to America. The late 19th century saw the rise of trade unionism and in 1889 the Social Democratic Party was founded. Sweden maintained neutrality throughout the First World War but suffered economic hardship because of blockades. In 1929 the first social democratic government came into office and this party came to dominate Swedish politics in the twentieth century. Sweden claimed neutrality again during the Second World War.

1946–1950 might justly be called the great age of social reform in Sweden. The social democrats introduced comprehensive laws that were to form the basis of the welfare state and Sweden steered its famous 'Middle Way' during the Cold War by adopting the best political and economic aspects of both socialism and capitalism. By means of tax reorganisation there was a wider and more even distribution of wealth but plans for the nationalisation of industry were not enforced.

In the latter half of the twentieth century Sweden has become increasingly integrated into international political and economic affairs. In 1952 the Nordic Council was founded between the Scandinavian countries to promote cooperation between the Nordic parliaments. In 1971 Sweden declared its intention not to seek membership of the European Community on grounds that it wished to preserve its neutrality. In 1995 Sweden got round this by adopting observer status in the Western European Union (the defence arm of the EU). An estimated 70% of Swedes are still currently opposed to abandoning their traditional neutrality). Sweden flashed briefly into the World headlines in 1986 following the inexplicable assassination of the Swedish Prime Minister, Olof Palme, who was succeeded by Ingvar Carlsson. In 1991 the Conservatives held a brief three-year term in office, coinciding with severe economic problems in Sweden, but the Social Democrats under Ingvar Carlsson were returned to office again in 1994, the same year in which Sweden voted to join the European Community.

Economy

Sweden's Gross National Product per capita is one of the world's highest, but about 60% of the gross domestic product passes through the public sector and includes the payments of welfare benefits. As a result of the extensive welfare programme taxes and welfare contributions in Sweden are some of the steepest in the world. Since 1983 Government involvement in the distribution of national income has lessened and the majority of enterprises are privately owned. Sweden is highly dependent on international trade and exports account for about 30% of the gross domestic product. Although formerly most of Sweden's exports were in the form of raw material or semi-manufactured products (steel, pulp and cut wood), today finished goods dominate the market, in particular engineering goods like cars and telecommunications equipment. Major imports are engineering products, chemicals, textiles and imported foodstuffs include coffee, tea, fruit and fish.

Most of Sweden's major industrial companies are international and because Swedish industry has tended to invest more abroad than at home some industries (among them Volvo and Electrolux) employ more cheap foreign labour than native Swedes. About 800,000 workers are employed in private industry in Sweden but half that number again work in Swedish industry abroad.

The traditional Swedish industries of agriculture, forestry and fishing have declined in the second part of the twentieth century whilst industry and manufacturing have developed. However, the biggest growth area has been in services and administration in particular in the public sector. Sweden is well-endowed with natural resources including wood, hydroelectric power and metallic ores, which are the historical backbone of Sweden's industrial economy. 50% of electric energy comes from hydroelectric sources and 45% from nuclear sources, making Sweden one of the highest users of nuclear power per capita in the world. Following a 1980 referendum Sweden is aiming to eliminate the use of nuclear power by 2010. Northern Sweden has large mineral resources and the state-owned company Luossavaara Kirunavaara at Kiruna in Lapland manages about 90% of the total production capacity of the iron ore deposits. Parts of Nordland have a wide range of metal mines including zinc, gold, copper and lead.

Just under 6% of Sweden is cultivated for farming and the most profitable agricultural land is in southern Sweden. In the south potatoes, vegetables, sugar beet, oilseeds, wheat and barley are the main crops whilst in the north, up to the Arctic Circle, hay and potatoes are the dominant crops. Generally, animal products are more important than arable products and dairy cows are found throughout Sweden. Pig farming and poultry tend to be concentrated more in the extreme south. Swedish farms have some of the world's highest yields. About 3.7% of the population is employed in the agricultural sector which accounts for about 1.3% of the gross domestic product.

Approximately 55% of land in Sweden is covered by forest with the main trees being spruce and pine. 50% of Swedish forest land is in private ownership with the remainder being divided evenly between company and public ownership. Since the 19th century forestry in Sweden has been conducted on a sustained-yield basis which is very strictly enforced. The average growing time for a new tree is 70 years in the south and 140 years in the north. Forestry work was once a winter occupation for farmers but today it is carried out all year round by professional foresters. About 37,000 people are employed in the forestry industry. Sweden is one of the main world exporters of wood products and manufactures a wide variety of them including pulp and paper, furniture and prefabricated houses.

Fishing plays a small part in the Swedish economy. The centre for the fish market and the major fishing harbour is Gothenburg. Major fish products are salmon, herrings, cod, plaice and mackerel. Sweden's main manufacturing industry is engineering, in particular the transport industry. The aerospace and automotive industries have major plants in south central Sweden and the big Swedish names are Volvo in Gothenburg and Saab-Scania in Trollhätten. Other main products are communication equipment and metal, plastic and glass products. Both the pharmaceutical and biotechnology industries are growing in Sweden as is the petrochemical industry based around Stenungsund. Before the 1980s petrochemicals accounted for 25% of the value of Sweden's total imports but now account for less than 5%. Whilst the construction and food processing industries in Sweden continue to play a part in the economy, the textile and shoe industries have declined because of competition from cheap imports.

The early 1990s have been a difficult time for the Swedish economy with unemployment reaching record levels of 14% and a national debt amounting to 80% of the gross domestic product. In 1992 the Swedish National Bank raised interest rates by 500% overnight to defend the Swedish Krona against speculation. Two fifths of manufacturing jobs were lost in the recession although since 1993 Sweden has shown marked signs of recovery.

Government

Sweden has a multi-party democratic system and a constitutional monarchy. The monarch (currently King Carl XVI Gustaf)) has only a ceremonial role and political power rests with the *Riksdag* (parliament) and the government. The Swedish constitution was revised in 1975 and is based on four basic laws: the Instrument of Government, the Act of Succession, the Freedom of the Press Act and the Riksdag Act. The main principles of the Swedish constitution are representative democracy, popular sovereignty and parliamentarianism. The prime minister is appointed by the speaker of the Riksdag but must be approved for office through a vote of parliament. The cabinet is appointed by the prime minister and is responsible for all government decisions. There are at present 13 ministries which are relatively small and administration and the implementation of legislation are dealt with by central administrative agencies. The Riksdag can make amendments to the constitution if there is the support of one third of the Riksdag. The Riksdag is a unicameral parliament which is elected every four years (three years prior to 1995), usually in September. The 349 members of the Riksdag are elected by proportional representation. The voting age is 18 and turnout is usually exceptionally high, averaging 90%.

The five main political parties are split into two blocs with the Social Democrats and the Left Party (formerly the Communist Party) representing the socialists and the Conservatives, the Centre and the Liberals representing the more right-wing group. In addition, there is now an up-and-coming Green Environment Party in Sweden. There is a quota rule in Swedish politics which excludes parties with less than four per cent of the national vote or less than 12% of the votes in at least one electoral district. By far the most dominant party of the twentieth century has been the Social Democratic Party. Closely allied with the trade unions, the party was in power from 1932–76 (with a brief loss of power in 1936) and from 1982–1991. In 1991 the Conservative Party came to power under Prime Minister Carl Bildt, coinciding with Sweden's worst economic crisis since the 1930s and in 1994 the Social Democrats under the former Prime Minister Ingvar Carlsson were re-elected. Nonetheless, the Social Democrats who founded Sweden's 'cradle to grave' social welfare state have been forced to make welfare cutbacks in the hope of reviving the Swedish economy.

The role of the ombudsman is very important in Swedish affairs and a Parliamentary Ombudsman monitors and investigates suspected cases of abuses of authority by civil servants. The majority of government documents are open to inspection by the press and the public at any time.

Northern Sweden is home to the five Swedish Lapp or *Sami* communities. Like the Norwegian Lapps, the Swedish Lapps have their own parliament which meets at Gällivare within the Arctic Circle. The rights of the Lapps have been recognised by statute since 1650. The younger Lapps are struggling to maintain their unique cultural and racial identity and are finding support from the nation's Greens.

Whilst Sweden has traditionally been part of the Nordic bloc of countries which have kept a certain distance between themselves and the rest of Europe, it is now forming closer ties with western Europe. Sweden applied for membership of the European Community in July 1991 and signed the European Economic Area agreement in the same year. Sweden is a member of the European Free Trade Association and has strong international trading links. Sweden became a member of the European Union by a narrow majority vote (52% to 47%) and joined on 1 January 1995. Thus joining Finland and Denmark as the trio of Scandinavian countries which are now part of the EU.

Historically, Sweden has remained neutral and has kept out of wars for about 180 years but this policy became less clear cut in 1994 when Sweden signed the NATO Partnership for Peace following the completion of negotiations to join the European Union.

Geographical Information

Sweden occupies the eastern sector of the Scandinavian peninsula and covers a total area of 173,732 sq miles/449,964 sq km. At twice the size of the United Kingdom, Sweden is Europe's fourth largest country, stretching 1000 miles/1600 km from north to south and averaging 250 miles/400 km from west to east. About half of the land is covered in forests interspersed with nearly 100,000 lakes and numerous rivers. The eastern coastline is studded with thousands of tiny, wooded islands which have remarkably similar shapes due to the action of glacial ice. Sweden shares most of its western border (1000 miles/ 1600km) with Norway and in the far north shares a small border with Finland. Sweden is separated from Denmark by a mere ten miles at the narrowest point in the Oresund strait leading into the Baltic Sea. There has been strong environmental opposition to the plan to build Europe's longest bridge between Copenhagen and Malmö but this is going ahead in the interests of Sweden's closer ties to the the European Union which it will undoubtedly help to forge.

Sweden lies on northerly latitudes (the same as Alaska) and about 15% of the country lies above the Arctic Circle.

Sweden is divided into three traditional regions: Norrland in the north covers about three fifths of the country and is primarily an area of mountain and forest. Svealand in central Sweden contains lowland in the east and highlands in the west, and Götaland in the south contains the Småland highlands and the rich fertile plains of Skåne. The Lapps or Sami in the north do not recognise national boundaries and move freely between Norway, Sweden, Finland and Russia. One fifth of the country, particularly in the south west is covered by peat and bog land. In addition to the three traditional regions, Sweden is divided into 24 Län or counties. The Scandinavian mountains between Norway and Sweden form a natural physical border and are the source of Sweden's chief rivers, most of which flow southeastwards towards the Gulf of Bothnia or the Baltic Sea. The longest of these is the Klar-Göta River which rises in Norway and flows for 447 miles to the North Sea. Many of the rivers, except in the far north where they are protected, are a source of the nation's hydroelectric power.

Population

The present population of Sweden is approximately 8.6 million giving it one of the lowest population densities in Europe. The average number of inhabitants per square km is 21 although in northern Sweden the average can be as low as one person per square km. 70% of the country has a density of six inhabitants or less per square km although in Stockholm the average is 3,655. The annual rate of population increase declined during the 1980s but the trend has been slightly upwards in the early 1990s. The increase is accounted for mainly by increased immigration levels and Sweden has approximately 1 million immigrants of whom 60% are Finnish. Immigration is becoming increasingly more strictly controlled. Sweden has two minority groups of indigenous peoples: the Lapp population of about 15,000 who are scattered throughout Sweden's northern interior, and the Finnish speaking people of the northeast along the Finnish border.

Until 1870 fewer than 10% of the Swedish population lived in urban areas. Economic growth after World War II led to a dramatic migration from the countryside to the towns and cities resulting in a depopulation of rural Sweden. There is a very big demographic divide between the north and south with over 90% of the population living in the south of the country and 85% of these in cities and urban areas. The majority, 1.5 million, live in the capital Stockholm whilst 734,000 live in Gothenburg on the south western coast and 480,000 in Malmö in the far south.

Climate

Despite being on the same latitude as parts of Greenland, Sweden enjoys a relatively mild climate thanks to the southwest Atlantic winds warmed by the North Atlantic currents. High pressure systems to the east create sunny summers but cold winters and there are periodic shifts in climate because of the interaction between the Atlantic currents and the high pressure systems. Differences in latitude and altitudes create considerable regional differences. The northern interior is particularly cold in winter experiencing up to eight months of snowfall with temperatures falling as low as-20°F to-40°F-30 to-50°C. Between November and May the Gulf of Bothnia freezes over. In southern Sweden temperatures are milder in winter (averaging 0° C/32° F) with irregular snowfall. Coastal waters rarely freeze in the south. There is less variation in summer climates — Haparanda in the north has an average temperature of 59° F/ 15° C and Malmö in the south averages 63° F/ 17° C.

Rainfall varies from 28 inches/ 700 mm on the east coast to 40 inches/1000 mm on the western slopes of southern Sweden. There is rainfall throughout the year but the wettest period is from late summer to autumn.

Regional Guide

Sweden can be divided into three traditional regions: Norrland, Svealand and Götaland, and into 24 counties. Because of the low population density, the country can be divided into the following fairly large areas:

Stockholm and Environs

Stockholm is the most beautiful of the Nordic capitals and arguably one of the most beautiful in Europe. Built on 14 small islands, Stockholm is a spacious city of parkland, water, old buildings and new state-of-the-art architecture. The old quarter, Gamla Stan, with its medieval twisting streets and waterside walks contrasts with the glass and steel skyscrapers of modern Stockholm. With over 50 museums and galleries Stockholm is a city of culture but also contains a strong rural element in its many parks and lakes. For a relatively small city with a small population Stockholm has a varied and lively nightlife and sources of entertainment. Most Stockholmers live in the high-rise apartments in the surrounding forested suburbs and commute to the centre via the efficient transport infrastructure. The city is clean and safe and pollution is kept to a minimum. Out at sea from Stockholm is the archipelago comprising hundreds of tiny islands with beaches which are a popular tourist resort in summer. An hour away from Stockholm to the north is the cathedral and university town of Uppsala which is regarded as the country's religious and historical centre. About two and a half miles north of Uppsala is the ancient pagan settlement of Gamla Uppsala with royal burial grounds dating back to the 6th century, making it a kind of Swedish Stonehenge.

The South East, Gotland and Öland

The south east of Sweden below Stockholm is a forested region containing the two counties of Östergötland and Småland. The centre of Småland is home to the delightfully named 'Crystal Kingdom' which is based around the town of Växjö. The Crystal Kingdom refers to the local glassblowing factories for which the region is famous.

Gotland and Öland are Sweden's only two major islands. Öland is connected to the mainland at Kalmar by bridge and is a very popular tourist attraction in summer. The island bears a surprising resemblance to the Netherlands, having flat green countryside and over 400 windmills. Wooden cottages, castles, fortresses and burial mounds give it an historic charm which keeps the tourists coming. Gotland is also a popular tourist resort frequented by Stockholmers in search of a good time. The capital Visby was an early Viking Settlement and was the hub of the Swedish traders in the Hanseatic League in the twelfth century.

The Southwest and Göteborg (Gothenburg)

The south of Sweden contains extensive forests and two of the largest lakes: Lake Vänern and Lake Vättern. The landscape is relatively flat and is more similar to that of Denmark which is just a stretch of water away. The coastal beaches make it a popular holiday resort for the Swedes and the area is also graced by attractive ageing towns and cities of which the principal one is Gothenburg. Gothenburg (Göteborg to the Swedes) is the second largest city in Sweden with a population of 500,000 and is a ship building city, fishing harbour and the landing point for the Harwich ferries. Beyond the inelegance of the shipyards it is one of Sweden's most attractive cities. South of Gothenburg are the three provinces of Halland, Skåne and Blekinge. They are rather different in character from the rest of Sweden, several centuries of being under Danish rule setting them apart. Skåne in particular has a distinctive dialect and customs and there is even an independence movement within the province. The port town of Helsingborg is literally only a few minutes ferry ride away from the Danish port town of Helsingør. The region is generally flat and contains some of Sweden's most fertile farming country.

The East Coast

North of Uppsala, the east coast forms the edge of the Gulf of Bothnia, a narrow corridor of water that separates Sweden from Finland and stretches up to Haparanda on the Sweden/Finnish border. Towns are small and spaced out on the coast and depend mainly on fishing for their livelihood. The principal coastal towns are Gävle, Sundsvall, Umeå and Luleå although none of them is particularly big. Umeå and Luleå are modern manufacturing centres but Gävle, Hudiksvall and Skelleftel retain some of Sweden's heritage in the form of old wooden buildings. The area enjoys clean beaches and crystal clear water.

Central and Northern Sweden

From north of Lake Vänern through the Arctic Circle to the north Norwegian border you get the picture postcard image of Sweden. The area is characterised by rural counties with tiny populations living amongst forests and lakes with reindeer for the local wildlife. The central province of Dalarna is known as the 'Folklore District' and is a place of forests, mountains, lakes and painted wooden farmhouses. It is the favoured site for the midsummer celebrations and home to traditional Swedish naïve religious paintings. The traditional region of Norrland stretches from the northern border 620 miles/1000 miles south and is a vast tract of wide open spaces. More than 30% of the area is virtually uninhabited but the far north above the Arctic Circle is home to the Swedish Laplanders. Although once nomadic reindeer herders, the majority of Lapps now have permanent homes. Technology and the modern world have encroached on the traditional way of life and even helicopters may be used to round up the reindeer these days.

The most northern Swedish city is Kiruna, home to the nation's huge iron ore mines. Kiruna has the world's largest underground iron mine at 310 miles/500 km long. Spread over an area half the size of Switzerland, Kiruna is sometimes called the 'world's biggest city' although the population is small and it is also home to the Laplander museum. Also of note in northern Sweden are the towns of Gällivare, another iron ore mining town and Jokkmokk which is the Lapp cultural centre and host to the great 400-year-old Lapp winter market in February. Norrland is characterised by mountainous ranges to the west, forests and moorlands in the centre and wild rugged coastline to the east. However, Sweden's excellent transport system means that it is relatively accessible even by public transport. There are two main national parks in northern Sweden, the most stunning is Sarek which is Sweden's highest mountain area with over 90 peaks and is home to arctic animals like elk, bear, wolverine, lynx and the Arctic fox. Slightly less impressive is the Muddus National Park which is less mountainous and more forested.

Residence and Entry Regulations

The Current Position

Until recently foreign nationals who wanted to live and work in Sweden were faced by a daunting amount of red tape and fairly limited work opportunities. Most work opportunities for the casual foreign worker were only to be had during the summer from mid-May to mid-October when a special work permit allowed students under 30 to do vacation work in Sweden. In the past, all prospective foreign workers with the exception of other Scandinavians had to have a firm offer of work before going to Sweden and work permits were usually only given for a limited period. Now that the regulations of the European Economic Area (EEA) and the European Union have come into force in Sweden the whole work situation has changed for nationals of member states who now enjoy most of the same rights to live and work in Sweden as native Swedes. Effectively EEA and EU nationals no longer need a work permit.

Residence Permit — EU Nationals

Citizens of the European Union and the EEA can stay in Sweden for up to three months without a residence permit although they should be able to support themselves financially during this period. Those wishing to extend their stay beyond three months must apply for a residence permit (*uppehållstillstånd*). This is done through the local police station and you will need to present a passport (or identity card for citizens of Belgium, France, Italy, Luxembourg, the Netherlands, Germany or Austria) and proof of employment. If your employment is permanent, a residence permit is granted for five years. If it is not permanent it will be granted for the period of employment.

Family Members

The following family members of EEA/EU nationals working in Sweden are entitled to enter the country and apply for a residence permit:

husband/wife or partner.
Children under 21 or children who are dependent on parents for their livelihood eg those with disabilities.
Dependent parents.

Family members can obtain a work permit by producing the following documents:

Passport or identity card.
A certificate confirming the relationship.
For dependents, a certificate confirming the dependency issued by relevant authorities in the home country.

Those entitled to live in Sweden are also entitled to work without a work permit. Family members may usually remain in Sweden after the decease of the employee.

Note: Partners of a citizen of an EEA/EU country who come from a country outside the EEA/EU must have been granted a residence permit before arrival in Sweden.

Entering to Work — EU Nationals

Sweden is subject to the European Union regulations concerning the free movement of labour. EU nationals can enter Sweden with the intention of looking for work and do not need to have secured an offer of employment or a work permit before entering the country. EU nationals have the same rights as Swedish citizens as regards pay, working conditions, access to housing, vocational training, social security and trade union membership. Families and dependants have similar rights.

When entering Sweden to work you will need to obtain a national registration number (*personnummer*) which is a digit number consisting of your birthdate and a four digit code. Registration numbers are issued by the tax authorities and you should visit your local tax office (look up *lokala skattemyndigheten* in the pink pages of the phone book). You should take your residence permit and passport/identity card with you. The tax office will also issue you with a tax card (*skattsedel*) which will levy the appropriate level of taxes to be deducted from your pay.

Transferring Unemployment Benefit

If you have been claiming unemployment benefit for at least four weeks before you go to Sweden you can continue to claim it there for up to three months whilst you look for work. Before you leave you should inform your local job centre of your intention to look for work in Sweden and pick up the form E303 which will secure the payment of your unemployment benefit whilst in Sweden. Your job centre will advise the DSS Overseas Branch who will determine whether you qualify for benefit to be paid to you abroad. When you arrive in Sweden you should register with a Swedish employment office within seven days and bring the completed E303. It should be borne in mind that the cost of living in Sweden is very high and your unemployment benefit may not be sufficient to live on whilst you are looking for work. For further details consult the DSS leaflet SA29 *Your Social Security insurance, benefits and health care rights in the European Community*, available from job centres.

Useful Addresses

Department of Social Security: Overseas Branch, Longbenton, Newcastle upon Tyne NE98 1YX; tel 0191-213 5000.
National Social Insurance Board (Riksförsäkringsverket, RFV): 103 51 Stockholm; tel 8 786 90 00.

Entering to Start a Business

EU citizens are free to enter Sweden for up to three months with the intention of setting up a business. Citizens of the European Union may run their own business in Sweden on the same conditions as Swedish citizens. This also applies to agencies, branches and subsidiaries. All businesses must be registered with the Registrar of Companies (851 81 Sundsvall; tel 60 18 40 00) and you should include a certificate of registration from the Registrar of Companies or the Swedish Patent and Registration Office (Box 5055, 102 42 Stockholm; tel 8 782

25 00) when you apply for a residence permit. See Chapter Seven *Starting a Business.*

Students

Students who are members of the European Union and European Economic Area are entitled to a residence permit for the duration of their studies in Sweden but must have adequate means of financial support. A student may work whilst studying and partners and dependents will be granted a residence permit for the duration of the student's studies provided that they have adequate means of support. Residence permits for students are usually granted for one year at a time and this is renewable. If the period of study is shorter, students should take out comprehensive sickness insurance.

Pensioners

Pensioners from EEA and EU countries and family members will be given a residence permit if they can prove that they have adequate means of support — the equivalent of a normal Swedish basic pension — and enough to cover housing costs after tax. See also *Retirement* Chapter Five.

Residence Only

Citizens of the EEA/EU will be granted a residence permit to live in Sweden without working if they have adequate means of financial support and will not have to rely on the social welfare system. Proof will be required in the form of bank deposits or through the another party guaranteeing the livelihood of the applicant and his/her family.

Non-EU Nationals

US, Canadian, Australian and New Zealand Citizens can enter Sweden for up to three months without a visa but must have a valid passport. Note: the three-month period begins from the time you enter any Scandinavian country. Whilst most nationals of other foreign countries are not required to have a visa to enter Sweden, they should check with the embassy in their own country first. Non-members of the European Union will still have to face the stringent regulations regarding the employment of foreigners in Sweden. In practice this usually means that you should have secured a job and been given a firm written offer of employment before coming to Sweden. The offer of employment should include details of working hours, pay, length of employment and accommodation arrangements. Once you have been made a firm offer of employment you should contact the nearest Swedish embassy or consulate for a work permit. It is quite common for the embassies to interview you regarding your application.

The Swedish National Labour Markets Board (AMS) usually considers the work permit application and will assess the current state of the Swedish labour market when making a decision. If a work permit is granted it will usually limit you to a specific employer, a specific job and a specific length of stay in Sweden. Work permits are rarely granted for longer than one year at a time but these can be renewed if the circumstances under which they were given still apply.

Useful Addresses

The Swedish Immigration Board, (Statens Invandrarverket): PO Box 6113, S)600 06 Norrköping; tel 11 15 60 00.
The Swedish Embassy: 11 Montagu Place, London W1H 2AL; tel 0171-724 2101.

Setting Up Home

Moving to Sweden with the intention of buying or renting a home is not particularly common and information and agencies geared towards moving there are quite hard to find. Estate agents and banks in Britain will probably not be able to provide much help and you will probably need to go through the Swedish channels. Sweden's entry into the European Union grants member citizens the same rights of access to housing as Swedish citizens.

How do the Swedes Live?

The standard of housing is very high in Sweden and Sweden's housing policy is based on giving everyone the opportunity to own their own home at a reasonable price. In the mid-1960s the Swedish parliament introduced the 'million programme' whereby more than one million flats were built over a period of ten years. In 1984 the government embarked on a programme of updating and improving all dwellings which lacked proper fittings and conveniences and also sought to adapt flats for energy conservation and for the use of the elderly and disabled and to install lifts. In 1993 they began a new programme of repair, conversion and extension work, and whilst this was partly to boost employment in the building sector, it will ensure that Sweden's housing continues to be of a very high standard.

The average number of dwellings per thousand inhabitants is 470. There are 3.8 million households in Sweden and 4.0 million dwellings. The average household consists of 2.2 persons and single households are the largest group, accounting for about one third of all households. Almost as many dwellings consist of just two persons. There are several reasons for the low occupancy rate: it is rare in Sweden for more than two generations to live together and Swedish housing policy seeks to help the elderly continue to live in their own homes for as long as they wish. Most elderly people live in one or two person households. It is also usual for grown-up children to find their own accommodation relatively quickly when they leave home, although this is becoming more difficult in metropolitan areas.

The majority of Swedes live in urban areas and about 30% of the population lives in the largest cities of Stockholm, Gothenburg and Malmö. 40% of the population live in towns of at least 2,000 inhabitants and 30% live on farms or in small village communities.

With a small population and so much empty space the Swedes can afford to be generous when it comes to living area. Government policy laid down in the 1960s states that dwellings should be sufficiently large for no more than two persons to occupy the same room, excluding the kitchen and living room, and just under 100% of households and flats conform to this standard. The average living space per person is 47 square metres with approximately two rooms per inhabitant. Most people in major towns live in apartments and about 2.1 million dwellings are in blocks of flats. Sweden has a large number of big country houses, especially in the southern provinces and the area around Lake Mälaren in particular has a large number of castles and manors dating from the 16th to the

18th century. In central Sweden traditional painted wooden farmhouses are preserved as part of Sweden's heritage.

Whilst more than 70% of the population live in towns or cities, over 22% of Swedes own a second vacation home in the countryside. Housing generally is of a very high standard and Swedish cities are noted for being carefully and tastefully planned. About 40% of the population live in subsidised housing. Recent economic setbacks in Sweden have affected some sectors of the population badly and such is Sweden's reputation for welfare provision that the fact that there are now people sleeping rough on the streets of Stockholm has been reported in the foreign national papers.

The local authorities are responsible for providing social care in housing areas eg child care facilities and are responsible for the planning of how land is used. Residents have the same rights as landowners and property-owners to appeal against planning decisions.

The standard of living in Sweden is generally very high but this is matched by an equally high cost of living. After Norway and Denmark, Sweden has the highest cost of living in the European Economic Area. Areas which are particularly expensive include housing, alcohol, tobacco and food.

Where to Look for Accommodation

If you are arranging to work abroad before moving to Sweden you should consult your prospective employer as regards accommodation. Prior to Sweden's membership of the European Economic Area employers usually had to demonstrate to the appropriate authorities that they had arranged accommodation for the prospective foreign employee or that the employee had somewhere to live. In practice many jobs abroad will come with their own accommodation — this is particularly true for temporary or casual work such as au pair, nanny, home help, farm work and hotel and catering work. Most employers advertising in the international press will either provide accommodation or be prepared to help you find it on arrival. Another invaluable source of information will be other foreign workers and asking around should provide something. Swedish people generally are friendly and helpful, if on the surface reserved, so don't be afraid to ask — they'll probably also relish the opportunity of being able to practise their excellent language skills.

More formal means of finding accommodation are through Sweden's daily papers where property is advertised extensively. The largest circulation dailies which carry listings are: *Expressen* (Stockholm) *Svenska Dagbladet* (Stockholm), *Goteborgs-Posten* (Gothenburg) and *Sydsvenska Dagbladet* (Malmö). Advertisements for accommodation can be placed via Frank L Crane Ltd (International Press Representation, 5-15 Cromer Street, Grays Inn Road, London WC1H 8LS; tel 0171-837 3330).

Types of Tenure

There are three kinds of tenure in Sweden: ownership, tenant-ownership and rental. The majority of single or two-family houses are owner-occupied. 40% are rented and about 15% are tenant owned. Tenant-owners are members of a non-profit making organisation which provides its members with accommodation (usually flats). Special regulations regarding tenant-ownership means that members must make an initial capital investment in the property and then pay monthly charges to cover the cost of the organisation's loan and capital expenditure. Tenant-owners are usually responsible for their own maintenance and can sell the property, usually at a price determined by themselves.

Finance

Raising finance for a Swedish mortgage in Sweden will prove difficult if you are not intending to reside there and likewise in Britain if you are intending to reside abroad so you should discuss your situation with a financial advisor before taking any steps. In Sweden mortgages are arranged on similar lines to British mortgages and you will need to discuss your individual needs with the finance company or bank.

Recent economic difficulties in Sweden have affected the housing market as much as anything else. The most notable development has been the decision to privatise the country's largest mortgage lenders *Statshypotek* (Box 7675, S-103 95 Stockholm; tel 8 723 24 00). As Sweden's largest mortgage lender Statshypotek has a lending volume of 320 billion SEK — one sixth of the total sum lent by banks and Swedish institutions in Sweden-and 93% of its lending is to house buyers of whom there are 750,000.

Taxation

A tax reduction of 25% of interest outgoings is allowed for interest expenses on owner-occupied houses and tenant-owned homes. Property tax is levied at 2.5% of the assessed value of multi-family blocks of rented and tenant-owned accommodation and at 1.5% for single-family dwellings. New and renovated homes qualify for a ten year property tax reduction. Property is assessed every six years and the assessed value equals 75% of the market value. A capital gains tax of 15% is levied on profits from the sale of owner-occupied and tenant-owner property.

Housing Allowances

Pensioners and low-income families with children are entitled to housing allowances. Approximately 26% of families with one child receive housing allowances and 30% with two children or more receive it. The recession in Sweden means that the number of people receiving housing allowances is rising.

Renting Property and Municipal Housing Corporations

About 40% of Sweden's dwellings are rented and almost all rented dwellings carrying tenancy rights are to be found in blocks of flats. Standards regarding the cost of renting property are carefully monitored in Swedish housing property under the utility value provisions legislation. This ensures that the rent for a flat may not be significantly higher than that of another flat in the same area which is of roughly the same value. In public housing (usually flats), the rent is set by negotiation between the corporation and the tenant organisation. Public housing rents usually include the cost of maintenance, management and capital expenditure. In privately owned property the rent is also usually set by negotiations between the landlord and a tenant organisation but costs incurred by the landlord are not normally taken into account. Usually tenants enjoy right of tenure and in some cases may transfer their rented flat to another person when they move on. In the past the costs of rent in the private and public sector have been on comparable levels although the rent-setting system is now becoming rather looser. Nonetheless, Sweden's renting system is generally favourable towards tenants and tenants rights are respected.

The availability of rented accommodation in Sweden varies throughout the country. Finding rented accommodation in Stockholm is quite difficult but rather easier in Gothenburg and Malmö and most vacant apartments will be found in the suburbs. You can advertise for rented accommodation in local and regional papers or go through municipal and private housing companies (look under *bostadsföretag* in the yellow pages). To find a sublet apartment through an agency look in the yellow pages of the telephone directory under *bostadsförme-dling* — there is a fee for this service. Subletted apartments can be found through newspaper adverts and are comparatively easy to find.

The current average yearly rent for an apartment in Sweden is 635 SEK per square metre. The average monthly rent (including heating) for a flat with three rooms and a kitchen is 3,970 SEK and for a four bedroom house with a kitchen is 4,740 SEK. In Stockholm the average rent is slightly higher. Modern flats built in the past five years are about 20% higher than the average flat rental. These costs are subject to change.

Nearly every municipality in Sweden has its own public housing company and public housing companies own about 50% of all rented flats in Sweden. The public housing companies are an integral part of Sweden's housing and social welfare policies and the homes they own are available to all. Further advice and information on this can be obtained from The Swedish Tenants Association (Box 7514, S-103 92 Stockholm; tel 8 791 02 00, fax 8 20 53 24. (visiting address: Norrlandsgatan 7).

Purchasing Property

If you can afford to buy property in Sweden you should find the purchasing procedure relatively straightforward. Real estate brokers (the equivalent of estate agents) can be found through the daily papers or in the yellow pages of the phone book under *Fastigshetsmäklare*. The two leading nationwide housing companies are HSB and Riksbyggen which can be found in local phone books. For more details about real estate brokers in Sweden and for a list of local brokers contact the Swedish Association of Real Estate Brokers (Box 1487, S-171 28 Stockholm; tel 8 734 6700).

For those with more exclusive tastes, occasionally Sweden's tiny islands come up for sale in the international press. After Canada's islands, Sweden's islands are reputed to be some of the most affordable. Impoverished Swedish aristocrats occasionally put their ancestral homes up for sale. The majority of these are found in the southwest of Sweden. Sormland Manor, 130 miles southwest of Stockholm was advertised in the international press recently for 4.3 million SEK ($555,000). For that you get 46 hectares of forests and farmland, two guesthouses and an artist's studio.

Contracts

You should always ask for a written contract when buying or renting accommodation in Sweden but you will have certain specified rights even if you do not have a contract.

Legal

Anyone considering purchasing property in Sweden should take proper legal advice from a lawyer who is familiar with Swedish house purchase and conveyancy law. See under useful addresses for English speaking Swedish lawyers who handle property purchase.

Useful Addresses

Folke Brandt Advokatbyrå: PO Box 7086, 402 32, Gothenburg 7; tel 031 11 34 78, fax 031 13 53 73.

Advokatfirman LJB: PO Box 465, Linköping S-58105; tel 013 11 01 05, fax 013 14 12 20.

Herslow and Holme HB: Södra Tullgatan 3, Box 4307, S-203 14 Malmö; tel 040 10 14 60, fax 040 97 42 10.

Malmström and Malmenfelt Advokatbyr̃ AB: 4th and 5th floor, Hovslagargatan 5B, PO Box 1665, 111 96 Stockholm; tel 8 679 69 50, fax 8 611 57 55.

Utilities

Most Swedish homes are fully equipped with the latest modern amenities: 73% of the population have a washing machine, 93% a freezer and 43% a dishwasher. The number of telephones, videos, cars, boats and second homes per person is amongst the highest in the world and Sweden holds the world record on the percentage of the population owning a mobile phone (currently 10.86%). There are high standards of heating and insulation in Sweden which, given the climate, is probably a good thing. The electrical current in Sweden is 220 volts and plugs usually have two round prongs. About three-quarters of the present housing stock in Sweden has been built since 1940 and the majority of older houses have been modernised. Consequently most houses are well-equipped with utilities. Just under 100% have their own running water, central heating, WC and bath or shower. In apartment blocks it is usual for there to be laundry facilities in the basement for general use although the amount of time you can spend using them is fiercely regulated by elderly ladies employed as laundry attendants.

Removals

Moving houses is inherently traumatic and moving abroad potentially even more so. The process will be greatly simplified if you can reduce your possessions to the contents of a car boot but this is not always practical, particularly if you are moving abroad for a long period. Even though Sweden is the home of pine furniture costs of setting up a home from scratch in Sweden will be very expensive and you may not particularly like the Ikea look anyway. Set against this is the fact that moving abroad is also expensive-moving to Sweden could cost several thousand pounds. If you choose to move your worldly goods to Sweden choose an experienced removals company with international experience. The British Association of Removers produce a useful leaflet for anyone thinking about moving overseas. Send an SAE to the address below. European Community Law states that legitimate household items can be imported duty free.

Useful Addresses

The British Association of Removers: 3 Churchill Court, 58 Station Road, North Harrow, Middlesex HA2 7SA; tel 0181-861 3331.

Scotpac International Moving: Security House, Abbey Wharf Industrial Estate, Kingsbridge Road, Barking, Essex IG11 0BT; tel 0181-591 3388, fax 0181-594 4571.

Allied Pickfords: 490 Great Cambridge Road, Enfield, Middlesex BN1 3RZ; tel 0181-366 6521.

Gauntlett International Ltd: Gauntlett House, Catteshall Road, Godalming, Surrey GU7 1NH; tel 01483-428982.

Exporting a Vehicle

If you intend to take your car abroad for more than 12 months it is regarded as a permanent export. Vehicles kept or used in Britain are registered at the Driver and Vehicle Licensing Centre at Swansea. Before you go you should complete the form V5 registration document (available from the Centre or from your local vehicle registration office) to show your intended date of export. The form should be returned to your local office or the headquarters at Swansea. You will then receive the V561 *Certificate of Export.* Allow at least one month for the processing of your application. If you do not intend to take your vehicle abroad for more than 12 months you must take a V5 registration document with you.

When it has been checked that you are the owner of the vehicle you will be issued with a *Certificate of Registration* (V3790) which will cover you whilst you are driving abroad. You must fix a sticker on the back of your car indicating nationality eg GB for Britain.

If you expect to have to relicense your vehicle before you return to Britain you should apply by post on the form V10 (available at post offices and registration offices) before you go. Send it to a main post office in Britain at least six weeks before the new licence should start. You will need to provide both your British and foreign address on the V10. A foreign MOT is not acceptable for a British vehicle licence application. For further details on driving and importing cars to Sweden contact the Swedish Embassy (11 Montagu Place, London W1H 2AL; tel 0171-724 2101).

Importing Pets

Regulations for importing a dog or cat to Sweden are fairly strict. Cats and dogs may only be imported if they comply with the terms of an import permit which is issued by the National Board of Agriculture Division for Contagious Diseases (see below). All dogs and cats must have an Export Health Certificate prior to being exported to Sweden. The application form must be sent to the local Animal Health Office (the address of your nearest one is available from the Ministry of Agriculture — see below for address). On receipt of the application the office will issue the certificate to your nominated veterinary surgeon who will complete the certificate. Dogs and cats must be given a permanent tattoo marking or an implanted microchip for the purposes of identification and must be treated for internal parasites 14 days before they are exported. All dogs and cats will be examined by a vet on arrival in Sweden. Should the animal need to be in quarantine, quarantine stations are sited at Stenungsund, Solleftea, Furulund and Vallentuna. For further details contact the Ministry of Agriculture who provide a leaflet on importing dogs and cats to Sweden.

Useful Addresses

The National Board of Agriculture: Division of Contagious Diseases, S-551 82 Jonkoping.
Ministry of Agriculture, Fisheries and Food: Animal Health (International Trade) Division B, Hook Rise South, Tolworth, Surbiton, Surrey KT6 7NF; tel 0181-330 4411.

Daily Life

Sweden is one of the most efficient states in Europe and life in Sweden has a justifiable reputation for running smoothly. Red tape is kept to a minimum — passports can be issued in ten minutes providing the applicant has the necessary information, registering a car under another name takes two weeks, the results of blood tests are usually given on the same day as the test was taken, divorces take one or two months (there is a compulsory six-month trial separation if children are involved), a phone can be installed in five days although cancellation takes only one hour, marriages can take place within a day providing there is no hindrance and birth registration forms are completed and sent off by the hospital without you having to raise a finger. If all that sounds too good to be true, it gets better — even the trains run on time. Nonetheless, moving to any foreign country necessarily involves upheaval and a period of getting to grips with new customs and a new way of life. Whilst some initial disorientation is inevitable, what follows is an overview which may help you deal with some of the basic day to day realities which influence life in Sweden.

The Language

Like most of their Scandinavian cousins, the Swedes seem to have an impressive facility for acquiring foreign languages. English is taught extensively in Swedish schools from the third year of education and you should have no trouble making yourself understood amongst all sectors of the population (with the possible exception of the very young and the elderly). The influence of British and American television in Sweden means that many Swedes hear English spoken daily and many prefer listening to the words in English rather than relying on the translation of the subtitles.

The Swedish language is a north Germanic language and shares similarities with Norwegian, Danish and Icelandic but there has also been a Finnish, French and English influence. Regional dialects in Sweden are gradually being eroded through the influences of education and the mass media. Spoken Swedish is most noted for its tone or pitch which gives it a distinctive singsong sound. There are three letters of the alphabet which are peculiar to Sweden: ä, ö and å, all of which come after the letter z in the alphabet. Swedish is amongst the more widely spoken of the Scandinavian languages (an estimated 17.5 million people speak it world-wide) and it is understood by many people in Norway and Denmark. Those wanting to learn Swedish will find books and tapes readily available and may find that it is on offer at local evening classes. Both the Berlitz Language Schools and Linguarama offer courses in Swedish (see below) at regional areas in Britain and Linguaphone offer a course of tapes/compact discs and books for home-study. Provision for learning Swedish in Sweden is well developed and if you want to take advantage of it you should contact your local education authority in Sweden (see useful addresses). Students who wish to study at a Swedish university can arrange for an examination through the municipal adult education scheme or can take the Swedish Language Test for Academic Purposes. Details of this can be obtained through embassies or through the Institute for English-speaking Students in Sweden (see under useful addresses). Immigrants eg those with Swedish partners, or refugees are entitled to free Swedish classes for three hours a day. These are available throughout Sweden and are run by the SFI (*Svenska För Invandrare*) available through the immigration service (see useful addresses).

Useful Addresses

Linguarama: Queen's House, 8 Queen Street, London EC4N 1SP; tel 0171-236 1992, fax 0171-236 7206.

The Berlitz School of Languages: 79 Wells Street, London W1A 3BZ; tel 0171-580 6482.

The Linguaphone Institute Limited: St Giles House, 50 Poland street, London W1V 4AX; tel 0171-287 4050.

The Institute for English-speaking Students: University of Stockholm, 106 91 Stockholm; tel 8 16 20 00.

The Swedish Immigration Board (Statens Invandrarvark): PO Box 6113, S-600 06 Norrköping; tel 11 15 60 00.

The National Agency for Education: Skolverket, S-106 20 Stockholm; tel 8 723 32 00.

Schools and Education

Despite having one of the most expensive school systems in the world, education in Sweden has incurred considerable criticism from within the country. One of the more controversial issues towards the end of the 1980s was the fact that pupils were not given marks before the eighth grade because of the belief that this created competition instead of cooperation whereas in the upper secondary schools pupils were marked every term. There has also been criticism about the level of education and knowledge that pupils attain. Reform of these issues was central to the education policies of the 1991-1994 Conservative government but before this the Social Democrats had instituted reforms within education and the 1990s have marked a period of upheaval and change within Swedish schools. Until very recently all schools in Sweden were free and there were no state grants for private education but the Conservative government enabled parents to choose for the first time whether to send their children to private or public schools. Parents opting for the independent sector are issued with vouchers worth at least 85% of the cost of state education. As a result there has been a large increase in the number of private schools in Sweden in recent years. Details of private schools in Sweden can be obtained from *Lararforbundet* (tel 8 733 6500).

Primary and Secondary Education

Compulsory primary education was introduced into Sweden as early as 1842. Today the majority of Swedish children attend pre-school for one year followed by a compulsory nine years of comprehensive school (*grundskola*) from the age of seven although from 1997 the age will be lowered to six. Until 1995 the comprehensive school system was divided into three stages of three years each: lower, middle and upper. Now that these divisions have been done away with pupils will be evaluated in the fifth and ninth grades. About 90% of all children continue from the comprehensive school to the upper secondary school (*gymnasieskola*). In the upper secondary school the curriculum is divided into university and vocationally oriented programmes which take place over three years. In recent years this curriculum has been revised and is now aimed at being more knowledge oriented and vocational courses which used to take two years now take three. Unlike in some countries books and lunches are provided free in Swedish schools.

Higher Education

Sweden has an impressive 13 major universities and the oldest at Uppsala was founded in 1477. Higher education is available at 30 locations throughout Sweden. A unified educational system was introduced in 1977 which created greater integration between the universities and other institutions of higher education. Most undergraduate programmes run for four years. About 35% of those completing upper secondary school continue directly on to some form of higher education although the government is trying to increase this figure. Course fees are paid throughout the higher education system up to doctorate level although most students pay for their own board and lodging and books. Government grants and loans for education are widely available and no one is excluded because of lack of money. Sweden has a good record on research, particularly in science and technology and a large proportion of research funds come from business. About 14,000 young adults a year attend one of Sweden's 128 Folk High Schools. These are mainly residential colleges with individual education programmes in more vocational subjects.

Adult Education

About one fourth of the adult population in Sweden has a higher education. Continuing and adult education play an important part in Swedish life. An average of one in three adults is engaged in some kind of educational programme available at folk high schools, on courses run by government and employment agencies or through one of the eleven nationwide adult education associations. Adult education receives subsidies from central and local government and is usually affiliated with a special interest organisation or a political party. Study circles are very popular in Swedish adult education — these are run as informal gatherings of adults with a common educational interests and attract government funding. Radio and television courses are available for people who are unable to attend education centres. For further details contact the Folk High School Information Centre (Box 740, S-101 35 Stockholm; tel 8 796 00 50, fax 8 21 88 26; visiting address is Västmannagatan 1).

International Education

A number of English-speaking schools cater for children whose parents have temporarily moved to Sweden (see below). International schools offer the International Baccalaureate which is an international curriculum and university entrance exam. British schools in Sweden offer a British style education and exam system. A few Swedish schools offer the Swedish national curriculum but have an international section which offers the Baccalaureate. The children of foreigners domiciled in Sweden who attend Swedish schools are entitled to lessons in both their own native language at school and extra Swedish tuition. If you want information about state schools you should contact the local education authority (*Skolverket*) which will be in the telephone directory. For Stockholm contact *Skolverket:* (S-106 20 Stockholm; 8 723 32 00). For general information about schools in Europe contact the European Council of International Schools (21 Lavant Street, Petersfield, Hampshire GU32 3EL; tel

01730-268244). For information about the International Baccalaureate in Sweden contact The Associate Regional Director for Europe (International Baccalaureate Nordic Countries, Johannesgatan 18, 11138 Stockholm; tel 8 24 00 51, fax 8 24 00 52).

Useful Addresses

British Primary School in Stockholm: Ostra Valhallavägen 17, S-S-182 62 Djursholm, Stockholm; tel 8 755 23 75, fax 8 755 26 35 (Takes boys and girls aged 3-12. Language of instruction is English and offers the UK national curriculum).

International School of Stockholm: Johannesgaten 18, S-111 38 Stockholm; tel 8 24 97 15, fax 8 10 52 89 (takes boys and girls age 4-15. Language of instruction is English and offers the US and UK national curriculum).

Hvitfeldtska Gymnasiet: International Section, Rektorsgatan 2, S-411 33 Gothenburg; tel 31 778 64 52/4, fax 31 81 17 97 (Takes boys and girls aged 16-20. The language of instruction is English and offers the National curriculum and the International Baccalaureate).

English Junior School: Lila Danska Vägen 1, S-41274 Gothenburg; tel 31 40 18 19 (takes boys and girls age 5-13. The language of instruction is English and offers a British Education).

Kungsholmen's Gymnasium: Bergslagsväen 80, S-161 54 Stockholm-Bromma; tel 8 87 00 92, fax 8 87 00 16 (takes boys and girls age 15-19. The language of instruction is English and offers a National curriculum and the International Baccalaureate).

Sigtunaskolan Humanistiska: Laroverket (International Section), PO Box 508, S-193 28 Sigtuna; tel 8 592 501 35, fax 8 59 25 15 25 (takes boys and girls age 13-19. The language of instruction is English and offers the National curriculum and the International Baccalaureate. Has boarding facilities).

Media and Communications

Newspapers and Magazines

Swedes are avid newspaper readers and the average newspaper circulation is 534 per thousand. The most popular daily is the *Expressen* with a daily circulation of 566,000 followed by the independent liberal newspaper *Dagens Nyheter* with a circulation of 407,126 followed by the conservative *Svenska Dagbladet* with a circulation of 217,282. In Gothenburg the most popular paper is the liberal *Göteborg-Posten* (circulation 187,000) and in Malmö it is *Sydsvenska Dagbladet* (circulation 148,000). Apart from the national newspapers Sweden has a wide selection of regional papers and popular, trade and organisational magazines. Magazines published by the trade union organisations reach a wide readership and play an important role in public debate. Traditionally Swedish papers have been linked to political parties and this is still true to some extent (a number of papers are party owned) but in Sweden priority is given to critical monitoring of people in power and this has been aided by the Freedom of the Press Act which was enshrined in Swedish law in the revisions of the Constitution in 1974. The Act guarantees the protection of anonymous sources, gives journalists freedom of access to public documents and establishes procedures in trials involving freedom of the press issues thus making it very difficult to win large monetary judgements against journalists. A press ombudsman supervises the adherence to ethical standards within the press. Despite a large number of state subsidies for the press many smaller publications have been forced to shut down in the economic recession of the 1990s in Sweden.

British newspapers are available in Stockholm and a wide selection of foreign publications can be found at the Press Centre (Gallerian: Hamngatan, Sveavagen 52, Stockholm) and at the Central Station.

Useful Addresses

Expressen: Gjorwellsgatan 30, S-105 16 Stockholm; 8 73 83 00, fax 8 619 04 50.

Dagens Nyheter: Rålambsvägen 17, S-105 15 Stockholm; 8 738 10 00, fax 8 54 57 90.

Svenska Dagbladet: Rålambsvaggen 7, S-105 17 Stockholm; 8 13 50 00, fax 8 51 15 24.

Göteborgs-Posten: Polhemsplatsen 5, S-40502 Gothenburg; tel 31 62 40 00, fax 31 15 87 91.

Sydsvenska Dagbladet: Krusegaten 19, S-20505 Malmö; tel 40 28 00 00, fax 40 18 36 65.

Television and Radio

Radio and Television in Sweden come under the umbrella of the Swedish Broadcasting Corporation which was modelled on the BBC. The main TV channels are *Kanal* 1, TV2 and the Nordic channel TV3 which is also available in Denmark and Norway. Private companies can broadcast TV via satellite and cable to a large proportion of Swedish households. The Swedish Broadcasting Company is mainly financed by household licences and until recently paid advertising on state television was prohibited but there is now a commercial channel, TV4, which has commercial advertising. There are many imported foreign programmes on Swedish TV and you can usually tune into a familiar English or American soap opera even inside the Arctic Circle.

Swedish Radio has expanded in recent years. Radio Sweden (7.38 MHz) has an impressive range of foreign language broadcasts and from late September to late March you can hear English daily from 5.15 pm to 5.45 pm and 10.30 pm to 11pm on weekdays and there is an additional English broadcast from 9.30 pm to 10 pm at the weekend. In the Summer there is a daily news broadcast in English at 1 pm on 1179MHz. You can also tune into the BBC World Service on 61.95MHz. Radio Bandit blasted onto the Swedish airways in 1994. Bandit is an all-English commercial radio station owned by Americans.

The Postal System

The Swedish postal system is highly efficient. Post offices in Sweden are usually open Monday to Friday from 9.30 am to 6pm and from 10 am to 1 pm on Saturdays. The post office at the Central Station in Stockholm is open Monday to Friday 7 am to 10 pm and on Saturdays and Sundays from 10 am to 7 pm. The main post office in Stockholm (Vasagaten 28-34 and Master Samuelsgatan 70; tel 8 7812055) is open Monday to Friday from 8 am to 6.30 pm and on Saturday from 10 am to 2 pm.

Post boxes in Sweden are yellow. For enquiries about the postal system in Stockholm ring 8 781 20 05. All post offices can provide the post code list (*postnummer katalog*).

Telephones

Post offices generally do not have telephone facilities but there are a few *Tele* or *Telebutik* telephone offices including the *Telecenter* at the Central Station in Stockholm which is open daily from 8am to 9pm from where you can make long-distance telephone calls. There are three methods of payment for public phone calls: money (currently accepts 1 SEK and 5 SEK), *Telefonkort* (Telephone card) and credit card. *Telefonkorts* can be bought from *Telebutiks* and hospitals. Pay phones are widely available in Sweden and new orange pay phones are replacing the old green ones. A local call currently costs a minimum of 2SEK.

To call abroad dial 009 followed by the country code, when you hear the tone dial the area code (often the first digit is not required) followed by the number. To call Sweden from abroad dial 00 46. For operator assistance call 0019-all operators speak good English. For directory enquiries in Sweden call 07975 and for other foreign enquiries cal 0019.

Area Codes:

Stockholm 8, Gothenburg 31
Malmo 40, Uppsala 18

Emergency Numbers

In an emergency call 90 000 for the police, fire brigade or ambulance. The number is free and you will not need coins for a call box. In the case of serious illness or death, Radio Sweden on KHZ 6065 can broadcast urgent messages in emergencies.

Remember that in a Swedish telephone directory the letters ä, ö and å come after the letter Z.

Cars and Motoring

Roads

Roads in Sweden are well maintained and away from cities and towns can often be empty for many miles at a stretch. Sweden's 49,600 miles/80,000km of road networks range from four lane motorways on the busiest stretches, *motorled* or highway, conventional two lane roads and *grus* or gravel roads which tend to be rather more off the beaten track. The motorway network is fairly small (744 miles/1200km) and where the motorways run out the *motorled* take over. Effectively the motorled are two-laned main roads with hard shoulders. The hard shoulders are used as additional lanes in the event of overtaking (the driver being overtaken moves onto it). The E4, Arctic Highway, is Sweden's main route and runs from north of Stockholm through Uppsala and continues right the way up the coast to Harapanda on the Finnish border. Driving west from Stockholm, the E3 leading into the E18 provides a direct route to Oslo and neighbouring Norway. There are also major routes to Norway from Sweden via the E75 from Sundsvall to Trondheim, on the E79 which goes from Umeå to Mo-i-Rana and on Route 98 which links with the E4 after Luleå and goes directly to Narvik via Kiruna, linking with route 70. Sweden's south coast is served by a good network of major and minor roads (reflecting the greater size of the population in the south) which go all around the coastline and directly over from east to west. Further north roads become progressively fewer and large tracts of land are not served by road although all towns and cities can be reached. Areas around the coast have more roads than in the interior.

Petrol is available throughout Sweden although you should stock up on a full tank if you are covering long distances, particularly in the north, and as a precaution it's a good idea to carry a can of spare fuel. Petrol is sold in 95 octane lead-free (*Blyfri* in Swedish), 96 octane (three star), 98 octane (four star) and diesel. The majority of petrol stations are self-service-this is indicated by the sign *Tanka Själv*-and many have automatic pumps (*Sedel Automat*) which can be used 24 hours a day. Automatic pumps are usually slightly cheaper. Payment is by inserting a 100 SEK note. The sign *Konto* on a pump indicates that it is for local account holders. Many petrol stations stock basic foodstuffs and newspapers.

Minor roads in the north can become impassable in winter and studded tyres and snow chains are recommended for mountainous and difficult terrain.

Breakdowns and Accidents
Members of British motoring organisations receive accident and breakdown service if they pay for extra cover in Europe. The AA operates a Five Star Service and the RAC operates Reflex. In Sweden the major motoring organisation is *Motormännens Rikförbund* and the main accident and insurance organisation is *Larmtjäst* (see under useful addresses). When there is an accident in Sweden it is mandatory to exchange names and addresses with the other party involved even in the case of non-serious accidents. The main hazards to look out for on Swedish roads are wild animals wandering on to the road-notably reindeer in the north and elk in the north and further south. They can be particularly hard to spot in bad light and at twilight. As elks can weigh as much as 120 stone both you, and your car, will know if you collide with one. Elks are involved in one-fifth of Swedish road accidents. For emergencies, accidents and insurance ring the *Larmtjänst* (free on 020 910040) or the police (on 90 000). You do not have to inform the police if an accident is not serious but if you consider it to be you should call them.

Driving Regulations
Speed limits in Sweden are: 110kph/68mph on motorways, between 90kph/56mph and 70 kph/43mph on other roads and 50kph/31mph in built up areas. In the summer (mid-June to mid-August) speed limits on motorways are dropped to 90kph on most routes. Driving on motorways forms part of the Swedish driving test.

Driving is on the right in Sweden and the main rule is to give way to traffic approaching from the right unless the road signs indicate otherwise. Drivers of right hand drive cars should adjust their headlights so that the beam sweeps to the right. Dipped headlights are obligatory both by day and by night. The driver and all passengers must use seat belts.

Drink-Driving
Drink-driving regulations in Sweden are some of the toughest in the world and the best policy is simply not to drink and drive. The police have the power to stop drivers at any time to take a breathalyser test. The legal limit is a mere 20mg/100ml — less than one can of beer. Random breath tests are routine and if you are over the limit (a mere 0.02% of the blood alcohol content) you can expect fines, loss of licence and sometimes imprisonment. Driving with a blood alcohol level over 1.5% can lead to one year's imprisonment. Driving under the influence of drugs incurs comparable punishment levels. Foreigners are no exception to this and pleading ignorance of Swedish law will not solve the problem.

Driving Licences
European Commission directives making licences fully transferable come into force in July 1996. Until then an international driving permit is needed for those wanting to drive abroad. In Britain this can be obtained from the Automobile Association (AA — see below) by holders of a full British licence. You will need to produce your driving licence, a passport-sized photo signed on the back and

the appropriate fee. Alternatively you can apply through the Drivers Vehicle Licensing Centre (see useful addresses). Other nationals who do not have a British driving licence should make applications to the country where their licence was issued.

In Sweden new vehicle checks take place every three years, followed by a two-yearly check and then yearly checks. Drivers are given an appointment at a government centre where their cars are given a twenty-minute road and mechanical inspection — this costs about £30. The certificate of road worthiness, insurance and tax are all due at the same time making them difficult for drivers to forget.

Insurance

All vehicles registered abroad must carry international liability insurance and an accident report form. These are available from motoring organisations. You can, if need be, buy temporary insurance cover at the border. Swedish Insurance companies operate the Larmtjänst organisation which also offers an emergency breakdown service.

Useful Addresses

The Automobile Association: Head Office, Norfolk House, Priestley Road, Basing-stoke, Hampshire RG24 9NY; tel 01256-20123, fax 01256-493389.

The Royal Automobile Club: PO Box 700 Spectrum, Bond Street, Bristol BS99 1RB; tel 01272-232340.

DVLC (The Driver and Vehicle Licensing Centre): The Exports Section, Swansea SA99 1BL; tel 01792-783100.

Motormañnnens Rikförbund: Sturegatan 32, 102 48 Stockholm; tel 8 78 23 80, fax 8 663 89 21.

Larmtjänst: Tegeluddsvägen 100, 115 87 Stockholm; 8 78 37 000.

Transport

Rail

To get to Sweden by rail, there is a daily service from London Victoria for the Dover-Ostend ferry or from London Liverpool Street Station which links with the Harwich-Hook of Holland crossing. Connecting trains take you to Copenhagen where there is an on-going service to Sweden via ferry and connecting train. You can also catch the ferry and hydrofoil service from Copenhagen to Malmö. For further details contact the Swedish Travel Council (73 Welbeck Street, London W1M 8AN; tel 0171-487 3135; fax 0171-935 5853).

The Swedish State Railway Company (*Statens Järnvägar* or SJ; telephone 020 75 75 75 for details in Sweden) operates one of Europe's most efficient, punctual and scenic train services. Bookings can be made through the Norwegian State Railways in London. There is a coordinated rail and bus service in Sweden which covers 1,000 towns and cities within the country. The southern part of Sweden has the most railway stock, reflecting the bigger population there. The network stretches from Malmö in the south to Kiruna in the north. Swedish trains have been substantially upgraded in recent years and innovations include sleeping cars with en suite toilets and showers, family coaches with play areas for children and even cinema coaches for trains travelling to the north of Sweden. The Rolls Royce of the Swedish railway system is the new X2000 high speed train which at speeds of 125 mph can take you from Stockholm to Gothenburg in three hours. There is a supplement for travelling on the X2000 but as facilities include newspapers, headphones and office facilities it's probably well worth the extra if your time is so valuable that you carry out business on the move. Many trains require reservations particularly on long journeys and these can usually be made up to the time of departure. There are frequent departures of the Inter Nord trains which travel between the three Scandinavian capitals of Stockholm, Copenhagen and Oslo. These trains travel through both the day and the night and have first and second class compartments, restaurant cars and cafeterias.

Useful Addresses
Norwegian State Railways: 21-24 Cockspur Street, London SW1Y 5DA; tel 0171-930 6666.
British Rail European Departure Office: Victoria Station, London SW1; tel 0171-834 8511.

Air
British Airways and the Scandinavian airline SAS operate daily flights from London Heathrow to Stockholm and Gothenburg. There is also a service to Stockholm and Malmö from Gatwick. SAS operates frequent daily services to Europe, USA and Canada.

Useful Addresses
British Airways: PO Box 10, Hounslow, Middlesex TW6 2JA; tel 0181-897 4000.
SAS Scandinavian Airlines: SAS House, 52–53 Conduit Street, London W1R 0AY; tel 0171-734 2040.
SAS Reservations New York: Ticket Office C/O Continental Air Lines, 100 East 42 Street, New York, USA; tel 212 682 3180.

Domestic Flights
Internal air travel can save a considerable amount of travelling time in Sweden, particularly in the north where towns are far apart. The main agents for internal flights are SAS Scandinavian Airlines and Linjeflyg which cover over 40 destinations. Passengers can get half price fares at off-peak times and the so-called 'micro-fares' which are return flights can knock up to 60% off the price but these can only be bought in Sweden and must be booked two weeks in advance.

Useful Addresses
Linjeflyg: Box 550, S-190 45 Stockholm Arlanda; tel 8 797 5000.
SAS Arlanda: Box 54, S-190 45, Stockholm Arlanda; tel 8 797 5050.

Boats and Ferries
There are frequent ferry services to Sweden from Britain and the rest of Europe. Scandinavian Seaways operates a regular service all year round from Harwich to Gothenburg as well as from Newcastle to Gothenburg in the summer. Alternatively, Stena Line has several ferry services to Europe from where boat, car or coach transport can take you to Sweden. Scandinavian Ferry lines operate the ferry route from Elsinor in Denmark to Helsingborg in Sweden. This crossing should take 25 minutes but it is very busy and can take up to an hour. There are several other connecting ferry and hydrofoil services from Denmark to Sweden including Kastrup (Copenhagen airport) to Malmö, Grenå to Halmstad, Varberg and Helsingborg and Frederikshavn to Gothenburg.

Useful Addresses

Scandinavian Seaways: Scandinavian House, Parkeston Quay, Harwich, Essex CO12 4G; tel 01255-240240.

Scandinavian Seaways: 15 Hanover Street, London W1R 9HG; tel 0171-493 6696.

Sealink-Stena Line: Charter House, Park Street, Ashford, Kent TN24 8EX; tel 01233-647047.

The archipelago off Sweden's coastline has given rise to almost an armada of local boat services and there are ferry services from the mainland to the islands throughout the coastal regions. For further details and for sailings along Sweden's Göta Canal which links the Baltic Sea with the North Sea contact Norwegian State Railways (see above for address).

Buses and Public Transport

In summer there is a daily coach service to Sweden from London via Amsterdam and a service three times a week during the rest of the year. It takes 47 hours to get to Stockholm. For further details contact Eurolines (52 Grosvenor Gardens, London SW1; tel 0171-730 8111.

There is a network of express bus services which link towns and cities in southern and central Sweden. There are also regular services from Stockholm to the north. The main operator is *Swebus* (Gullbergs Strandgata 34, S-41104 Gothenburg; tel 031 10 38 20). Smoking is not allowed on any buses.

Most Swedish towns and cities have a reliable and relatively cheap public transport system and in some cities buses operate 24 hours a day. You pay the driver as you enter. Bus services are the mainstay of urban transport but Gothenburg and Norrköping also have trams and Stockholm is serviced by a comprehensive underground called the *Tunnelbana* which is centred on *T-Centralen* station. Transport in Stockholm is operated by *Storstockolms Lokal-trafik* (SL) (Nortullsgatan 6; tel 8 600 10 00).

Banks and Finance

Swedish banks operate on a similar system to British banks and opening a bank account should be a relatively straightforward affair but you will need to obtain a personal identity number from the tax office first (see Chapter Two *Residence and Entry Regulations*). Banks are highly computerised and the 'Bank-giro' (ie a system of credit transfer between banks) clearing system facilitates the transfer of money from one bank to another therefore cheques tend to be used less in Sweden than in other countries. The Swedish post office also operates a post-giro system and the major Swedish bank Norbanken provides its banking service through the post office as well as through its other branches.

Opening hours in banks are generally from 9.30 am to 3 pm Monday to Friday and also between 4 pm and 5.30 pm on Thursdays although branches in larger cities may stay open until 5.30 pm. Banks are closed on Saturdays. Major credit cards are accepted throughout Sweden and Eurocheques backed by a guarantee card are accepted in banks, restaurants and shops.

The Currency

The Swedish currency is the Swedish Krona (plural kronor) which is usually abbreviated to Kr in shops or SEK to differentiate it from the Norwegian and Danish Krone and the Icelandic króna. The Swedish Krona divides into 100 öre. Coins are issued in values of 50 öre and in 1, 5 and 10 kronor. Bank notes are printed in values of 10, 20, 50, 100, 500, 1000 and 10,000 kronor.

Transferring Funds to Sweden

There are no limits on the amounts of Swedish or foreign currency which can be imported into Sweden but currently not more than 6,000 SEK in Swedish notes and currency may be exported. The transfer of foreign money to a Swedish bank can usually be effected within 48 hours via telephone.

Taxation

The Swedish tax system includes numerous direct and indirect taxes and charges. Taxes in Sweden have a reputation for being very high and this is a reputation which is justified. Amongst other things, taxes go towards funding the cradle to grave welfare state. In 1988 the overall tax burden was about 55% of the GDP, making it amongst the highest in the world. Since then Sweden has undergone major tax reforms which came into effect in 1991 and 1992. Effectively the tax reforms abolished national income tax for the majority making employees liable only for local (municipal) income tax. The current average rate of local income tax is 31% and marginal income tax has been reduced to a maximum of 50%. Those on a high income (over 198,700 SEK) are still liable for national income tax which stands at about 20%.

The most important indirect tax is value added tax VAT (known as *moms* in Sweden). To make up for lost revenue the government has extended VAT to a wide variety of services not previously included and increased VAT on others that had previously had a lower rate. Taxes have also been imposed on private pension savings and on pollution emissions for the first time. VAT on most goods and services is at 25%.

There is also an extensive system of employer contributions to cover the welfare system which includes payment for pensions, health benefits and social insurance.

Useful Addresses

The Inland Revenue: EC Unit (Room S20), Somerset House, London WC2R 1LB.
Local Tax Office (Farsta): Box 70297, 107 22 Stockholm; tel 8 714 20 00, fax 8 714 12 70. The visiting address is Folkungagatan 44.

Health Care and Insurance

Health Insurance and Hospitals

British and EU citizens working and living in Sweden are entitled to health care in Sweden on the same terms as Swedish citizens. All Swedes are covered by the national health insurance system which provides medical care, medicine, hospitalisation and most dental services either free of charge or at a small cost.

Sickness Benefit

All employees in Sweden are entitled to taxable cash benefits during periods of illness. The social security system pays between 75 and 90% of a person's normal income when they are sick. From 1992 employers were made responsible for the first two weeks of sick pay, partly as a way of combatting heavy levels of absenteeism. There is no compensation for the first day of absence from work and sick pay for the second and third day amounts to 75% of the normal income. For the rest of the period it is 90%. From the fifteenth day sickness allowance is paid by the social insurance office. Freelance and self-employed workers receive sickness allowance from the social insurance office from the start. This works out at nothing for the first day, 65% of the usual income on the second and third day and 80% from the fourth day for a year. A national occupational injury insurance system pays all health care costs for work related accidents.

About 9% of the GDP goes on health care and health care in Sweden is generally of a very high standard. Since the 1980s there has been a move away from the infrastructure of big hospitals and a movement towards decentralising health care as much as possible. This in turn has lead to an increase in community health care centres and the introduction of a system of family doctors. Responsibility for health care, both inpatient and outpatient, is the responsibility of the 23 county councils and three large municipalities. Everyone has the option of registering with a general practitioner of their choice and every district has at least one local health centre with doctors and district nurses. If you need a doctor you should contact the *Vårdcentral* (primary health care district). There are about 27,000 doctors in Sweden of whom 5% are in private practice. When registering with or calling a doctor you should check that they are affiliated to the *Försäkringskassan* (Swedish National Health Service) or you may end up paying for a private practitioner. Virtually all doctors and staff will speak English.

There is a small fee for a visit to a doctor. If you need any medicine you should obtain a prescription from the doctor and take it to the chemist (*Apotek*). Prescriptions cost up to 130 SEK but costs for prescribed drugs and medical treatment exceeding 1,600 SEK a year will be refunded. Maternity, child health care and stays in hospital are free.

Emergencies

If there is an emergency you should go to the casualty department (*akutmottagning*) of the nearest major hospital but otherwise you should consult the local health clinic. In more remote districts where there is no hospital you should go to the local clinic. Ambulances can be called free on 90 000. The fee for a visit to an *akutmottaging* is currently 200 SEK.

Dentists

There is a set fee for dental services of 660 SEK per hour. Dental surgeries are indicated by the word *tandläkare*. Main cities operate an emergency out of hours dentist service.

Useful Numbers (Stockholm)

Doctor on Duty: tel 8 644 92 00
Anti-poison services: tel 8 33 12 31
Queries about medical care: tel 8 644 92 00
24 hour chemists: Stockholm: 8 21 89 34; Gothenburg: 31 80 44 10; Malmö: 40 19 21 13.
For Aids Information (freephone): 020 78 44 40
Emergency Dental Services: Stockholm: 8 654 11 17; Gothenburg: 31 80 31 40; Malmö: 40 33 35 00.

The E111

If you are intending to go to Sweden to look for work you should obtain an E111 from the post office or department of social security before you leave. The E111 enables you to receive urgent medical treatment free of charge. The E111 is valid for three months and will cover you if you are not registered as a Swedish citizen. The form is primarily for emergency medical care.

Private Medical Insurance

Some health insurance companies provide private health insurance for those living abroad. In Britain insurance can be arranged through BUPA (British United Provident Association) head office: BUPA, 23 Essex Street, London WC2 8AX; tel 0171-353 521) or the Private Patients Plan (Philips House, Crescent Road, Tunbridge Wells, Kent TN1 2PL; tel 01892-512345).

For information on health care benefits in Sweden contact: National Social Insurance Board, (Riksförsäkringsverket, RFV, 103 51 Stockholm; tel 8 786 90 00, fax 8 11 27 89).

Social Security and Unemployment Benefit

Social Security is something of a way of life in Sweden which might have some claim to be the original Welfare State. The overall aims of the welfare system are to distribute income more evenly over each individual's life cycle, to narrow the gaps between social classes and to provide a good standard of living for everyone. In return for high taxes Swedes are provided with a broad section of generous welfare benefits — so generous in fact that many Swedes are beginning to question what they see as an unhealthy dependency on the 'nanny welfare state'. The shortcomings have been highlighted in recent years following Sweden's economic depression and the Social Democrat Government has had to look for ways of cutting down expenditure on welfare.

Child Care

Child care in particular is excellent and parents who stay at home to look after their children qualify for payment by the state of ten months of 80% of their previous income (formerly 90%) and an additional month on 90% of their normal income. There are tax-free child allowances for every child up to the age of 16 and families with three or more children receive an additional payment. Parents get up to 60 days leave per year to look after sick children and are paid at about 80% of their normal wage. Day-care centres and pre-school child care are widely available and day-centres typically stay open between 6 am and 6.30 pm. The state funds up to 90% of the cost of pre-school care. For local details look up *barnomsorg* in the green pages of the local telephone directory. Responsibility for social welfare services rests primarily with the municipalities.

Social Security Benefits

Under the European Economic Area Agreement, and latterly the EU agreement, member nationals are entitled to the same social security rights in Sweden as the Swedes. When you start work in Sweden (for a Swedish employer) you will contribute to the Swedish Social Security System and will therefore have right to the benefits.

Unemployment

Most working people in Sweden have unemployment insurance through their trade unions. Everyone with an income contributes 1% of their income as a directly levied tax toward unemployment benefits. Unemployment benefits are generally high at 80% of the previous salary although this represents a drop from 90% in 1994. UK citizens who are unemployed and want to have their benefit transferred to Sweden see Chapter Two *Residence and Entry Regulations*.

When you live and work in Sweden you will be linked in to the social insurance system and will be contributing to the system by paying taxes. There are two types of insurance. You can choose between insurance offices connected with the unions (*akassorna*) or those run by the state (*arbetsmarknadskassen*). The main difference between the two is that you join the former whilst in work and the latter when you are out of work.

If you become unemployed whilst in Sweden you should register with your nearest local employment office which will advise you about labour market schemes and claiming unemployment benefit. You will probably need to complete a E301 form stating your periods of employment and unemployment before coming to Sweden and you can obtain and fill out this form before you go to Sweden.

There are two forms of unemployment benefit. The most favourable is the *dagpenning* which is related to your previous income and by which the unemployed person receives 80% of their previous income for a period of 300 working days with a maximum payment of 12,408 SEK a month. To qualify for dagpenning you must have been employed for five of the previous twelve months, have worked at least 75 hours in each month and have contributed 1% of your income into the unemployment insurance system.

If you do not meet these requirements you may be entitled to another form of unemployment benefit — *KAS/grundbelopp* or cash labour market assistance. This is calculated on your previous working hours. Both kinds of benefit are taxable.

Note: the future of the unemployment benefit is uncertain and there are likely to be a number of changes in the coming years.

Useful Addresses

Department of Social Security: Overseas Branch, Longbenton, Newcastle upon Tyne NE98 1YX; tel 0191-213 5000.

National Social Insurance Board (Riksförsäkringsverket RFV): 103 51 Stockholm; tel 8 786 90 00, fax 8 11 27 89. The visiting address is Adolf Fredriks Kyrkogata 8.

Local Government

Sweden is divided into 286 *Kommuner* (municipalities) each having an elected assembly and the right to levy income taxes. Kommuner deal with matters concerning schools and social and public housing services. Elections for the Kommuner coincide with the four year national elections. Since 1976 immigrants who have been resident in Sweden for three years are entitled to vote in the Kommuner elections.

Between the national and municipal governments are the County Councils. Sweden is divided into 24 *län* or counties whose principal responsibility is to administer regional transport, public health and the medical services. County governors and county administrative boards are elected by the national government.

Crime and the Police

As with the rest of Scandinavia, crime in Sweden is very low. In the unlikely event of crime call the police free on 90 000 and ask for *polislarm*. The Police

Headquarters for Stockholm is located on Agnegatan 33-37; tel 8 769 30 00. There are local stations in the city at Bryggargatan 19, and at Tulegatan 4. Non-emergency numbers are: Gothenburg 031 61 80 00 and Malmö 041 20 10 00.If you are arrested you should inform the nearest embassy or consul immediately. A person can be detained for six and in some cases twelve hours without orders from a prosecutor. After orders from a prosecutor they can be held for another day and sometimes longer. At this stage they have the right to contact a solicitor and a court must decide whether the person is to be detained or set free. You are entitled to legal representation in Sweden. About 15,000 people are sent to prison each year and the most common offence is drink-driving. This is a reflection on the stringent penalties rather than on the fact that Swedes are more prone to drink and drive than other nationalities. Between 25 and 50% of those currently serving prison sentences are there for drug related offences. Drug abuse is not particularly prevalent in Sweden but possession and dealing incur severe punishment. The most serious punishment in Sweden is life imprisonment although this is usually commuted to between 12 and 16 years.

The Judicial System

Courts are organised on three levels: Local courts (*tingsrätter*) courts of appeal (*hovrätter*) and the Supreme Court (*högsta domstolen*). All criminal and civil cases start in the local courts and may subsequently be taken to the courts of appeal. Only cases involving issues of major interest are taken to the supreme court. The equivalent of jury members in Swedish courts are lay assessors who work with legally trained judges and also participate in decisions on sentencing. There are also administrative courts in Sweden which deal with cases involving taxes, social insurance etc. You can turn to any lawyer for one hour of discounted legal advice. Look up *advokatbyråer* in the yellow pages of the phone book. Sweden also operates an extensive legal aid system for those who cannot afford legal costs.

Social Life

The Swedes have a reputation for being reserved, even shy, and to some extent this reputation is justified but the majority will be overwhelmingly helpful when approached. Angry displays are rare in Sweden and there is some statistical evidence to suggest that aggressive behaviour and loud confrontations in the home and the workplace occur less often in Sweden than in many other countries. Swedish humour ranges from the scatological to the slapstick but it is rarely vindictive. There is a tendency amongst the Swedes to run themselves and their country down a little but they will not appreciate it if an outsider tries to join in.

Sweden is a socialist state and class barriers and racial divisions are kept to a minimum. Attitudes in Sweden are fairly liberal as one would expect in an enlightened socialist country (not to mention the fact that it was the original home of the blue movie and the the massage parlour). Homosexual couples were allowed a recognised form of marriage in Sweden for the first time in 1994, although they are not allowed to adopt children and lesbian couples may not receive artificial insemination. Equality is an important facet of Swedish society and children's rights are enshrined in law.

Entertainment and Culture

Cultural activities reach all parts of the country through travelling theatre, concerts and exhibitions. The country's cultural institutions are state subsidised.

There are over 300 museums throughout Sweden and each municipality has its own public library which is free of charge. Stockholm is home to symphony orchestras and the national opera and theatre. Famous contributors to Swedish culture include classic writers such as August Strindberg and the more homely Astrid Lindgren, the children's author most famous for the *Pippi Longstocking* series. Additionally, film maker Ingmar Bergman and composer Wilhelm Stenhammar are revered internationally.

Whilst there are night clubs and concerts in Stockholm, Sweden's nightlife is decidedly low key with many people preferring to go to an evening class. Western and jazz music are fairly popular and the old-fashioned dance band is rather more in evidence than heavy metal rock bands but pubbing and clubbing is popular with those in their late teens and early twenties. Like their Norwegian cousins, Swedes are great outdoor lovers and right of public access to the countryside is upheld in national law (*Allemansrätten*) which translates literally as every man's right.

Second, country homes are common in Sweden and outdoor sport is also popular, particularly cross country skiing, football and orienteering. Sports organisations receive extensive subsidies from the state although facilities are much better in the south than in the north.

Religion
90% of the Swedish population belong to the Lutheran Church. All Swedish citizens are automatically registered in the Church at birth providing that one parent is a member. Even though only about 5% of the population actually attends church and religion is generally considered to be far less important in Sweden than in many other countries, few people actually bother to opt out of the church. An annual subscription to the Church is automatically deducted in taxes and the Church also derives revenue from its ownership of lands and forests.

There are many other smaller denominations in Sweden, the largest of which is the Pentecostal Movement with over 100,000 followers. Immigrants have swelled the ranks of non-Christian groups which include 50,000 Moslems, 2,000 Buddhists and 2,000 Hindus.

There are English language church services in Sweden at St Peter and St Sigfrid Anglican/Episcopal Church (Strandvagen 76, Stockholm; tel 8-663 82 48 which has services on Sundays at 11am) and at Santa Clara Church, International Church of Stockholm (Klara Ostra Kyrkogata, Stockholm; tel 8 723 30 29 which has services on Sunday at 9am). In Gothenburg the Anglican Church of St Andrews is a popular meeting point for expatriates.

Shopping

The main Swedish cities have pleasant indoor shopping malls complete with fountains and cafés. Urban centres usually have the ubiquitous department stores of Åhlens and Domus and the popular clothing chains of Hennes and Gullins. The Swedes enjoy a high standard of living and shopping is a major leisure activity.

Usual shopping hours on weekdays are 9am to 6 pm and 9am to 1pm on Saturdays but in practice many shops will stay open longer, particularly on Saturdays and many stores have late opening on Thursdays up to 7pm.

Food and Drink
Sweden is home to the designer sandwich or Smörgås, an elaborate work of art on bread. Probably the most famous Swedish food export has been the *smörgåsbord*

(literally sandwich table) — a large buffet affair usually served at lunchtime and washed down with beer. Fish is a popular item on Swedish menus and is served in many varieties as is game (mainly elk or *älg* and reindeer or *ren*). Breakfast usually consists of coffee and two or three kinds of bread, cheese and meat. Lunch, eaten between noon and 2 pm is often the main meal of the day in Sweden. It is usually *husmanskost* (home cooking) and tends to be staple, filling fare such as meat and potatoes with salad. Dinner is usually a fairly light meal. Coffee and cakes form a popular snack in Sweden.

Sweden's policies on alcohol are restrictive; a reminder perhaps of the days when alcoholism was such a problem that rationing had to be introduced. Wine, spirits and beer can only be bought through the state controlled shops *Systembolaget* where you have to queue. If you come away feeling as if you're indulging in a wicked vice don't worry — that is how it is intended. The *Systembolaget* are open Monday to Friday from 9am to 6pm (sometimes 7pm on Thursday) and there is always a long queue on Friday night and before festivals.

Public Holidays

1 January — New Year's Day   6 January — Epiphany
Good Friday, Easter Sunday and Easter Monday
1 May — May Day, Whit Sunday and Whit Monday
Midsummer Day (approx 21-22 June but varies)
All Saints' Day
25 December — Christmas Day
26 December — Boxing Day

Retirement

Sweden has one of the best records in the world in terms of caring for its senior citizens but there has been concern in recent years over the increasing number of elderly people placing a heavy burden on the medical and welfare system. A growing percentage (currently 18%) of the population is over 65 years old. This is partly due to the fact that in Sweden shares with the rest of Scandinavia some of the highest longevity rates in the western world. The average life expectancy of a man is 74.9 and for a woman 80.5 years.

To choose to retire to Sweden is not particularly common — both the weather and the high cost of living tend to militate against it. Nonetheless, retired people can expect to enjoy a high standard of living and social care throughout their retirement. Many elderly people in Sweden are able to continue living in their own homes thanks to an extensive system of home help services. Every municipality employs workers who help the elderly, as necessary, with cleaning, shopping, cooking and personal care. Pensioners pay for this service according to their means. Other benefits for pensioners include housing allowances, home adaptation grants and on-call warden services where needed. You can gain further information about retiring in Sweden by contacting the *Pensionärens Riksorganisation* (Box 3274, S-10365 Stockholm; tel 8 24 49 60).

The retirement age in Sweden is expected to be raised from 60 to 62 to cope with increased costs. Everyone of retirement age is entitled to a basic pension regardless of whether they have worked or not. In addition most people also receive an income-related supplementary pension (ATP). The basic pension is financed by both employees and employers and the State pays an income-related supplementary pension financed from employer pay roll fees. The two pensions are inflation-linked and are intended to provide two thirds of a pensioner's average real earnings during their 15 best years of income. People with disabilities (both mental and physical) are eligible for public pensions at an earlier age if there is no appropriate sheltered housing available.

As with so many other state institutions in Sweden, the ATP system has been the subject of debate and criticism in recent years and there has been concern that slower economic growth and a higher proportion of ATP recipients to the labour force means that funds may prove insufficient to meet pension obligations in the next twenty to thirty years. There may therefore be the need in the future for a larger element of individual retirement savings and for individual private pension plans. However, as of 1994 it was agreed by parliament that everyone should be entitled to a basic pension of 74,000 SEK which is taxable and in addition a sum calculated on life income will be granted.

Residence Requirements

Since 1 January 1992 pensioners from EU states have been free to live wherever they wish in the European Union provided that they have adequate means of financial support. Sweden's membership of the EU in 1995 has brought it in to line with regulations on these matters. Currently, the Swedish regulations state that a pensioner from any EEA country and his/her family members will be granted a residence permit if they can show that they have adequate means of support which is at least the equivalent of a normal basic Swedish pension after tax. Additionally they must be able to prove that they have enough assets after tax to cover their housing costs. Proof will be required in the form of bank balance statements etc.

Pensions

If you become entitled to a state pension before leaving the UK you can arrange to have it paid to you in Sweden although you should bear in mind that it will be linked to British levels. People who have moved to Sweden before retirement but have continued to pay British national insurance contributions will qualify for a British pension but if they have paid into the Swedish welfare system they will be entitled to a Swedish pension. To claim a solely British pension after retiring you should apply to the DSS (Overseas Branch, Longbenton, Newcastle upon Tyne, NE98 1YX; tel 0191-213 5000) and arrange for your pension to be paid into a designated bank account every month. To claim a combined British and Swedish pension the Swedish and British authorities must exchange records and calculate how much is payable to you from each country. For further details consult the DSS leaflet SA29 *Your Social Security, Health Care and Pension Rights in the European Community.*

For further details about pension rights in Sweden contact the National Social Insurance Board (RFV, 103 51 Stockholm; tel 8 786 90 00, fax 8 11 27 89).

Entertainment

The number of fellow British expatriates is relatively small in Sweden and unless you speak the language opportunities for entertainment may be limited. Whilst nearly every town is served by visiting theatres and concerts, these will be of little benefit to you unless you speak Swedish. Additionally, long hours of darkness in winter and snowy and icy conditions may render Sweden rather depressing. The BBC World Service provides radio entertainment in the English language and programmes and frequency charts can be obtained from London Calling (PO Box 76, Bush House, London WC2 4PH). If your Swedish is good enough you could take out a subscription to the Swedish Pensioners' magazine *Pensionären* which is published ten times a year and contains articles and information of interest to those who are retired (write to Pensionärens Riksorganisation Box 3274, S-10365 Stockholm; tel 8 24 49 60). The British Embassy (Skarpögatan 6-8, S-115 93 Stockholm; tel 8 667 01 40) will be able to put you in touch with fellow expatriates and specifically British clubs, societies and forms of entertainment.

Offshore Banking

If you are considering retiring to Sweden you should take specialist financial advice regarding your monetary situation. One tax-free investment worth considering is offshore banking. Many high street banks and building societies offer long-term accounts in tax havens such as the Channel Islands and Gibraltar. The minimum amount of money deposited is usually more than £500 and interest can be paid monthly or annually.

Useful Address

Nationwide Overseas Ltd: PO Box 217, Market Street, Douglas, Isle of Man; tel 01624-606095, fax 01624-663495.

Abbey National: 237 Main Street, Gibraltar; tel 00-350 76090.

NatWest Expatriate Service: PO Box 12, 2nd Floor, National Westminster House, 6 High Street, Chelmsford, Essex CM1 1BL; tel 01245-355628.

Health

The Swedish health care system is excellent and well geared to the needs of the elderly. According to EU regulations you should receive health care on the same basis as a Swedish citizen (see *Daily Life* for more details on Swedish health care).

Wills and Death

Anyone considering moving abroad should put their financial affairs in order first and make sure that there is a will to prevent complications in the event of death. Death in a foreign country is necessarily more complicated to deal with than in the home country, particularly because there may not be relatives there to deal with the situation. In the event of a death contact the embassy who will be able to offer assistance.

SECTION II

Working in Sweden

Employment
Types of Work
Business and Industry Report
Starting a Business

Employment

The Employment Scene

Sweden operated government programmes to combat unemployment as far back as the outbreak of the First World War. Then as now they were aimed at promoting jobs for everybody and providing incentives for occupational mobility. The presiding ethos of Swedish labour market policy is the activation principle or the work-for-all strategy which gives priority to ensuring that everyone who can be is employed and if not that unemployed people should be placed in labour market programmes. There is an extensive number of employment programmes, training opportunities and job placement schemes for the unemployed which are offered by the Employment Service which is the main instrument of the government labour market policies.

Sweden is currently emerging from its worst recession in recent history and still has some way to go before it can be said to have truly recovered. There are now some signs of recovery in the economy and the employment situation, although Sweden is certainly not clamouring for foreign workers at the present. This should be borne in mind when applying for work.

Over the past 100 years Sweden has evolved from being a largely agrarian country into a modern, efficient and technologically advanced nation. Only 3.4% of the population now work in agriculture and farming, 37.3% work in the private services, 33.9% in the public services, 19.5% in manufacturing and mining and 5.9% in construction. The labour force participation is 79%. 80% of men are employed and 77% of women. The main focus of growth in the Swedish employment sector has been in the public sector and in the private sector to a lesser extent. Manufacturing and agriculture are examples of sectors where employment has shrunk.

UK citizens can work in Sweden on both a long and short-term basis. The work may be full or part-time but if it is part-time you should make sure that you will be earning enough to live on bearing in mind Sweden's very high cost of living. It is not as common for foreigners to work in Sweden as it is in other parts of the European Union and in the past, foreigners working in Sweden have mainly been undertaking short-term vacation or voluntary work or have been filling a gap in the labour market that cannot be filled by native Swedes. Consequently there are fewer opportunities for foreign workers in Sweden than in other parts of the European Union.

Residence and Work Regulations

Sweden's membership of the European Economic Area and subsequent membership of the European Union effectively removes barriers for nationals of member states who want to look for work in Sweden. A work permit is no longer required and citizens of the EEA and EU countries can enter Sweden with the intention of looking for work and should be given equal rights as regards employment as Swedish citizens. Some kinds of work e.g. those connected with national security such as the army will remain open only to Swedes. Anyone who wishes to stay in Sweden for more than three months must apply for a residence permit (see Chapter Two, *Residence and Entry Regulations.*

Skills and Qualifications

You can obtain up-to-date information on the comparability of Swedish and British professional qualifications from the European Division of the Department of Trade and Industry (Ashdown House, 6th Floor, 123 Victoria Street, London SW1E 6RB; tel 0171-215 5354). For information about the comparability of academic qualifications you can get in touch with the National Agency of Higher Education in Sweden (Department of International Affairs, *Verket för Högskoleservice*, VHS, Box 45503, 104 30 Stockholm; tel 8 453 50 000, fax 8 34 27 25). You should be aware of the fact that in Sweden, graduates are usually expected to have a degree which is directly relevant to the job for which they are applying. For vocational training such as catering, construction and agriculture contact the Comparability Coordinator of the Employment Department (TS1E 1, Moorfoot (Room E603), Sheffield S1 4PQ; tel 0114-259 4144) who can provide a fact sheet to aid comparability of skills.

The Department of Trade and Industry can issue you with a certificate which will validate your qualifications in other EU countries but there is a fee for this — about £50. It is useful to have your qualifications translated into Swedish although the majority of Swedish employers will understand English.

A number of professionals need authorisation from the Swedish authorities before they can practice in Sweden. Whilst this may change following Sweden's membership of the European Community, the following professionals should contact the appropriate board:

Health care professionals (doctors, dentists, dental hygienists, nurses, midwives, physiotherapists, chiropractors, opticians, pharmacists, psychologists, psychotherapists and speech therapists) should contact The National Board of Health and Welfare (160 30 Stockholm; tel 8 783 30 00, fax 8 783 30 06. The visiting address is Linnégatan 87). When you contact the board you will be sent a form which you should complete and return with proof of your qualifications.

Vets must be approved by the Swedish Board of Agriculture (*Statens Jordbruksverk*: 551 82 Jönköping; tel 36 15 50 00, fax 36 11 51 14. The visiting address is Vallgatan 8).

Sources of Jobs

Newspapers and Directories

UK Newspapers & Directories

Adverts for Swedish jobs in the British press are relatively rare and looking there is probably not the best method of finding work in Sweden. However *Overseas Jobs Express* (available on subscription only from Premier House, Shoreham Airport, Brighton BN43 5FF; tel 01273-440220, fax 01273-440229) has a substantial section of job adverts around the world and you may well see something for Sweden. Casual and temporary jobs can be found in the *Directory of Summer Jobs Abroad*, teaching jobs in *Teaching English Abroad* and au pair and nanny jobs in *The Au Pair and Nanny's Guide to Working Abroad*. All these publications are available from Vacation Work Publications (9 Park End Street, Oxford OX1 1HJ; tel 01865-241978, fax 01865-790885).

Of the daily quality newspapers, *The Guardian*, *The Times* and *The Independent* all carry some adverts for work abroad and the international English language papers, *The European* and *The International Herald Tribune* also carry adverts for jobs abroad.

Swedish Newspapers

The morning daily *Dagens Nyheter* has the biggest number of adverts for job vacancies. *Svenska Dagbladet* and *Dagens Industrie* concentrate mainly on business. In Sweden, Sunday is the most important day for publishing job advertisements. You may consider taking out subscriptions to the main daily papers. The current rates for a three-month subscription are: *Dagens Nyheter* (105 15 Stockholm; tel 8738 10 00, subscriptions 8 738 17 25, fax 8 656 47 22, subscriptions fax 8 619 00 65) 1,834 SEK by airmail, 1,429 SEK by surface mail and Sundays only for three months is 318.50 SEK by airmail, 260 SEK by surface mail; *Svenska Dagbladet* (105 17 Stockholm; tel 8 13 50 00, subscriptions 8 13 53 45, fax 8 13 58 01, subscriptions fax 8 61 9 00 65) 1378 50 SEK by airmail, 1063.50 SEK by surface mail and Sundays only for three months 234 SEK by airmail and 188.50 SEK by surface mail; *Dagens Industri* (Box 3177, 103 63 Stockholm; tel 8 736 56 00, subscriptions 8 723 06 70, subscriptions fax 8 20 51 33) costs 2,250 SEK for six months (six days a week) by airmail.

Local and regional papers are also useful sources of jobs in Sweden.

Platsjournalen and *Nytt Jobb* are two publicly financed magazines containing vacancies and information about the Swedish labour market You can subscribe to them at the National Labour Market Board, Publishing Service, 171 99 Solna; tel 8 730 60 00, fax 8 730 68 42. The visiting address is Sundbybergsvägen 9). You can also find these papers at job centres throughout Sweden.

Advertising in Newspapers

The European offers an advertisement service whereby you can seek jobs anywhere in the European Union free of charge. The maximum word number is 60 words in which you should include who you are, your qualifications and languages and preferred place of work as well as a passport sized photo (contact the European Classified Advertisement Department, 200 Gray's Inn Road, London WC1X 8NE; tel 0171-418 7878, fax 0171-7113 1835).

You can advertise in Swedish newspapers for employment although this is not a particularly common practice in Sweden. For *Dagens Nyheter* contact the UK advertising rep: Powers Overseas Ltd (46 Keyes Place, Dolphin Square, London SW1V 3NA; 0171-834 5566). For *Svenska Dagbladet* contact Frank L Crane (5-15 Cromer Street, Gray's Inn Road, London WC1H 8LS; tel 0171-837 3330) and for *Dagens Industri* contact David Todd Associates Ltd (tel 0171-538 5811).

Professional Associations

Although most professional associations will not provide direct help with finding work abroad they may be able to provide useful information and contacts. The majority will also have a counterpart association in other European Union States. Details of professional bodies can be found in the *Directory of Trade Associations and Professional Bodies* in the UK which is available at most reference libraries. A few of the more mainstream ones are listed below.

Useful Addresses

The Biochemical Society: 7 Warwick Court, Holborn, London WC1R 5DP.
The British Computer Society: 13 Mansfield Street, London W1M 0BQ.
The British Medical Association: BMA House, Tavistock Square, London WC1H 9JP.
The Chartered Institute of Bankers: 10 Lombard Street, London EC3Y 9AS.
The Chartered Institute of Building: Englemere Kings Ride, Ascot, Berks SL5 8BJ.

The General Dental Council: 37 Wimpole Street, London W1M 8DQ.
The Institute of Actuaries: Napier House, 4 Worcester Street, Gloucester Green, Oxford OX1 2AW.
The Institute of Chartered Accountants: Chartered Accountants' Hall, Moorgate Place, London EC2P 2BJ.
The Institute of Chartered Secretaries and Administrators: 16 Park Crescent, London W1N 4AH.
The Institute of Civil Engineers: 1-7 Great George Street, London SW1P 3AA.
The Library Association: 7 Ridgmount Street, London WC1E 7AE.
The Royal College of Nursing: Henrietta Place, 20 Cavendish Square, London W1M 0AB.
The Royal College of Veterinary Surgeons: 32 Belgrave Square, London SW1X 8QP.
The Royal Insitute of British Architecture: 66 Portland Place, London W1N 4AD.

Professional Journals and Magazines

You can find a comprehensive list of UK trade magazines which may contain adverts for jobs abroad in media directories such as *Benn's Media Directory for the UK* which is available in most reference libraries. *Benn's Media Directory for Europe* contains a comprehensive list of Swedish trade journals and magazines (for example *Civilingenjören* for graduate engineers) which contain adverts aimed at a specialist field. These adverts are likely to be in Swedish.

Employment Organisations

The Swedish State Employment Service

The Swedish labour market comes under the aegis of the Employment Service which is the fundamental instrument of government labour policies. About 90% of all job vacancies in Sweden are reported to the Employment Service. The Swedish Labour Market Administration (*Arbetsmarknadsverket*) has about 380 employment offices (*Arbetsformedlingen*) throughout Sweden which deal with about 35% of all vacancies and between 85-90% of unemployed people make use of them. 60% of all job seekers are registered at the offices which are the equivalent of UK job centres and offer placements and job counselling services. Other facilities include the two employment magazines *Platsjournalen* and the more specialised *Nytt Jobb*. The Swedish employment service is highly computerised and every employment office has access to a computer terminal with a list of vacancies (*platsautomaten*) and up-to-date information about jobs. There is also a telephone line *AF-Direkt* whose staff can give information in Swedish or English about vacancies throughout the country. The line is open during weekdays 9am-7pm and is free of charge. Telephone 020 34 34 34.

Information about new vacancies can be sent to your home address. You do not have to be registered at an employment office to find out about vacancies and use the facilities but you must be registered if you want to claim unemployment benefit. The main employment office is in Stockholm (Arbetsformedlingen City, Vasagatan 28-34, 101 30 Stockholm; tel 8 21 43 00) but for regional employment office details look under *Arbetsformedlingen* in the telephone directory. A major international employment office is at Sergels Torg 12, Box 7763, S-10396 Stockholm; tel 8 20 03 50.

When you register with the employment office you will be required to specify the kind of job you are looking for and you will often be expected to narrow your choice down to one specific type of work. This tends to be a binding choice in the employment service which may only offer you help in finding the nominated job so think it through carefully before hand.

Private Swedish Agencies
Private job agencies have been allowed to operate in Sweden since July 1993 and only a few exist. There are two types of agencies apart from public offices: private agencies which supply mostly office staff and union agencies which deal mainly with salaried personnel such as engineers. To find an agency look under *Arbetsförmedlingar* in the yellow pages of the local telephone directory.

UK Employment Organisations
In Britain you could try contacting the Federation of Recruitment and Recruitment Services Ltd (FRES: 36-38 Mortimer Street, London W1N 7RB; tel 0171-323 4300) which is a trade association of private agencies and has lists of private agencies which place people in work in Europe. There may be a charge for this service.
Euroadviser Network: You can contact UK jobcentres for information and advice on working in Sweden. Jobcentres can put you in touch with Euroadvisers who are UK employment service staff with specialist knowledge about work in the EEA and the EU. They have computer contact with their counterparts in Sweden and have access to the latest labour market information.

The Application Procedure
Finding a job via personal contacts and through word of mouth is fairly common in Sweden. Speculative applications are also quite common but it is usual to make a telephone call first and talk to the personnel officer or someone in middle to senior level management. This way you make yourself known to them and raise any questions you may have and they can find out what kind of person you are. When you write enclose your CV, a letter of application, copies of qualifications, references and work samples if appropriate. Letters should be typed and to the point (put the details on your CV). In interviews you should be prepared to answer questions about yourself, your education and work experience and you will probably be expected to ask some questions at the end of the interview so have some prepared. Some employers may conduct interviews in Swedish.

Permanent Work

At the time of going to press there is not a large demand for permanent employees from other European nations. The main possibilties seem to be as teachers or as employees of multi-national companies. The *Business and Industry Report* (see below) gives some idea of the main industries where jobs are likely to be found.

Medical
Information on registration requirements for foreign doctors and nurses are available from the Swedish Board of Health and Welfare (RT-enheten, 106 30 Stockholm). However, according to the Board, openings for foreign personnel are very restricted. In all cases you will probably improve your chances, if you locate the institutes, medical schools, hospitals etc. best known for your speciality and apply to the head of the department directly.

Teaching
Teaching English
There are fewer opportunities for teaching English as a foreign language in

Sweden than in other parts of Europe, notably the south, and standards of English in Sweden are generally very high. Nonetheless, attending adult evening classes is a way of life in Sweden and many Swedes like to have the opportunity to practise their English in a group gathering. Since 1955 the Folk University of Sweden has placed British teachers in a network of adult education centres for one academic year. Centres are extramural departments of the Universities of Stockholm, Uppsala, Gothenburg, Lund and Umeå and there are branches in many other small towns, including in the far north. Students are varied, ranging from the unemployed to business people and from housewives to pensioners. The Folk universities hire teachers aged between 22 and 40, preferably with a teaching qualification, and guarantee the number of hours you will work over a nine month period. Wages are not particularly high (between £10 and £15 per class) although you should earn enough to live on and the work is not particularly onerous, consisting of 45-minute lessons usually spread over four evenings. For further details contact International Language Services (address below). Those prepared to work in the far north will receive favourable consideration and the absence of a TEFL qualification may be waived if you can convince them that you are prepared to stick it out. You may be able to find freelance teaching work when in Sweden to supplement your income and extend your stay in Sweden by arranging another teaching job before the first one has expired.

Another alternative is to try ringing around colleges of further education and commercial language schools although you should bear in mind that you may be interviewed in Swedish. Addresses can be obtained from the National Agency for Higher Education (address below) or look under *Språk* in the yellow pages. You will be in a particularly strong position if you can offer business English to corporate clients and business English attracts higher wages of about £30 per hour. Terms begin in September and January and you should time your application to coincide with these.

Other Teaching Jobs
Qualified primary and secondary school teachers who want to teach abroad English or international schools abroad should contact the European Council of International Schools (21 Lavant Street, Petersfield, Hampshire GU32 3EL; tel 01730-268244). Teachers should have a minimum of two years teaching experience. See *Education* in *Daily Life* for a list of British and international schools in Sweden.

Useful Addresses
International Language Services: 36 Fowlers Road, Salisbury, Wilts SP1 2QU; tel 01722-331011, fax 01722 328324).
The National Agency for Higher Education (Verket för högskoleservice, VHS); Box 45503, 104 30 Stockholm; tel 8 728 36 00, fax 8 34 27 25.
The Folk High School Information Centre: Box 740, 101 35 Stockholm; tel 8 796 0050, fax 8 21 88 26. The visiting address is Västmannagatan 1.
The Institute for English Speaking Students: University of Stockholm, 106 91 Stockholm; tel 8 16 20 00.

Professional
Those with a professional qualification could write to the relevant professional organisation in Sweden which may be able to provide sources of jobs. Accountants and translators are authorised by the Swedish Board of Trade.

Useful Addresses
The Swedish Bar Association for Lawyers: Box 27321, 102 54 Stockholm; tel 8 24 58 70, fax 8 660 07 79.

The National Association of Swedish Architects: Norrlandsgatan 18, 111 43 Stockholm; tel 8 679 27 60, fax 8 611 49 30.

The Swedish National Board of Trade: Box 1209, 111 82 Stockholm; tel 8 791 05 00, fax 8 20 03 24/.

The Swedish Institute of Authorised Public Accountants: Box 6417, 113 82 Stockholm; tel 8 23 41 30, fax 8 34 14 61.

The National Board of Health and Welfare: 160 30 Stockholm; tel 8 783 30 00, fax 8 783 30 06.

The Swedish Board of Agriculture: 551 82 Jönköping; tel 36 15 50 00, fax 36 11 51 14.

Temporary Work

Au Pair and Domestic Work

Perhaps better known for providing au pairs than for looking for them, Sweden's demand for domestic help is not particularly high. This is mainly because child care provision is extensive and available to all sectors of society. There is some demand for domestic employees in Sweden although this is mainly amongst the wealthier sectors of the population who are to be found in the large houses in southern Sweden. For Au pair agencies placing people in Sweden see addresses below. You can also approach the nearest job centre and ask about vacancies. Adverts for staff are not particularly common but Swedes are fairly approachable and knocking on doors can sometimes obtain results if you can summon up the courage to do it. Even if you are turned down, it will usually be done in a pleasant way.

If you enter into a formal agreement to work as a domestic or au pair within a household you will be covered by the 1970 Act on domestic work which states that you should not normally work more than 40 hours per week and you cannot be expected to do more than 48 hours overtime within a four week period or more than 300 hours during a calender year. Your employer must keep a record of your overtime and pay you accordingly either in wages or time off in lieu. You are entitled to 36 hours of continuous time off every week and usually this will be at weekends. Employees who are under 18 may not work more than ten hours during a 24-hour period.

Domestic employees are entitled to a written contract. Average weekly wages are between £30 and £40 a week whilst qualified nannies can earn between £60 and £150 a week. If the contract is indefinite, one month's notice is required from either side. You will have the right to a written reference when you leave.

Useful Addresses

Euro-Pair: Heathside, Downs Way, Tadworth, Surrey KT20 5DU; tel 01737-813330.

North South: 28 Wellington Road, Hastings, East Sussex TN34 3RN; tel 01424 422364.

People and Places: Trewornan Farm, Wadebridge, Cornwall PL27 6EX; tel 01208-816652.

Smarties Agency: 2A St James Road, Kingston upon Thames, Surrey KT1 2AA; tel 0181-541 1384.

Farm Work

Just over 3% of the Swedish population work in farming and agriculture. The main types of agriculture are arable, pigs, mixed and dairy and horticulture including tree nurseries, greenhouse produce and vegetables. The National Federation of Young Farmers' Clubs can arrange placements on Swedish farms for young farmers and horticulturalists. To qualify for a place on the programme you should be aged 18-28, have had two years experience of farming (one of which could be at college), have a valid driving licence and intend to make a career in agriculture or horticulture. Placements are for between three and 12 months all year and as far as possible the work is matched with individual interests. Participants live in with the farming family and receive board and lodging and a basic wage of 2,500 SEK after tax. There is a registration fee of £85 and you will have to provide your own travel expenses and insurance. Places are limited. For further details contact the International Farm Experience Programme (YFC Centre, National Agricultural Centre, Stoneleigh Park, Kenilworth, Warwickshire CV8 2LG; tel 01203-696584).

Hotel and Catering

It is possible to go to Sweden to look for work in the hotel and catering trade. Most hotel work will be found in the holiday resorts around the south coast, particularly around Örebro, Åre, and Linköping. Of the main cities, Stockholm and Gothenburg have the largest number of hotels. If you decide to do an on-the-spot job hunt you should contact the nearest employment office which can provide up-to-date details of the latest vacancies but it is also feasible to tout around the hotels themselves. If you are working in a behind the scenes position, for example as a chambermaid or in the kitchens, you should not find lack of knowledge of Swedish too much of a barrier although it may prevent you from moving on to better things. The average wage is about £900 a month for an average working week of 40 hours. Much of this type of work is seasonal and accommodation is usually provided which should help towards the Swedish high cost of living. An alternative is to write to hotels prior to the season, stating your interests and any relevant qualifications. A list can be obtained from the Swedish Travel Council (73 Welbeck Street, London W1M 8AN; tel 0171-487 3135; fax 0171-935 5853).

Sweden is served by an extensive coastline and 46 ferries regularly travel to and from Sweden's 25 ports. In the past foreigners have found jobs working aboard the cruisers and ferries plying across the Gulf of Bothnia to Finland and the Baltic States. Additionally there are the ferries which take tourists island hopping around the archipelago off Stockholm and there is the Göta Kanal tourist route which links the Baltic with the North Sea via Sweden's two largest lakes, Vänern and Vättern. As well as catering, some of the ships need staff for entertainment such as DJ-ing. Whilst there is no formal procedure of application, you could enquire about jobs on board at the Swedish job centres, approach the boats in person and ask to speak to the captain or make a speculative application. You can obtain addresses of ship companies from the Stockholm Tourist Office (Arenavägen 41, Box 10134, 121 28 Stockholm-Globen; tel 8 725 55 00).

Voluntary Work

There are a few opportunities for voluntary work in Sweden. *Internationella Arbetslad* which is the Swedish branch of the Civil International Service recruits volunteers to take part in international work camps in Sweden. Work varies from manual labour to social activities and there are usually study themes attached to the work camps. Work camps last for two weeks between June and September. Applicants should be over 18 and be prepared to work hard for 35-40 hours a week. Food and accommodation are provided but you will have to pay your own fares and insurance.

Foreningen Staffansgarden is a community for adults with learning disabilities which takes on between five and ten volunteers a year to work in the community. Work is varied and covers all aspects of daily life including cooking, cleaning and farming. The minimum age limit is 19 and the minimum length of stay is six months although preference is given to applicants who can stay for one year. Board and accommodation are provided in the first six months and a small wage is paid thereafter.

Useful Addresses
International Arbetslag (IAL): Barnangsgatan 23, 11 641 Stockholm.
Foreningen Staffansgarden: Box 66, Furugatan 1, 82060 Delsbo.

Aspects of Employment

Salaries
There is no statutory minimum wage in Sweden and wages are usually fixed by collective agreements or by individual agreements between the employer and employee. Blue collar workers are normally paid according to hours worked on a fortnightly or weekly basis whilst white collar workers are usually paid a fixed monthly salary. Wages are not automatically adjusted to the cost of living although alterations in the cost of living are taken in to account when collective agreements are made.

In 1993 the annual labour costs for an industrial labour amounted to 237,800 SEK (about £19,800) of which 172,800 SEK (about £14,400) consisted of wages, 50,800 SEK was withheld by the employer for income tax payments and an additional 65,000 SEK was paid by the employer on behalf of the worker towards welfare costs.

For white collar workers in the business sector the employee's gross salary was 252,500 SEK (about £21,000) of which 94,600 SEK was withheld in income tax and social welfare contributions came to 99,700 SEK.

As a rough guide (and subject to change), the average incomes for adult employees in the following areas are:

Construction industry — 173,000 SEK (about £14,416)
Commerce, hotels and restaurants — 139,000 SEK (about £11,583)
Finance, insurance and estate agency — 180,000 SEK (about £15,000)
Public administration and service industries — 138,000 SEK (about £11,500)

Working Conditions
The average working week in Sweden is 40 hours and employees are entitled to at least 36 hours of leisure time in a seven-day period, usually at weekends. Employees are entitled to have a break during working hours and should not work more than five hours in a row. There may be exemptions to this for example in the case of those who work at sea or in road transport but generally the supervision of working conditions is carefully monitored by the National Board of Occupational Safety and Health and the implementation of laws governing working conditions are supervised by Labour Inspectorates. Salaried employees often have shorter working days in the summer. Employees are entitled to at least 25 days paid holiday per year and in addition there are 12 public holidays. At least four weeks of continuous leave should come during the period between June and August unless there is a collective agreement to the contrary. There is no legislation regarding work on Sunday in Sweden but generally most employees do not work at the weekend.

The 1991 Sick Leave Act entitles employees who are unable to work due to sickness to receive sick pay from their employer from the second to the thirteenth day of illness after which payment becomes the responsibility of the national health insurance system. On the first two to three days payment is 75% of normal remuneration and 90% of normal remuneration from the fourth to the fourteenth day. All employees are covered by a compulsory national insurance system against occupational accidents and diseases. The insurance fee is collected through the tax system and also covers accidents occurring on journeys connected with work.

Contracts
Verbal or even tacit contracts are legally binding in Sweden but it is still advisable to get a written one. The employer is legally obliged to inform you in writing within a month of your start of employment about rules and conditions for employment. The information must give the name and address of your employer, the details of your work assignment, the duration of employment, period of notice, rights to paid vacation, working hours and any relevant collective agreements. Under the 1982 Act on Security of Employment employees can only be dismissed on objective grounds (unless there is a statement in the contract that states otherwise eg temporary employment). Objective grounds include serious breach of rules, non-authorised absence from work, crime in the workplace and an inability to cooperate at work. Non-objective grounds include sickness, pregnancy, minor offences and crimes not related to the workplace. Employees have the right to a minimum of one month's notice from the employer in the event of dismissals and employers have a similar expectation from employees. The period of notice increases with length of service and rise in the age of the employee. Regulations regarding unfair dismissal are very comprehensive and you should approach your union representative if you feel you have been unfairly treated or make use of the ombudsman system which is prevalent throughout Sweden.

Part-time
There are no specific rules about part-time employment in Sweden but part-time contracts are as legally binding as any other kind of contract and employees who work part-time are entitled to the same rights and duties as other employees.

Private Employment Agency Workers
Those employed by private employment agencies are entitled to the same rights and duties as all other employees. The employment agency is classed as your employer. If you have voluntarily left an employment and become employed by an employment agency you may not be leased out to your former employer for at least six months after you have left that employer.

Etiquette in the Workplace
Many Swedes hate notions of nationalism and national character, believing that this is only a step away from racial stereotyping nonetheless it will not be appreciated if you criticise Sweden or the Swedes to their face. Generally matters are conducted along smooth lines and fuss is kept to a minimum. Interview studies have revealed that in the workplace loud confrontations are less frequent than in many other countries and politeness and respect are the norm amongst all sectors of the workplace. Less of a distinction is made between workers and management in Sweden than say in Britain. A strong history of trade unionism means that worker's opinions are represented and listened to when important decisions are being made and bosses frequently consult with their employees so the preferred leadership style is consultative. The furniture designers Ikea in particular have operated on egalitarian principles where all employees are

encouraged to contribute to company development and where top executives fly economy class, giving it a rather Swedish *Body Shop* image. Attitudes in Sweden tend to emphasise the importance of the group rather than the individual. Whilst it is normal for Swedes to work hard during working hours it is recognised that people have duties towards their families and other groups so there is an annual limitation on overtime (about 200 hours a year). In general, handshaking is *de rigueur* when doing business and the majority of Swedish business men and women will not deafen you with hype — their disarming honesty can take a bit of getting used to. A Swedish business meeting will usually start on time and the small talk that is customary in many countries is usually by-passed.

Trade Unions

Trade unions were first formed in Sweden in the 19th century and are an important feature of Swedish labour relations. The central organisation for the workers is the Swedish Trade Union Confederation or LO and for employers it is the Swedish Employers Confederation or SAF. There are a number of other unions representing professional and white collar workers of which the most important are the Confederation of Salaried Employees (for white collar employees) and the Confederation of Professional Associations (mainly for university educated white collar employees). The LO is the largest confederation in Sweden representing almost 85% of blue collar workers and comprising 21 trade unions nationwide. The LO and SAF came to a joint agreement in 1938 whereby the interests of workers and employers should be protected. The agreement has undergone some modification since but labour relations in Sweden are on the whole good. About 90% of employees belong to a union. Labour and employer organisations are hierarchically structured at local, regional and central levels and as well as overseeing working conditions form an important political power factor in Swedish society.

Useful addresses

The Trade Union Confederation (LO): Barnhusgatan 18, 105 53 Stockholm; tel 8 796 25 00, fax 8 796 02 56.
The Employers Confederation (SAF): Södra Blasieholmen 4a, Stockholm; tel 8 762 60 00, fax 8 663 75 20.
Confederation of Salaried Employees (TCO): Linnegatan 14, Stockholm; tel 8 782 91 00, fax 8 663 75 20.
Confederation of Professional Associations (SACO): Box 2206, 103 15 Stockholm; tel 8 613 48 00, fax 8 24 77 01.

Women in Work

The number of women with paid jobs currently stands at 48% of the labour market and is soon expected to equal that of men in Sweden. 85% of mothers with pre-school children work and this is made possible through extensive child care facilities. The average woman's working week is shorter than that of men and currently stands at 32 hours. This is accounted for largely by the fact that over 90% of Sweden's part-time workers are women. There are still fairly traditional divides between male and female occupational choices — 90% of all engineers, architects, electricians and mechanics are men and women predominate in areas such as clerical work, pre-school teaching, secretarial work, kitchen work and nursing. Whilst women enjoy a relatively good representation at middle management levels they are under represented at higher levels and very few women hold top leadership positions in companies and trade unions. Politically women are relatively prominent in elected bodies such as parliament and the municipal and county councils. The Social Democratic Party has roughly equal numbers of male and female representatives and has pledged itself to actively campaigning for higher female representation in the European Union. Swedish law prohibits sexual discrimination and employers are obliged to take active measures to promote equality in the work place.

At the time of going to press a mother is guaranteed 100 per cent of her income a year after the birth of her child, and she does not have to be married to receive this. However, in line with current cutbacks this is going to be reduced to 75% of income.

Business and Industry Report

Sweden is at present recovering from the worst European recession in recent years. Unemployment was kept low in the 1980s thanks to a strong business sector, the growth of the public sector and a proactive labour market policy. The deregulation of the financial markets after 1985 followed an unsustainable credit and property boom and led to the inevitable credit squeeze with the result that the Swedish economy became overheated and then slid into recession. The recession began to make itself felt in the early 1990s when unemployment soared from just 1.6% to 14% (including 5-6% on government work schemes). Between 1990 and 1993 the unemployment figures rose by 500,000. Towards the close of 1994 unemployment started a slow downward turn to about 13.3% of whom 7% were openly unemployed and 5.5% were in labour market measures. The main sectors affected have been manufacturing and construction. Production and manufacturing dropped by 17% from 1989 to 1993 but began to rise again in 1993. Inflation stands at a relatively low 2.9% although the budget deficit is high, accounting for 12.9% of the GDP. Sweden also has a substantial public debt of 83% of the GDP. The Social Democratic Party which came to power in 1994 is implementing a series of public spending cuts and austerity measures in an effort to stabilise public debt (which at present accounts for nearly 100% of the Gross National Product) by 1998.

Decades of social democratic rule in Sweden were founded on a massive public sector but in recent years, following the election of the Conservative government, there has been a large swing towards privatisation of Swedish industries, beginning with the flotation of a 48% interest in the steel group SSAB in 1992. After some teething troubles, privatisation has caught the Swedish public's imagination and it is likely that although the Social Democrats have regained power there will be further privatisation.

After three years of recession, Swedish industry started to make a comeback in 1994 thanks largely to the success of its exports. The industrial sector has recovered more than 80% of the production loss suffered in 1990 up to the end of 1992 and the situation is tentatively optimistic for the future. In 1993 Stockholm shares rose by 35% following a drop in interest rates from 13 to 7.4% and a massive devaluation of the Krone. Swedish exports are expected to increase by 18% between 1994 and 1995. Sweden's entry into the European Economic Area in 1994 followed by entry into the European Union in 1995 has boosted trade and industry in Sweden by increasing trade opportunities, reducing red tape and removing tariff restrictions. The abolition of restrictions on cross border acquisitions and overseas investments led to some notable investments by Sweden including Stena's acquisition of the British Sealink Ferries and *Svenska Cellulosa's* purchase of the German Conglomerate *Feldmühle G. Nobel* although the proposed merger between Swedish Volvo and French Renault proved to be abortive. In turn there have been increasing signs of foreign investment in Sweden. A climate of greater investment confidence in Sweden should bring both increased domestic investment and a spur to much needed foreign investment in the country.

The Swedish economy is heavily dependent on foreign trade and Western Europe and North America are the main Swedish export markets. The biggest trading partners are Germany, the UK, the USA and the Nordic countries of Denmark, Norway and Finland. Sweden's main sources of imports are the UK and Germany. Major imports include machinery and equipment for industry, office machinery, petroleum and petroleum products and iron and steel. Principal exports include road vehicles, medical and pharmaceutical products and general industrial machinery. The shares of about twenty of Sweden's major companies are traded on foreign stock markets and include big names like Astra, Electrolux, Ericsson and Volvo.

The following section provides a guide to some of the most important Swedish industries.

Engineering

Engineering forms a significant sector of Swedish industry. About 445,000 people are employed in engineering and 62% of its products are exported. The industry is mainly concentrated in southern and central Sweden and includes several of Sweden's largest industrial companies including Asea. In 1988 Asea linked with Switzerland's Brown Boveri to form the world's largest electrotechnology group, ABB. Another giant is SKF which has elevated the humble ball bearing to a major industry-Sweden is currently the world leader in roller bearings and employs about 150 British managers at a senior level. Electrolux has become a household name in household appliances and is amongst the world's largest producers. After the motor industry, mechanical engineering is the most important subsector of Swedish engineering, followed by electrical products (telecommunications and household appliances) and metal goods. The electrical products industry in particular has been a growth area in Sweden and about 60% is exported. Telecommunications account for 40% of Sweden's electrical industry and the giant Ericsson has been particularly popular with American investors who now control 30% of the shares. Medical electronics and computers are amongst the fastest growth areas.

The Automotive Industry

The automotive industry is the most important subsector of engineering and is dominated by the two Swedish giants Volvo and Saab-Scania. Exports from the Swedish automotive industry account for 14% of total Swedish merchandise exports and it employs about 82,000 employees.

Volvo has made a remarkable come-back since the company experienced its highest ever losses between 1988 and 1993 when car sales fell from 340,000 to 125,000. This has been achieved at a price and Volvo was forced to shut two of its three Swedish plants and cut 15,000 staff from the workforce. Efficiency has been sharply improved in the process with the number of hours taken to produce a car reduced from 70 to 40. In 1994 Volvo announced its decision to drop its strategy of expansion into other markets and decided to concentrate solely on motors, including cars, trucks, buses and engines. Volvo is currently producing 320,000 large cars and 12,000 medium-sized cars annually and has managed to turn deficits into solid profits.

Similarly Saab has had to make a substantial number of cuts, reducing the workforce by half to about 7,300 and reducing hours needed to produce a car by more than 70% for some models. In 1989 the US owned General motors and Saab-Scania signed an agreement spinning off the Saab division into a new company Saab Automobile AB with Saab Scania and GM each owning 50%.

The signs for both Saab and Volvo are good although their shared traditional selling points — environmental friendliness and safety — are fast being caught up with by competitors.

Both Volvo and Saab-Scania produce heavy engines and aircraft components.

Arms Industry

Despite a long history of neutrality, Sweden has the Nordic region's largest defence industry. With a population the same size as Los Angeles, Sweden ranks as a major producer of defence technology. The defence industry is undergoing extensive restructuring and reductions following the end of the Cold War and there has been a move towards cooperation amongst the four Nordic countries of Sweden, Denmark, Norway and Finland in the production of defence equipment. It is expected that Sweden's contribution will be largely in the field of artillery. Car giants Saab have produced fourth generation aircraft of which the most recent is the JAS 39 Gripen fighter plane. Sweden's main armaments company is Bofors whose annual sales in 1993 amounted to 1.54 billion SEK. Following 30% cut backs over the past five years, Bofors signed a cross-border agreement with Giat industries in France in 1994 to cooperate on the development of a new long-range artillery system.

Chemicals

About 75,000 employees work in the chemical industry and 47% of chemical industry products are exported. In total, the chemical industry (including rubber and plastic products) produces more than 10% of Sweden's industrial output. The most important subsector of the industry is pharmaceuticals which account for 2% of the country's total industrial production and employs about 10,000 people. Exports are very important in the pharmaceutical industry and some firms export 80-90% of their products. Current major areas of research include eye-surgery products (Kabi-Pharmacia), genetic engineering (KabiGen), dialysis (Gambro) and drugs for cardiovascular, gastrointestinal and respiratory diseases (Astra).

Biotechnology also forms a significant part of the Swedish industry and Swedish biotechnological specialities include plant breeding (Hilleshög and Weibulls), waste water treatment and metal (Boliden), animal husbandry (Alfa-Laval) and processes for the manufacturing of plastics and other chemicals (Nobel Industries, Perstorp, Biotechnics). The chemical industry has played a significant role in Sweden's attempts to deal with domestic pollution.

The chemical industry appears to have weathered the worst of the recession-chemical and drug shares rose by an average of 11% in 1993. At the beginning of 1994 *The Financial Times* speculated that the pharmaceutical industry looks set to become one of Sweden's most promising industrial sectors for future expansion on global markets and predicted that the two main pharmaceutical companies Astra and Pharmacia would thrive in the 1990s. Astrea's three main growth areas are in core products for gastrointestinal, respiratory and cardiovascular diseases. Pharmacia is Europe's eighth largest pharmaceutical company and was privatised in 1994. Pharmacia produces a range of products aimed at niches within health care including growth hormone treatment, ophthalmic surgery, nutrition, allergies, anti-smoking drugs and drugs to prevent blood clotting.

Mining

Mining is a centuries old tradition in Sweden but has declined in importance since the mid-1970s. The mining industry employs about 12,000 people and exports 52% of its products, accounting for about 2% of the total industrial value. The major mining company is the state-owned LKAB. Sweden also produces large quantities of copper, lead, zinc, silver, gold and other non-ferrous metals which are mined in northern Sweden, principally from mines owned by Boliden (a subsidiary of Trelleborg). Trelleborg has been badly hit by depressed nickel and copper prices in the 1990s and has faced a bigger struggle against the recession than many other Swedish companies.

Steel
With its large engineering industry, Sweden is amongst the world's largest per capita steel consumers. 30,000 people work in the steel industry which exports about 80% of its products and accounts for 4% of the country's total industrial value. Approximately 60% of the production was ordinary steel and the rest was in the form of alloys. The steel industry has undergone extensive restructuring and modernising and large investments have been made in research and development. The biggest ordinary steel producer is SSAB whilst Avesta has effected a merger with British Stainless Steel. Sandvik is the main producer of speciality steels.

Forest Products
Sweden's exports of pulp, paper and paperboard products are the third largest in the world and European Community forms 80% of the exports market. About 57,000 employees work in the paper industry which exports 70% of its produce and accounts for 8% of the total industrial value.

Over half of Sweden is covered in forests and forest products have long been a mainstay of the Swedish economy. About half of all woodland is in private ownership with the rest belonging to the state, church and municipal governments.

The Swedish pulp and paper industry has undergone numerous mergers and has made large investments in the EU through the acquisition of Felmühle and Reedpack by Stora and SCA. Ten per cent of all paper production within the EU is manufactured by Swedish subsidiaries and the pulp and paper giants are SCA, Stora and MoDo. The annual total production of pulp and paper comes to 12 million tonnes of which 10 million tonnes are exported (8.45 million to the EU) and the rest is for domestic consumption. The Swedish pulp and paper association, Skogsindustrierna, has begun to express concern regarding recent moves in Sweden to increase the recycling of paper and fears that this will lead to a fall in domestic demand for virgin wood fibres for pulp and paper. Increasing environmental awareness in Sweden means that the country currently recycles almost half its yearly paper consumption of 1.9 million tonnes. There are also fears that recycling in the EU may increase, leading to a greater expansion of the paper-producing capacity in EU countries which would have detrimental effects on the Swedish paper industry. On the plus side, membership of the European Union was particularly important for the pulp and paper sector as, following Finland's membership, Swedish forestry executives were concerned that they would lose out to their main European competitor in the European arena if they were left outside the Union. Within Sweden there has been criticism of the management of forests and changes are being implemented in forestry techniques with a view to creating a more 'green' industry.

Wood products account for 8% of the industrial value but of these only 31% of products are exported. The wood products industry employs about 67,000 employees and unlike the paper industry consists mainly of small firms. About 500 sawmills account for 97% of sawn timber production. Furniture producers Ikea have become as much a symbol of Sweden as Abba and Volvo and the company which started as a mail order business is now the biggest furniture group in the world with 120 stores in 25 countries. Described as 'cheap without the nasty', Ikea has stayed ahead by marketing furniture at prices 20-30% lower than its competitors. Recent economic difficulties and increased threat from low-budget competitors mean that Ikea has had to pare down costs by 10% and has had to make redundancies for the first time but profits are continuing to rise and plans are underway for the exploitation of new markets in Eastern Europe and the Far East.

Food Processing

81,000 people work in the food processing industry which is dominated by a relatively small number of companies. These include producer cooperatives such as the Federation of Swedish Farmers (LRF), the Swedish company Procordia and subsidiaries of the better known multi-national companies. The importation and sale of alcoholic beverages comes under the state controlled shops Systembolaget. Stockholm has so far rejected EU demands to scrap its state alcohol monopoly because of fears of drunkenness blighting Sweden but home-distilling is so endemic that even the local supermarkets sell flavourings (mainly to disguise the paint-stripper taste). Ownership of food processing industry has become increasingly concentrated but employment has maintained a steady figure. Imports greatly exceed exports which are around 6%. Food processing accounts for 12% of the total industrial value added.

Regional Employment Guide

Sweden is a large country with a small population of whom 90% lives in the south and 85% in cities and urban areas. Consequently there is an inevitable divide between employment opportunities in the north and south. What follows is a general round-up of major work areas:

Fishing is concentrated largely around the south coast with Gothenburg as the leading fish harbour and fish market. The pulp and paper industry developed originally around the mouths of rivers around Lake Vänern and the Gulf of Bothnia although new plants have been built around the coasts of southern Sweden. Historically the metal industry has been dependent on water power and forest land (which gives charcoal fuel) which determined the location of iron mills. Oxelösund and Luleå on the coast are home to twentieth century iron and steel mills. The main plants of the automotive and aerospace industries are situated in south-central Sweden. Volvo has its headquarters in Gothenburg and Saab-Scania in Trollhättan whilst heavy vehicles are produced in Södertälje and aircraft in Linköping. Electrics and the electronic industry are based mainly around Stockholm and Västerås. The forested areas of Southern Sweden are home to the small plastic, metal and glass processing plants. The petrochemical industry is based at Stenungsund on the west coast and the pharmaceutical and biotechnology companies are located near leading medical research centres in the south.

Directory of Major Employers

For a full and detailed list of British owned subsidiaries operating in Sweden contact The Swedish Trade Council (Box 5513, S-114 85 Stockholm; tel 8 783 8500). For an exhaustive list of Swedish companies and their products consult the directory *Kompass Sverige* which should be available in most main reference libraries.

The Automobile Industry
Berix Svenska AB: Överby, S-461 70 Trollhätten; tel 0520 972 30.
Industri Motor AB: Box 42098, S-126 12 Stockholm; te 8 744 03 35.
Saab-Scania AB: S-461 80 Trollhätten; tel 0520 850 00.
SP-Maskiner AB: Box 322, S-341 26 Ljungby; tel 0372 811 85.
Volvo Penta AB: S-405 08 Göteborg; tel 031 23 54 60.

Swedish Banks
Nordbanken Finans AB: Box 7455, S-103 92 Stockholm; tel 8 787 65 00.
Statshypotek AB: Box 7675, S-103 95 Stockholm; tel 8 723 24 00.
SwedeCorp: Box 3144, S-103 62 Stockholm; tel 8 677 66 00.
Skandinaviska Enskilda Banken AB: S-106 40 Stockholm; tel 8 763 50 00.

Chemicals
Center Pac AB: Box 70, S-283 00 Osby; tel 0479 126 40.
CRC Chemicals Sweden AB: Kryptong 14, S-431 153 Mölndal; tel 031 87 55 20.
Dinol AB: Box 149, S-281 22 Hässleholm; tel 0451 800 00.
Kemetyl AB: Box 47320, S-100 74 Stockholm; tel 8 18 00 90.
Lyckeby Stärkelseförädling AB: Box 75,Karlshamn; tel 0454 150 20.
Salko Kemi AB: Box 415, Stockholm; tel 8 613 08 64.

Clothing and Footwear
JC Inköps AB: Box 55034, S-500 05 Borås; tel 033 17 28 00.
Samhall Avebe AB: Box 90118, S-120 21 Stockholm; tel 8 723 54 00.
Tegma AB: Kopparbergsg 29, S-214 44 Malmö; tel 040 802 00.

The Furniture Industry
Bjärnums Möbelfabriker Hokus Pokus AB: Box 22, S-280 20 Bjärnum; tel 0451 214 60.
Hyllteknik AB: Box 73, S-432 22 Alvesta; 0472 118 05.
Ikea Svenska Försäljnings AB: Box 200, S-260 35 Ödåkra; tel 042 25 26 00.
TUVE Möbler AB: Box 72, S-283 00 Osby; tle 0479 11835.

Fish Processing
Abba AB: S-456 81 Kungshamn; tel 0523-390 00.
ITOCHU Corporation Stockholmskontoret: Box 12801, S-112 97 Stockholm; tle 8-13 08 75.
Marubeni Scandianvia AB: Box 16128, S-103 23 Stockholm; tel 8-613 11 00.
Nissho Iwai (Nordic) A/S: Kristinelunddsg 16, S-411 37 Göteborg; tel 031-81 05 35.
Norrfrys AB: Box 804, S-953 28 Haparanda; tel 0922-114
Scandsea International AB: Box 1234d, S-Helsingborg; tle 042-12 06 40.
Seafood House AB: Grosshandlarv 1, S-121 73 Johanneshov; tle 8-722 30 80.
Svenska Nestle AB: S-267 81 Bjuv; tle 042-860 00.
Westerberggruppen AB: Box 50579, S-202 15 Malmö; tel 040-18 23 45.

Industrial Machinery
Ferm AB: Harpsundsv 166 — 168, S-124 59 Bandhagan; tel 8 86 04 80.
Göteborgs Hydrauliksevice AB: Ångpanneg 3, S-417 05 Göteborg; tel 031 23 53 90.
Hydraulik Consult AB: Box 8080, S-163 08 Spånga; tel 8-760 29 30.
ITT Flygt AB: Box 1309, S-171 25 Solna; tel 8 627 65 00.
Lindstam Motor AB: Box 42098, S-126 12 Stockholm; tel 8 647 25 75.
Mecman Gillberg Hydraulik AB: Hemg 57, S-784 73 Borlänge; tel 0243-840 50.
Mitsui & Co Scandianvia AB: Box 5750, S-114 87 Stockholm; tel 8-679 56 78.
Svensson & Co AB Gunnar: Box 99, S-131 07 Nacka; tel 8-716 27 50.

VOAC Hydraulics Trollhätten AB: Box 943, S-461 29 Trollhätten; tel 0520-935 00.
Volvo Penta AB: Gropegårdsg, S-405 08 Göteborg; tel 031-23 54 60.
Zander and Ingström AB: Box 12088, S-102 23 Stockholm; tel 8-80 90 00.

Insurance
Skandia Group Insurance Co Ltd: Sveav 44, S-103 50 Stockholm; tel 8 788 10 00.

Legal Services
Folke Brandt Advokatbyrå: PO Box 7086, 402 32, Gothenburg 7; tel 031 113478.
Advokatfirman LJB: PO Box 465, Linköping S-58105; tel 013 110105.
Herslow and Holme HB: Södra Tullgatan 3, Box 4307, Malmö S-203 14; tel 040 101460.
Malmstrm and Malmenfelt Advokatbyr AB: 4th and 5th floor, Hovslagargatan 5B, PO Box 1665, Stockholm 111 96; tel 08 679 6950. *Styrbjörn Gärde Advokatbyrå:* Box 5208 Nybrogatan 34, S-102 45 Stockholm; tel 8 665 00 40.

Mineral Mining
Ahlsell Mineral AB: Box 10154, S-121 28 Stjo,-Globen; tel 8-789 16 00.
Industrimineral AB: Sågve 12, S-Åkersberga; tel 8 540 885 50.
MINELCO AB: Box 58, S-951 21 Luleä; tel 0920-381 60.
Nilsson & Söner Grait AB: Box 2003, S-593 02 Västervik; tel 0490-131 10.
NORDKALK KALCIUM AB: Box 30022, S-200 61 Malmö; tel 040-36 18 90.
Skandiviska IFAB Filtrering AB: Hangarv 9, S-423 37 Torslanda; tel 031-92 20 70.
Växjö Åkericentral Ek Förening: Arabyg 37, S-352 46 Växjö; tel 0470-101 65.

Media and Newspapers
Expressen: Gjorwellsgatan 30, S-10516 Stockholm; 8 73 83 00.
Dagens Nyheter: Rålambsvägen 17, S-10515, Stockholm; 8 738 10 00.
Svenska Dagbladet: Rålambsvaggen 7, S-10517, Stockholm; tel 8 13 50 00.
Göteborgs-Posten: Polhemsplatsen 5, S-40502, Gothenburg; tel 31 624 00.
Sydsvenska Dagbladet: Krusegatan 19, S-20505 Malmö; tel 40 28 00 00.

The Pulp and Paper Industry
Holmen Paper AB: Vattengränden 2, S-601 88 Norrköping; tel 011 23 50 00.
Klippans Finpappersbruk AB: Västerg 1, S-352 30 Växjö; tel 0470 512 00.
MoDo Paper AB: S-891 80 Örnsköldsvik; tel 0660 750 00.
Polynova Nordic KB: Box 32021, S-452 21 Stockholm; tel 8 744 25 60.
Stora Feldmühle Hylte AB: S-31400 Hyltebruk; tel 0345 190 00.
Tumba Bruk AB: S-147 82 Tumba; tel 8 530 695 00.
Wisaforest Sverige AB: Arstaängsv. 17, S-117 43 Stockholm; tel 8 762 94 00.

Pharmaceutical Products
Astra AB: S-151 85 Södertälje; tel 8 553 260 00.
Kemetyl AB: Box 47320, S-100 74 Stockholm; tel 8 18 00 90.
Kabi Pharmacia AB: Rapsg. 7, S-751 82 Uppsala; tel 018 16 30 00.
Nobel Chemicals AB: S-691 85 Karlskoga; tel 0586 830 00.
Chemotechnique Diagnostics AB: Box 3903, S-100 54 Stockholm; tel 8 24 76 50.

The Wood Industry
Göteborgs List & Träindustri AB: Långavallsg 2, S-424 57 Angered; tel 031 30 03 00.
Jarl-Trä AB: S-361 93 Broakula; tle 0471 402 75.
Niab Hestra AB: Box 119, S-330 27 Hestra; tel 0370 352 90.
Skogsägarna Västerbotten-Örnsköldsvik, Ek Förening: Box 4076, S-904 03 Umeå; tel 090 15 67 00.
Tarkett Svenska AB: Box 4538, S-19104 Sollentuna; tel 8 92 89 80.
Töreboda Limträ AB: Box 49, S-545 21 Töreboda; tel 0506 116 10.

Starting A Business

The Swedish government's attitude towards foreign investment and ownership is favourable. Sweden's traditional position as a neutral nation enjoying good relations with other countries is complemented by a heavy emphasis on foreign trade and former laws restricting foreign ownership of companies and real estate have been abolished.

Sweden has always had a high level of dependence on foreign trade and direct investments abroad by Swedish companies have grown at an astounding rate since the 1970s. A very high proportion of Swedes work abroad — about 590,000 in the mid 1990s — and of these, 55% work in the EU countries and 18% in North America. The vast majority are employed in subsidiaries of Swedish manufacturing companies. An important result of the rise in Swedish corporate capital spending abroad is an increased access to foreign markets generally.

Foreign direct investments in Sweden have increased manifoldly over the past decade. In the mid 1990s the Nordic countries, France, the Netherlands, the United Kingdom, Germany and the United States are the major countries making foreign investments in Sweden. Sweden's accession to the European Economic Area followed by membership of the European Community in 1995 means that foreign direct investment in Sweden is likely to increase in the 1990s following the abolition of regulations regarding foreign acquisitions. Under the agreement of the EEA and EU, member countries constitute one large market and the free movement of goods, services, people and capital is guaranteed.

The number of persons in Sweden employed in firms where foreign owners controlled 50% or more of the shares increased by over 100% from 113,000 to 230,000 between 1980 and 1990. In the same period foreigners acquired the majority share in 925 Swedish firms. The expansion of the foreign-owned sector in Swedish industry is almost entirely due to foreign acquisition of Swedish firms.

Sweden is still recovering from its worst recession since the 1930s but the worst of the recession appears to have been short-lived (it lasted from 1990 to 1993). The signs for continued recovery are good thanks to the power of Swedish exports. Whilst unemployment is still high (about 14% including those on government work schemes) and the economic picture is still overshadowed by the budget deficit and national debts as well as a decrease in consumer spending there is some optimism for the future of trade with Sweden, particularly in the light of the EU membership.

Sweden is an advanced industrial nation whose workforce is well educated and efficient and the majority speak good English. The communication and transport infrastructure is well developed. In summary, the main market advantages for British investors include historical trade links, good communications, English is widely spoken, cultural compatibility, membership of the EEA and EU and Sweden is a major importer with many multi-national companies. Market inhibitors include recent recession, perceived geographical remoteness, a small domestic market and overall high costs.

Procedures Involved in Buying or Starting a New Business

Preparation from Scratch

Anyone contemplating starting or buying a business in Sweden should seek appropriate help from expert sources (see addresses below). The Swedish government is particularly open to foreign investment and a number of sources can provide useful information for the prospective entrepreneur. Fact sheets on Swedish industry and on its various branches can be obtained from the Swedish Institute which acts as an information service for Sweden. The Institute can also provide general up-to-date information on the Swedish economy, foreign policy and the labour market. Much of this information is disseminated through the embassies. The Department of Trade and Industry can provide a number of useful publications for UK traders (see also under exports), including Country Profiles and trade briefs. Barclay's Bank can provide a detailed country account of current economic trends and the medium-term outlook in Sweden. Worldwide accountants Ernst and Young provide a detailed booklet *Doing Business in Sweden* which covers most aspects of setting up a business. The Business and Industry Information Group (*Näringslivets Ekonomifakta AB*) provides information about the process of setting up a business in Sweden. Information on Swedish tax laws for business purposes can be obtained from the National Tax Board (*Riksskatteverket RSV*). Details on Swedish business can be obtained from the Swedish Trade Council which is the national service organisation for all exporters of goods and services and has missions in many countries. The Council can provide information about customs and imports regulations and is particularly involved in setting up trade links between Swedish exporters and foreign firms. For those intending to employ staff, the trade union of employers, SAF, operates an information department from where information on these matters can be obtained.

Useful Addresses

The Swedish Institute: Hamngatan, Stockholm; tel 8 789 20 00, fax 8 20 72 48.
The Department of Trade and Industry: 1-19 Victoria Street, London SW1H
  0ET; tel 0171-215 5130, fax 0171-215 5611.
Barclay's Bank PLC: The Librarian, Economics Department, PO Box 12, 1
  Wimborne Road, Poole, Dorset BH15 2BB; tel 01202-671212.
Ernst and Young: Apex Plaza, Forbury Road, Reading RG1 1YE; tel 01734-
  500611, fax 01734-507744.
The Business and Industry Information Group: Box 1666, S-111 96 Stockholm;
  tel 8 762 7050.
The National Tax Board: Tritonvägen 21, S-171 94 Solna; tel 8 764 8000.
The Swedish Trade Council: Box 5513, S-114 85 Stockholm; tel 8 783 8500.
The Swedish Trade Council: 73 Welbeck Street, London W1M 8AN; tel 0171-
  935 9601, fax 0171-935 4130
SAF: Information Department, S-103 30 Stockholm; tel 8 762 64 90, fax 8 762
  60 00.

Registration

All new businesses in Sweden must be Registered with the Registrar of Companies (*Registreringsverket*). The purchasers of the new business must provide the company's name, registered address, the company's fiscal year-end, the number and nominal values of the shares (where appropriate), any restrictions on their transfer and the names and addresses of the directors and the auditor. Formation of a limited company usually takes one month and there is a registration fee of about 1,000 SEK. The company should also register with the tax office and social security office and where appropriate with the Patent and Registration Office (*Patent-och Registreringsverket*).

Useful Addresses

Register of Companies: S-851 81 Sundsvall; tel 60 18 40 00.
The National Tax Board: Tritonvägen 21, S-171 94 Solna; tel 8 764 80 00.
The National Social Insurance Board: Adolf Fredriks Kyrkogata 8, S-103 51 Stockholm; tel 8 786 90 00.
The Patent and Registration Office: Trade Marks Department, Box 5055, S-102 42 Stockholm; tel 8 782 25 00.
Local Tax Office (Farsta): Box 70297, 107 22 Stockholm; tel 8 714 20 00, fax 8 714 12 70. The visiting address is Folkungagatan 44.

Regional Trade Associations

Sweden has 12 local Chambers of Commerce which are run as independent private organisations representing industry and commerce in their areas. About 10,000 companies are members and the chambers assist with internal Swedish matters and promote trade between Sweden and other countries. The Swedish Trade Council promotes exports through the commercial departments of Swedish embassies abroad and through its own offices. The Council acts in cooperation with other Swedish export organisations and helps foreign companies who want to trade with Sweden. The Federation of Swedish Commerce and Trade is a private federation of 1,300 companies. The Federation promotes trade and imports and has a special foreign trade department.

Useful Addresses

The Swedish Trade Council: Box 5513, S-114 85 Stockholm; tel 8 783 8500.
The Federation of Swedish Commerce and Trade: Box 5501, S-114 85 Stockholm; tel 8 783 8039.

Choosing an Area

When you have decided on a business idea and carried out the appropriate market research you will need to consider where to locate your business. As the *Regional Employment Guide* in Chapter Six indicated, the overwhelming majority of the population and businesses are to be found in the south and this will probably influence your choice of location to a very large degree. Whilst costs in the north may be generally cheaper it should be born in mind that the population is much smaller and therefore labour supplies may be scarce. A certain remoteness in the north would also pose an increase in transport costs. However, there are more financial incentives on offer to businesses choosing to locate in rural areas where the economy is weaker. In general your type of business enterprise will influence your choice of region for example a retail business would tend to be within reach of cities. The Swedish Regional Development Fund (Box 23155, S-104 35 Stockholm; tel 8 15 14 00) can provide advice for those considering locating a business away from major urban areas.

Raising Finance

If you are intending to reside in Sweden you will find it difficult to raise finance with a British Bank. However Swedish banks will lend money to foreign businesses. The Swedish banks have undergone a number of changes in recent years including the elimination of several regulatory restraints with the view to becoming more competitive in the international environment following Sweden's membership of the EU. One result has been an increasing number of commercial banks which are the leading source of short-term finance and about one half of their loans are made to businesses. Because of the importance of foreign trade to Sweden, Swedish banks have a reputation for efficiency in handling foreign currency transactions. Banking is highly computerised and the bank-giro system is very common. Foreign individuals and entities may generally buy shares in Swedish banks. Following several scandals in the early 1990s finance companies are restricted in their activities. Other sources of credit include the National Pensions Fund whose assets exceed the combined assets of all commercial banks and which can provide long-term financing to companies. Insurance companies also have significant influence in capital markets.

Useful Addresses

Nordbanken Finans AB: Box 7455, S-103 92 Stockholm; tel 8 787 65 00.
Statshypotek AB: Box 7675, S-103 95 Stockholm; tel 8 723 24 00.
SwedeCorp: Box 3144, S-103 62 Stockholm; tel 8 677 66 00.
Skandinaviska Enskilda Banken AB: Kungsträdgårsgatan 8, S-106 40 Stockholm; tel 8 763 80 00, fax 8 763 95 66.
Enskilda Corporate: 2 Cannon Street, London EC4M 6XX; tel 0171-236 6090, fax 0171-588 0929.
SwedBank: S-105 34 Stockholm; tel 8 22 23 20, fax 8 11 90 13.
Atle Forvaltnings AB: Box 7308, 103 90 Stockholm; tel 8 24 62 10.
Alfred Berg: Birger Jarlsgatan 7, Box 70447, S-107 25 Stockholm; tel 8 723 58 00, fax 8 611 16 81.
Alfred Berg: 85 London Wall, London EC2M 7BU; tel 0171-256 49 00, fax 0171 920 9126.
The HSBC Group: Box 7615, Birger Jarlsgatan 10, S-10394 Stockholm; tel 8 614 59 00, fax 8 611 00 46.

Investment Incentives

The main sources of grants and financial aid for foreign investors have traditionally been the Regional Development Fund (*Utvecklingsfonden*), the Swedish Industrial Development Authority (*SIDA*) and the Swedish National Board for Industrial and Technical Development (*NUTEK*). However, Sweden's entry into the EU has meant that grants and aid have been reduced in order to comply with EU regulations. Investors should therefore contact these organisations directly to discuss individual requirements.

Useful Addresses

The Swedish Regional Development Fund: Box 23155, S-104 35 Stockholm; tel 8 15 14 00.
The Swedish Industrial Development Authority: Birger Jarlsgatan 61, S-105 25 Stockholm; tel 8 728 61 00.
The Swedish National Board for Industrial and Technical Development: S-117 Stockholm; tel 8 775 40 00.

Business Structures

Companies

Limited liability companies (*aktiebolag* or AB) are used by the vast majority of business enterprises in Sweden. There are about 300,000 ABs in Sweden and the limited liability company is classed as a separate legal entity and is also considered to be a separate entity for tax purposes. They are regulated by the Accounting Act and by the Companies Act and it is expected that they will conform to European Commission guidelines in the future.

Partnerships

There are two types of partnerships: the *handelsbolag* (HB) and the *Kommandit-bolag* (KB). Partners in an HB have unlimited liability whereas in a KB one or more partners has unlimited liability. Profits and losses of a partnership are divided among partners according to their agreement or according to the Partnership Act. Individuals are taxed on their shares of the net income but for the purposes of VAT, the partnership constitutes a separate entity.

Joint Ventures

A joint venture is not classed as a legal entity in Sweden but as a contract or agreement. In Sweden a joint venture is an agreement between two or more parties to carry out an enterprise together. Joint ventures must form either a limited liability company or a partnership and the choice is often influenced by tax considerations. A limited liability company is taxed directly but partnerships are not directly taxed though individual partners are taxed on their share of the profit.

Trusts

A trust (*stiftelse*) is formed when the founder appoints separate and independent property for a particular use. The tax authorities recognise three types of trust: privileged, family and others. Only a privileged trust is exempt from tax and more than 80% of its activities must benefit the public and it must use over 80% of its income over a five-year period as evidence that it is active.

Branches of Foreign Companies

A parent company operating within its country of origin may apply to form a branch company in Sweden. Branches are generally subject to the same rules as companies resident and domiciled in Sweden. Branches should maintain separate books, appoint a manager who is domiciled in Sweden and appoint an auditor who is a certified public accountant in Sweden.

Ideas For New Businesses

Although the Swedish economy is currently rather flat because of the recession, Swedish companies still need to import capital equipment and supplies. The top six major UK exports to Sweden currently include petroleum and petrol products, electrical machinery, office machines and ADP equipment, road vehicles, iron and steel and general industrial machinery and equipment therefore businesses which trade in these goods will have an advantage.

The Department of Trade and Industry identifies the following consumer goods as areas of opportunity for potential traders in Sweden: clothing, furniture (particularly reproduction) and foodstuffs. Clothing has especial potential because the Swedish manufacture of home-made clothes and shoes has declined due to heavy competition from abroad and British fashions are particularly favoured in Sweden. Other areas which the DTI is exploring include automotive components and accessories and the food and drink sector. Another area of potential is in establishing language schools specialising in business English as there is a big demand for this. Areas such as Gothenburg which have a large English-speaking expatriate community offer potential for the establishment of typically English/Irish pubs and eating places although food and alcohol costs may make this a rather expensive proposition. There is a high level of environmental concern in Sweden which may provide openings for the selling of environmentally friendly products.

Exporters

The Scandinavian desk of the Department of Trade and Industry (1-19 Victoria Street, London SW1H 0ET; tel 0171-215 5103, fax 0171-215 5611) provides help and information to potential exporters to Sweden. For a fee they can provide reports on specific countries, market information and details of import procedures. Now that Sweden is part of the European Union, the free quarterly magazine *Single Market News* can be a useful source of business news and regulations concerning the single market. The DTI also publishes a number of general booklets and trade briefs free of charge and has a Market Information Centre Library (Room 150, Ashdown House, 123 Victoria Street, London SW1; tel 0171-215 5444) which can be visited between 9.30am to 5.30pm Monday to Friday by those with a business address.

Running a Business

Employing Staff

Contracts: The important point to remember about contracts in Sweden is that even a tacit agreement can be considered legally binding. In practice many employment contracts are verbal although it is in everyone's interest to have a written contractual agreement drawn up. According to European Community directives employers are obliged to inform the employee in writing about the terms of the employment within a month from the beginning of the employment. This information should include the following:

Name and address of employer and employee and the date on which the employment starts and the place of work
The employees duties and the nature of the position (ie open-ended or fixed-term contract)
Notice period or date of termination of the contract
Methods and amount of payment
Hours of work and holiday
Any applicable collective agreement
Conditions for work abroad if the job abroad lasts more than one month.
The employer must give the employee one month's notice of any changes to the above conditions.

Under the 1982 Security of Employment Act it is possible to employ staff for a probationary period of not more than twelve months. Employment can be terminated before the end of the probationary period by both parties without the need to give a reason. In other cases of employment, under the 1982 Act employees may only be dismissed on objective grounds eg gross misconduct and the employer is obliged to consult and inform the employee and the relevant trade union in connection with a termination of an employment contract. The employee and trade union may challenge the dismissal through the courts. An employee may not be dismissed on grounds of pregnancy or sickness. Both the employer and the employee are entitled to a minimum of one month's notice and this period increases with length of service.

Trade Unions: About 90% of the labour force belongs to a union. The central organisation for the workers is the Swedish Trade Union Confederation or LO and for employers is the Swedish Employers Confederation or SAF although there are a number of other unions representing professional and white collar workers. The right to strike is guaranteed in the Swedish constitution unless it is forbidden by collective agreement and a strike does not terminate the employment contract but only suspends it for the duration of the action. In practice strikes are rare because of negotiation procedures which are built into the system.

Labour Relations: According to the 1976 Co-Determination Act, employees have far-reaching rights as regards representation, information and negotiation whilst the employer also has rights to negotiate with the trade union. The 1987 Board Representation for Employees in Private Enterprises states that in private enterprises employing more than 25 people employees can be represented by two representatives on the board of directors. In companies employing more than 1,000 people, three employee representatives may be appointed. The representatives enjoy the same standing as the other members of the board. An employee who is subject to a work dispute has the right to assistance from her/his trade union but employees who are not members of a trade union have to find legal assistance elsewhere. The disciplinary powers of employers are fairly circumscribed by the Co-determination Act and an employee cannot incur any other penalty than damages for a breach of discipline and the burden of proof rests with the employer. An employee may only be dismissed for gross misconduct.

Employee Training: The 1974 Employee's Right to Educational Leave entitles every employee to leave of absence from employment for educational purposes. The Act applies to both public and private sector employees but does not entitle the employee to paid leave and nor does the Act cover purely private studies. The Act does not place any restriction on the duration of leave but the employer may be able to defer the leave for up to six months by negotiation. The Act is currently undergoing revision and some of the statutory provisions can be modified by collective agreement.

Wages and Salaries: There is no minimum wage in Sweden and wages are fixed by collective agreements or by individual agreements between employers and employees. Amendment of remuneration can only be done through collective agreements and the employer is obliged to inform the employees in writing of any amendments one month in advance.

Social Security Contributions: There is an extensive system of employer contributions to cover the welfare system which includes payment for pensions, health benefits and social insurance. Whereas a full-time industrial worker pays about 31% of gross salary in direct tax, the employer also pays nearly 40% on top of the pay rolls to the government to cover a wide range of social insurance benefits. Employers withhold social security contributions at source and forward them to the appropriate authorities in the following month.

Paid Holiday:
All Swedish employees are entitled to a minimum of 25 days paid holiday a year and in addition there are twelve public holidays.

Taxation

In January 1992 Sweden effected significant tax reforms which lowered the national tax rates for both individuals and companies and broadened income tax and indirect tax bases. The principle taxes in Sweden are direct tax and indirect tax.

Direct Taxes: These include national income tax which is levied on companies based on the results of their annual accounts with some adjustments made for tax purposes and individual income tax.

Individual Income Tax: Individual income tax is a local tax levied at a flat rate of about 31% (but which can differ from area to area) and a national income tax which is levied on those in higher income brackets (the current threshold amount is over 198,700 SEK) who are still liable for national tax which stands at about 20%. Payment is withheld at source by the employer. Amounts withheld are paid to the authorities in the following month.

Corporate Income Tax: Corporate income tax is currently 30% and this is levied on all corporate income including interest, royalties and domestic and foreign dividends. For most companies the income year is the calendar year although income years ending on 30 April, 30 June and 31 August are permitted. A company should normally file a preliminary return before 1 December of the year before the income year.

Capital Gains Tax: Capital Gains Tax is a uniform 30%. The gain on sales of stock is fully taxable irrespective of the period of ownership. A gain on the sale of real property is taxed as income for business.

Net Wealth Tax: There is also a net wealth tax on assets such as real estate, bank balances, bonds and shares etc. This tax is proportional and is payable on taxable assets exceeding 800,000 SEK.

Indirect Tax: The principle indirect tax is VAT (MOMS in Sweden) which is generally levied at a rate of 25% on taxable sales of both goods and services.

Legal Advice
Anyone contemplating doing business in Sweden should take specialist legal advice, preferably from a lawyer who is familiar with Swedish business law. The following English-speaking law firms specialise in Swedish business law:

Useful Addresses
Styrbjörn Gärde Advokatbyrå: Box 5208, Nybrogatan 34, S-102 45 Stockholm; tel 8 665 00 40, fax 8 665 00 41.
Advokatfirman LJB: PO Box 465, S-58105 Linköping; tel 013 11 01 05, fax 013 14 12 220.
Herslow and Holme HB: Södra Tullgatan 3, Box 4307, S-203 14 Malmö; tel 040 10 14 60; fax 040 97 42 10.
Malmström & Malmenfelt AB: Hovslagargatan 5B, Box 1665, Stockholm 11196; tel 8 679 69 50, 8 611 57 55.

Accountancy and Auditing Advice
Swedish law requires that under the Accounting Act of 1976 companies, partnerships and sole proprietors must comply with
the following requirements:

Account for all transactions and prepare accounts in a systematic and chronological order with appropriate supporting documents.
Prepare annual reports.
Retain all accounting material in Sweden for ten years.
A company's annual report must be filed with the Registrar of Public Companies within one month of the company's AGM. It must be signed by the director and certify that the annual report and appropriation of profit were approved by the shareholders at the annual meeting.

Financial Reporting: The usual financial year is 12 months. Under the Accounting Act a business must prepare a financial statement at the end of each financial year. The statement should include a balance sheet and a statement of earnings with appropriate notes.

Audit Requirements: The annual reports of every limited liability company must be audited. The auditor must appoint at least one certified public accountant. The auditor's report must include the following:

Approval of the balance sheet and statement of earnings.

Approval of the board's proposed allocation of earnings for the distribution of dividends

A discharge of responsibility for the members of the board with respect to their administration of the company for the fiscal year.

Swedish auditors are also required to express an opinion on the director's and chief executive's administration.

The accountancy firm Ernst and Young have many branches and associates throughout Sweden and provide the booklet *Doing Business in Sweden* which contains detailed information on auditing and accounting in Sweden.

Useful Addresses

Ernst and Young: Apex Plaza, Forbury Road, Reading RG1 1YE; fax 01734 507744.

Ernst and Young: Box 3143, Adolf Fredriks Kyrkogata 2, S-103 62 Stockholm; tel 8 613 90 00, fax 8 10 57 38.

The Association of Authorised Auditors: Box 6417, S-113 82 Stockholm; tel 8 23 41 30.

The Swedish Accounting Standards Board: Box 7831, S-103 98 Stockholm; tel 8 787 80 28.

Personal Case Histories

Denmark

Camilla Marsden

Camilla Marsden a 25-year-old fashion student has a Danish boyfriend and for the five years in which she has been studying she has regularly taken casual work in Denmark during the vacations. She is hoping to work for Clare, a Danish fashion company which has offices in London as well as in Denmark, but she would like to live and work in Denmark once her studies are completed. We asked her:

Have you managed to learn to speak Danish?
Yes, but with some difficulty. The pronunciation is similar to German but the grammar is simpler than that of English. Danish uses a lot fewer words than English so the main problem for a foreigner learning it is that the same words mean different things depending on the context. There is no problem learning Danish in Denmark as there are plenty of evening classes for foreign students. I took one at Copenhagen University.

What kind of jobs have you been able to find and was the language a problem initially
The language is not really a problem as everyone in Denmark speaks such good English. I found jobs by looking in the newspapers, using the phone book and turning up in person at local businesses. Having a Danish boyfriend was useful as he was able to help me decipher newspaper adverts and ask around for me. I worked for three months at a time in various jobs including waitressing and serving in a bakery.

How do you find the working conditions?
Employers in Denmark are more laid back than in Britain; perhaps this is because there is less bureaucracy concerned with running a small business and so they seem more laid back than in the UK. The working week is shorter than in some countries. The Danes reduced it to 35 hours a couple of years ago to get more people into jobs. There is also a minimum wage in Denmark which is about £7.50 an hour. I earned this as a waitress plus 13% of tips. As I am still a student earning under £3,000 a year I don't pay tax which is otherwise very high at 50%.

Is it easy to find accommodation?
When you arrive there are hostels in Copenhagen where you can rent a room cheaply. I managed to find a two-bedroomed flat with kitchen and bathroom for £180 per month in a reasonable area of Copenhagen. Housing is definitely cheaper in Denmark, especially to buy — it's about half the price of UK property.

How do you find the social life?
Danish people are very sociable and they tend to have lots of dinner parties. Friday and Saturday nights are the busiest nights for socialising. After a meal with friends at your own or someone else's home you usually go out on the town (if you can afford it). There are hundreds of pubs, clubs and cafés in which to spend the night hours. It is possible to stay out all night if you want to. Eating out is very expensive by British standards but if you are earning a Danish salary it will not seem as pricey.

How do you find the Danes?
Danes are very friendly and they are more than helpful to foreigners and they seem genuinely interested in people from other countries.

Any other comments about daily life in Denmark?
Coming from Britain where you have to fill in forms for everything Denmark is quite a change. Here you hardly have to fill in any forms. For instance my Danish boyfriend only had to fill in one form for his student grant which is paid monthly for three years. There are no renewal forms for each term or year.

Finland

Dr Bernadette Ferry

Bernadette Ferry, was a 25-year-old immunologist from Glasgow when she wrote a speculative job application to the head of the transplantation department at the the Medical Institute of Helsinki. The institute is part of Helsinki University. She was offered a one-year contract which was extended to two years. We asked her:

Was there a language problem?
Nearly everyone speaks English so it was not a problem to communicate, except with some of the very old. But if you want to integrate you need to speak Finnish. I took an evening course at the university. There are courses run especially for foreigners which are free or for which there is a nominal charge depending on your circumstances.

Did you manage to speak Finnish?
Yes, but it is a very difficult language to learn.

How did you find accommodation?
I was very lucky as the university found it for me. I spent the first three weeks in ordinary student accommodation which was completely free. Then I was moved to a very nice flat which I shared with two Finns, a law student and the other who was studying French and German. It was very cheap, about £110 per month which included everything. There was even a laundrette in the basement and also a sauna. You could have a sauna every day if you wanted for no extra charge. Nearly all apartment buildings have such facilities which are paid for by all the tenants.

What were the working conditions like?
They were fine and I would recommend the Helsinki medical insitute as a place to work. However, the university canteen was another matter. Finnish insitutional food is completely bland and presentation is not considered important. Meat is very expensive so communal canteens tend to serve a monotonous menu in which milk products, potatoes and black pudding feature heavily. The best thing you can say about lunch is that everyone stops work for it and it can be quite sociable.

What's it really like living and working in Finland?
Really difficult. Ask any foreigner working in Finland and they will say the same. I think it's a combination of a very harsh climate and the fact that the Finns are hard to get to know. You have to dig really hard. Foreigners like me are used to spontaneity and humour. Finns are very private people and they tend to be conformist. Socialising is really difficult because there a few pubs or the equivalent where people can congregate so it's really hard to meet Finns outside working hours. In Finland people don't have many dinner parties, probably because food is so expensive. Social gatherings tend to take place in restaurants which is even more of an expense so it is only done occasionally. The two worst things I remember about Finland are the grim climate and how expensive it is compared with the UK.

What alteratives are there for amusement in the long winters?
Finns, especially the young people and students are very cultured. They love cinema, concerts, opera etc. Many buy a season ticket for the Finlandia Hall. Outside Helsinki there is virtually nowhere to socialise. It is important if you take a job in Finland to live as close to the centre of Helsinki as possible.

Have you any other comments on life in Finland for Foreigners?
Just to reiterate that it is very difficult. Most foreigners are diplomats, multi-national company employees, academics or teachers. Anyone who can get accommodation provided for them should do so as otherwise housing costs and the cost of living are extremely high. Buying and running a car is also very costly. In Helsinki public transport is excellent and cheap and if you live near the centre and use public transport you should not have any problems getting around.

Iceland

Janet Bridgeport

Janet Bridgeport is 23 and works for a riding school. She worked on a pony trekking farm in Iceland during the summer having gone there initially as a tourist.

How easy was the Icelandic bureaucracy?
I managed to bypass most of it because I went there on a British passport as a visitor then found work by chance at a trekking centre near Hvollsvollur in the south. Now that Iceland has joined the EEA things are much simpler as you don't need a work permit. Technically, I suppose I wasn't actually an employee because the only payment I received was in kind — board and lodging.

What chances led you to take work in Iceland?
I was staying at a guest house in Hvollsvollur where they told me that the farm next door had a trekking centre. Because I'd worked with horses and wasn't in any rush to get back home I went and knocked on their door and asked them if they needed any casual help for the summer. I was really amazed when they said they'd take me on but a lot of the horse riding guests spoke English so I suppose that weighed heavily in my favour.

How did you find the social life and the Icelanders?
I don't think anyone goes to the Icelandic countryside for the wild night life. There was a swimming pool and a café in the nearest town but there's really very little to do and you end up making your own entertainment. My employer's extended family were staying with him so there were always lots of people

around and in Iceland neighbours are always popping round for a meal and a drink — it took me quite a while to work out who was family and who wasn't.

Television and videos are quite popular and I'd heard that the Icelanders read a lot although I didn't see much evidence of it. I met some other foreign workers who were working on Icelandic farms who didn't seem to be having a very good time and were bored. I think I was lucky in this respect. And of course there was always the horse riding which was great. The Icelanders I met were very nice but a bit reserved at first. My employer was excellent and trusted me totally to get on with things. I've met other people who find Icelanders a bit grim but that was never my experience.

What is your advice for someone thinking of going to work in Iceland?
Try to fix up a job first, preferably with accommodation because the cost of living is very high. Also it's probably not a good idea to go in winter as I can imagine that would be a bit miserable.

Norway

Moira Mitchell
Moira Mitchell is 29 and spent eight months working for the British Council in Oslo as an administration assistant before studying modern languages at university. Her mother is Norwegian and both her parents have retired to Norway. Moira now works as an office manager for a Norwegian software company in Britain.

Is the Norwegian bureaucracy easy to deal with?
It's a lot simpler now of course because of Norway's EEA membership. However, for me it wasn't a problem anyway as I was working for the British Council which deals with all the necessary documentation for its staff. Tax regulations were a bit more complicated — I was taxed by both Britain and Norway as, at the time I was there, there was no dual tax arrangement which there is now thank goodness.

How easy was it to get work?
Very easy. A friend of mine in Norway sent me an advert for a job with the British Council which had appeared in a Norwegian newspaper and I applied. I wasn't even interviewed in person although they did interview me on the phone.

Was it easy to find accommodation?
I was lucky because the same friend who had told me about the job also helped me to find somewhere to live. I rented a room in a house and although the cost of renting was high, the standard of housing in Norway is correspondingly high. Buildings in Norway tend to be better constructed than in Britain — I never went in to a draughty house in Norway.

How did you find the social life and the Norwegians?
I tended to socialise mainly with people from work. Most of them were British although some were married to Norwegians. There aren't many pubs as such in Norway although there are bars but these tend to be very expensive. People usually go to each others houses more because it's cheaper and it's also part of Norwegian culture. The cinemas in Oslo are very good and you get lots of English and American films. Norway's also great for sports and the outdoor life if you're in to that sort of thing. I was there in winter when people tend to stay in much more and hibernate.

People can get very depressed because it's so dark and cold. Norwegians generally are very down to earth and friendly and it's a case of 'what you see is what you get'. Outside Oslo the smaller rural communities tend to be very conservative so it could get a bit repressive.

What is your advice for others thinking of going to Norway?
The most important thing is to make contact with other people. Join a club and throw yourself into the local culture because that can make so much difference to how you feel about the place. Also it's probably not a good idea to move there in winter as it can seem really harsh and cold whereas in summer it is totally different.

Sweden

Charlotte Rosen
Charlotte Rosen is 27, British and works in marketing. She has a degree in international politics and has lived and worked in Australia, the United States and Hong Kong. She worked as an English teacher in Sweden for one and a half years and has a Swedish fiancé.

How easy is it bureaucratically to move to Sweden now it is in the EU?
Things are a lot simpler now that Sweden is part of the European Union. Before, you had to be interviewed at the Swedish Embassy in Britain if you wanted to go and live and work in Sweden. Also you don't need a residence permit to live in Sweden if you are living there with a Swedish partner, but you do need to have a national identity number for most things.

Sweden is bureaucratic in the sense that you have to fill in forms for most things but generally things are dealt with smoothly and efficiently. The Swedes are great sticklers for fairness and so people are treated on a strictly first come first served basis.

How did you go about finding work?
I had visited Sweden several times before going there to work so I knew quite a lot before I went but I also did as much as possible to prepare myself before going. I knew that I wanted to teach English when I got there so I took a TEFL course in London beforehand. After I'd been in Sweden for about six weeks I looked through the yellow pages for language schools and sent off my CV in English which wasn't a problem because everyone speaks English really well. I was offered several interviews, including by the British Institute. Many of them said they were interested but the terms only start in September and January so you have to time your applications quite carefully.

How important is it to speak Swedish when looking for a job?
Learning Swedish can be a big help when looking for work and when I went to Sweden I signed up with the SFI (Swedish immigration Service) which is an organisation that teaches Swedish to immigrants. Because I was living with my partner I was entitled to go on it although I had to get a national ID number first. The organisation gave me three hours of free Swedish classes a day. All the English language schools wanted to interview in Swedish but they were very accommodating and prepared to switch to English when necessary. Part of the reason why they interview in Swedish is to see how committed you are to staying in the job; a willingness to learn the language is taken as an indication that you are committed to staying.

How did you find Swedish accommodation?
It is generally cheaper than in Britain and of a very high standard. I lived with

my fiancé in Gothenberg where it is fairly easy to rent a flat but more difficult to rent a house as people tend to buy them. Most flats are unfurnished but a peculiarity of Sweden is that when people move houses they tend to leave behind some household appliances like fridges, even if they are fairly new.

How did you find the Swedes?
The Swedes are generally fairly reserved and can be very polite and proper although they don't see themselves like that. Even if someone goes absolutely wild at a party they'll probably still ring you up the next day to thank you for it. I found that you often have to make the first move but if you do they are usually very friendly and helpful. I can honestly say that I left liking most people.

How did you find the social life?
The social life generally is quite low-key. Where I was in Gothenburg there is a big English-speaking community (mainly Americans, Australians and Irish) but they tend not to socialise much with the Swedes. As I was joining my fiancé in Sweden I inherited his friends most of whom were couples. The Swedes aren't big on going out. The 18-23 age range go pubbing and clubbing but people older than that tend to meet in private homes — that's partly because it's so expensive to go out for a meal or a drink. Lots of people go to evening classes and I joined a dance studio and took up road running which was also a way of meeting people. Sailing is also popular and everybody skis.

People were very friendly but I found that relationships didn't tend to develop outside the activity. There are quite a lot of expat clubs and the British Consul can provide lots of contacts.

I joined the American Women's Club where I found a lot of support and they provide a monthly news letter with lots of information and practical help. There's also an Anglican Church in Gothenburg called St Andrews which is a good place for meeting people and they have lots of groups including an Amnesty International Group which operates in English.

What advice would you give to someone thinking of living and working in Sweden?
I think it's very important to start to learn the language before you go — it makes life much easier in the initial stages. It's also a good idea to make contact with fellow expats to give you support and it's a good idea to join a club or get a job to prevent boredom. I found I went through stages of really disliking Sweden and everything about it and then coming round to liking it so I also think it's important to take a longer term view and give yourself time to adjust.

Vacation Work also publish:

	Paperback	Hardback
The Directory of Summer Jobs in Britain	£7.95	£12.95
The Directory of Summer Jobs Abroad	£7.95	£12.95
Adventure Holidays	£5.95	£10.95
The Teenager's Vacation Guide to Work, Study & Adventure	£6.95	£9.95
Work Your Way Around the World	£9.95	£15.95
Teaching English Abroad	£9.95	£15.95
The Au Pair & Nanny's Guide to Working Abroad	£8.95	£14.95
Working in Ski Resorts — Europe & North America	£8.95	£14.95
Kibbutz Volunteer	£5.95	£8.95
The Directory of Jobs & Careers Abroad	£9.95	£15.95
The International Directory of Voluntary Work	£8.95	£14.95
The Directory of Work & Study in Developing Countries	£7.95	£10.95
Live & Work in France	£8.95	£14.95
Live & Work in Australia & New Zealand	£8.95	£14.95
Live & Work in the USA & Canada	£8.95	£14.95
Live & Work in Germany	£8.95	£11.95
Live & Work in Belgium, The Netherlands & Luxembourg	£8.95	£11.95
Live & Work in Spain & Portugal	£8.95	£11.95
Live & Work in Italy	£7.95	£10.95
Travellers Survival Kit: Russia & the Republics	£9.95	–
Travellers Survival Kit: Western Europe	£8.95	–
Travellers Survival Kit: Eastern Europe	£9.95	–
Travellers Survival Kit: South America	£12.95	–
Travellers Survival Kit: Central America	£8.95	–
Travellers Survival Kit: Cuba	£9.95	–
Travellers Survival Kit: USA & Canada	£9.95	–
Travellers Survival Kit to the East	£6.95	–
Travellers Survival Kit: Australia & New Zealand	£9.95	–
Hitch-hikers' Manual Britain	£3.95	–
Europe — a Manual for Hitch-hikers	£4.95	–
The Traveller's Picture Phrase-Book	£1.95	–

Distributors of:

Summer Jobs USA	£10.95	–
Internships (On-the-Job Training Opportunities — in the USA)	£19.95	–
Sports Scholarships in the USA	£17.95	–
The Directory of College Accommodations USA	£5.95	–
Emplois d'Ete en France	£7.95	–
Making It in Japan	£8.95	–
Jobs in Japan	£9.95	–
Teaching English in Asia	£8.95	–

Vacation Work Publications, 9 Park End Street, Oxford OX1 1HJ
(Tel 01865-241978   Fax 01865-790885)